1. 2. *Phylacteries*. 3. *A Jew in his Phylacterial dress reciting the forms of prayer*. 4. *Mezuzah*. 5. *A Talismanic figure*.

London, Published by Longman, Rees, Orme & C.ͦ August 1827.

THE REASONS

OF

THE LAWS OF MOSES,

FROM

THE "MORE NEVOCHIM" OF MAIMONIDES.

WITH NOTES, DISSERTATIONS, AND

A LIFE OF THE AUTHOR.

BY JAMES TOWNLEY, D. D.

AUTHOR OF "ILLUSTRATIONS OF BIBLICAL LITERATURE," &c. &c.

◆

Quemadmodum adhuc viget, ita in omne ævum vigebit, MAIMONIDIS *memoria.*——BISHOP CLAVERING.

◆

THE LAWBOOK EXCHANGE, LTD.
Union, New Jersey
2001

ISBN 1-58477-168-2

Printed in the United States of America
on acid-free paper

The Lawbook Exchange, Ltd.
965 Jefferson Avenue
Union, New Jersey 07083-8605

Please see catalogue at rear of this volume
or our website www.lawbookexchange.com
for a selection of our other fine facsimile reprints
of classic works of legal history.

Library of Congress Cataloging-in-Publication Data

Maimonides, Moses, 1135-1204.
    [Dalalat al-ha'irin, English. Selections]
    The reasons of the laws of Moses: from "More nevochim" of Maimonides / [translated]
by James Townley.
    p. cm.
    Includes bibliographical references (p.) and index.
    ISBN 1-58477-168-2 (cloth: alk. paper)
    1. Commandments (Judaism) 2. Commandments, Six hundred and thirteen. I.
Townley, James, 1774-1833. II. Title.

BM520.7 .M67213 2001
296.1'8--dc21

                                      00-066334

THE REASONS

OF

THE LAWS OF MOSES,

FROM

THE "MORE NEVOCHIM" OF MAIMONIDES.

WITH NOTES, DISSERTATIONS, AND

A LIFE OF THE AUTHOR.

BY JAMES TOWNLEY, D. D.

AUTHOR OF " ILLUSTRATIONS OF BIBLICAL LITERATURE," &c. &c.

—◆—

Quemadmodum adhuc viget, ita in omne ævum vigebit, MAIMONIDIS *memoria.*——BISHOP CLAVERING.

—◆—

LONDON:

LONGMAN, REES, ORME, BROWN, AND GREEN, PATERNOSTER-ROW ;
AND JOHN COCHRAN, 108, STRAND.

1827.

LONDON:

PRINTED BY JAMES NICHOLS,
WARWICK SQUARE, NEWGATE STREET.

PREFACE.

———

THE LAWS AND INSTITUTIONS OF MOSES constitute the earliest and most original system
of ecclesiastical and civil jurisprudence and
polity, with which the world has ever been
favoured. Suited to the genius, the habits, and
the circumstances of the people to whom they
were delivered, they comprize not merely a code
of political and moral regulations, for the wise
and prosperous conduct of the Jews, as a distinct
and peculiar people; but rules of economy, for
the promotion of their health and domestic comfort. Justly claiming to be a revelation from
God, they are marked with the authority, and
inculcate the unity, purity, and goodness, of
JEHOVAH; and promise that temporal prosperity
to the obedient, which the enactments of no
other legislator ever dared to propose. Designed
to introduce another religious dispensation, many
of the rites were symbolical in their character,
and being succeeded by a series of prophetic
enunciations, served gradually to develope the

scheme of human redemption by the incarnation
and death of the MESSIAH.

Amongst the innumerable commentators and
expounders of the Mosaic writings, *Maimonides*
deservedly ranks among the foremost for intelligence and learning. His fame as a writer on
Jewish Literature and Antiquities, is fully
established by the sanction of the learned of different ages and countries, whether Jews or Christians, who constantly refer to him as indisputable
authority on every topic of Hebrew Legislation
and Tradition. His writings are multifarious and
voluminous; but in none of them do we discover
more extensive knowledge or sounder judgment,
than in his *More Nevochim,* or " Teacher of
the Perplexed." Of this work, which contains
critical remarks on Hebrew Words and Phrases,
and explanatory observations on Jewish opinions,
no portion is more deservedly esteemed or does
greater credit to the writer, than that which is
devoted to the examination of the " Reasons of
the Laws of Moses." Yet it is a singular fact,
that, although this part has been uniformly
referred to, and quoted by almost every writer
on the Mosaic Institutes, no entire English
translation has ever yet appeared; and the reader
of the various interesting extracts made from it
by Bishop Patrick, in his learned and valuable

Commentary, as well as by others of considerable note, has only to regret that he is not in
possession of the whole exposition.

Impressed with a conviction of the importance
and general excellence of this compendious
defence of the Ritual of Moses, the translator,
without pledging himself to the absolute correctness of every opinion maintained by the author,
has attempted to give a faithful, but not a servile
translation of it. The copies of the work which
were before him, were R. Samuel Aben Tybbon's
Hebrew edition, with the triple Rabbinical commentaries of RR. Shem Tob, Ephodæus, and
Karshakas, printed in folio, at Jaznetz, in 1742,
—and the Latin versions of Justinian, and Buxtorf, the former in folio, printed in 1520, at
Paris, by Jodocus Badius Ascensius, in a beautiful Gothic character; the latter, in quarto,
printed at Basle, by J. J. Genath, in 1629.—In
a few instances, the translator, from motives of
delicacy, has ventured to abridge the details of
the author, but has generally inserted them in
the Notes, from Buxtorf.

To the Translation, are prefixed a LIFE OF
MAIMONIDES, with several DISSERTATIONS on
different subjects connected with the object of
the work ; and which, with the NOTES appended
at the close, the translator trusts, will serve to

elucidate the views and positions of the author, and occasionally to rectify what has been regarded as erroneous or uncertain.

In presenting the result of his labours to the public, the Translator is far from wishing to depreciate any similar works which have been previously published. The principal publications of this nature, accessible to the English reader, (except those which are restricted to the Antiquities or Customs of the Jews,) are, Michaelis's "Commentaries on the Laws of Moses," 4 vols. 8vo., translated from the German, by Dr. Smith; Lowman's "Rational of the Ritual of the Hebrew Worship;" Shaw's "History and Philosophy of Judaism;" Graves, "On the Four last Books of Moses," 2 vols.; Woodward, "On the Wisdom of the Egyptians," 4to.; Fergus, "On the Reasonableness of the Laws of Moses;" Atkins's "Attempt to illustrate the Jewish Law;" Jahn's "Biblical Archæology," translated from the German, by T. C. Upham; Fleury's "Manners of the Israelites," by Dr. A. Clarke; and the "Commentaries" of Bishop Patrick and Dr. A. Clarke. For although other Commentators have occasionally explained and defended the Mosaic Ritual, these have exhibited the greatest learning and research.

These works have each their respective excellencies; and all of them have eludicated, with considerable talent and effect, the objects they severally proposed. These, however, have been various : *Michaelis* proposes to consider the Mosaic Laws, not as a Theologian, but as a Civilian ; *Graves*, and *Shaw* vindicate their Divine Authority against Infidels; *Lowman*, and *Fergus* defend their general importance ; *Woodward* refutes the opinions of Dr. Spencer, in his work, " De Legibus Hebræorum ;" and *Jahn* and *Fleury* illustrate the Jewish Antiquities. Maimonides's work, therefore, though brief, enters more into detail, and exhibits more fully than the others, the sentiments of the intelligent and learned of the Hebrew nation, on the reasons and peculiar objects of their Ceremonial Law.

To the reader who wishes to pursue the subject beyond the range of English authors, the present writer would recommend, amongst others, Dr. Spencer's learned work, " De Legibus Hebræorum ;" and Sir John Marsham's " Canon Chronicus Ægyptiacus," &c. corrected in some of their peculiar opinions by Witsius's " Ægyptiaca ;" and Meyer's Treatise, " De Temporibus et Festis Diebus Hebræorum ;" Cunæus, " De Republica Hebræorum ;" and Bochart's " Hierozoicon," a work replete with various and recondite information.

In concluding his prefatory remarks, the Translator is aware that a work commenced and completed amidst the interruptions of official duties, must have occasion to claim indulgence for defects; but assured by former approbation, that his consciousness of a sincere desire to serve the best interests of mankind, will be met by corresponding candour, he submits the present Translation and accompanying Dissertations and Notes, with confidence to the public, hoping that the Blessing of the God of Jacob will accompany this attempt to vindicate the wisdom, and equity, and benevolence of Institutions Divinely authorized, and solemnly promulged.

CONTENTS.

b

LIFE

OF

MAIMONIDES.

——

RABBI MOSES Ben Maimon or Maimonides, called also Rambam from the initials of his name, and Moses *the Egyptian* from his long residence in Egypt, was born at Cordova in Spain, in the year 1131, or according to some 1133, of the Christian era. His father, who was descended from an illustrious line of ancestors, sustained the office of judge among his own nation; and by his knowledge of jurisprudence, and the ability and integrity with which he executed the difficult and important duties of the magistracy, secured the respect of Christians as well as Jews.

The education of young Maimonides appears to have been conducted, at first, under the immediate superintendence of his father; but a series of domestic quarrels having subsequently obliged him to quit the paternal roof, he placed himself under the care of the most learned Jewish teachers, and studied, with sedulous attention, the Mosaic Law, and its various Talmudical and Rabbinical commentaries. After devoting some years to the pursuit of Hebrew learning, he attached himself to the great Arabian philosopher and physician Averroes, as one of his pupils and disciples. With these advantages, and possessing a mind vigorous, penetrating, and acute, he not only made uncommon pro-

B

gress in Rabbinical literature, but excelled also in the mathe-
matical, metaphysical, and medical sciences; and added to
a knowledge of the Hebrew and Arabic languages,
an acquaintance with the Chaldee, Turkish, and Greek,
beside the other more modern dialects of the countries in
which he resided. As his knowledge was profound, so
his reading was extensive and various, having read not
only the works of the most celebrated Rabbins of his own
nation, but also the writings of Plato, Aristotle, Themis-
tius, Galen, and of the Philosophers in general.

The astonishing talents and learning of Averroes produced, in Maimonides, an esteem and attachment, disinterested and unconquerable; so that when a violent persecution had been raised against Averroes, and he had been
removed from the Chief Magistracy of Cordova by the
influence of the Mussulman doctors, who suspected him of
defection from the Mohammedan faith, Maimonides continued the offices of friendship, and, sooner than discover
his place of concealment, submitted to a voluntary exile
from his native country and early associates, and withdrew
into Egypt where he principally resided during the rest of
his life. To this steady devotion to the interests of his
teacher and friend, we ought, probably, to attribute the
calumny raised against Maimonides by the zealots of his
nation, that he had apostatized from the religion of his
fathers and embraced the peculiarities of Islamism;—
a calumny industriously propagated by his enemies, so that
one of them, a Spaniard, named Abu-Arab, a man of eminent talents, coming to reside in Egypt, embittered his
latter days, by renewing the charge of apostacy, with such
determined enmity, that at length the Sultan summoned
Abu-Arab into his presence and silenced him, by defending Maimonides, and deciding, that even if he had professed himself a disciple of Mohammed, during a time of
violent persecution, he ought not to be regarded as an apostate, for that " whatsoever is done involuntarily and by

violence, in matters of religion, ought to be considered as nothing." It must, however, be acknowledged that this principle, though one which had been maintained by our author himself, in an Epistle addressed to his persecuted countrymen, is founded too much on the doctrine of *expediency*, and too much fraught with the most danger-ous consequences, to have been a sufficient apology for a false profession of Islamism, if so foul a prevarication had been proved against him.

On removing to Egypt, Maimonides settled at Cairo, where, for want of other employment, he was at first reduced to the necessity of trading as a jeweller. But neither penury nor persecution could repress his ardour for study; for, in the midst of complicated troubles, he continued and completed his *Commentary on the Mishna* or ORAL LAW,* which he had begun in Spain, at the age of twenty-three; and prior to which he had composed a *Commentary* on certain portions of the GEMARA, that has been unfortu-nately lost, probably at the period of his removal from Spain.

After some time, his great merit introduced him to the notice and esteem of the Sultan Alphadel, who appointed him his physician, and allowed him a pension. In an epistle to his friend, R. Samuel Aben Tybbon, he thus describes the daily occupations of his elevated station:—" I gene-rally visit the Sultan every morning; and when either he, or his children, or his wives are attacked with any disorder, I am detained in attendance the whole of the day; or, when any of the nobility are sick, I am ordered to visit them. But, if nothing prevent, I repair to my own habi-tation at noon, where I no sooner arrive, exhausted, and faint with hunger, than I find myself surrounded with a crowd of Jews and Gentiles, nobles and peasants, judges and tax-gatherers, friends and enemies, eagerly expecting

* See the *Dissertation on the Rabbinical Writings.*

B 2

the time of my return. Alighting from my horse, I wash my hands, according to custom, and then courteously and respectfully saluting my guests, entreat them to wait with patience whilst I take some refreshment. Dinner concluded, I hasten to enquire into their various complaints, and to prescribe for them the necessary medicines. Such is the business of every day. Frequently, indeed, it happens, that some are obliged to wait till evening, and I continue for many hours, and even to a late hour of the night, incessantly engaged in listening, talking, ordering, and prescribing, till I am so overpowered with fatigue and sleep that I can scarcely utter a word."

At the command of the Sultan, he translated the works of the celebrated Arabian physician, AVICENNA or IBN SINA; a copy of which is said to be preserved at Bologna, with the following titular inscription: " ABENSARA: translated by our master, Moses the son of Maimon, whose memory be blessed !"

His residence at the court of the Egyptian Prince, enabled him not only to protect the Jews, by his influence with the Sultan, but also to found an academy for his nation at Alexandria, which he appears to have countenanced and promoted by his personal superintendence and instructions. The celebrity of the institution drew students from various parts of Egypt, Judea, and Syria, who, attracted by the fame of Maimonides, rejoiced in the opportunity afforded them of becoming his scholars. This desire of benefiting by the advantages of the Alexandrian academy continued, with increasing ardour, till persecutions, being raised by the Mohammedans against the Jews, rendered it unsafe for strangers to visit Egypt, and even induced some to assume the character of Mohammedans who secretly retained their preference for Judaism.

The multifarious engagements of our learned physician, numerous and toilsome as they were, could not divert him from his favourite studies of Hebrew jurisprudence and literature; we therefore find him labouring with indefatigable diligence and patience on a digest of the Jewish laws, collected from the immense and confused compilations of the *Talmud*. This great work he entitled *Yad Hachazakah*, "The strong hand," or *Mishneh Torah*, "The Mishnical Law :"* it has been several times printed; and is held in high estimation as an excellent compendium of the laws and decisions of the Talmud.

Another work of still greater interest and value, was his MORE NEVOCHIM, or "Instructor of the Perplexed," which he completed in his fiftieth year, and to which he appears to have brought the most profound learning under the direction of the soundest judgment. It is a critical, philosophical, and theological work, in which he endeavours to explain the difficult passages, phrases, parables, allegories, and ceremonies of the Old Testament; and is rendered particularly important, by " an excellent Exposition of the grounds and reasons of the Mosaic Laws," † to which many of our most eminent Biblical critics and commentators have been deeply indebted.‡ It was written originally in *Arabic*, by Maimonides, and afterwards translated into *Hebrew*, with his approbation, by his friend and disciple, R. Samuel Aben Tybbon, author of an Hebrew translation of *Euclid*, and other learned works. A Prospectus of an edition of the *Arabic*, to be accompanied with a Latin version and notes, was circulated by the eminent Orientalist Dr. Thomas Hyde; but not meeting with sufficient encouragement, he abandoned the design. The Prospectus has been since reprinted in the *Syntagma* of Dr. Hyde, by Dr. Gregory Sharpe. In 1520, Justinian, Bishop of Nebio, published a Latin

* See Dissertation on the Rabbinical Writings.

† Graves' Lectures on the Pentateuch, i. 320. note.

‡ See Hyde De Veterum Persarum, &c.—Patrick's, Dodd's, &c. Commentaries.—Selden. De Diis Syriis, &c.—Young on Idolatrous Corruptions.—Spencer. De Legibus Heb. &c. &c. &c.

translation of this work, in folio, beautifully printed with a Gothic type, by Badius Ascensius, at Paris. The younger Buxtorf undertook a new version of the Hebrew into Latin, which was printed at Basil, by J. J. Genath, 1629, 4to. with a Preface including a biographical account of the author. The Hebrew, accompanied with Rabbinical commentaries, was printed at Venice, in 1553, and at Jaznitz, in 1742: other editions also have been printed at different times, which it is unnecessary to particularize.

On the first appearance of the *More Nevochim*, and especially after its translation into Hebrew, by R. Samuel Aben Tybbon, it met with the most violent opposition from many of the more bigoted and pharisaical Rabbins, owing to its author having preferred Scripture and Reason, to the dogmas and decisions of the Talmudical and Rabbinical doctors, in the explanation of Scripture phraseology and precepts. Rabbi SOLOMON, who presided over the synagogue, and the other Rabbins of Montpelier, in France, were among the most violent opponents of the writings of Maimonides. Professing themselves defenders of the Talmud, they omitted nothing that could discredit our author, or render him suspected of maintaining erroneous and dangerous doctrines. They even burnt his books, and excommunicated those who read them, or applied themselves to the study of foreign languages and science. This violent procedure was determinately resisted by the Rabbins of Narbonne, who anathematized R. Solomon, and two of his disciples who had been the most active in seconding the views of their teacher. Exasperated by this act, R. Solomon and his adherents appealed to the other synagogues of France; and, having engaged them in their interest, induced them to return the anathema, by publicly excommunicating the Rabbins of the synagogues of Languedoc. The Rabbins of Narbonne, resolute in their defence of Maimonides and his *More Nevochim,* immediately delegated the celebrated Rabbi David Kimchi to visit the synagogues of Catalonia and Arragon, and endeavour to prevail upon them to vindicate their illustrious countryman against the machinations of his furious enemies. Rabbi Kimchi undertook the mission, after having fruitlessly endeavoured to effect a reconciliation between the contending parties. Before he had proceeded far on his journey, he was seized with an illness, which prevented him from visiting the synagogues in person: but by his letters and influence he so far accomplished his object, that although some individuals of eminence and learning warmly espoused the cause of R. Solomon and his associates, all the principal synagogues of Spain united in the anathema, denounced against the Rabbins of France, who had combined their efforts to suppress and discredit the writings of Maimonides. R. Solomon, in the mean time, irritated by this vigorous opposition to his designs, ventured on the desperate measure of applying to the Christians to aid his determination of destroying or preventing the reading of any of the works he had condemned. For this purpose he appealed first to the common people, and then to the ecclesiastical dignitaries, assuring them that certain heretics had sprung up among the Jews, who entertained dangerous opinions, and expressing an earnest wish that they might be treated as the Christians treated such characters among themselves, by burning both them and their works. For some time the Jews were brought into great contempt and danger; but the decisive and united censure of the Spanish synagogues produced a revolution in the public mind in favour of Maimonides and his writings; for the Rabbins of France, astonished and alarmed by the proceedings of the Rabbins of Spain, withdrew their censure, revoked the decrees which had been passed at Montpelier, and consented to cancel the Epitaph on the tomb of Maimonides, who had been some time deceased, because it was there declared that he was *excommunicated*. The contest, however, did not entirely cease for several years, but was continued with more or less virulence till the year 1232, when it finally terminated.

The *More Nevochim* was the last great literary work in which our author engaged, unless, indeed, we except an accurate transcription of the PENTATEUCH made with his own hand, and designed to serve as an exemplar for the scribes of the Law. Of this transcription, Maimonides himself has stated, if the account given in an ancient manuscript be correct, that having frequently remarked, with pain, the very inaccurate and faulty manner in which the manuscripts of the Law, in use in Egypt, had been copied, he transcribed the *Books of Moses* with his own hand, from a most valuable and accurate copy, written before the destruction of Jerusalem, that other copies might be made by his disciples, and dispersed among the Jews who were settled in Egypt, that they might by this means be furnished with true copies of the Divine Laws. After completing his transcription, he visited Chalons, in Burgundy, and there obtained sight of a transcript of the Law, written by the hand of EZRA, *the priest and scribe.* With this venerated copy of the Pentateuch, he collated that which he himself had written, and found it to agree with it in every particular; and so great was his joy on the occasion, that he vowed to celebrate the event by an annual feast.

Some doubts, indeed, have been raised against the truth of this relation, from the fact not being stated in certain of his writings, in which it is supposed such an occurrence would have been noticed, if it had taken place; but if the transcripts were made, as is not improbable, towards the close of his life, it could not be noticed in works composed prior to the event.

Our great author died in Egypt, at the age of seventy, and was buried in the *Land of Israel.* For three days successively there was a general mourning among the

Egyptians as well as the Jews; and the year in which he died, was called *Lamentum Lamentabile.* " From Moses to Moses," say the Rabbins proverbially, " there never arose one like unto Moses."—" The memory of Maimonides," says Dr. Clavering, Bishop of Peterborough, " has hitherto flourished, and will continue to flourish for ever."*

* Bartalocci Bibliotheca Mag. Rabbinica, tom. iv. pp. 86—110, *Romæ,* 1676-93.—Buxtorf Maimonidis More Nevochim, in Præfat.—Buxtorfii Biblioth. Rabbin.—Clavering, Maimonidis Tractatus Duo, &c. Dissertatio de Maimonide.—Basnage's History of the Jews, B. vii. ch. 8.—Wolfii Biblioth. Heb. tom. i. p. 834. Hamburgh et Lips. 1715, 4to.

DISSERTATION I.

ON THE

TALMUDICAL AND RABBINICAL WRITINGS.

———◆———

THE principal compilations and writings of the Jewish Doctors are the TALMUDS,—the TARGUMS,—DIGESTS *of Hebrew Jurisprudence,*—COMMENTARIES ON THE SCRIPTURES,—and the MASORA and CABALA.

1.—THE TALMUDS.

THERE are two Talmuds, designated from the respective places where they were compiled, the *Talmud of Jerusalem* and the *Talmud of Babylon.*

The *Jerusalem Talmud* was compiled in the year of Christ, 230, (or, according to some, in the year 300,) for the use of the Jews living in Judea, by Rabbi Jochanan, who for many years presided over the Synagogues of " the land of Israel."—It comprises a much smaller number of doctrinal and legal questions and decisions than the later Talmud of Babylon; and, being written in the peculiar dialect of Judea, is difficult to be understood. On these accounts the voluminous Talmud of Babylon is preferred to the earlier Talmud of Jerusalem, by the Jews in general, among whom the Jerusalem Talmud is become so completely obsolete, that the use of the term " *Talmud"* is almost exclusively appropriated to the Talmud of Babylon.—

The Jerusalem Talmud was printed at *Venice*, in 1523, by D. Bomberg, in 1 vol. folio ; and again, with marginal glosses, at *Cracow*, 1609, in 1 vol. folio.

The *Talmud of Babylon* was compiled for the use of Jews dwelling in Babylon and other foreign countries, and completed about A. D. 500. It is an immense work, containing the Traditions of the Jews, their Canon Law, and the questions and decisions of the Hebrew Doctors relative to their doctrines and usages. This Talmud has been several times printed :—in 1520, in 12 vols. folio, including the Comments of Jarchi, Ben Asher, and Maimonides, by D. Bomberg, at *Venice :*—in 1581, by Frobenius, at *Basil*, in which those passages are expunged that were directed against Christianity :—at *Cracow*, in which the passages left out in the *Basil* edition were restored :—at *Amsterdam*, in 1644, by Immanuel Benbenisti, in large quarto, on two kinds of paper : (Wagenseil says, there were two editions, one correct, the other incorrect :) but the best edition is said to be that printed at *Berlin* and *Francfort*, in 12 vols. folio, 1715.

The *Talmuds* are composed of the *Mishna*, or Oral Law, which is the text, and the *Gemaras*, or decisions of the Jewish Doctors on the Mishna, prior to the compilation of the Talmuds.

The *Mishna*, or Oral Law, consists of the traditionary explanations of the Law of Moses, said to have been given by God himself to Moses, on Mount Sinai, who transmitted them by Oral communications, through Aaron and his sons, to Joshua and the Prophets, and by them to the members of the great Sanhedrim, who committed them in a similar way to their successors, till the time of *R. Judah Hakkadosh*, or the *holy*, who flourished about A. D. 150 : of whose compilation of the Mishna, *David Levi*, (" Ceremonies of the Jews," p. 285,) gives the following account : —" Rabbi *Judah Hakkadosh* was the compiler of the Mishna ; for, having seriously considered the state of our

nation in his time ; and also perceiving that the captivity
had already continued a long time ; (he having lived about
100 years after the destruction of the temple ;) and that
those learned in the Oral Law began to decrease : And
justly apprehending that the face of affairs might one day
grow worse, he came to the resolution of compiling and
digesting into one body, all those Doctrines and Practices
of our church, which had been preserved and conveyed
down to posterity by Oral Tradition, from the time of the
Elders and the Prophets, the men of the Great Synagogue,
and also the Mishnical Doctors down to his own time.　All
these he committed to writing and arranged under *six*
general heads, called *Sedorim*, orders or classes."— " As
soon as the Mishna was committed to writing," adds the
same learned Jew, " it was received by all our nation with a
general consent, and was so universally approved of by
them, that it was embraced as an authentic body of the
LAW, (as it undoubtedly was, being delivered by God to
Moses as an explanation of the Written Law, and handed
down by tradition, as already shown,) and taught in all
our public schools in the Holy Land, as also in Babylon."

The *Gemaras* are expositions of the Mishna ; for the
Mishna, being delivered in aphorisms or short sentences, as
not being intended to be committed to writing, but delivered by tradition, was thought to need some larger explica-
tions to render it the more easy and intelligible.　" This
task," observes the author already quoted, " was begun
within a short time after its first publication, by several of
the most eminent and learned men in the nation, who, in
their respective ages and schools, taught and expounded
to their scholars the meaning of those short sentences, and
illustrated all the difficult and less obvious passages of the
Mishna, with proper and useful Comments ; and those
Comments and Expositions are, what we call *Gemara*,
that is, the *Complement*, because, by them the Mishna is
fully explained, and the whole traditionary doctrine of our

law and religion completed ; for the *Mishna* is the text, and the *Gemara* is the comment, and both together is what we call the *Talmud.*"—The comments thus collected by R. Jochanan in the third century of the Christian era, and appended to the Mishna, constitute, with it, the *Jerusalem Talmud ;* and the comments and expositions collected by R. Ashe and his successors in the presidentship of the Jewish academy at Sora, and completed about the year 500, form, with the Mishna, the *Babylonish Talmud ;* and are sometimes called *the Talmud,* though without the text, or Mishna. The *Mishna,* or text, is the same in both Talmuds, the difference being in the *Gemaras* or Comments.

The *Mishna* has been frequently printed separately, with and without commentaries :—two editions, in folio, were printed at *Naples,* in 1492, with the commentary of Maimonides, by Joshua Solomon of Soncini :—another edition, with the Comments of Maimonides and Bartenora, was published at *Venice,* A. D. 1606, in folio, and again with brief and useful scholia in 1609, in 8*vo.*—There have also been separate portions printed both by Jews and Christians ; those by Christians are generally accompanied with translations, chiefly in Latin, except two titles or sections—*Shabbath* and *Eruvin,* in English, by Dr. Wotten, accompanied with learned notes, in a rare and valuable work, entitled, " Miscellaneous Discourses relating to the Traditions and Usages of the Scribes and Pharisees in our Blessed Saviour Jesus Christ's time." 2 vols. 8*vo., London,* 1718.—The most complete and useful edition of the entire Mishna, is that by Surenhusius entitled, " MISCHNA, sive totius Hebræorum Juris, Rituum, Antiquitatum, ac Legum Oralium Systema. Heb. et Lat. cum Commentariis *Maimonidis, Bartenoræ* et *aliorum:* Interprete, Editore et Notatore, *Guil. Surenhusio.*" *Amst.* 1698—1703, 6 volumes folio.—" This is a very beautiful and correct work," says a learned commentator and bibliographer,* " necessary to the library of every biblical critic and divine.   He who has it, need be solicitous for nothing more on this subject."

The *Talmuds,* being compiled by men of various talents and learning during a course of successive ages, contain, as we might justly expect, many highly figurative illustrations of Jewish opinions, many extravagant and absurd expositions of Scripture, and violent invectives against Christ and Christianity, with numberless fabulous relations and additions to Scripture facts.   The English reader who wishes to form an opinion of the ridiculous fables and monstrous absurdities, to be found in these volumes and other Rabbinical works, may consult the Rev. J. P. Stehelin's " RABBINICAL LITERATURE ; or, the Traditions of the Jews, contained in their Talmud and other mystical Writings." *London,* 1748, 2 vols., *8vo.*—The Talmudic writings have, of late, however, found an ingenious defender in *Mr. Hyman Hurwitz,* who, in an *Essay* prefixed to his " HEBREW TALES," has advocated the cause of the Hebrew writers with considerable ability and learning ; and in the " Hebrew Tales" themselves has presented the reader with several pleasing and important apologues, selected from their writings, and conveyed in an elegant and spirited translation.

But whatever may be the judgment formed of the contents of the Talmuds, it must be matter of regret to every candid lover of literature, that they should have been so frequently and vigorously prohibited and suppressed ; for, "if the *Talmud* was received with great applause by the Jews," says the Rev. J. P. Stehelin, " the Christians looked upon it as a book very pernicious, abounding with ridiculous fables, insignificant decisions, and manifest con-

* Dr. Adam Clarke.

tradictions. The Emperor Justinian in his 14th *Novel*; Lewis the Saint, King of France in the year 1240.; Philip IV., King of Spain; the Popes Gregory IX.; Innocent IV.; Honorius IV.; John XXII.; Clement VI.; Julius III.; Paul IV.; Pius V.; Gregory XIII.; Clement VIII.; &c., forbade the reading of it. The Cardinal Inquisitors at Rome, by a decree made in the year 1563; and confirmed afterwards, in the year 1627, ordered all the copies of it to be burnt. In consequence of which, the famous library of the Jews at Cremona was, in the year 1569, plundered, and about 12,000 copies, as well of the Talmud, as of other Rabbinical books, committed to the flames." (Pref. p. 27.)*

Towards the close of the tenth or the commencement of the eleventh century, the Talmud was translated into *Arabic* by order of Haschim II., Caliph of Cordova, who committed the translation to R. Joseph, the disciple of R. Moses, usually called *Moses clad with a sack*, from having been thus meanly clothed when his great learning and talents were first discovered.

2.—THE TARGUMS.

THE Chaldee word *Targum* means *translation* or *interpretation*, but is chiefly appropriated to the versions or translations of the Scriptures into the East-Aramæan or Chaldee dialect. For, after the Babylonish captivity, it was the practice of the Jews, that when the Law was "read in the synagogue every Sabbath-day," in pure Hebrew, an explanation was subjoined to it in Chaldee, in order to render it intelligible to the people, who had but an imperfect knowledge of the Biblical Hebrew.—There are ten Targums or Paraphrases still extant, on different parts of the Old Testament: These are,

* See also "Illustrations of Biblical Literature," vol. i. p. 184; ii. pp. 179, 479; iii. p. 20.

1. *The Targum of Onkelos ;* which was probably executed about the time of the Christian era, or a few years previously, as Onkelos, who was a Jew by birth and highly esteemed for his learning and probity, is said to have died eighteen years before the destruction of Jerusalem. " It is a strictly literal version, word for word, of the original text" of the Hebrew Pentateuch, into pure Chaldee. It was printed with the Pentateuch, in folio, 1482, *Bonon.*—The best edition will be found in Buxtorf's Hebrew Bible, 2 vols, *Basil,* 1620 ; or in the London Polyglott, vol. i. taken from the above, *London,* 1657, 6 vols. folio.

2 *The Targum of Jonathan Ben Uzziel, on the Prophets ;* that is, on *Joshua, Judges, Samuel,* and *Kings,* called by the Jews the *former* Prophets ;—and *Isaiah, Jeremiah, Ezekiel,* and the *twelve minor Prophets,* called the *latter* Prophets.—" This Targum is a paraphrase rather than a version, and contains many of the writer's own glosses on the text ; besides which, several stories are inserted which discredit the work."—The author, Jonathan the son of Uzziel, who was nearly contemporary with Onkelos, is said to have been educated in the school of Rabbi Hillel, grandfather to Gamaliel, at whose feet the Apostle Paul was "brought up."—To attach the greater authority to this Targum, the Jews assert, that, whilst its author was composing it, there was an earthquake for forty leagues around him ; and, that if a bird happened to pass over him, or a fly to alight on his paper whilst writing, it was immediately consumed by fire from heaven, without any injury being sustained either in the Rabbi's person or his paper ! The earliest printed edition of part of this Targum was that published with the PROPHETÆ PRIORES, folio, *Leiræ,* 1494 ; but the whole was published by Buxtorf in his *Hebrew Bible,* folio, 2 vols., 1620. This, and the *London Polyglott,* contain the best editions of this Targum.

3. *The Targum of the Pseudo-Jonathan,* so called from being *falsely* ascribed to *Jonathan Ben Uzziel,* from whose

paraphrase of the Prophets it differs so exceedingly both in style and diction, as well as in the frequent introduction of legendary stories, and occurrences long subsequent to the time of Jonathan, as to place its *pseudo* character beyond a doubt.—It is a diffuse and paraphrastic version of the *Pentateuch*, and was first printed at Venice, and afterwards at Basle. Since then it has been printed at Hanover, 1614, and at Amsterdam, with the Targums of Onkelos and Jerusalem and the Commentary of R. Solomon Jarchi:— It was translated into Latin, in the sixteenth century, by Anthony Ralph de Chevalier.

4 *The Jerusalem Targum ;* so denominated from being written in the dialect of Jerusalem, or that which was spoken by the Jews after their return from the Babylonish Captivity. The author and date of it are unknown, but it does not appear to have been written earlier than the seventh century, and some have thought not till the seventh or eighth, or even the ninth century. This Targum is not a continued paraphrase of the entire *Pentateuch*, on which it is written, but of certain parts only, occasionally omitting whole verses or chapters, and sometimes offering explanations of single words or sentences; it has therefore been supposed, by several learned philologers and critics, to have been compiled by various authors, and formed from extracts and collections. It was translated into Latin by Chevalier, and by Francis Taylor.—This Targum was published by Buxtorf in his Great Rabbinical Bible, *Venice,* 1547, *folio,* and by Walton in the London Polyglott, 1657, with an improved Latin translation. A Latin version was printed at London, 1649.

5. *The Targum of Rabbi Joseph,* surnamed the *Blind,* ruler of an academy in Syria, who flourished in the fourth century. It is a paraphrase on the books of *Chronicles* written in the Jerusalem dialect. The best edition of this Targum, is that published by David Wilkins, from a

manuscript in the University library at Cambridge, *Amstel.* 1715, 4*to.*

6. The *Targum on certain books of the Cetubim,* or Hagiographa or Holy Writings,* viz. *The Psalms, Proverbs, and Job;* is ascribed by some Jewish writers to Rabbi Joseph the Blind, though others affirm the author to be unknown. The style of it is barbarous and unequal, and intermixed with Syriac, and Greek, and Latin words, so that none but the most skilful even of the Jews can read it.—It has been published in Latin by Arias Montanus and others.

7. The *Targum on the Megilloth,* or books of Ecclesiastes, Song of Solomon, Ruth, Lamentations of Jeremiah, and Esther. The dialect is that of Jerusalem, and appears not to have been written earlier than the sixth century. The author of it is unknown.

8, 9, 10. *Targums on the book of Esther.*—Of these three Targums, the first has been printed in the Antwerp Polyglott, the second in the London Polyglott, and a Latin version of the third by Francis Taylor, London, 1655.— The first is said to be the least diffuse, and the least corrupted by legendary fables and traditions. They are all of late date, and their authors uncertain.

3.—DIGESTS OF HEBREW JURISPRUDENCE.

Of this kind are the Compendiums and Abridgments of the Mishna or Talmuds. Notices of the titles and authors of most of these will be found in Buxtorf's *Bibliotheca Rabbinica,* connected with his work *De Abbreviaturis Hebraicis.* Franeq. 1696, 8*vo.* Among these are,—אלפסי *Alphesi,* compiled by R. Isaac Ben Reuben, who died A. D. 1103, and printed at Cracow, 1597, in folio, with the Commen-

---

* The books of Scripture denominated *Cetubim* by the Jews, and *Hagiographa* by the Greeks, include the Psalms, Proverbs, Job, Song of Solomon, Ruth, Lamentations of Jeremiah, Ecclesiastes, Esther, Daniel, Ezra, Nehemiah, and Chronicles.

taries of RR. Solomon Jarchi, Jonas and Nissim;—אשרי Asheri, composed by R. Asher, who died at Toledo, A. D. 1328;—and משנה תורה Mishneh Torah, by Joseph Karro, printed at Venice, 1577, in folio , a work in great repute among the Jews.—But the digest most esteemed both by Jews and Christians, is the great work of Maimonides, entitled יד חזקה Yad Chazakah, or The Strong Hand, in which the whole Talmud is compendiously and systematically abbreviated and explained in elegant and easy Hebrew.—It was printed at Venice in 4 vols. folio, 1574; and again at Amsterdam, 4 vols. folio, 1702. A list of the titles or sections of each volume, pointing out those that have been translated into Latin, with the names of the translators, is given by Dr. Wotton in his " Miscellaneous Discourses relating to the traditions and usages of the Scribes and Pharisees,"&c.—Vol. ii. pp. 273—277, London, 1718, 8vo.

Towards the close of the seventeenth century, M. Colbert, the great patron of letters under Lewis XIV. King of France, engaged M. Lewis de Compiegne de Veil, a learned converted Jew, to translate the whole of this work into Latin. In 1678, he printed nine titles or sections, in Latin, at Paris, in a quarto volume, under the title of *Majemonidis Tractatus de Cultu Divino*; reprinted in CRENII *Fasciculi—Fascic.* 6. 7. Rotterdam, 1696, 8vo.—with the addition of three other titles or sections by the same translator. Having embraced Protestantism, M. De Veil came to England about the year 1680, and proceeding with his work, published six new titles or sections, which he entitled *Majemonides de Sacrificiis*, London, 1683, 4to. to which he subjoined the title or section of *Consecration of New Moons and Intercalations*, printed fourteen years before at Paris. He also translated and published Abarbanel's *Preface* to his *Commentary on Leviticus*, and other works

c 2

of a similar nature. It must, however, be regretted that his
design of translating and publishing the whole of Maimonides's *Yad,* was never completed, for want of greater encouragement, since the translation of the whole would have
afforded an easy and useful introduction to a knowledge of
Talmudic theology and jurisprudence, which, as Dr. Lightfoot has clearly shown in his *Horæ Hebraicæ et Talmudicæ,*
and other works, may be rendered eminently useful' in
elucidating the peculiar phraseology of the New Testament.

4.—COMMENTARIES ON THE SCRIPTURES.

THE most celebrated Jewish Commentators, are R.
Solomon Jarchi, R. Abram Aben Ezra, R. David Kimchi,
R. Moses Bar Nachman, R. Levi Ben Gersom, R. Saa-
dias, and R. Isaac Abarbanel or Abravanel.

R. SOLOMON ISAACI or IARCHI, called also *Rashi,* by
an abbreviation of his name, was born in France, at the
commencement of the twelfth century. He devoted himself to the study of the Scriptures and the Talmud; and
visiting Italy, Greece, Palestine, Persia, Tartary, Russia,
Germany, and other foreign countries, embraced every
opportunity of acquiring information relative to Rabbinical
literature, which he employed with great applause in his
academical disputations after his return from his travels.
His Commentaries are highly esteemed by the Jews, who
designate him, *the Prince of Commentators;* but, being
obscure in their style and interspersed with Talmudical
fictions, they are less regarded by Christians. He died at
Treves, in 1180, and his remains were conveyed to Prague,
in Bohemia.

R. ABRAM ABEN EZRA, surnamed *the Wise,* was a
native of Spain. He is said to have been an excellent
astronomer, philosopher, physician, poet and grammarian,
as well as a valuable interpreter of Scripture, and intimately

acquainted with the Jewish Cabala. His expositions being literal and grammatical, are highly valued both by Jews and Christians. He died about A. D. 1174.

R. DAVID KIMCHI, called from a technical abbreviation of his name *Radack*, was born in the province of Narbonne, at that time subject to Spain: this is the reason why Kimchi is generally accounted a Spaniard. His father, a learned author, was the virulent enemy of the Christians, but, happily, was not followed by his son in the bitter opposition manifested in his various writings. He was the able and successful defender of Maimonides, especially in the famous dispute between the French and Spanish Jews, relative to the MORE NEVOCHIM; (See *Life of Maimonides*, p. 19 *ante;*) and, as a commentator, secured public approbation by his sedulous attention to the grammatical sense of the Sacred Scriptures; his Commentaries on the PSALMS and on ISAIAH have been noticed with peculiar approbation.—He flourished about A. D. 1190.

R. MOSES BAR NACHMAN, frequently called *Ramban*, from the abbreviation of his name, and sometimes also *Nachmanides*, was born at Gerona, in Catalonia, about A. D. 1194. After studying Law and Physic, he applied himself to the mysteries of the Cabala, and became one of its most strenuous advocates. His Commentaries are consequently full of Cabalistic and allegorical expositions. His reputation in his native country was exceedingly great, but towards the close of life he exchanged his honours for retirement, and withdrew to Jerusalem, where he resided till his death, after having built a synagogue. The time of his decease is uncertain, different authors placing it in different years.

R. LEVI BEN GERSOM, or *Ralbag*, was a native of Provence, in France, though of Spanish extraction, Moses Bar Nachman being his maternal grandfather. He was a physician by profession, but, being fond of theological pursuits, wrote largely on various topics of divinity, and compiled a Commentary esteemed for its historical, literal, and philosophical explanations: his Exposition of the *Pentateuch* is that which is the most generally valued. He died at Perpignan, A. D. 1370.

R. SAADIAS, surnamed *Gaon,* or the *Excellent,* was a native of Al Fiumi, in Egypt, where he was born about A. D. 892. He became Rector of the Academy of Sora, and General Superintendent of the Babylonian schools in 927, and discharged his important trust with considerable honour and success. He was the author of a " literal and faithful" ARABIC translation of the OLD TESTAMENT, or certain portions of it, besides writing Commentaries on *Job, Daniel,* and the *Song of Solomon,* and composing several *Grammatical* and other works. He died A. D. 942.

R. ISAAC ABARBANEL or ABRAVANEL, was a Portuguese Jew, born at Lisbon, A. D. 1437. His father, who was a person of considerable rank, gave him the most liberal Jewish education, and such were his talents and improvement, that he was occasionally consulted by Alphonsus V. of Portugal. But on the decease of that sovereign, persecution raged with such violence against the Jews, that Abarbanel was obliged to fly into Italy, and from thence to various other places; and, after a life of chequered fortune, he died at Venice, A.D. 1508, aged 71. His writings, which are voluminous, including his Commentary, are held in considerable estimation both by his own nation, and by Christians. From his rank and birth, he is sometimes called *Don Isaac Abarbanel.*

Separate editions have been published of the principal Commentaries of the preceding authors: and most of them will be found accompanying the Great Bibles published by D. Bomberg and J. Buxtorf.

5.—THE MASORA.

THE *Masora* is a system of criticism invented by Jewish theologians to preserve the true reading of the sacred text. The Hebrew doctors assert, that when God gave the Law to Moses, on Mount Sinai, he taught him, first, its *true reading*, and, secondly, its *true interpretation*; the former of which is the subject of the *Masora*; the latter of the *Mishna* and *Gemara*. " This system is one of the most artificial, particular, and extensive comments ever written on the Word of God; for there is not one *word* in the Bible that is not the subject of a particular gloss, through its influence: Their *vowel-points* alone add whole conjugations to the language. The *Masorites* or *Mazoretœ*, as the inventors and perfecters of this system are called, were the first who distinguished the books and sections of the books of Scripture into verses. They numbered not only the chapters and sections, but the verses, words, and letters of the text, and marked the middle verse of each; the amount of these enumerations they placed at the end of each book respectively, either in numeral letters, or some symbolical word formed out of them. They have also marked whatever irregularities occur in any of the letters of the Hebrew text, such as the different size of the letters, their various positions and inversions, &c. endeavouring to find out reasons for these irregularities, and pointing out the mysteries which they supposed to be in them; they are also regarded as the authors of the *Keri* and *Ketib*, or marginal corrections of the text in the Hebrew Bibles.

The *Masora*, or collection of critical notes upon the text of the Hebrew Bibles, was at first written in separate rolls, but afterwards was abridged in order to place it in the margin. This abridgment was called the *little Masora*, (Masora parva,) or the *great Masora*, (Masora magna,) according as it was more limited or copious; and the omitted parts which were added at the end of the text, were denominated the *final Masora*, (Masora finalis.) The compilation of these Masoretic criticisms, is supposed to have been commenced about the time of the Maccabees, and to have been continued to about the year of Christ, 1030.

The first printed edition of the Masora, was in Bomberg's Great Hebrew Bible, printed at Venice, in 1526, in 2 vols. folio, and again in 1549, under the direction of R. Jacob Ben Chaim, a learned Jew, of Tunis. A Latin translation of his celebrated preface may be seen in Dr. Kennicott's *Second Dissertation*, pp. 229—244. The Jews call the Masora, *the Fence* or *Hedge of the Law*, from its being a means of preserving it from corruption and alteration.

6.—THE CABALA.

The *Cabala* is a mystical mode of expounding the Law, called by the Jews, *the soul of the soul of the Law*, many of them preferring it to the Scriptures, or Mishna, which they term *the soul of the Law*. It was delivered to Moses, say the Hebrew doctors, by the Divine Author of the Law, who not only favoured him with the Oral Explanation of the Law or Mishna, but also added a mystical interpretation of it, to be transmitted, like the Mishna, by tradition, to posterity. The *Mishna*, say they, explains the manner in which the rites and ceremonies of the Law are to be performed; but the *Cabala* teaches the mysteries couched under those rites and ceremonies, and hidden in the words and letters of the Scriptures. They divide this mystical science into thirteen different species; and by various transpositions, abbreviations, permutations, combinations, and separations of words, and from the figures and numerical powers of letters, imagine the Law sufficient to instruct the Cabalistic adept, in every art and science.

The principal interpretations and 'commentaries of the Cabalists, are contained in the book ZOHAR, said to have been written by Rabbi Simeon Ben Jochai, who died about A. D. 120 ; but it is probably of a much later date. An edition of it was printed at *Mantua*, 1558, 4*to*. and another at *Cremona*, 1559, folio. Those English readers who wish for further information relative to the *Cabala*, may consult Basnage's *History of the Jews*, B. iii. c. x—xxviii. pp. 184—256. *London*, 1708, folio,—and Gaffarel's *Unheard-of Curiosities*, passim, 8*vo*. both of them translated from the French.*

* See Surenhusii Mischna, in Præfat.—Waltoni Prolegomena.—Basnage's History of the Jews.—Buxtorfii Bibliotheca Rabbinica.—Relandi Analecta Rabbinica.—Levi's Ceremonies of the Jews.—Kennicott's Dissertations on the State of the Printed Hebrew Text.—Lewis's Hebrew Antiquities.— Prideaux's Connexion of the History of the Old and New Testament.— Clarke's Succession of Sacred Literature.—Horne's Introduction to the Critical Study of the Scriptures, &c. &c.

DISSERTATION II.

ON THE

ZABIAN IDOLATRY:

OR,

ANCIENT WORSHIP OF THE STARS.

———

ZABIANISM ; or, as it has been variously denominated
Zabaism, Sabæanism, or *Sabaism,* consisted in the
worship of the Sun and Moon, and of the other planetary
bodies, and was the most ancient and most widely spread
of any of the forms of Pagan idolatry. From the period
of its origination, it appears to have been associated with
superstitious rites and ceremonies of a symbolic or incantatory nature, and not unfrequently of the most obscene and
revolting character, varying according to the circumstances
and habits of the people by whom they were practised. By
the Jews, these idolaters were designated, from the nations
in their vicinity, and their superstitious practices condemned, as " *the ways of the Amorites.*" In subsequent
ages when other modes of idolatry prevailed almost
universally, this more early practice was denominated
ZABIANISM, most probably from the Hebrew word צבא
(*tzaba,* a host,) the sun, and moon, and stars being usually
called the *Host of Heaven.**

* Pocockii Specimen Hist. Arab. p. 139.

Intimations are given in the Holy Scriptures, that this deviation from the worship of the ONE TRUE GOD, and that its attendant practices, took place at a very early period. Job vindicates himself from all suspicion of idolatry by the most solemn asseverations :—" If I beheld the Sun when it shined, or the Moon walking in brightness, and my heart hath been secretly enticed, or my mouth hath kissed my hand : this also were an iniquity to be punished by the judge; for I should have denied the God that is above." (Job xxxi. 26 — 28) From this passage Dr. Hales argues, that Zabianism was at that period punishable by the public law ; and the Rev. G. Townsend, in his learned Dissertations " On the Origin, Progress, and Decline of Idolatry,"* observes, that " Moses, it is well known, wrote the Pentateuch, to continue the knowledge of the true God among the Israelites. As they were surrounded by idolatry in its most corrupt and odious form, he never loses sight of its superstitious observances. Unless, indeed, we understand the history of the times when Moses wrote, we lose much of the beauty and interest of his narrative. In perusing the Pentateuch, we must never forget, that idolatry had become almost universal, and that Moses, by his laws, as well as by his example, constantly endeavoured to guard his people from the contagion. Many expressions therefore, which otherwise, in a narrative so brief, as that of Moses, might appear unnecessary, were, at the time they were written, of the utmost consequence. Thus, when in the account of the Creation, Moses adds, ' He made the stars also ;'—and, ' thus the heavens were finished, and all the host of them ;' he evidently means to say to the wor-

* Classical Journal, No. XLVI. p. 332, and No. XLIV. p. 324. See also, " Young's Historical Dissertation on Idolatrous Corruptions in Religion," vol. i. pp. 30—35.

shippers of the Tsabaoth,* Your gods are inferior to Jehovah, for they are the work of his hands."

Some learned men have even supposed, that the worship of the heavenly bodies prevailed, almost universally, at the the time of the general Deluge, and was the occasion of the destruction of the old world by that dreadful judgment. This was the opinion of Onkelos, Maimonides, and other celebrated Rabbins, who interpret the words relating to the birth of Enos, (Gen. vi. 11.) "Then began men to call on the name of the Lord;" by translating them, "In those days men seceded from calling on the name of the Lord," by which they understand, "that the most glorious name of God was then given unto creatures." In this interpretation, they are followed by the very learned Selden. Lightfoot also translates the passage, "Then began profaneness in calling on the name of the Lord:" and Heidegger, in his eighth Dissertation on the Theology of the Cainites, and the Antediluvian Idolatry, adduces many arguments to prove that Idolatry was the corruption before the flood. This view of the perversion of Divine worship by the Antediluvians, has likewise been thought to be forcibly corroborated by the degree of perfection attained by the Chaldeans at so very early a period after the Deluge, and at a time when the Postdiluvians must have been much occupied in choosing their new settlements. "Burnet, justly observes in his Archæologia," says Mr. Townsend, "that, 'it is reasonable to believe that the Antediluvian fathers were not utterly foolish, and ignorant of the sciences. Of these, whatever they might have been, Noah was the heir.' Whatever the aged Patriarchs knew, was most probably communicated to Noah. He was the inhabitant of both worlds, and transferred the lamp of the sciences from one to the other. Mr. Maurice too, in his 'Memoir on the Ruins of Babylon,' very justly observes, (p. 22,) 'The very early proficiency of

* Or Host of Heaven.—ED.

the Egyptians and Chaldeans in astronomy, can only be accounted for by the supposition that a considerable portion of the Antediluvian arts and sciences, among which must be numbered astronomy, was, by the permission of Providence, preserved on tablets of stone to illumine the ignorance and darkness of the earliest Postdiluvian ages.' To suppose that our Antediluvian ancestors, for sixteen hundred years together, could be uninterested spectators of the celestial bodies, would be to imagine them destitute of common curiosity."*

Gale (*Court of the Gentiles*) supposes the Zabian idolatry to have arisen from indistinct and misunderstood traditions; his words are:—" It will be necessary to consider, though but cursorily, the rise and progress of all *Idol-Gods* and *Idolatry*: all of which is comprehended, by some learned men, under these two common heads of *Zabaism* and *Hellenism*. *Zabaism*, so termed from the Zabii, a sect of Chaldean philosophers, was the first and more natural piece of idolatry, which consisted in a religious worship given unto the sun, moon, and stars, stiled in Scripture, the Hosts of Heaven. *Hellenism*, which superadded hereto an infinity almost of fictitious and coined gods, was of more late date, and proper to the Grecians, most skilful in the art of making gods. As for *Zabaism*, which gave a Deity and Divine worship to the sun, moon, and stars, it began very early, even in the infancy of the church, and had made good progress in the world about the age of Job and Moses, as appears by Job xxxi, 26, 27; as also by Deut. xi. 6.—and as Owen, (Theolog. Lib. 3. c. 4, p. 188, &c.) observes, this Pagan humour, of idolizing these glorious celestial bodies, seems to have had its rise from some broken traditions, conveyed by the Patriarchs touching the dominion of the sun by day, and of the moon by

---

* Classical Journal, No. XLII. pp. 323, 324.—Young On Idolatrous Corruptions in Religion, vol. i. pp. 7, 8, 15, *Lond.* 1734, *8vo.*—Waltoni Polyglott. tom. i.—Onkelos in Gen. iv. 26.

night; according to Gen. i. 16 and Psalm cxxxvi. 7, 8, 9, where the sun and moon are stiled the ' greater lights' not only by condescension to vulgar capacities, as some will have it, but from their peculiar office, the Sun being appointed to govern by day, and the Moon by night. So that albeit the Moon be, in regard of its substance and borrowed light, inferior to many of the stars, yet, by virtue of its office, it is above them, and so termed a ' greater light.' Now it is very probable, that the fame of this dominion, conferred by God on the Sun and Moon, was diffused amongst the Gentiles, first in the oriental parts; whence their corrupt imaginations, very prone to idolatry, conferred a deity on these creatures which to them seemed most glorious. Thence they termed the Sun מלך *Moloch*, or *Melec*, the *King;* also בעל *Baal*, the *Lord;* and אל *El, God*, (whence the Greek ʽηλιος the *Sun:*) likewise בעל שמים *Bel Sames, Lord of Heaven;* and עליון ʽελιουν *Eliun*, the *Most High*, all which are names, which the Scripture gives the true God of Israel, and, without all peradventure, had their original thence." *

The almost immemorial antiquity of this species of idolatry is not only maintained by the concurrent testimony of the most ancient accredited authors, profane as well as sacred, but also by the remains, which have been discovered in various countries, especially in the East, of symbolic representations of sidereal objects of religious veneration. Of these, the engraved cylindrical signets recovered and brought from the East by Capt. Lockett, Mr. Rich, and others, from the sites of the ancient Babylon and Nineveh, and from Phenicia, and deposited in various European museums, are curious and interesting specimens. Landseer, in his erudite " Sabæan Researches," supposes these signets to

* Gale's Court of the Gentiles, Part I. Book ii, Chap. 1, pp. 105, 106.—Oxon. 1669, 4to.

have been engraved for the purpose of exhibiting the state
of the heavens at the time of the birth of the persons
to whom the signets respectively belonged; "and hence the
astrological priest who registered the birth of a Babylonian
child, also cast his nativity; and, in so doing, assigned to
him the subject of his future signet."—Some of the horoscopical signets which he has examined, he regards as being
more than *three thousand* years old, and defends the conjecture by learned astronomical calculations.—"There is a
remarkable conformity," he observes, "between our antique
cylindrical monuments and the earlier poets, prophets, and
astronomers, with regard to the comparative veneration, in
which the extra-zodiacal asterisms were held in the remoter
periods of time: and the impressive coincidence at which we
here arrive, between the art and literature of far distant
ages and nations—between that practice of the Chaldean
astronomers which may be safely inferred from the more
ancient of the cylindrical engravings; and that habitual
observation of the stars which is recorded of the patriarchs,
prophets, and philosophers, of the Sacred Scriptures and
of Greece,—I repeat, the impressive coincidence between
these, at which we here arrive,—is probably the best of all
evidence that is now attainable, on a subject so remote in
time and place, and so recondite in its nature."*

Dr. Long, whose great astronomical knowledge rendered
him deservedly celebrated, expresses a similar opinion of
the antiquity of the Zabian idolatry: "The most ancient
idolaters," says he, "are, with great probability, thought by
some learned men to have received the name of Zabii from
worshipping the host of heaven;" and subsequently adds,
" I have before observed, that Zabaism, or the worship of the
host of heaven, was the most ancient kind of idolatry; the
custom of deifying dead men was later, though that also is

---

* Landseer's Sabæan Researches, pp. 55, 104, 242, 250, 251, 327, *et
passim.*—London, 1823, 4*to.*

very ancient."* The antiquity of *Uranolatria*, or wor-
ship of the heavenly bodies, is also maintained by Selden,
(*De Diis Syris*, c. 3,) Beyer, (*Additamenta* ad cap. 3.
Joh. Seldeni,) Pococke, (*Specimen Historiæ Arabum,
Notæ*, p. 138,) Hyde, (*Hist. Relig. Vet. Persar.* c. 1,)
Prideaux, (Connection of the History of the Old and New
Testament, p. 1. b. iii,) and other learned Orientalists.

Zabianism, or Sabæanism, was not only the most ancient
species of idolatry, but extended its influence more universally than any other. " This religion," says Mr. Young,
" having taken its rise in Chaldæa, was soon carried into
Egypt, and from thence into Greece. It spread itself to
the most distant parts of the world, and infected not only
the eastern and western Scythians or Tartars, but the
Mexicans too, for there the Spaniards found it when they
first came amongst them."† Traces of this worship are still
found in the island of Ceylon, where it is termed *Baliism*,
a word of uncertain etymology, but which will remind an
antiquary of the names of *Baal*, *Bel*, and *Bal*, given to the
sun,‡ by the Chaldeans and other ancient nations, and the
Baltan or *Bealteine* fires of Ireland and Highlands of
Scotland.§ These Singhalese worshippers of the stars are
few in number, and generally conceal their opinions. " The
worship consists, entirely, of adoration to the heavenly
bodies; invoking them in consequence of the supposed
influence they have on the affairs of men. The (Singhalese)
priests are great astronomers, and believed to be thoroughly
skilled in the power and influence of the planets." Among
the valuable paintings, illustrative of the religious opinions
of the native inhabitants of Ceylon, brought from thence by

* Long's Astronom. B. ii, chap. 2, p. 179: B. iii, chap. 3, p. 194.
† Young on Idolatrous Corruptions in Religion, Vol. i. p. 35.
‡ See Selden De Diis Syris, Syntag. 2. et Additamenta Beyerii. *Amst.*
1680. 12*mo.*
§ See Ency. Perth. *in voc.* and the authorities referred to in that work, and
Toland's History of the Druids, Let. 2. pp. 101—106.

Sir Alexander Johnstone, are several referring to the worship just described.*

Abulpharagius affirms, that the major part of the ancient Greeks were Zabians, (Græcorum plerique *Sabii* erant,) worshipping the stars, and forming idolatrous representations of them.† This opinion is supported by R. P. Knight, Esq. in "An Inquiry into the Symbolical Language of Ancient Art and Mythology," in which he remarks, "The primitive religion of the Greeks, like that of all other nations not enlightened by Revelation, appears to have been elementary; and to have consisted in an indistinct worship of the sun, the moon, the stars, the earth, and the waters, or rather to the spirits supposed to preside over those bodies, and to direct their motions, and regulate their modes of existence."‡ In this he follows the early Heathen and Christian writers, who assert that the principal persons among the ancient Greeks held the sun, and moon, and stars, to be gods; which, Plato assures us, was the species of worship prevalent among the greater part of barbarous nations.§ Landseer, further states, that the "ancient Sabæan faith in the stars, is well known to have reached from the lands of Nimrod and Jemsheed, westward through that of Canaan, to the shores of the Mediterranean: southward to the straits of Babel-mandel, and the Erythrean ocean; and northward to the farthest extremities of Scythia."||

The superstitions accompanying this mode of idolatry, varied among different nations and at different periods, as is fully proved by the mythology of the Greeks, and

* For this information I am indebted to the Rev. Benjamin Clough, an intelligent and learned Wesleyan Missionary, in Ceylon, one of the translators of the Cingalese Scriptures.

† Greg. Abul Pharajii Hist. Dynast. a Pocock, p. 6, *Oxon*, 1663, 4*to*.

‡ Classical Journal, No. XLV. March, 1821, p. 1.

§ Eusebii Præparat. Evang. Lib. i. c. 9, and iii, c. 2.—tom. I. *Coloniæ* 1688, folio.

|| Landseer's Sabæan Researches, Essay viii. p. 264.

D

Romans, and others, as detailed by their best and most authentic historians, as well as by those who have expressly treated upon the rites and ceremonies of the ancient idolatries. Eusebius, in his " Præparatio Evangelica," has discussed this point with considerable learning; and the names of Grotius, Jablonsky, Bryant, Leland, and many others among the moderns, are too well known to need eulogium. I shall, therefore, only add from General Vallancey, who supposes IRELAND to be the ancient *Thule*, and to have derived its idolatrous worship from the Carthaginians, that, " The chief deity of the Carthaginians was Baal, Beal, or Bel, the Sun, to whom they offered human sacrifices. The chief deity of the Heathen Irish was Beal, the sun, to whom also they offered human sacrifices. The sacrifice of beasts was at length substituted among the Carthaginians; the same custom, we learn from the ancient Irish historians, prevailed in this country. The month of May is, to this day, named *Mi Beal teinne*, i. e. the month of Beal's fire; and the first day of May is called *la Beal teinne*, i. e. the day of Beal's fire. These fires were lighted on the summits of hills, in honour of the sun; many hills in Ireland still retain the name of *Cnoc greinne*, i. e. the hill of the Sun; and on all these are to be seen the ruins of Druidish altars. The Carthaginians did not represent *Baal*, as they had him before their eyes daily in all his glory; they made their addresses immediately to him according to the ancient rite. No idol of Baal is ever mentioned by the ancient Irish historians, or was any ever found since Christianity was introduced." *

To show the peculiar fitness of the Mosaic Ritual for eradicating the opinions and practices of the Zabii from the congregation of Israel, forms an important part of the design of Maimonides in the ensuing treatise translated from his celebrated MORE NEVOCHIM, or " Teacher of the Perplexed." For this interesting exposition, he

* Essay on the Antiquity of the Irish Language, p. 19, 1772, 8vo.

was peculiarly qualified by his extensive and intimate acquaintance with the works extant amongst the Egyptians and Arabians on the subject of the Zabian idolatry; his profound knowledge of the Talmudical and Rabbinical writings; his opportunities of investigating the idolatries of Egypt during his residence in that country; and his uncommon acuteness and energy of mind, joined to his patience in research and soundness in judgment. " Maimonides," observes Mr. Townsend, " was the first who endeavoured to solve the mysteries which had so long perplexed the world. He perused, he tells us, with great attention, all the ancient authors on the rise and progress of idolatry. . He did this, to explain the reasons of the enactment of those ordinances and rites of the Jewish Law which appear to have no meaning, unless they are considered in connexion with the idolatrous customs of the surrounding nations."*—The result of these investigations is comprised in the following treatise, which, with every allowance for Jewish prejudices, presents one of the best compendiums of expository remarks on many of the Mosaic Precepts, with which we are acquainted, and fully justifies the eulogiums which have been passed upon him by the learned of different ages and countries.

* Classical Journal, No. XLII. June, 1820, p. 322.

DISSERTATION III.

ON

THE ORIGINALITY

OF THE

INSTITUTIONS OF MOSES.

———

IT has been justly remarked by an ingenious writer, that they who suppose Moses himself to have been " the author of the institutions civil or religious that bear his name; and that in framing them he borrowed much from the Egyptians or other ancient nations, must never have compared them togther, otherwise they could not but have perceived many circumstances in which they differed most essentially from them all."—That a correspondence subsisted between some of the Mosaic ordinances and the customs of other people, is granted, but that they were derived from the practices of idolatrous nations appears inconsistent and absurd. The true source of the similarity is to be traced to those primitive revelations and patriarchal examples retained by the Israelites and corrupted by the Gentiles;—whilst the striking and radical opposition discoverable between the most important parts of their respective systems of worship and religious service, mark, with indubitable evidence, the design of the Deity to separate the one from the other. It is only necessary to give to the following instances of the dissimilarity betwixt the Laws and Institutions of Moses and those of other nations, the consideration they merit, to be fully convinced, that the Mosaic ritual was vastly

superior to every other, and formed with too much con-
trariety to other systems ever to have been borrowed from
them.

1. No heathen ever conceived an idea of so great an
Object as that of the Institutions of Moses, which appears
to have been nothing less than the instruction of all mankind in the great doctrine of the Unity and Moral Government of God, as the Creator of the world, and the common Parent of all the human race, in opposition to the
polytheism and idolatry which then prevailed, which,
besides being grossly absurd in its principles and leading to
endless superstitions, threatened the world with a deluge
of vice and misery.—For this purpose the Hebrew nation
was placed in the most conspicuous situation, among all
the great civilized nations of the earth, which were universally addicted to idolatry of the grossest kind, to divinations, necromancy, and other superstitions of a similar
nature, and practised as acts of religion ; some of their
rites abominably licentious, and others most horribly cruel,
yet enjoined as the necessary means of recommending the
persons that performed them to the various objects of their
worship.

As all mankind imagined that their outward prosperity
depended upon the observance of their respective religions,
that of the Hebrew nation was made to do so in the most
conspicuous manner as a visible lesson to all the world.
They were to prosper beyond all other nations while they
adhered to their religion, and to suffer in a manner equally
exemplary and conspicuous in consequnce of their departure from it. Of this, all mankind might easily judge.

These great ideas occur in the sacred books of the
Hebrews, and no where else. They are all distinctly advanced by Moses, and more fully unfolded in the writings of the
later prophets. But certainly nothing so great and sublime
could have been suggested to Moses, from any thing that he
saw in Egypt, or could have heard of in other countries.

2. In no system of Religion, besides that of Moses, was *purity of Morals* any part of it. All the heathen religions were systems of mere ceremonies, and the sole business of the Priests was to attend to those rites, which were so far from being favourable to morals, that they were of the most impure and abominable nature.

The contrary to this appears, not only in the Ten Commandments, but in all the Writings of Moses. The purest morality, the most favourable to private and public happiness, was the principal and ultimate object of the whole system. Sacrifices, and ceremonial observances of every kind, are always represented as of no signification without morals. Such precepts as these, " Be ye holy, for I am holy;"—and, " What does the Lord require of thee, but to do justly, and to love mercy, and to walk humbly with thy God?"—could never have been borrowed from any heathen system of Religion. The Writings of Moses, and of the Prophets that succeeded him, are in these respects *a great Original.*

3. No where in all the heathen world could Moses have heard of such a sublime *Worship*, as that which he introduced. The Hebrews alone had one single object of their worship, one altar, one precise ritual, one only place for the meeting of the whole nation at the great public festivals. In no other country in the world were the *public festivals* instituted in commemoration of such great events, respecting their history and the divine origin of their religion. It is also peculiar to this nation, that directions for the celebration of them were reduced to writing at the time of their institution, so that there never could be any uncertainty about the *origin* or the *reasons* of them. These festivals were three, the Passover, on their deliverance from their state of servitude in Egypt, when the first-born of all the Egyptians were destroyed, and all theirs preserved ; the Pentecost, on the giving of the Law from Mount Sinai ;

and the Feast of Tabernacles, in commemoration of their living in tents or booths during their travels through the Wilderness.

No heathen festivals were so well adapted to important events as these. The festivals of the heathens were numerous and perplexing. More than sixty were celebrated by the Athenians; the origin and reasons of their institution were uncertain, and none of them were to answer any important moral purpose. The heathen festivals were also in general celebrated in a manner the most disgusting to modesty and common sense. Even the wise Athenians celebrated the festival of Cotytto with such rites, as demonstrated that the object of their worship delighted in nothing so much as lewdness and debauchery.—*Potter's Antiquities of Greece,* p. 409.

It would be easy to multiply examples of the indecency and absurdity of the festivals of the heathen, and those of Greece were chiefly borrowed from Egypt. Why did not Moses the same? Such arts would no doubt have been acceptable to his people, naturally prone to sin like others; and this is evident from his own history of the Israelites joining in the worship of Baal-Peor. So far, however, was the Jewish legislator from yielding to such compromising suggestions, that in the place of the infamous rites and orgies inseparable from Egyptian festivals, the Jewish festivals were united with inviolable principles of morality, which were constituted solemn acts of religion, and, in their purport and manner of observation, perfectly distinguished the Israelitish congregations from the other families of mankind.

4. In no other country was the *Place,* and other circumstances of the public worship, so well calculated to inspire a profound respect for the object of it, as among the Hebrews. No heathen temple could be compared with the Temple of Solomon, or even the tabernacle of Moses, erected in the wilderness, designed only for temporary use,

and portable. The dress and office of the High Priest, and the whole of the Ceremonials annexed to the Priesthood, were in the highest degree striking and impressive, and far beyond any thing of the kind in the heathen world.

When the nation was in the wilderness, even then an order and solemnity were observed, for which there was no precedent. The place of the tabernacle was in the centre, each of the twelve tribes had its prescribed place on the North or South, the East or West side of it. The Levites had their station nearest to it, and were employed in taking it down, carrying, or erecting it. They were not, however, allowed to touch the most sacred utensils, this duty remained solely with the priests. To them also exclusively appertained the carrying the ark, the place of which was the Holy of Holies, and over which was the place where the immediate presence of God was manifested.

How different from this were the most solemn processions of the heathens, when they carried the images of their gods from place to place, generally, at least, in the East, on the idea of giving them an airing, or amusing them with an excursion from their temples! (*Asiatic Researches*, vol. i. p. 292.) In time of public danger, they made a public feast in the temples, and the statues of the gods were brought in rich beds with pillows, and placed in the most honourable parts of the temple, as the principal guests.—*Kennett's Antiquities of Rome*, p. 84.

The Ark of the Hebrews was never removed on any such ideas as these. It contained no *image* to which such an excursion or entertainment could apply; and, after the building of the temple, it was never on any occasion removed out of it. Before this it had, by the order of God, been carried by the priests to the brink of the river Jordan, the waters of which were divided as their feet touched them; and on some solemn occasions it was permitted to be carried as a token of the Divine presence; and from the wonders thus wrought, the Hebrews must have had a much higher idea of the object of their worship, than any of the heathens could have of theirs.

5. *Sacrificing* was a mode of worship more ancient than idolatry, and instituted, as there are the strongest reasons to believe, by the Deity himself, as soon as the guilt of man made such an offering necessary. But this universal practice was greatly corrupted by the heathen, who introduced superstitious customs, thus teaching the worshippers to reverence and fear the creature rather than the Creator, all of which were excluded from the religion of the Hebrews; while their sacrifices assumed a greatness, and excited an elevated hope, by manifesting that they were the pattern of heavenly things, and shadows of good things to come, when "a body should be prepared for him" who was the substance of them all.

The heathen sacrifices were different according to the rank of the particular deity to whom they were offered. (*Potter*, p. 216.) No distinction of this kind was suffered to offend the Holy One of Israel. With the heathens there was an order of Priests called *Haruspices*, whose sole business it was to examine the entrails, especially the liver, and to *divine* success, or the contrary, from the appearance. No such superstition dishonoured the moral Governor of the world in the Hebrew ritual.

We read of nothing among the heathen from which Moses could take such distinctions of offerings as we read in his institutions — The *burnt-offerings*, *sin-offerings*, *peace-offerings*, or of the *heaving*, or *waving* of them. These therefore, he could not borrow from them. These positive institutions by which the people were thus disciplined, Christian believers now know, and the whole Jewish nation might know, answered a divine purpose, and, as a school-master, brought the worshippers to Christ.

Lastly: Among all the Heathen, especially in the time of Moses, *Human Sacrifices* were considered as the most acceptable to the gods; but in the law of Moses nothing is mentioned with greater abhorrence, and they are expressly declared to have been a principal cause of the expulsion of the idolatrous inhabitants of Canaan. The *right* of the Deity indeed, to claim the life which He has given, in any way that may please him, is evident, and is intimated by the command given to Abraham, to offer up Isaac. But when the faith of the Patriarch was proved, the offering was declined, and a ram substituted in his place.

6. If the heathen had any *Temples* before the time of Moses, which is uncertain, and not probable, they were constructed in a very different manner from the tabernacle, or the temple of Solomon. We no where read of *such divisions* as that of the Hebrew temple; of such a *symbol of the divine presence* as the covering of the Ark between the Cherubim, in the Holy of Holies; there was no *table of shew-bread*, nor such a candlestick as was in the holy place. The fire and the lamps, also, evidently had their use, as appointed by Moses, but though sacred, there was nothing in them to divert the reverence of the worshipper from the invisible Jehovah. This could not be said of the perpetual fires, either of the Persians, or of the Vestals at Rome: These were debasing superstitions.

7. Both the Hebrews and the heathen allowed *the Privilege of Asylum* to those who fled to their temples. But with the heathens this was carried to a length equally superstitious and dangerous to the community; because, whatever was the crime with which any person was charged, the criminal could not be apprehended, and much less could he be punished, without incurring the vengeance of the Deity, who, it was supposed, protected him. (*Potter's Antiquities*, p. 201.) But no person, charged with any crime, was protected by flying to the altar of the Hebrews, except till the cause could be heard by regular judges; when, if he appeared to be guilty, he was ordered to be

taken from the altar itself, and put to death. Even the City of Refuge could not protect him, who was found, upon inquiry, to have killed his neighbour with design.

8. Had Moses copied any thing from the heathen, he would probably have introduced something of their *Mysteries*, which were rites performed in secret, and generally in the night; to which peculiar privileges were annexed, and which it was deemed the greatest crime to reveal. The most remarkable of these mysteries were the Eleusinian, which were celebrated at Athens every fourth year. Whatever these rites were, (and they were of a very suspicious nature,) it was made death to reveal them, and if any person, not regularly initiated, was present at this exhibition, he was put to death without mercy. Vile as these mysteries must have been, according to the habits of the initiated, yet it was taken for granted, that those who had performed them, lived in a greater degree of happiness than other men, both before and after death.—*Potter's Antiquities*, vol. i. p. 389.

Nothing like this can be found in the Institutions of Moses. There was no *secret* in the Hebrew ritual. Every thing is described in the written law; and though none but the Priests could enter the holy place, and none the Holy of Holies, besides the High Priest, every thing that was done by them there, is as particularly described, as what was to be done by the people without.

9. The heathen had their *Oracles*, as well as the Hebrews; but the difference between them was very great. With the Hebrews, the responses were in a clear, articulate voice, free from ambiguity, and given only on solemn occasions, and with a solemnity becoming a message from God. They were also perfectly gratuitous, and confined to no particular time. But the Oracles of the heathen were always obscure, and generally ambiguous, delivered in a frantic manner, only at particular seasons, and always attended with great expence.

10. The heathen had also their *Purifications*; but how very different from those of the Hebrews! Nothing was used by them for this purpose, but pure water, evidently emblematic of inward purity. The only obscure article, in this respect, was that prescribed for cleansing after the touch of a dead body, on which occasion the water was mixed with the ashes of a red heifer; and certainly there was no precedent for this among the Egyptians, or any other nation. But the heathen used mixtures continually, and with such superstitious regard to particulars, as evidently taught the worshippers to reverence the creatures used, instead of the Creator. The purifications also among the Hebrews tended to recommend cleanliness, and consequently to promote health; but some of the most sacred rites of the heathen were filthy and disgusting,—as the *Tauribolium*, in which the person so *purified*, was covered with blood, his hair and his garments full of it, and in this condition he continued as long as he could, without washing himself or changing his dress!

11. Religion directed the choice of proper articles of *Food*, both with the heathen and the Hebrews; but with the latter, the most wholesome food was allowed, and nothing was forbidden for any reason which tended to nourish superstition. But no good reason can be given for the Egyptians abstaining from mutton, the Syrians from fish, the Hindoos from the flesh of cows, or the Priests, in some countries, from the flesh of animals of any kind. The only reasons given tended to superstition. The Hebrew priests also were not obliged to practise any peculiar austerities. They might drink wine, except during the time of their actual ministrations. They might marry and have families. The heathen priests on the contrary, (*Potter*, p. 391,) were obliged to submit to austerities equally superstitious, cruel, and debasing.

12. Moses assigned no part of the national worship to *Females*, but in the heathen temples there were Priestesses

as well as Priests, and the Oracle at Delphi was always delivered by a woman. In this respect a very striking difference exists between the heathen and the Hebrew worship.

13. Where, in all the world, could Moses have obtained the idea of his *Annual Fast*, for the purpose of a general confession of sin? Where could he find any thing like the striking lesson exhibited on that occasion, first of the dreadful wages of sin, and secondly of the removal of it, by the fine emblems of a goat sacrificed, as suffering the penalty, and another goat dismissed, over the head of which the confession had been made? Many rites of the heathen were celebrated with the appearance of grief and deep affliction, but for no such moral purpose; on the contrary, the worshippers soon passed to every species of licentiousness. Such were the festivals of Adonis in the East and in Greece, but it was only a commemoration of his death in the first instance, and of his re-animation in the second.

14. *A weekly Sabbath,* continually reminding the Hebrews of the Creation of the world in six days, as opposed to the general opinion of the Heathen, that the world had existed from eternity, without any intelligent author :—a *Sabbatical Year,* reminding them, that the country they occupied was not their own but God's, who only gave them the use of it under such terms as he thought proper :—and a *Jubilee,* (to be mentioned hereafter,) were institutions peculiar to the Hebrews, and what Moses could not have borrowed from any other nation.

15. Had Moses borrowed any thing from the heathen, he could not have overlooked their various modes of *Divination, Sorcery, and Witchcraft;* their omens, their distinctions of days into lucky and unlucky, &c. But so far are we from finding any thing of this kind in the writings of Moses, that they are spoken of with the greatest abhorrence, and they who learn of the heathen, are ordered to be put to death.

In fact, the truth of the Mosaic revelation appears, in few points more strongly and forcibly than in this ; for the edicts which were repeatedly enacted against every species of it, the peremptory statutes which interdicted wizards, soothsayers, and those pretending to familiar spirits, and forbad, as unworthy of the veracity of the God of Israel, every artifice by which the public mind had been led astray, are no unimportant vouchers of that inspiration which Moses claimed, being corroborative in every point of the legal mode of ascertaining the Divine will, by Urim and Thummim, which he records.   The belief, indeed, of fatidical responses, appears to have been so deeply rooted, and to have acquired such strength from the long adoption of divination and oracles, that possibly the Israelites would have attached no credit to a system in which every mode of obtaining divine responses had been wanting ; but miracles, and visible proofs of the attending Deity, had so completely authenticated the disclosure of their law, that they were supplied with superabundant evidences, that the answers returned to the High Priest, within the precincts of the sanctuary proceeded, indubitably, from God.   Hence, instead of wearing amulets, talismans, and other fancied repellents of evil, like their former oppressors, they were taught to seek protection in obedience to the divine commandments, and desired to bind the law of God as a sign on the hand, and as frontlets between the eyes, and to write it on their houses and gates.

16. The general system of *Civil Government* laid down in the institutions of Moses, is essentially different from any thing that he could have seen, or heard of, in his time, and infinitely more favourable to personal liberty, and consequently to justice, truth, and happiness.

In the time of Moses, all the neighbouring countries, of any note, were governed by kings, whose will, as far as appears, was the only law.   But the government instituted by Moses, was a government of *fixed laws*, and those laws reduced to *writing*, so that they could not but have been universally known; and nothing was left to the arbitrary will of any man, whatever office he might hold in the state. In all this, a noble example was set to the world; and we find, in fact, that civil and personal liberty have been regarded in every nation in proportion as the Scripture has been regarded. The government of the Hindoos is the very reverse of that of Moses, being evidently calculated, as Sir William Jones has justly observed, to throw all power into the hands of the despot and the priests, while the rest of the nation were kept in ignorance and slavery.

The Hebrew government was a Theocracy: God was their King, not only as creatures, but as a nation. As, however, a deviation, through the unfaithfulness of the people, from this divine constitution, was foreseen, provision was made for it; and, among other guards against the abuses of power, the King was requested to write, with his own hand, a copy of the laws by which he and the rest of the nation were to be governed. Their kings were thus the lieutenants of Jehovah, nor did any king of Judah, even the most addicted to idolatry, make any alteration in the laws of the kingdom. The priests received no power by the civil governors; God determined by Moses the duties and the privileges of each; and no classes of men were ever more different from each other, than the Brahmins among the Hindoos, and the order of priests among the Israelites; this all unprejudiced persons, who are in the smallest degree attentive to the subject, must acknowledge.

17. If Moses had borrowed his religious institutions from Egypt, or any other nation, he would probably have adopted some of their *Civil Laws*, as those relating to persons, property, &c. But we find no such resemblance in those of any nation, ancient or modern. The privileges

of the Sabbatical year, and of the Jubilee, are wholly of a civil nature, and they must have been an admirable security for personal liberty, and the property of families. No Hebrew could bind himself in a servile state for more than seven years, nor could he alienate his landed property for more than fifty. In consequence of this, though a family might suffer by the imprudence or extravagance of the head of it, the evil had a limit, for all estates at the Jubilee reverted to their original proprietors.

The laws relating to theft, robbery, and personal injuries, are by no means the same with those of other nations, and they are all admirable for their equity. The abominable vices of sodomy and bestiality, are punishable with death by the law of Moses, but not by those of any ancient legislator; and they are eminently calculated to preserve the real dignity, and prevent the degradation of mankind.

18. In all ancient nations there were trials by various *Ordeals*, in which the accused person was supposed to be guilty, unless fire or water did not injure him. This is the case among the Hindoos, who hold this mode of evidence in the highest veneration. In the institutions of Moses we find one trial by ordeal, but it is so essentially different from any that was in use in other countries, that it could never have been borrowed from them. This was in the case of a wife suspected of adultery. To satisfy the husband in this case, the wife was made to drink a quantity of water, in which was put some dust from the ground, and the scrapings of a writing, containing a denunciation of divine judgments to be instantly inflicted in case they were guilty. But besides that recourse was had to this mode of trial only in defect of proper evidence, all that can be objected to, even by those who do not believe in any divine interposition, is, that the guilty person might remain unhurt: a striking contrast this to the cruel and unjust ordeals of the heathen.

From this general view of the subject, and the comparison might have been extended to many more particulars, it is manifest, that the laws of Moses are truly *original;* and that their superiority to those of other nations, even the most famed for wisdom, especially if we consider the high and certain antiquity of these laws, is an evidence of their divine origin ; and that Moses truly was, according to his own declarations, *only the instrument of* JEHOVAH. His appeal to the people, thus taught of God, has all the boldness of truth, and need never fear detection or contradiction. " Behold ! I have taught you statutes and judgments, even as the Lord my God commanded me, that you should do so in the land whither ye go to possess it. Keep, therefore, and do them, for this is your wisdom and understanding in the sight of the nations, which shall hear all these statutes, and say, Surely this great nation is a wise and understanding people. For what nation is there so great, who hath God so nigh unto them, as the Lord our God is in all things that we call upon him for ? And what nation is there so great, that hath statutes and judgments so righteous as all this law, which I set before you this day ?" Deut. iv. 5—8.*

* For the observations in this Dissertation, I am indebted principally to a valuable pamphlet, *On the Originality of the Mosaic Institutions,* printed in Northumberland, America, 1803, 8vo. and Dr. Wait's *Course of Sermons preached before the University of Cambridge.* Lond. 1826.

E

DISSERTATION IV.

ON

THE MOSAIC DISTINCTION OF ANIMALS.

———————

THE Jewish Legislator, in the eleventh chapter of Leviticus, specifies various Beasts, Birds, Fishes, and Reptiles, which he distinguishes by the terms CLEAN and UNCLEAN : the " clean" are permitted to be eaten, but the " unclean" are forbidden. He also lays down certain rules for distinguishing, generally, those that are " clean " from those that are " unclean."—According to the position so ably defended by Maimonides, these distinctions are not arbitrarily marked, or causelessly enjoined, but originate in sacred wisdom, and are designed to promote the welfare of the nation on whom they are enforced.—It may therefore increase our conviction of the wise and salutary tendency of the Mosaic economy, to glance at the nature of the tests established for ascertaining the legal purity or impurity of animals in general ; and to enquire into the reasons for adopting the distinction.

I.—THE SYSTEM OF DISCRIMINATION.

1. WITH respect to *Quadrupeds*, Moses reduces the rules of distinction to the natural and simple ones of *the form of the foot* and *the chewing of the cud*. All beasts that have their feet completely cloven, above as well as below, and at the same time ruminate or chew the cud, are

"clean:" those which have neither, or want one of these distinguishing marks, are " unclean."—But as there are some cases in which doubt may arise whether they do fully divide the hoof, or ruminate, as in the case of the *hare*, &c., the legislator, in order to prevent difficulties, authoritatively decides the point, by distinctly specifying which of such animals shall be eaten, and which shall be forbidden.— On this system of distinction, Michaelis, in his *Commentaries on the Laws of Moses*, observes, " That, in so early an age of the world, we should find a systematic division of quadrupeds so excellent as never yet, after all the improvements in natural history, to have become obsolete, but, on on the contrary, to be still considered as useful by the greatest masters of the science, cannot but be looked upon as truly wonderful."*

2. The systematic distinction of *Fishes*, is equally clear and simple as the former. All that have *scales and fins* are " clean" or lawful to be eaten, all others "unclean" or forbidden.

3. With regard to *Birds*, no particular characters are given for dividing them into classes, as " clean," or "unclean;" but judging from those which are specified, so far as the obsolete nature of the Hebrew names will permit, it will be found, that those which live on grain are not prohibited; and as these are the domesticated kinds, we might almost express it in other words—that birds of prey, generally, are rejected, that is, those with crooked beaks and strong talons ; whether they prey on lesser fowls or animals, or on fish : while those which eat vegetables are admitted as lawful. So that the same principle is maintained to a certain degree, among birds as among beasts."†

* Michaelis's Commentaries, translated by Dr. A. Smith, vol. iii. Art. 204, p. 233. *London*, 1814, *8vo.*

† Scripture Illustrated, by C. Taylor: cited by Harris, in Natural History of the Bible, Dissert. iii. *London*, 1824, *8vo.*

4. With respect to *Serpents, Worms, Insects,* &c., it is declared, that "all creatures that creep, going upon all four; and whatsoever goeth upon the belly; or whatsoever hath more feet than four among creeping things, are an abomination." An exception, however, is made with respect to those winged insects, which besides four walking legs, have also two longer springing legs, (*pedes saltatorii,*) and under the denomination of *locusts* are accounted clean.

5. Besides the general distinctions already noticed, another is made relating to whatsoever goeth upon his *paws* among all manner of beasts that go upon all four; being therefore pronounced unclean. The literal translation of the Hebrew would be *palms* or *hands,* and therefore probably refers to those animals whose feet resemble the hands or feet of the human being, such as apes, monkeys, &c., and all creatures of that genus; together with bears, lions, cats, dogs, and frogs, &c. &c.*

II.—REASONS OF THE DISTINCTION OF "CLEAN" AND "UNCLEAN."

VARIOUS reasons have been adduced for the legal distinction betwixt *clean* and *unclean* animals, by those learned men, who have made this part of the Jewish polity their peculiar study; and although it must be acknowledged that some of them have been too fanciful in some of the positions which they have advocated, and that others have ramified their enquiries into unnecessary minuteness, and have even weakened their arguments by attempting to prove too much, still it will be found by the candid investigator that there are some great and leading reasons for these dietetic distinctions, in which all the best writers are agreed, and which we may therefore safely consider as sound and

---

* See Dr. A. Clarke's Commentary: *in loc.*—Lewis's Antiquities of the Heb. Republic, vol. iii. c. 19. p. 211.

scriptural, as well as rational. The sum of these is, that these distinctions were intended *to prevent idolatry,—to promote the health and comfort of the people,*—and *to influence the moral character of the nation.*

1.—TO PREVENT IDOLATRY.

THE Israelites having sojourned in Egypt amongst gross idolaters for several ages, had become so deeply imbued with the idolatrous principles of the people, and so habituated to their practices, that it required the most solemn and reiterated injunctions and threatenings to check their strong propensity to adopt the idolatrous manners of the Egyptians and other surrounding nations. The distinction of animals into " clean" and " unclean," aided the accomplishment of this great and desirable object, since it took away the very foundation of all commerce with other people: For those who can neither eat nor drink together, are never likely to contract an intimacy; nor was it probable that the Israelites would look upon those animals as deities worthy of being worshipped, upon which they fed daily. But not only were they permitted to eat such as were usually adored by the Egyptians, they were also taught to look upon others with religious detestation, which were accounted sacred and held in the highest veneration by them. " Most of the creatures," says the erudite Lewis, " which are pronounced *unclean*, were such as were in high esteem and sacred among the heathen; as a swine was to Venus, the owl to Minerva, the hawk to Apollo, the eagle to Jupiter, and even the dog to Hecate; which gave occasion to Origen justly to fall into admiration of the wisdom of Moses, who so perfectly understood the nature of all animals, and what relation they had to demons, that he declared all those to be unclean which were esteemed by the Egyptians and other nations to be the instruments of divination, and those to be *clean* which

were not so : (*Origen contra Celsum*, lib. iv.) and if in the
time of Moses such creatures were not sacred to demons,
it is a greater wonder that he should mark out those as
impure, which proved to be so sacred to after ages ; as a
great number of birds mentioned in Porphyry, who says,
The gods used them as heralds to declare their mind to
men, and several other creatures mentioned by other
authors, as peculiarly appropriated to other deities."* It
is well known, that the lion, wolf, dog, cat, ape, and
even frogs, otters, rats, beetles, and flies, as well as serpents and fishes, were held in idolatrous veneration by the
Egyptians and other nations,† and for which they were
thus satyrized by Juvenal, a Pagan Roman himself:

> How Egypt, mad with superstition grown,
> Makes gods of monsters, is but too well known :
> One sect, devotion to Nile's serpent pays ;
> Others to Ibis that on serpent preys.
> Where, Thebes, thy hundred gates lie unrepair'd,
> And where maim'd Memno's magic harp is heard ;
> Where these are mould'ring, lest the sots combine
> With pious care a monkey to enshrine !
> Fish-gods you'll meet with fins and scales o'ergrown ;
> Diana's dogs ador'd in ev'ry town,
> Her dogs have temples, but the goddess none :
> 'Tis mortal sin an onion to devour,
> Each clove of garlic is a sacred pow'r.
> Religious nations sure and blest abodes,
> Where ev'ry orchard is o'er-run with gods.
> To kill is murder, sacrilege to eat
> A kid or lamb. ‡ ——

The restrictions, therefore, which were made with
respect to diet, especially by the division of animals into

---

* Lewis's Antiq. of Heb. Republic, vol. iii. b. 6, p. 203. See also Bruce's
Travels, vol. v. Appendix pp. 163—167, 4to.

† Marshami Chronicon, sec. ix. p. 162, Lipsiæ, 1676, 4to.—Bryant's
Observations upon the Plagues inflicted upon the Egyptians, *passim.*—Beloe's
Herodotus, *Euterpe*, vol. i. p. 300.

‡ Dryden's Juvenal, Sat. xv.

" clean" and " unclean," were eminently calculated •to
prevent intimacies with the Egyptians and Canaanites and
other idolaters, and to prevent their " table from becoming
a snare ; and that which should have been for their welfare
becoming a trap." (Psalm lxix. 22.) It has, consequently,
been well remarked, that " this statute, above all others,
established not only a political and sacred, but a physical
separation of the Jews from all other people. It made it
next to impossible for the one to mix with the other, either in
meals or in marriage, or in any familiar connexion. Their
opposite customs in the article of diet not only precluded
a friendly and comfortable intimacy, but generated mutual
contempt and abhorrence. The Jews religiously abhorred
the society, manners, and institutions of the Gentiles,
because they viewed their own abstinence from forbidden
meats, as a token of peculiar sanctity, and of course
regarded other nations, who wanted this sanctity, as vile
and detestable. They considered themselves as secluded
by God himself from the profane world, by a peculiar
worship, government, law, dress, mode of living, and
country. Though this separation from other people, on
which the law respecting food was founded, created in
the Jews a criminal pride, and hatred of the Gentiles ; yet
it forcibly operated as a preservative from heathen idolatry,
by precluding all familiarity with idolatrous nations."*
" Ye shall therefore," said JEHOVAH, " put difference
between clean beasts and unclean, and between unclean
fowls and clean ; and ye shall not make your souls abominable by beast or by fowl, or by any manner of living
thing that creepeth on the ground, which I have separated
from you as unclean : and ye shall be holy unto me ; for I
the LORD am holy, and have severed you from other
people that ye should be mine." Levit. xx. 25, 26.

* Tappan's Lectures, quoted in Harris's Natural Hist. of the Bible. Dissertation iii. p. 27.

2.—TO PROMOTE HEALTH AND COMFORT.

In the distinction of animals into " clean" and " unclean," particular reference appears to have been made to their suitableness for food, those being accounted " clean" which afforded a considerable proportion of wholesome nutriment, and those being condemned as " unclean," which were of a gross and unwholesome nature. " While God keeps the eternal interests of man steadily in view," observes a learned Commentator,* " he does not forget his earthly comfort ; he is at once solicitous both for the health of his body and his soul. He has not forbidden certain aliments because he is a Sovereign, but because he knew they would be injurious to the health and morals of his people. *Solid-footed* animals, such as the *horse*, and *many-toed* animals, such as the *cat*, &c. are here prohibited. Beasts which have *bifid* or cloven-hoofs, such as the *ox*, are considered as proper for food, and therefore commanded. The former are *unclean*, *i. e.* unwholsome, affording a gross nutriment, often the parent of scorbutic and scrophulous disorders; the latter *clean*, *i. e.* affording a copious and wholesome nutriment, and not laying the foundation of any disease. *Ruminating* animals, *i. e.* those which *chew the cud*, concoct their food better than the others, which swallow it with little mastication, and therefore the flesh contains more of the nutritious juices, and is more easy of digestion, and consequently of assimilation to the solids and fluids of the human body : on this account they are termed clean, *i. e.* peculiarly wholesome and fit for food. The animals which do not *ruminate* do not concoct their food so well, and hence they abound with gross animal juices, which yield a comparatively unwholesome nutriment to the human system. Even the animals which have *bifid* hoofs, but do not chew

* Dr. Adam Clarke's Comment. on Levit. xi.

the cud, such as the *swine;* and those who chew the cud,
but are not *bifid,* such as the *hare* and *rabbit,* are by Him,
who knows all things, forbidden, because He knew them to
be, comparatively, innutritive.——On the same ground he
forbad all *fish* that have not both *fins* and *scales,* such as
the *conger, eel,* &c. which abound in gross juices, and fat,
which very few stomachs are able to digest."

" One of the most distinguishing traits in the character of
Moses, as a legislator," says a celebrated French writer,
" and one in which he was the most imitated by those who
in after ages gave laws to the Eastern world, was his constant attention to the health of the people. He forbad the
use of pork, of the hare, &c. of fish without scales whose
flesh is gross and oily, and all kinds of heavy meat, as the
fat of the bullock, of the kid, and of the lamb; an inhibi-
tion supremely wise in a country, where the excessive heat
relaxing the fibres of the stomach rendered digestion peculiarly slow and difficult."*

" The flesh of the *eel* and some other *fish,*" says Larcher,
" thickened the blood, and by checking the perspiration
excited all those maladies connected with the *leprosy ;*" and
even goes so far as to suppose that this was the reason why
the Egyptian priests proscribed certain kinds of fish and
caused them to be accounted *sacred,* the better to preserve
the people from eating so unwholesome a kind of food :†
—and Plutarch gives a similar reason for *swine* being held
in general abhorrence by them, notwithstanding they sacrificed them at the full moon, to the Moon and to Bacchus,
" The milk of the *sow,*" he remarks, " occasioned leprosies,
which was the reason why the Egyptians entertained so
great an aversion for this animal."‡—The innutritive

* M. de Pastoret. Moyse, considere' comme Legislateur et comme Moraliste.
Chap. vii. p. 528. Paris, 1788, 8vo.

† Beloe's Herodotus, *ut sup.*

‡ Ibid. vol. i. pp. 231, 272.

quality of the animals forbidden is also learnedly defended by *Michaelis* in his *Commentaries on the Laws of Moses,* Vol. iii. article 503, pp. 230, 231 ;—and by *Wagenseil* in his *Tela Ignea Satanæ,* in *Carminis R. Lipmanni Confutat.* pp. 555, 556, who observes that the Jews not only considered the eating of *pork* as inducing the *leprosy,* but regarded the very name of *swine* as ominous, and avoided naming it if possible; and that the Talmudists say, " If a child sucks the milk of a sow it will become leprous."—

From these and similar views of the dietetic character of theMosaic distinction of animals into "clean"and " unclean," Lowman judiciously observes, that " the food allowed the Hebrew nation, as an holy people, were the gentler sort of creatures, and of most common use, such as were bred about their houses and in their fields, and were, in a sort, domestic : they were creatures of the cleanest feeding, and which gave the most wholesome nourishment, and were of a better taste, and might be had in greater plenty and perfection by a proper care of their breeding and feeding : they seem, therefore, naturally fit to be chosen as a better kind of food : and if it became the Hebrews as an holy nation, to have any ritual distinction of foods, could any thing have been devised more proper than to prefer such foods as were the best foods, most easy to be had, and in the greatest perfection, most useful and most profitable to the industrious husbandman ? Was not this much better than to give encouragement to hunting of wild beasts and following birds of prey, no ways so fit for food nor so easy to be had, and hardly consistent with the innocency and mildness of a pastoral and domestic life ? Such a difference as the ritual makes between foods, was wisely appointed to encourage the improvement of their ground, to contribute to the health of their bodies, and to the ease of their employment in life, no inconsiderable part of the blessings of the promised land."*

* Lowman, Rational of the Ritual of the Hebrew Worship, p. 220.

3.—TO INFLUENCE MORAL CHARACTER.

THIS object was promoted in the Mosaic distinction of animals,—by impressing the minds of the Israelites with the conviction that as they were chosen by God to be " a peculiar people," it was their duty to endeavour to become " a holy nation;"—by prohibiting the eating of those animals, which by their gross and feculent nature as food would induce or increase any vicious propensities;—by symbolizing the dispositions and conduct to be encouraged and cultivated, or to be abhorred and avoided;—and by gradually weaning the mind from the superstitious influence produced by the manners of the Egyptians, and restoring it to soundness and spirituality.

The following extracts will show, that these reasons have received the sanction both of Jewish and Christian writers of different countries and in different ages.—*Levi Barcelona*, a Rabbinical writer, says, " As the body is the seat of the soul, God would have it a fit instrument for its companion, and therefore removes from his people all those obstructions which may hinder the soul in its operations ; for which reason all such meats are forbidden as breed ill blood ; among which if there may be some whose hurtfulness is neither manifest to us nor to physicians, wonder not at it, for the faithful Physician who forbids them is wiser than any of us."*—*Aristeas*, in his *History of the Septuagint*, states, that when sent by Ptolemy Philadelphus, to procure translators of the Sacred Books of the Jews into Greek, for the royal library, Eleazer, the high-priest, in answer to his enquiries respecting the Law of Moses, gave the following explanation of the precepts concerning " clean" and " unclean" animals : "Moses," he observes, " hath very well

* Precept lxxix. quoted in Harris's Nat. Hist. of the Bible. Dissert. iii, p. 29.

and wisely ordered all things to the honesty of living, having regard to purity and cleanliness, and to the correction and amendment of manners: and as for birds and flying fowls, he hath permitted us to eat ordinarily of such as are tame, and are different from others in neatness and cleanliness, and that live upon grains and seeds;—and such as he hath forbidden us to eat, are wild and ravenous, living upon flesh and carrion, of proud natures, inclined to rapine and prey, and such as by force set upon others, and seek not their living, but to the damage, hurt, and injury of the other poultry who are gentle and tame. Our law-maker, therefore, noting this by way of similitude, and by a borrowed way of translation, taken from the nature of such fowls, hath pronounced them unclean and infectious, as being willing to reduce and bring all things to the consideration of purity and cleanliness of the soul, to the end that every one being admonished by ordinary and domestic examples may understand how it behoveth us to use equity and justice; and that it is not granted to man, be he never so strong, powerful, proud, bold, and audacious soever, to ravish by force any thing from another, nor to do any injury to any person; but that it is convenient he should order the course of his life in imitation of the fowl I have spoken of, who live by grain, leading a tame and tractable life; and that it is not lawful to vex and trouble any person of our own kind, nor ravish his goods by force, as do those beasts he hath prohibited us to eat; and not to use violence in any case, which is figured by the nature of beasts, not wholly void of sense." And again, " Where he hath licensed us eating the flesh of four-footed beasts, who have *two*, and the hoofs *cloven*, the import is, that we ought to direct our operations to justice and bounty: by this *cloven hoof* figuring to us the distribution of rewards and punishments. He hath added further, that they should be such as *chew the cud*, by which he manifestly admonisheth us to have this rumination in memory, and in the course of our life ; for what signifieth the *chewing of the cud*, but that we ought still to have in our minds a continual revolving of our lives and actions, and so, by a frequent meditation, the duties to which we are obliged, and what we owe to all ?"*

The early Christian Fathers abound with similar representations of the tropological or figurative nature of these distinctions. *St. Barnabas*, in *his Catholic Epistle*, thus explains the design of these Mosaic precepts. " Why did Moses say, ' Ye shall not eat of the swine, neither the eagle, nor the hawk, nor the crow ; nor any fish that has not a scale upon him ?' I answer, that under this outside figure, he comprehended three spiritual doctrines that were to be gathered from thence. Therefore David took aright the knowledge of his threefold command, saying in like manner, (Psalm i,) ' Blessed is the man that hath not walked in the counsel of the ungodly ;'—as the fishes, before mentioned, in the bottom of the deep in darkness : ' Nor stood in the way of sinners ;'—as they who seem to fear the LORD, but yet sin, as the sow :—' And hath not sat in the seat of the scorners ;' as those birds who sit and watch that they may devour."† This interpretation of the first Psalm is copied by *Clemens Alexandrinus*, in his *Stromata*, lib. ii. with the addition of many similar expositions of the Mosaic precepts ;‡ and Eusebius, in his *Præparatio Evangelica*, lib. viii, has transcribed from *Aristeas*, the interpretations of the high-priest Eleazer.§ *Origen* observes, " There is scarcely any thing more extraordinary in the

* Aristeus's History of the Septuagint : Englished from the Greek, by Rev. Dr. John Done, pp. 76—84. Lond. 1685, 24mo.

† Wake's Apostolical Epistles:—Epist. of St. Barnabas, pp. 286, 289. Lond. 1693, 8vo.

‡ Clement. Alexand. Stromat. Lib. ii. p. 389. Lib. vii. p. 718. Coloniæ, 1688, fol.

§ Eusebii Præpar. Evan. Lib. viii.

writings of Moses, than his distinctions in the nature of
animals; whether the relations subsisting between the
different species and demons be considered as revealed to
him by God, or discovered by his own observations. For
in these distinctions, he places, in the class of *unclean*, all
those which are made use of in their divinations by the
Egyptians and other nations; and ranks almost all others
among those that are considered *clean*. Thus, the wolf,
the fox, the serpent, the eagle, the hawk, and other similar ones, are, according to Moses, unclean; and commonly, both in the Law, and in the Prophets, these animals
are designed to represent whatever is most wicked in the
world."*   *Justin Martyr* also says, " He (God) has
likewise commanded you to abstain from certain meats,
that, even whilst you eat and drink, you might have God
before your eyes."†   *Tertullian* likewise has the following
remarks, with which we shall conclude this article : " If
the Law takes away the use of some sorts of meat, and
pronounces creatures unclean, that were formerly held quite
otherwise, let us consider that the design was to inure them
to temperance, and look upon it as a restraint laid upon
gluttons, who hankered after the cucumbers and melons of
Egypt, whilst they were eating the food of angels. Let
us consider it too as a remedy at the same time against
excess and impurity, the usual attendants on gluttony.
It was partly likewise, to extinguish the love of money
by taking away the pretence of its being necessary for
the providing of sustenance. It was, finally, to enable
men to fast with less inconvenience upon religious occasions, by using them to a moderate and plain diet."‡

---

* Origen contra Celsum. Lib. iv. p. 124.

† Justin Martyr's Dialogue with Trypho, the Jew, translated by H.
Brown, vol. i. sec. 20, p. 98.   Oxford, 1755, 8vo.

‡ Tertullian adv. Marc. lib. ii. c. 18. *in fine*, quoted in Harris's Nat.
Hist of the Bible, Dissert. iii.

The reader who wishes to pursue this subject more at large, may consult with advantage Spencer *De Legibus Hebræorum:* Michaelis's *Commentaries on the Laws of Moses:* Young's *Historical Dissertation on Idolatrous Corruptions in Religion:* Harris's *Natural History of the Bible, Dissertation iii.;* and the authors to whom they respectively refer.

DISSERTATION V.

ON

THE PROHIBITION OF BLOOD.

———

THE Reasons for the Prohibition of eating Blood were various, and may be distinguished as *Moral, Physical,* and *Typical.*

I.—MORAL.

1. ONE very principal reason for prohibiting blood to be eaten was, beyond all doubt, *to prevent idolatrous practices.* For blood was regarded as the food of demons, not only by the nations immediately bordering upon the dwellings of the Israelites, but by other idolaters in different parts of the world. Maimonides has stated at large the super- stitions of the Zabii, in offering blood as a sacrifice to the infernal objects of their worship.* R. Moses Bar Nachman (on Deut. xii. 23,) says, " They gathered together blood for the devils, their idol gods, and then came themselves and ate of that blood with them as being the devil's guests, and invited to eat at the table of devils, and so were joined in federal society with them; and by this kind of com- munion with devils, they were able to prophesy and fore- tel things to come."† Similar practices obtained also among the Romans, since Horace thus satyrizes the super- stitious rites of his countrymen :

* See More Nevochim, Lib. iii.
† Young on Idolatrous Corruptions in Religion, vol. i. p. 235.

Canidia with dishevell'd hair,
(Black was her robe, her feet were bare,)
With Sagana, infernal dame!
Her elder sister, hither came.
With yellings dire, they fill'd the place,
And hideous pale was either's face.
Soon with their nails they scrap'd the ground,
And fill'd a magic trench profound,
With a black lamb's thick streaming gore,
Whose members with their teeth they tore,
That they may charm the sprights to tell
Some curious anecdotes from hell.

FRANCIS'S HORACE.—Sat. 7. Book i.

The sacred books of the *Hindoos* exhibit traces of the same kind of worship formerly prevailing amongst them. In the *Asiatic Researches*, vol. v., is a translation of the " *Rudhiradhyaya* or Sanguinary Chapter" of the *Calica Puran*, by W. C. Blaquiere, Esq., from which the following are extracts:

" Birds, tortoises, alligators, fish, nine species of wild animals, buffaloes, bulls, he-goats, ichneumons, wild boars, rhinoceroses, antelopes, guanas, rein-deer, lions, tygers, men, and *blood* drawn from the offerer's own body, are looked upon as proper oblations to the Goddess *Chandica,* the *Bhairăvăs,* &c.—The pleasure which the Goddess receives from an oblation of the blood of fish and tortoise, is of one month's duration, and three from that of a crocodile. By the blood of the nine species of wild animals, the Goddess is satisfied nine months, and for that space of time continues propitious to the offerer's welfare.—That of the lion, rein-deer, and the human species, produces pleasure which lasts. a thousand years.—The vessel in which the blood is to be presented, is to be according to the circumstances of the offerer, of gold, silver, copper, brass, or leaves sewed together, or of earth, or of tutenague, or of any of the species of wood used in sacrifices. Let it not be presented in an iron vessel, nor in one made of the hide of

F

an animal, or the bark of a tree; nor in a pewter, tin, or leaden vessel.—Let it not be presented by *pouring it on the ground*, or into any of the vessels used at other times for offering food to the deity.—Human blood must always be presented in a metallic or earthen vessel; and never on any account in a vessel made of leaves, or similar substances."

2. Another reason why blood was to " be poured upon the earth as water," and not to be " eaten," appears to have been, that by this means the Israelites might be deeply and constantly impressed with the important truth, that God is *the sole Author and Disposer of Life*; and thereby maintaining a constant sense of dependance upon Him, and of gratitude to Him for his providential mercies. " God," says the learned *Calmet*, " reserved to himself the blood of all sacrifices as absolute Master of Life and Death." —Blood, being regarded as the organ of life, was therefore sacred to Him from whom life was derived: for " the blood is the life, and thou mayest not eat the life with the flesh." Deut. xii. 23, 24; Lev. xvii. 10—14.

The doctrine of the *Vitality* of the Blood, thus suggested by the Laws of Moses, does not appear to have been avowed by medical writers before A.D.1628, the time of the celebrated Harvey, the discoverer or reviver of the doctrine of the circulation of the blood, who, in his writings maintained the opinion, but was never much followed till Mr. Hunter, professor of Anatomy in London, defended the hypothesis with much acuteness and strength of argument, in his *Treatise on the Blood, Inflammation*, &c., London, 1794, 4to.—The arguments of Hunter were vigorously attacked by Professor Blumenbach of Gottingen, who fancied he had gained a complete victory over the defenders of the Vitality of the Blood. But his translator, Dr. Elliotson, in the Notes he has added to the Professor's *Institutions of Physiology*, (Sect. vi. pp. 43, 44, London, 1817, 2nd edition, 8vo.,) thus sums up what he regards as the true state of the question:—" The great asserter of

the life of the Blood is Mr. Hunter, and the mere adoption
of the opinion by Mr. Hunter would entitle it to the utmost
respect from me, who find the most ardent and independent
love of truth, and the genuine stamp of profound genius, in
every passage of his works. The freedom of the blood
from putrefaction while circulating, and its inability to
coagulate after death from arsenic, electricity and lightning, may, like its inability to coagulate when mixed with
bile, be simply chemical phenomena, independent of
vitality. But its inability to coagulate after death from
anger or a blow on the stomach, which deprive the muscles
likewise of their usual stiffness ; its accelerated coagulation
by means of heat ; perhaps its diminished coagulation by
the admixture of opium ; its earlier putridity when
drawn from old than from young persons ; its freezing
like eggs, frogs, snails, &c. more readily when once previously frozen ; (which may be supposed to have exhausted
its powers;) its directly becoming the solid organized substance of our bodies, while the food requires various
intermediate changes before it is capable of affording
nutriment; the organization (probably to a great degree
independent of the neighbouring parts) of lymph effused
from the blood ; and finally the formation of the genital
fluids, one at least of which must be allowed by all to be
alive, from the blood itself, do appear to me very strong
arguments in favour of the life of the blood."[*]

But whatever may be thought of the physiological dispute, the obligation remains inviolate ; for if we suppose
that when Moses says, (Levit. xvii. 11, 14,) " The life of
the flesh is in the blood :"—" it is the life of all flesh ;" he
only meant that " when the blood is withdrawn, life ceases,

* Blumenbach's Institutions of Physiology, translated by Dr. Elliotson.
Sect. 6, Notes, pp. 43, 44.—Dr. Hunter's arguments may be found in
an abridged form in Dr. A. Clarke's Commentary on Levit. xvii. 11, and
Encyc. Perth. art. *Blood.*

—that it is necessary to the life of animals," it still remains a duty to pour the blood upon the earth as the significant symbol of absolute dependance upon God for life and every blessing; blood being "the most important fluid of the animal machine,—a fluid, which *excites the heart* to contraction, which distributes *oxygen* to every part, and conveys the *carbon* to the excretory vessels, giving rise, by this change, to *animal heat :* which originally supplies the materials of the *solids*, and afterwards their *nourishment* . from which all the *fluids* with the exception of the crude [or chyle] are *secreted* and derived."*

3. A third reason which may be adduced for the prohibition of blood, is, that it served *to check cruel and savage customs, and prevent the unrestrained indulgence of barbarous and ferocious inclinations.*—The Jewish Rabbins assert that the prohibitory injunctions relating to blood were originally designed to suppress a practice, which, they say, obtained even in the time of Noah, of eating raw flesh, and especially of eating the flesh of living animals cut or torn from them and devoured whilst reeking with the warm blood.†—Plutarch, in his *Discourse of eating flesh,* informs us, that it was customary in his time, to run red-hot spits through the bodies of live swine; and to stamp upon the udders of sows ready to farrow, to make their flesh more delicious; and Herodotus (l. iv.) assures us, that the Scythians, from drinking the blood of their cattle, proceeded to drink the blood of their enemies. It is even affirmed that both in Ireland, and the Islands and Highlands of Scotland, the drinking of the blood of live cattle is still continued or has but recently been relinquished. Dr. Patrick Delaney says, "There is a practice sufficiently known to obtain among the poor of the kingdom of Ireland. It is customary with them to bleed their cattle for food in

* Ibid. Sect. 2. p. 8.
† See the following Translation.

years of scarcity:"* and the *Analytical Reviewers* observe, "It will scarcely appear credible at a future time, that at this day, towards the close of the eighteenth century, in the Islands, and some parts of the Highlands, [of Scotland,] the natives every spring or summer attack the bullocks with lances, that they may eat their blood, but prepared by fire." † The celebrated traveller, *Bruce*, relates with minuteness the scene which he witnessed near Axum, the ancient capital of Abyssinia, when the Abyssinian travellers whom he overtook, seized the cow they were driving, threw it down, and cutting steaks from it, ate them raw, and then drove on the poor sufferer before them.‡—Sir John Carr states, that "the natives of the sandy desart [between Memel and Koningsberg] eat live eels dipped in salt, which they devour as they writhe with anguish round their hands:"§ Major Denham also say, that "an old hadgi, named El Raschid, a native of Medina," who at different periods of his life "had been at Waday and at Sennaar, described to him a people, east of Waday, whose greatest luxury was feeding on raw meats cut from the animal while warm and full of blood."‖ And it is a well-known fact, that the savage natives of New Zealand continue to quaff the blood of their enemies when

* The Doctrine of Abstinence from Blood defended. p. 124, note. London 1734.—See also Revelation examined with Candour, vol. ii. p. 20. London 1732, 8vo.

† Analytical Review, vol. xxviii. July 1798.—Retrospect of the Active World, p. 105.

‡ Bruce's Travels, vol. iii. pp. 332—334. 8vo. See also some learned remarks by him on the present subject, vol. iv. pp. 477—481, in which he designates Maimonides as "one of the most learned and sensible men that ever wrote upon the Scriptures:" and an able defence of the statement of our author in Murray's *Life of Bruce*, p. 74, note.

§ Carr's Northern Summer or Travels round the Baltic in the year 1804, p. 436, London, 1805.

‖ Denham and Clapperton's Travels and Discoveries in Northern and Central Africa, vol. ii, p. 36, note. London, second edition, 1826, 8vo.

taken in battle.—To prevent such cruel and revolting
practices, the Divine Being enjoined, that animals destined
for food should be killed with the greatest possible
despatch, their blood be poured on the ground, and
the eating of blood religiously avoided ; and still more
deservedly prohibits such sanguinary food, from its baneful influence upon the dispositions of those whose vitiated
appetites or brutal superstitions led them to indulge
in gross and bloody repasts. For, as has been remarked,
"all animals that feed upon blood, are observed to
be much more furious than others ; "*—and Byron
(*Voyage*, p. 77.) tells us, that the men by eating what
they found raw, became little better than cannibals.†—
"Drinking of blood," says Michaelis, "is certainly not a
becoming ceremony in religious worship. It is not a very
refined custom, and if often repeated, it might probably
habituate a people to cruelty, and make them unfeeling with
regard to blood; and certainly religion should not give,
nor even have the appearance of giving, any such direction
to the manners of a nation."‡—We therefore add, in the
words of Dr. Delaney,§—" If God had not foreseen these
cruelties, corruptions, and inconveniencies, should we justly
deem him infinitely *wise?*   And if foreseeing them, he had
not yet prohibited them in their *cause*, (which was at once
the wisest and most effectual prohibition,) could we justly
deem Him infinitely *good* and gracious to his creatures ?
When therefore we find Him, infinitely wise in foreseeing,
and infinitely good in forbidding, such abominable practices,
do we hesitate to conclude such prohibitions to be the
effects of infinite wisdom and goodness ; or consistent with

* Delaney's Revelation examined with Candour, vol. ii. p. 21.

† Fergus's Short Account of the Laws and Institutions of Moses, p. 99,
note. Dunfermline, 1810, 8vo.—See also Marshami Chronicon, sec. ix, p. 185.
Lipsiæ, 1676, 4to.

‡ Michaelis's Commentaries on the Laws of Moses ;· vol. iii, p. 252.

§ Revelation examined with Candour ; vol. ii, p. 27.

any degree of wisdom and goodness in ourselves, to despise such commands, or to live in open avowed contempt of them ?"

II.—PHYSICAL.

BESIDES the *Moral* reasons already adduced for the prohibition of Blood, there are also others of a *Physical* nature relating to the health of the community, deserving of attention. For,

1. The Blood being highly *alkalescent*, especially in hot climates, is subject to speedy putrefaction; and consequently that flesh will be most wholesome and best answer the purposes of life and health, from which the blood has been drained; and will preserve its suitableness for food the longest.

2. Blood affords a very gross nutriment, and is very difficult of digestion; and in some cases it is actually dangerous to drink it; for if taken warm, and in large quantities, it may prove fatal, particularly bull's blood, which was given, with this view, to criminals, by the Greeks, "its extreme viscidity rendering it totally indigestible by the powers of the human stomach."—Valerius Maximus (lib. v, c. 6,) ascribes the death of Themistocles to his having purposely drunk a bowl of ox-blood, during a sacrifice, in order to avoid subjecting his country, Greece, to the king of Persia. It is true, the blood of animals does not always produce similar effects, but this may be owing rather to the smallness of the quantity taken, than to its not being injurious in its nature; or its malignity may be partially counteracted by the other dietetic substances with which it may be eaten.*

3. Those nations which feed largely upon flesh, are observed to be remarkably subject to *scorbutic diseases;*

* Dr. A. Clarke's Commentary on Levit. xvii. 11.—Michaelis's Commentaries on the Laws of Moses, vol. iii, article 206, p. 252.—Revelation examined with Candour, vol. ii, p. 23.—Encyc. Perth., article *Blood.*

and if physicians be right in ascribing such tendency to animal food in general when freely eaten, especially in the hotter climates, it must be acknowledged that the grosser and more indigestible juices of such food must have the greatest tendency to produce such injurious consequences, and blood as the grossest of all animal juices be the most inimical to health and soundness.*   To abstain, therefore, from all meat, from which the blood has not been drained, from whatever cause the blood has been retained in the animal, whether purposely by strangling or otherwise, must be much more conducive to health, than by yielding to a luxurious and vitiated taste and adopting a contrary practice.

3.—TYPICAL.

" The law was a shadow of good things to come," and " though not the very image of those things," was nevertheless designed to symbolize the great events of the Gospel dispensation.   Among the various types and figures of the Law was that of *Blood*, commanded to be poured out as " an atonement."—" The life of the flesh is in the blood, and, I have given it to you upon the altar to make an atonement for your souls: for it is the blood that maketh an atonement for the soul." (Lev. xvii. 11.)—On these words Bishop Patrick remarks: "The words, as they lie in the Hebrew, may well be translated, *Because the life of the flesh* (of any beast that is) *is in the blood*, therefore, *I have given it to you* (or appointed it for you) *upon the altar, to make an atonement*: which is as much as to say, The life of the beast lying in the blood, I have ordained it to expiate your sins, that by its death in your stead, your life may be preserved: and therefore I require you not to eat that, which is appointed for so holy an end."†—But as " the law made

---

* Revelation examined with Candour, *ut sup.*
† Patrick in loc.

nothing perfect," we are not to suppose that the blood of brute animals made an actual propitiation for sin, but only that the blood of bulls, and of goats, and of other animals, adumbrated the blood of Jesus Christ, which was " shed for many for the remission of sins," and who himself was the true "propitiation for the sins of the whole world." Nothing, therefore, could be more rational than the precept which enjoined, that a thing so sacred in its typical reference, as to be peculiarly appointed for "an atonement upon the altar," should not lose that honour and esteem which was due to it ; which it would most assuredly have done, had it been permitted to be eaten as a common nutriment.

We may, therefore, conclude this section in the words of a modern and very able writer : " To us these ancient references to things now distinctly seen, must yield incontrovertible demonstrations of the firm foundation of our faith : —the import of each former ordinance is resolved—every enigma and every symbol which darkened the Jewish dispensation, has passed away—we no longer require high-priests " daily to offer sacrifices, first for their own sins, then for those of the people," those continued exactions have been superseded by the one, full, perfect, and sufficient sacrifice, oblation, and satisfaction of the Son of God, who being constituted our High-Priest, after the power of an endless life; and having accomplished the purposes of his manifestation in the flesh, " is set down on the right hand of the throne of the Majesty in the heavens :" THERE, ever living to make intercession for us, He abideth a Priest for ever after the order of Melchizedek."*

As to the question of the *permanency* of the prohibition, different persons will judge very differently respecting it, according as they view it merely as a *ritual* precept, or as involving considerations both *moral* and *physical*. The former will at once decide on its temporary and evanescent

*Dr. D. G. Wait's Sermons. Sermon iii. p. 115.

character, and pronounce it to be no longer obligatory on the professors of Christianity : the latter, acknowledging its authority to have ceased as a ceremonial rite, are, nevertheless, inclined to regard it as still being of considerable importance and utility, and adopt a series of arguments, which, to say the least of them, are exceedingly plausible and deserving of attention. For, according to the advocates of the permanent nature of the injunction, Blood was forbidden in the Noahic grant of animal food, long prior to the Levitical institutions, and therefore not dependant upon them ; the Apostles enjoined on the first Gentile churches, to abstain, as " necessary things," from " things strangled and from blood," as well as from " fornication and meats offered to idols ;" the pouring out of the blood of slain animals may, with equal propriety, be regarded now, as formerly, as an acknowledgement of entire dependance upon God, as the Author and Disposer of life. There are still barbarous and savage nations to be influenced by the mild character and practices of Christianity, and bloody and inhuman customs to be subdued by its example and temper. The nature of blood itself remains unaltered, and consequently has still the same tendency to generate gross and scorbutic humours, though checked in their virulence by the difference in our climate and our general habits :—and blood is still, comparatively, an indigestible and innutritive aliment. Hence the supporters of this opinion are induced to believe, that to abstain from blood in every form is most consistent with temperance, prudence, and religious caution. But, *sub judice lis est* ; " Let every man be fully persuaded in his own mind ;" for " he that doubteth, is condemned if he eat."—Rom. xiv, 7, 23.

DISSERTATION VI.

ON

THE TYPICAL CHARACTER

OF THE

MOSAIC INSTITUTIONS.

———

THE adumbration of important moral truths by sensible symbols and representations, may be traced to the earliest periods, and to a divine original. In the garden of Eden, the tree of the knowledge of good and evil, and on the expulsion of our first parents from the garden for their violation of the easy test of obedience assigned by their Creator, the Cherubims who guarded the entrance to prevent return, were certainly symbolical in their character. In Patriarchal times, the appearance of the Divine glory or Shechinah passing between the divided animals, when God entered into covenant with Abraham, was similar in its nature, though its object was different. When, therefore, Jehovah instituted a ceremonial amongst the Jews, introductory to a more spiritual and perfect dispensation, it might naturally be expected that its character would be typical and prospective, symbolizing the principal events and truths of that superior and more sublime economy; in other words, that it should be " a schoolmaster to bring us to Christ."

In accordance with these views, the author of the *Epistle to the Hebrews*, has exhibited many of the coincidences or agreements between the Mosaic Ceremonial, and its glorious antitype, the Gospel; and has fully substantiated the principle of tbe representative nature of the Levitical persons, institutions, and ceremonies.

The fanciful similitudes in which the unbridled imagination of some divines has indulged, in the comparisons which they have instituted between the legal and evangelical dispensations, have too frequently marked rather the ardent piety of their authors, than their exercise of sober and well-disciplined minds; and led some to discard altogether, without sufficient caution, the idea of the shadowy and representative design of many of the institutions of Moses. But we can never justly reason from the misapplication of a principle, to the inconsistency and absurdity of the principle itself. The want of sobriety in writers on typical subjects, and the extravagance of some of their illustrative positions, can never, therefore, destroy the importance or utility of a judicious exemplification of the various points of agreement of the symbolical with the anti-typical dispensation. Such a view of the whole of the representative system of Moses is highly desirable; we therefore hail the appearance of such works as the Sermons of Chevalier, on the Historical Persons of the Old Testament,—and those of Dr. D. G. Wait, in which certain peculiarities of the Patriarchal, the Mosaic, and the Christian Dispensations are discussed with great learning and ability; whilst the excellent work of Mather, " The Figures and Types of the Old Testament," (London, 1705, 4*to.*) must ever retain its value, until superseded by some other more modern and complete. Under these impressions, the following brief observations are presented to the reader, as supplementary to the remarks of our learned Jewish author, Maimonides.

The whole of the Mosaic system was admirably suited to the state of a people just escaped from cruel bondage, and whose minds had been debased and sensualized by laborious servitude and idolatrous example; but who were destined by the providence of God, to be the depositaries of the Sacred Oracles, and the progenitors of the great Messiah. By its wise constitution, it at once served as a guard against idolatry, and as a typical economy to impress the mind with moral sentiments through the medium of sensible symbols, and adumbrate the advent of the Redeemer, and the glories of his kingdom, by its prospective institutions. The treatise of Maimonides sufficiently exhibits its *anti-idolatrous* character; but a few remarks in illustration of its *moral* and *prophetic* objects may not be deemed superfluous, as introductory to that treatise.

1. One of the first and most important moral considerations is, the necessity of *purity* or *holiness*, both in heart and conduct. For whether we regard the holiness and purity of the Divine Being as demanding an assimilation to his nature; or, the influence produced on our own happiness by the cultivation of purity in principle and practice, it will appear to be indispensably requisite in the true worshipper of God. " Ye shall be holy," saith the Lord, " for I am holy."—" Without holiness no man shall see the Lord."—" Blessed are the pure in heart, for they shall see God." These moral truths were, therefore, eminently symbolized by the various and frequent ablutions, and separations for legal defilement and uncleanness, instituted by the Levitical ceremonial.

For the *Ablutions* of the Israelites were instituted, not only on account of their propriety in those warm countries, but for the sake also of their *moral* signification, being impressively emblematical of inward purity and holiness:

For, from the Body's purity, the mind
Receives a secret sympathetic aid.

Few, indeed, could have been so ignorant, even under that obscure dispensation, as to imagine that these Ceremonies of it were instituted for their own sake merely, or from any intrinsic value or efficacy they possessed to sanctify the worshippers. They must have had a moral couched under them; and were intended to be emblematical of that Purity which was requisite to render their approaches to the Deity acceptable, and of the obligations upon them to impress their hearts with a sense of the purity and holiness of the God they worshipped. At the same time these ritual services had also a direct tendency to promote these valuable ends, and were admirably calculated to guard the Israelites against the use of those superstitious, and, some of them, barbarous rites, that obtained by way of *lustration*, in the worship of their Heathen neighbours. In particular, they were fond of purgations by wind, fire, and water; to which the poet seems to allude, when he says:

> Quin, et supremo cum lumine vita reliquit
> Non tamen omne malum miseris, &c.

> Ev'n when their bodies are to death resign'd,
> Some old inherent spots are left behind;
> A sullying tincture of corporeal stains,
> Deep in the substance of the soul remains,
> Thus are her splendours dimm'd, and crusted o'er
> With those dark vices, that she knew before.
> For this the souls a various penance pay,
> To purge the taint of former crimes away:
> Some in the sweeping breezes are refin'd,
> And hung on high to whiten in the wind:
> Some cleanse their stains beneath the gushing streams,
> And some rise glorious from the scorching flames.
> PITT'S VIRGIL, B. vi.

It was, therefore, the intention of the legal ablutions and separations, and other rites of a purifying character, to guard against idolatrous practices, and to eradicate idolatrous principles, and especially by the symbols of bodily lustrations to enforce that inward holiness, without which the whole system would have been vain and unacceptable to God.* See Levit. xv.—Numbers xix.

2. Nearly allied to the inculcation of Purity, is that of the *Mortification of inordinate and sensual appetites*, figuratively expressed in the Mosaic economy, by repeated restrictions, under particular circumstances, of gratifications lawful in themselves; and by the injunctions of frequent legal purifications after sensual indulgences, as well as by the ordinance of the painful rite of Circumcision.—See Exod. xix. 14, 15.—1 Sam. xxi. 4, 5.—Levit. xviii. 19.—Levit. xv. 16—18.

Circumcision, the first institution of which is recorded Gen. xvii. 10, 11, was the seal of the covenant made with Abraham, and designed to confirm his faith, and that of his posterity, in the promises made to him and them by the Divine Author of this typical rite. It served also as a mark of distinction from other nations; and having, like the other rites of Judaism, an important moral couched under it, reminded them of the promise of God, and encouraged them in his service, and at the same time intimated to them " the obligations they were under to mortify every irregular appetite, by representing the indulgence of these as incompatible with the character of a people devoted to God, or who would hope that their services would be acceptable to Him." Circumcision, then, was such a valuable mark in the flesh, as was very fit to be a sign to all the seed of Abraham, that they were to account themselves an

---

* See Shaw's Philosophy of Judaism, P. i. ch. i. p. 178, and Atkin's Attempt to illustrate the Jewish Law, pp. 211—237.—Lowman on the Hebrew Ritual, pp. 224—228. Those who wish to see the numerous *ablutions* and *Purifications* of the more modern Jews, as exemplifying the wisdom of Our Lord's censures on the *Tradition of the Elders*, will find themselves repaid by consulting *Surenhusii* MISCHNA, in *Seder Tahoroth*, or Order of Purifications ; or Dr. Wotton's Analysis of it in his *Miscellaneous Discourses*, vol. i. pp. 160—176.

holy nation, as his seed ; that they were obliged to keep up
an holy nation to Jehovah in that family, and in so doing
assure themselves of the peculiar favour of Jehovah, such
as He showed to their forefathers as their God ; and further
taught them, that the covenant between God and them,
required not barely a ceremonial holiness, but, what was
the true meaning of it, to circumcise their hearts, so as to
love and to honour the Lord their God with all their hearts,
and in all the acts of true righteousness and goodness."*

3. The *defection of man,* and the *necessity of atonement
by a vicarious sacrifice,* were strongly marked in the whole
of the sacrificial system, by which an innocent victim was
substituted for the guilty transgressor ; whilst the inferio-
rity of brute animals sacrificed in the stead of man, and
the constant recurrence of sacrifice, must impress every
rational and thinking person with a conviction, that it
was not possible that " the blood of bulls and of goats
should take away sins," and could, therefore, only be
deemed efficacious by an ulterior reference to a more worthy
and meritorious oblation, not hitherto offered, but to
which their faith was directed by the intimations of tradition and prophecy. " For the force of the reason is this, that
seeing the *effect* is to take away sin, it must have a *cause*
sufficient to produce it ; but the blood of bulls and of
goats, which was the principal thing in the legal annual
sacrifices, was no such cause, it had no such virtue; the
effect was so far above it, that there was no possibility that
such a *cause* should reach it. For every *cause* doth work
according to its power, as it is greater or less; but if there
be no power at all in respect of any particular *effect,* in
respect of that it can do nothing at all. The blood of bulls
and goats might be a *sign* of that blood that could take

* Lowman on the Hebrew Ritual, p. 217.—Shaw's History and Philosophy of Judaism, p. 78.—See also Mather's Figures or Types of the Old
Testament, pp. 173—184. Lond. 1705, 4*to.*

away sin; but take it away, or any ways actively concur to the taking away thereof, it could not. Such an effect, so great and glorious, and so beneficial to sinful man, must have some excellent and powerful *cause*, such as the blood of bulls and goats cannot be. As the beasts, so the blood was, morally, neither bad nor good, but indifferent; and, though offering and sprinkling of this blood was a rational act in the High Priest, yet it could give no moral, spiritual, or supernatural power to the blood: neither could the Priest have had any warrant to have made use of this blood, if God had not commanded him, and that to signify some better and far more excellent blood. Therefore, if we look upon the blood, and consider what it was, we cannot rationally imagine any power in it, either to satisfy Divine justice, or to merit any acceptation for that end from the Supreme Judge."*

How far the Jews themselves were aware of the inefficacy of their *expiatory sacrifices*, except as they had reference to the atonement that would be made by the great vicarious sacrifice of the Messiah, is not easy to decide. Were it possible for us to ascertain the manner in which the Levites studied the Law, and to discover their ideas of its symbolical sense, we might then reason with correctness, on their views of the ultimate reference of their piacular sacrifices. It is, however, certain, that the Prophetic books fully warrant the assertion, that the types were studied with reference to Him; and there is a variety of evidences in Isaiah, Jeremiah, and the minor Prophets, that they devoted their attention to the types; and the whole book of Ezekiel is constructed on a typical or allegorical model. The typical actions, by which they enforced their predictions on some occasions, were doubtless in unison with that

* Lawson's Exposition of the Epistle to the Hebrews, ch. ix. v. 4. pp. 199, 200. Lond. 1662, fol.

G

taste for symbols and typical imagery, which the nature of the Levitical institutions had excited in the public mind; and consequently shows, that this influence which they had acquired over the nation must have resulted from a long study of them. But whether the great body of the people discerned, though distantly and faintly, the great object of faith and the perfect oblation and sacrifice that he would offer or not; still it is certain from the language of Prophecy, as in the 53d chapter of Isaiah, and from the declarations of the author of the Epistle to the Hebrews, that some of the worthies of Israel saw and rejoiced in the day of Christ, with more or less distinctness of spiritual vision. (See Heb. xi.—John viii. 56.)*

For as the Jewish High Priest was a shadowy image of Jesus Christ, *our High Priest*, and the inner sanctuary of the temple was a figure of heaven itself; so also, the sacred incense which used to be burnt, both in the holy and in the most holy place, represented the prayers of the church, and hence the name of the thing signified is given to the sign, and those sacred odours are called " the prayers of the saints;" the burning of incense, therefore, before God, by the Jewish High Priest, in the inner sanctuary, prefigured our High Priest now in heaven, commending to God the prayers of his church.†

" The oracular type of URIM and THUMMIM,‡ was most eminently fulfilled in Jesus Christ, the only true High Priest, in and by whom alone God speaks his mind, and works his image in us. ' In him are hidden all the trea-

---

* Dr. Wait's Course of Sermons, Serm. ii, p. 48.

† Outram on Sacrifices, translated by J. Allen, p. 366.

‡ The *Breast-plate*, a garment peculiarly appointed for the high-priest, Exod. xxvii. 15. was, according to Dr. Lightfoot, " a rich piece of cloth of gold, an hand-breadth square, double, and set with twelve precious stones, in four rows, three in a row : these," he adds, " are called *Urim* and *Thummim*, Exod. xxviii. 30." The manner in which the answer was given, was not by any shining of the stones, or voice of an image, but by an audible

sures of wisdom and knowledge;' (Col. ii. 3.) and He is holy
and harmless, and separate from sinners. ' For such an
High Priest became us, who is holy, harmless, undefiled,
separate from sinners.' (Heb. vii. 26.) He wears the true
Urim and *Thummim* always upon his heart:—Illuminations and Perfections, Lights and Graces in the highest;
and we have nothing of either, but what we have from
him. Our Lights are from him. (2 Cor. iv. 6.—Matt. ix.
27.)—Our Graces from him.—' Of his fulness have all we
received, and grace for grace.' (John i. 16.)—' For the
Law was given by Moses,"—these legal shadows of terror
and darkness.—' But Grace and Truth came by Jesus
Christ:' (v. 17.)—GRACE, instead of legal terror and
rigour:—TRUTH, that is, accomplishments and perform-
ances, instead of shadows and promises, came by Jesus
Christ. It follows,—' No man hath seen God at any time,'
that is, by any light, or grace, or power of his own, ' but
the only begotten Son which is in the bosom of the Father,
He hath declared Him.' (v. 18.)—The true *Urim* and
Thummim is in the Pectoral of Jesus Christ; all our
illuminations and perfections are in him."*

5. The *temporary separation betwixt Jew and Gentile*,
and of the dispensation itself, was marked by the exclusive
character of the Jewish ritual, which forbade Gentiles to
offer the legal sacrifices unless initiated by the rite of circumcision; and which, by enjoining all the males to

voice from the presence or Shechinah: as " Moses heard the voice of one
speaking to him from off the mercy-seat." (Numbers vii. 29.) The names of
Urim and *Thumim* were given to denote the clearness and perfection of the
oracular answers; for *Urim* signifies *light*, and *Thummim*, *perfection*. For
these answers were not like those of the heathen oracles, enigmatical and
ambiguous, but always clear and manifest, and their truth ever certain and
infallible.—Lowman *on the Heb. Ritual*, p. 127.—Prideaux Con. part 1.
b. iii. p. 153. Lond. 1719, 8vo.

* Mather's Figures and Types of the Old Testament, p. 513.

appear *thrice* every year at Jerusalem, rendered the universal diffusion of Judaism impracticable. The *vail* too, which separated the people from the most Holy Place, indicated that universal access, even to the mercy-seat, was not yet permitted.

For although the peculiar construction of the tabernacle, and the exclusive character of the Jewish rites, might not have been sufficient of themselves to prove to the believing Israelite, that the Mosaic dispensation was temporary in its nature; yet, when connected with the Abrahamic promises and subsequent prophecies, it was demonstrably evident that those promises and prophecies could never be accomplished without an entire change of system, by throwing down the wall of separation between Jew and Gentile; nor a general entrance be opened into the immediate presence of the Divine glory, but by the rending of the veil which separated even the " holy" from the " most Holy Place." —" When, at the death of Christ," says Dr. A. Clarke, " the *veil* of the temple was *rent* from the top to the bottom, it was an emblem that the way to the holiest was laid open, and that the people at large, both Jews and Gentiles, were to have access to the holiest by the *blood of Jesus.*"—The writings of the Jews themselves also prove, that the impression produced on their minds by the promises and prophecies was similar to what we have supposed, and that they entertained an expectation of a general diffusion of Divine knowledge. In *Sohar Chadush*, it is said, " In the days of the Messiah, knowledge shall be renewed in the world, and the Law shall be made plain among all; as it is written, Jer. xxxi. 33, *All shall know me from the least to the greatest.*"—In *Midrash Yalcut Simeoni*, we find the following legend:—" The Holy Blessed God shall sit in Paradise and explain the law; all the righteous shall sit before Him, and the whole heavenly family shall stand on their feet; and the Holy

Blessed God shall sit, and the *new Law* which He is to give by *the Messiah,* shall be interpreted;"—and in *Sohar Levit.* " There shall be no time like this till the Messiah comes[[;]] and then the knowledge of God shall be found in every part of the world."*

6. The annual entrance of the High Priest into the Holy of Holies, and into the immediate presence of the She-chinah, or symbol of the Divine Glory, sprinkled with blood, and sprinkling the mercy-seat with blood, taught the people by a sensible representation that " without shedding of blood there could be no remission of sin," nor an entrance be administered into the " eternal inheritance of the saints in light."

" Of all the rites [of the Mosaic institute] *the sprinkling of the blood* was the most sacred; because by that act, the life of the victim was considered as presented to God the Supreme Lord of life and death:—and as the High Priest of the Jews carried the blood (the vehicle of the life or sensitive soul) of the victims, into the innermost sanctuary of the temple, as a sign of the previous immolation of them, and sprinkled it towards the mercy-seat; so our High Priest, in heaven itself, which that sanctuary prefigured, presents before God, not only the soul, but also the body, of the victim that was slain for our sins.—For the blood of those victims which were the principal types of Christ, was carried into the holy of holies which typified heaven itself."†

7. The principal FESTIVALS of the Jewish church were the *Passover,* the feast of *Pentecost,* and the feast of *Tabernacles.* The first of these was *commemorative* of the deliverance from Egypt, and the second of the promulga-tion of the Law on Sinai, as the last was, of the Israelites

* Dr. A. Clarke's Commentary on Eph. ii. 13. and Heb. viii. 11—13.
† Outram's Dissertations on Sacrifice, translated by John Allen.—Diss. i. c. xvi. p. 195; and Diss. ii. c. iii. p. 217. London, 1817, 8vo.

dwelling in booths or tabernacles in the wilderness. Of the *figurative* design of the two former of these festivals, there is no doubt ; the analogy between the Paschal Sacrifice and the sufferings of our Lord, between the Delivery of the Law and the Effusion of the Holy Spirit, having been remarked and acknowledged from the earliest period of the Gospel.—But the intention of the institution of the Feast of Tabernacles as a figurative festival, has not been so clearly explained. Some have supposed that it was designed to instruct the Israelites, " that they were but pilgrims and strangers here below, sojourners as it were in a strange land, passing through it to their own country, towards their own home."—The opinion, however, which seems most analogous to the objects symbolized by the other festivals, is that which regards it as shadowing forth the *conversion* and *restoration* of the Jewish nation. The Rev. Dr. Elrington has defended this view of its object with considerable ingenuity and force.—" That the Jews," says he, " annually observed three great festivals at Jerusalem, and that two of them, the Passover and the Feast of Pentecost, had a reference to events, which were to happen under the Christian dispensation, is well known. Hence, we are led to consider, whether the third solemnity was of a similar nature, and has received a similar completion. This was the Feast of Tabernacles, beginning on the fifteenth day of the seventh month ; when for seven days all that were Israelites born, were to dwell in booths, in remembrance of their dwelling in booths when they were brought out of the land of Egypt, and on the eighth day to return to their houses, celebrating it with great rejoicings. Levit. xxiii. 34, 35, 36, 42, 43.

" Now it is evident, that no circumstance attending the establishment of Christianity, had any resemblance to the journey through the wilderness, and the dwelling there under tents ; nor has any attempt been made, to prove a similarity of the sort. We must, therefore, either admit that this Feast of Tabernacles differs from the others, in having no prospective reference ; or we must seek in some future event its completion or antitype; and it will probably incline us to this latter opinion, when we consider, that the Jews will undoubtedly be brought back to Judea, when the fulness of the Gentiles shall be come in ; and if we suppose the season of the Feast of Tabernacles to coincide with that of their future return, as it appears to have done with their return from the Babylonish Captivity, we shall have a fulfilment of the three Jewish festivals completed finally in the conversion of the Jews to Christianity, which, with their return 'to their own land, will furnish a perpetual cause for thanksgiving and religious observance.

" Of the reference of this festival to the final restoration of the Jews, some of their traditions and practices may, perhaps, afford a further confirmation. It was their custom on the last day of the feast, to bring water from the fountain of Siloah, which the priests poured on the altar, singing the words of Isaiah, (xii. 3,) *With joy shall ye draw water from the fountain of salvation ;* which words the Targum interprets, *With joy shall ye receive a new doctrine from the elect of the just ;* and they appear from the preceding chapter, to relate to the final restoration of the Jews. The feast itself was also called Hosanna, *Save we beseech thee ;* and was the time when our Lord spoke the remarkable words mentioned in St. John, (ch. vii. 37, 38,) marking the relation which the ceremony of pouring out the water bore to his ministry. And among the traditions of the Jews we find that the defeat of Gog and Magog shall fall out upon the feast of Tabernacles, or that the consequent seven months cleansing of the land (Ezek. xxxix. 12,) shall terminate at that period; and there seems little reason to doubt the reference of that prophecy to the final restoration of the Jews."[*]

[*] Graves's Lectures on the Four last books of the Pentateuch, vol. ii. pp. 482—485. Lond. 1807, 8vo.

8. Of the emblematical and introductory nature of the Mosaic dispensation, and its adumbration of spiritual and Divine privileges, intimations were frequently given by prophetic explanations and promises. " I will raise them up a Prophet from among their brethren, like unto thee, and will put my words in his mouth." (Deut. xviii. 18, 19.) —" Behold the days come when I will make a *New* Covenant with the house of Israel; not according to the covenant that I made with their fathers." (Jer. xxxi, 31, 32, 33, 34.)—" Sacrifice and offering thou wouldest not, but a body hast thou prepared me." (Psalm xl. 6, 7, 8.) —" Yet once, it is a little while, and I will shake the heavens, and the earth, and the sea, and the dry land; and I will shake all nations, and the Desire of all nations shall come." (Haggai ii. 6, 7.)—"Behold to obey is better than sacrifice." (1 Sam. xv. 22.)—" The Lord God will circumcise thine heart." (Deut. xxx. 6.)

" If we, therefore, advert to the internal structure of the Law, which was accommodated to the temporary circumstances of the Israelites, restricted as it was from the nature of the times, and the genius of the people, who were thus appointed the guardians of God's truth and oracles, it will appear most eminently adapted to the pre-servation of the more ancient promises and revelations, and in every way fitted to be the connecting medium between the patriarchal economy and the Gospel. Its very deficiencies contained indications, that the end of its institution remained to be accomplished; its obscurities intimated, that its object and intent would hereafter be plenarily disclosed. Its whole catalogue of ceremonies was so constructed, that, surrounded as the Hebrews were by nations, who veiled their esoteric faith in external symbols or hieroglyphical devices, it was impossible that they should not have directed the inquirer, even at the time when they were confining him to the pure worship of the ONE ETERNAL GOD, to have sought in them a hidden and fuller signification; and, if at any time observant of the depravity of the Canaanite, or inquisitive respecting the superstitions of the house of bondage, the Israelite might have been induced to compare his legislative code with the laws of other communities, he must have perceived, that it had proceeded beyond the cultivation of the rest of the world; and could not have failed to have remarked, that it ranked above all others in a pre-eminent distinction, that, bearing the impress of divine revelation, it contained provisions for the future, and prefigured, in its whole body of services, a far more expansive, although distant communication from God to man. And although these evidences were dispersed through the whole economy, they nevertheless may be said to have been more especially comprised in the TYPES which rendered the sacrifices, oblations, and expiations, figurative of HIM, in whom they were ordained to receive their completion in the fulness of time: and as they supplied the student of Moses with the requisites to identify the true Messiah at his appearance, and established an union between the two Testaments, which then evinced both to have been revealed by the same All-wise Being, so they doubtless compensated to the Israelites for the absence of those mysteries and secret rites which the Gentiles had engrafted on Theology, and which even the divinely-taught Hebrew appears, from his numerous defections and his endless propensity to idolatry, to have required."*

* Dr. D. G. Wait's Course of Sermons, preached before the University of Cambridge, in the year 1825.— Sermon ii. pp. 40—45. Lond. 1826. 8vo.

DISSERTATION VII.

ON

THE LEPROSY.

———

THE LEPROSY derives its name from the Greek term λεπϱα (lepra) from λεπις (lepis) *a scale*, the body, in this dreadful disease, being covered with *thin white scales*, or *smooth shining patches*, so as to give it, in some instances, the appearance of *snow*. Nosologists class some species of this malady under the order *Squamæ*, or scaly diseases, and other species of it under the order *Tuberculæ*, or tubercular affections. That kind of Leprosy which is described by Moses in Leviticus xiii, appears to have been what was termed by the Greeks *Leuce*, (λευκη,) and by the Arabians *Albaras*, or more correctly *Baras*. In some instances it has been considered as assuming the form of *Elephantiasis*, and in others not appearing very dissimilar from the *Frambœsia*, or *Yaws*, of the West Indies.*

The *Leuce* or White Leprosy is thus described by Mr. Robinson, a medical practitioner of India:—" One or two circumscribed patches appear upon the skin, (generally the feet or hands, but sometimes the trunk or face,) rather lighter-coloured than the neighbouring skin, neither raised nor depressed, shining and wrinkled, the furrows not co-inciding with the lines of the contiguous sound cuticle.

* See Dr. T. Bateman's Practical Synopsis of Cutaneous Diseases: Order II. p. 25, and Order VII. p. 273. London 1819, 8vo., Fifth edition.

The skin thus circumscribed is so entirely insensible, that you may with hot irons burn to the muscle, before the patient feels any pain. These patches spread slowly until the skin of the whole of the legs, arms, and gradually often of the whole body, becomes alike devoid of sense : wherever it is so affected, there is no perspiration ; no itching, no pain, and very seldom any swelling. Until this singular apathy has occupied the greater part of the skin, it may rather be considered a blemish than a disease : nevertheless it is most important to mark well these appearances, for they are the invariable commencement of the most gigantic and incurable diseases, that have succeeded the fall of man : and it is in this state chiefly (though not exclusively) that we are most able to be the means of cure. The next symptoms—are the first which denote internal disease or derangement of any functions. The pulse becomes very slow, not small but heavy, 'as if moving through mud :'—the toes and fingers numbed, as with frost, glazed and rather swelled, and nearly inflexible. The mind is at this time sluggish and slow in apprehension, and the patient appears always half asleep. The soles of the feet and the palms of the hands then crack into fissures, dry, and hard as the parched soil of the country ; and the extremities of the toes and fingers under the nails are incrusted with a furfuraceous substance, and the nails are gradually lifted up, until absorption and ulceration occur. Still there is little or no pain; the legs and fore-arms swell, and the skin is every where cracked and rough. Contemporary with the last symptoms, or very soon afterwards, ulcers appear at the inside of the joints of the toes and fingers, directly under the last joint of the metatarsal or metacarpal bones, or they corrode the thick sole under the joint of the os calcis, or os cuboides. There is no previous tumour, suppuration, or pain, but apparently a simple absorption of the integuments, which slough off in successive layers of half an inch in diameter. A sanious discharge comes on ;

the muscle pale and flabby, is in turn destroyed; and the joint being penetrated as by an augur, the extremity droops, and at length falls a victim to this cruel, tardy, but certain poison. The wounds then heal, and other joints are attacked in succession, whilst every revolving year bears with it a trophy of this slow march of death. Thus are the limbs deprived one by one of their extremities, till at last they become altogether useless. Even now death comes not to the relief of, nor is desired by the patient, who ' dying by inches,' and a spectacle of horror to all besides, still cherishes fondly the spark of life remaining, and eats voraciously all he can procure: he will often crawl about with little but his trunk remaining, until old age comes on, and at last he is carried off by diarrhœa or dysentery, which the enfeebled constitution has no stamina to resist."*

In the *Elephantiasis*, to which the *Leuce* or *Baras* may be considered as having an affinity, and probably sometimes terminating in it, "the tubercles," when the malady has for some time proceeded, " begin to crack, and at length to ulcerate: ulcerations also appear in the throat, and in the nose, which sometimes destroy the palate and the cartilaginous septum ; the nose falls ; and the breath is intolerably offensive: the thickened and tuberculated skin .of the extremities becomes divided by fissures, and ulcerates, or is corroded under dry sordid scales, so that the fingers and toes gangrene and separate, joint after joint.—Aretæus and the ancients in general consider Elephantiasis as an universal *cancer* of the body, and speak of it with terror."† According to Dr. J. M. Good, this disease is called by the Arabians *juzam* and *juzamlyk*, though more generally, *judam* and *judamlyk*, from an Arabic root which imports erosion, truncation, excision. From Arabic the term *juzam* has passed into India, and is the common name for

* Ibid, pp. 311—313.
† Ibid, pp. 302, 303.

the same disease, among the Cabirajas, or Hindoo physicians, who also occasionally denominate it *Fisádi khún*, from its being supposed to infect the entire mass of blood, but more generally *khora.**

Maundrell, in a letter appended to his *Travels,* tells us, that at *Sichem,* (now *Naplosa,*) he saw several Lepers, who came begging to him all at the same time : " The distemper," says he, " as I saw it on *them,* was quite different from what I have seen it in England ; for it not only defiles the whole surface of the body with a foul scurf, but also deforms the joints of the body, particularly those of the wrists and ankles, making them swell with a gouty scrofulous substance, very loathsome to look upon. I thought their legs like those of old battered horses, such as are often seen in drays in England. The whole distemper indeed, as it there appeared, was so noisome, that it might well pass for the utmost corruption of the human body on this side the grave : and, certainly, the inspired penmen could not have found out a fitter emblem, whereby to express the uncleanness and odiousness of vice."†

Michaelis in his *Commentaries on the Laws of Moses,* (C. iv. Part ii. Art. 207, 208, 209, 210, 211,) has entered at large into a discussion of the nature of the Jewish Leprosy, and also shown with much force of reasoning the wisdom of the Mosaic regulations for the prevention of contagion, and reducing the virulence of the disease itself. He states that M. Peyssonel, a physician, was sent to Guadaloupe to enquire into the nature of the Leprosy that broke out in that island, about 1730 ; and details from him an account of the disease very similar to what has been already given ; to which M. Peyssonel adds,—" It has been remarked, that this horrible disorder has, besides, some very lamentable properties ; as, in the *first* place,

---

* Ibid, p. 317, note.

† Dr. A. Clarke's Comment. on Levit. xiii. 2.

that it is *hereditary;* and hence some families are more
affected with it than others : *secondly,* that it is *infectious;*
—*thirdly,* that it is incurable, or at least no means of cure
have hitherto been discovered."*

After the lapse of several thousand years, Leprosy is
still a common disease throughout all Syria : it was, of
course, endemic in Palestine, the country into which
Moses conducted the Israelites. In Egypt, where they
had previously dwelt, it is said to be still more frequent and
virulent. To this the climate, no doubt, contributed in
some degree. But other causes beside this may have tended
to increase its influence among the Israelites. They were
poor, and had been oppressed ; and cutaneous diseases, and
indeed almost all kinds of infectious disorders, prevail most
among the poor, because they cannot keep themselves
cleanly, and at a distance from infected persons. They
had also partly dwelt in the damp and marshy parts of
Egypt, and facts have proved that a very damp situation
will produce, if not leprosy itself, at least a disease very
similar to it. It is likewise material to notice, that their
residence along the Nile and the marshy districts, rendered
it easy for them to procure different kinds of fish, than
which nothing, it is said, more effectually spreads and
aggravates cutaneous disorders, if constantly or even frequently used as the entire or principal diet ; thus we find
at this day, in Norway and Iceland, a disorder, which, if
not leprosy, comes very near it in similarity of symptoms,
and which is ascribed to their eating great quantities of
fish.†

During the *Crusades,* numbers of the pilgrims and soldiers
who visited the East, were affected with severe cutaneous
diseases; by whom the Leprosy is said to have been imported

* Michaelis's Commentaries on the Laws of Moses, vol. iii. Art. 208. pp.
258—260.

† Ibid, pp. 273—277.

into Europe, and to have become extensively prevalent. It is certain that every country abounded with hospitals, established for the exclusive relief of that disease, from the tenth to the sixteenth century; and that an order of knighthood, dedicated to St. Lazarus, was instituted, the members of which had the care of lepers, and the controul of the Lazarettoes assigned to them, and ultimately accumulated immense wealth.* In 1179, the General Council of Lateran condemned certain of the clergy for preventing lepers erecting churches for themselves, notwithstanding they were prohibited from entering all other churches; and a decree was passed ordaining, that, wherever a sufficient number of lepers were living together, they should be allowed a church, a cemetery, and a priest, and should be exempted from paying tithes of the fruits of their gardens or of the cattle which they fed.† But we must not suppose that the immense numbers who were admitted into the Lazarettoes during the middle ages, were all afflicted with real leprosy, since almost every person affected with any severe eruption, or ulceration of the skin, was deemed *leprous*, and received into those institutions. " Indeed, there is little doubt," says Dr. Bateman, " that every species of cachectic disease, accompanied with ulceration, gangrene, or any superficial derangement, was deemed *leprous;* and hence that in the dark ages, when the desolation of repeated wars, and the imperfect state of agriculture, subjected Europe to almost constant scarcity of food, the numerous modifications of scurvy and ignis sacer, which were epidemic during periods of famine, and endemic wherever there was a local dearth, were in all probability classed among the varieties of leprosy; more especially as the last stage of the ignis sacer was marked by the occurrence of ulceration and gangrene of the

* Bateman's Practical Synopsis of Cutaneous Diseases, pp. 305, 306.
† Fleury, Histoire Ecclesiastique, Tom. xv, p. 412. Bruxelles, 1715, 12*mo.*

extremities, by which the parts were mutilated or entirely separated."*

On the statutes relating to the leprosy in *clothes* and *houses*, Michaelis very justly observes, that "when we hear of the leprosy of clothes and houses, we must not be so simple as to imagine it the very same disease which is termed leprosy in man.   Men, clothes, and stones have not the same sort of diseases ; but the names of human diseases are, by analogy, applied to the diseases of other things.   In Bern, for instance, they speak of the *cancer of buildings*, but then that is not the distemper so called in the human body.   The *cancer of buildings* is with equal propriety a Swiss, as the *leprosy of buildings* is a Hebrew expression."† The *house-leprosy* (Levit. xiv. 33—57) appears to have been very similar to those corrosive and destructive effects not unfrequently produced in houses placed in unfavourable situations by the action of damp and foul air, of which what is termed the *dry-rot* in timber may be adduced as an instance.—" Our walls and houses," the preceding writer remarks, "are often attacked with something that corrodes and consumes them, and which we commonly denominate *saltpetre*.   Its appearances are nearly as Moses describes

---

* Bateman's Practical Synopsis, p. 308.—" Sauvages, under the head of *Erysipelas pestilens*, arranges the fatal epidemic disease, which prevailed extensively in the early and dark ages, as the sequel of war and famine, and which has received a variety of denominations : such as ignis sacer, ignis Sancti Antonii, &c. &c. according to its various modifications and degrees of severity, or according to the supposed cause of it.   The disease was doubtless the result of deficient nourishment—a severe land-scurvy which was a great scourge of the ancient world, and often denominated *pestilence*."—" The name of St. Anthony seems to have been first associated with an epidemic disease of this kind, which prevailed in Dauphiné about the end of the 12th century. An abbey dedicated to that Saint had recently been founded at Vienne, in that province—and it was a popular opinion, in that and the succeeding century, that all the patients who were conveyed to this abbey were cured in the space of seven or nine days."—Ibid. pp. 134, 135.

† Michaelis, *ut sup.*

them. It is most frequently found in cellars, but ascends also into the higher parts of the building.—In Bern, Mr. Apothecary *Andreǎ* heard the people complain of a disease that in an especial manner attacked sand-stone, so as to make it exfoliate, and become as it were cancerous. They call it *gall*, and, in like manner, ascribe it to the saltpetre contained in the stone. It is not, properly speaking, saltpetre that is in these walls and buildings, but an *acid of nitre*, from which, by the addition of a *fixed alkali*, we can make saltpetre. The detrimental effects of this efflorescence in walls, or, if I may use the common name, of this saltpetre, are—the walls become mouldy, and that to such a degree, as in consequence of the corrosion spreading farther and farther, at last to occasion their tumbling down;—many things that lie near walls affected with saltpetre, thereby suffer damage, and are spoiled;—if the saltpetre be strong in those apartments wherein people live, it is pernicious to health, particularly where they sleep close to the wall.—The consideration of these circumstances will render the Mosaic ordinances on this subject easily intelligible. Their object was to check the evil in the very bud; to extirpate it while it was yet extirpable, by making every one, from the loss to which it would subject him, careful to prevent his house becoming affected with leprosy, which he could easily do, where the houses had no damp stone-cellars below ground; and thus also to place not only himself in perfect security, but his neighbours also, who might very reasonably dread having their houses contaminated by the infection."*—That Moses did not design to convey the idea that any leprosy in clothes and houses would infect any one, Michaelis thinks, is sufficiently proved, by ordering that when a house lay under suspicion of leprosy all the articles of furniture should be removed out of it, previous to its inspection; for if there

* Ibid. pp. 293—300.

H

had adhered any poisonous matter to the walls that could
pass to human beings, this would have been a most
extraordinary injunction, and the very way to a direct pro-
pagation of the infection.

The leprosy of *clothes* is described in Levit. xiii, 47—59,
as consisting of green or reddish spots that remain in spite
of washing, &c. and still spread, and by which the cloth becomes fretted and bare.—Dr. A. Clarke supposes that this was
most probably " occasioned by a species of small *animals*,
which we know to be the cause of the *itch :* these, by breeding in the garments, must necessarily multiply their kind,
and *fret* the garments, *i. e.* corrode a portion of the finer
parts, after the manner of *mites,* for their nourishment.—
He shall therefore burn that garment : There being scarcely
any mode of radically curing the infection. It is well known
that the garments infected by the *psora* or itch-animal, have
been known to communicate the disease, even six or seven
years after the first infection."*—The opinion of Michaelis
is not very dissimilar to that of the learned Doctor ; for
according to the information he received from an eminent
woollen manufacturer, the wool of sheep which die by
disease, and which is technically called *dead wool,* is apt to
breed vermin, especially when worn close to the body and
warmed by it ; he therefore conceives that it was an
additional proof of the consummate legislative policy of the
Mosaic institutes, to bring into discredit and disuse stuffs
already become thread-bare and fretted, and particularly in
climates which must have been so favourable to the rapid
multiplication of vermin.†—It may perhaps also lead the
reader to examine the subject still more fully, to remark,
that it is well known that if *cotton* or *linen* cloth be suffered
to remain long in a damp situation, it assumes an appearance

* Comment, *in loc.*
† Michaelis, *ut sup.*

similar to that described by Moses, and which is usually termed *mildew*, and is not only difficult to be removed by washing, but also frequently injures the texture of the cloth itself, as is frequently experienced to their loss by bleachers, in bleaching or whitening cloths of different descriptions.

DISSERTATION VIII.

ON

TALISMANS AND TALISMANIC FIGURES.

———◆———

THE almost universal prevalence of Idolatry in the early
ages of the world, was accompanied in most countries
by the dedication of representative images, to the deities
they worshipped. The sun, and the moon, and the stars,
the first objects of idolatrous veneration, had their representative idols, supposed to be under the special influence of
the planetary bodies to which they were dedicated, and
possessing through that influence a prophetic and powerful
character.—The astronomical pursuits of the Chaldeans, and
other oriental nations, aided the influence of idolatry, and
soon introduced the science of *Astrology* in all its ramifica-
tions, and induced the construction of horoscopical and talismanical images and figures. Figures of this description are
termed מגן (*magan*) by the Hebrews;—צלמניא (*tzel-
menia*), image or figure by the Chaldeans, Egyptians,
and Persians;—תלצמם (*talizmam*) or צלמם (*tzali-
mam*) by the Arabians;—and στοιχεια (*stoikeia*) by
the Greeks.—The Hebrew term *Magan*, properly signifies
a paper, or other material, drawn or engraved with
the letters composing the sacred name *Jehovah* or with
other characters, and improperly applied to astrological
representations, because, like the letters composing the
Incommunicable Name, they were supposed to serve as a
buckler or defence against sickness, lightning and tempest.*

———————

* Gaffarel. Curiositez Inouyes, ch. vi. pp. 106—111, 8vo. 1650.

A Persian writer, quoted by Dr. Hyde, defines the *Telesm* or *Talisman* to be "a piece of art compounded of the celestial powers and elementary bodies, appropriated to certain figures and positions, and purposes, and times contrary to the usual manner;" and Maimonides remarks, *images* or *idols* were called *Tzelamim*, not from their figure or form, but from the power or influence which was supposed to reside in them.*

The first construction of astrological or talismanic images, most probably arose from the wish of the idolaters to represent the planets during their absence from the horizon, that they might at all times have the opportunity of worshipping either the planetary body itself, or its representative. Their astrologers therefore, who appropriated particular colours, metals, stones, trees, &c. to the respective planets, formed images of such materials as were appropriated to the planets they were designed to represent, and constructed them when the planets were in their exaltation, and in a happy conjunction with other heavenly bodies; after which, they attempted, by incantatory rites, to inspire the fabricated symbols with the power and influence of the planets themselves.†—Manilius, a Latin poet, who lived in the reign of Augustus, wrote an astrological poem, still exant, explaining and defending the science and votaries of astrology. He supposes *Mercurius Trismegistus* to have been the inventor of Astronomy, and that the science being afterwards cultivated by the oriental princes and priests, they introduced Astrology as the result and perfection of their studies :

* Maimon. More Nevoch. Part I. c. i, p. 2.—Hyde, Syntagma, a Greg. Sharpe, Tom. i. p. 500, Oxon. 1767, 4to.

† Pocockii Specimen Hist. Arab. *note*, p. 140.— Hyde, De Veter. Persar. Relig. Cap. v. pp. 126—134.—Young On Idolatrous Corruptions, vol. i. p. 113.

SUCH were those wondrous men who first from far
Look'd up, and saw Fates hanging at each Star:
Their thoughts extended did at once comprise
Ten thousand revolutions of the skies ;
They mark'd the influence, and observ'd the power
Of every Sign, and every fatal Hour ;
What Tempers they bestow'd, what Fortunes gave,
And who was doom'd a King, who born a Slave ;
How aspects vary, and their change creates,
Though little, great variety in fates.
Thus when the Stars their mighty round had run
And all were fix'd whence first their race begun,
What hints Experience did to search impart
They join'd, and *Observation* grew to *Art ;*
Thus rules were fram'd, for by example shown
They knew what *would be*, from what had been done ;
They saw the stars their constant round maintain,
Perform their course, and then return again ;
They on their *Aspects* saw the Fates attend,
Their change or their *Variety* depend,
And thence they fix'd unalterable laws,
Settling the *same effect* on the *same cause.*

    *   *   *   *

The God or Reason which the Orbs doth move,
Makes things below depend on signs above ;
Though far remov'd, though hid in shades of night,
And scarce to be descried by their own light ;
Yet nations own, and men their influence feel ;
They rule the public and the private Will.*

Landseer (Sabæan Researches, pp. 54, 60) supposes
that many of the ancient engraved Babylonian or Chaldean
Signets, still preserved in the cabinets of the curious, were
originally designed as horoscopical representations of the
heavens at the time of the birth of the original possessor,
though destitute of any astral or magical influence. But
although Landseer and some others suppose, that the ancient
Chaldeans or Babylonians attributed no special or amuletic
influence to these Signets; it is certain that extraordinary

* Manilius, B. I. p. 4, and B. II. p. 52, London, 1697, 8vo.

power or influence was attributed, generally, to images or
figures formed or fabricated according to astrological principles. Tradition states that Terah, the father of Abraham, was a maker of " Talismans, or little images framed
in some planetary hour ;" and to which were attributed
certain occult and mysterious influences, as is evidenced by
the tale connected with this traditon, and frequently related
by writers on Hebrew Antiquities, from the *Bereshith
Rabba,* and other collections of Rabbinical Traditions.*

* The following is the elegant version of it given by *Hurwitz*, in his
interesting collection of Jewish Apologues and " Hebrew Tales :"—
" TERAH, the father of Abraham, was not only an idolater, but a
manufacturer of idols, which he used to expose for public sale. Being obliged
one day to go out on particular business, he desired Abraham to superintend
for him. Abraham obeyed reluctantly.—" What is the price of that god ?,"
asked an old man who had just entered the place of sale, pointing to an idol
to which he took a fancy.—" Old man," said Abraham, " may I be permitted to ask thine age !"—" Three-score years," replied the age-stricken
idolater.—" Three-score years !" exclaimed Abraham,—" and thou wouldest
worship a thing that has been fashioned by the hands of my father's slaves
within the last four-and-twenty hours !—Strange ! that a man of sixty
should be willing to bow down his grey head to a creature of a day !"—The
man was overwhelmed with shame, and went away. After this, there came a
sedate and grave matron, carrying in her hand a large dish with flour.
" Here," said she, " have I brought an offering to the gods. Place it before
them, Abraham, and bid them be propitious to me."—" Place it before them
thyself, foolish woman !," said Abraham : " thou wilt soon see how greedily
they will devour it." She did so. In the mean time, Abraham took a
hammer, broke the idols in pieces ; all excepting the largest, in whose hands
he placed the instrument of destruction. TERAH returned, and, with the
utmost surprise and consternation, beheld the havoc amongst his favourite
gods. " What is all this, Abraham ? What profane wretch has dared to
use our gods in this manner ?," exclaimed the infatuated and indignant
TERAH.—" Why should I conceal any thing from my father ?," replied the
pious son. " During thine absence, there came a woman with yonder offering
to the gods. She placed it before them. The younger gods, who, as may
well be supposed, had not tasted food for a long time, greedily stretched forth
their hands, and began to eat before the old god had given them permission.
Enraged at their boldness, he rose, took the hammer, and punished them for
their want of respect."—" Dost thou mock me ? Wilt thou deceive thy aged
father ?," exclaimed Terah, in a vehement rage.—" Do I then not know that

The learned Gregory supposes, that *Telisms* or magical images owed their origin to the false views entertained by the Gentile nations respecting the Brazen Serpent erected in the Wilderness :—" The Astrologers," says he, " had perceived that this God" (*i. e.* the God of the Jews) "had been pleased with the Brazen Serpent, which Moses the *Talisman* (so they would account him) set up upon a pole in the wilderness, (Numbers xxi. 8.,) and I need not stick to affirm, that the *Brazen Serpent* against the *Fiery Serpents* was the first occasion (I say not given, but) taken of all these Talismanical practices."*—But whether this erudite writer be correct or not in his conjectures, as to the origin of *Telesms* or *Talismans*, it is certain such images, constructed under certain positions of the heavens, were very generally used amongst the ancient nations, as the means of protection and safety, both to cities and persons. The Rabbis affirm that the *Blind* and the *Lame* mentioned 2 Sam. v. 6—8, were images written upon with the oath which Abraham and Isaac made to Abimelech, and that they were called " Blind" and " Lame," because "they had eyes and saw not, they had feet and walked not."† They were, therefore, most probably " *Stoichiodæ* or Constillated *Images of Brass*, set up in the recess of the fort, called in scorn, (as they were hated by David's soul,) the *Blind* and the *Lame ;* yet so surely entrusted with the keeping of the place, that if they did not hold it out, the Jebusites said they should not come into the house, that is, they would

they can neither eat, nor stir, nor move ?"—" And yet," rejoined Abraham, " thou payest them divine honours—adorest them—and wouldest have me worship them !" It was in vain Abraham thus reasoned with his idolatrous parent. Superstition is ever both deaf and blind. His unnatural father delivered him over to the cruel tribunal of the equally idolatrous NIMROD. But a more merciful Father—the gracious and blessed Father of us all— protected him against the threatened danger ; and Abraham became the father of the faithful." (Hurwitz's Hebrew Tales, p. 139: London, 1826, 8vo.)

* Gregory's (John) Works, c. viii. p. 41, London, 1671, 4to.

† Ibid, c. vii. p. 34.

never again commit the safety of the fort to such Palladiums as these."* The images of *Emerods* and *Mice,* sent with the Ark of JEHOVAH by the Philistines, (1 Sam. vi. 4, 5, 11, 17, 18,) appear to have been such Telesms or Talismanic figures, formed according to astrological rules.— Gregory details many instances of a similar nature. (*Works* c. vii., viii.) Dr. Adam Clarke observes, " It was a very common usage when a plague or other calamity infested a country, city, &c., for the magicians to form an image of the *destroyer,* or of the *things* on which the plague particularly rested, in gold, silver, ivory, wax, clay, &c. under certain configurations of the heavens; and to set this up in some proper place, that the evils thus represented might be driven away. These consecrated images were the same that are called *Talismans,* or rather *Telesms,* among the Asiatics. Mr. Locke" (and he might have added *Gregory*) " calls the diviners *Talismans!* but this is a pitiful mistake: the *image,* not the *fabricator,* was called by this name. —I have seen several of these *Talismans* of different countries; and such images were probably the origin of all the forms of gods, which, in after times, were the objects of religious worship. It is well known that Ireland is not infected with any venomous creatures; no serpent of any kind is found in it :—

> " No poison there infects, no scaly snake
> Lurks in the grass, nor toad annoys the lake.

" This has been attributed to a *Telesm,* formed with certain rites, under the sign *Scorpio.* Such opinions have been drawn from very ancient Pagan sources: *e. g.*—A stone engraved with the figure of a *Scorpion,* while the moon is in the sign *Scorpio,* is said to cure those who are stung by this animal. *Apollonius Tyanæus* is said to have prevented *flies* from infesting Antioch; and *storks* from appearing in

---

* Ibid, p. 34.

Byzantium, by figures of those animals formed under certain constellations. A *brazen scorpion*, placed on a pillar in the city of Antioch, is said to have expelled all such animals from that country : and a *crocodile* of lead is also said to have preserved *Cairo* from the depredations of those monsters. *Virgil* refers to this custom, (Eclogue viii. p. 80,) where he represents a person making two images, or *Telesms*, one of *wax*, another of *clay*; which were to represent an absent person, who was to be alternately *softened* or *hardened* as the *wax* or *clay* image was exposed to the fire.

> " Limus ut hic durescit, et hæc ut cera liquescit
> Uno et eodem igni ; sic nostro Daphnis amore.

" As this clay hardens, and this wax softens, by one and the same fire ; so may Daphnis, by my love.

" A beautiful marble figure of *Osiris*, about four inches and a quarter high, now stands before me, all covered over with hieroglyphics : he is *standing*, and holds in each hand a *scorpion* and a *snake* by the tails, and with each foot he stands on the neck of a *crocodile*. This, I have no doubt, was a *Telesm*, formed under some peculiar *configuration* of the heavens, intended to drive away both scorpions and crocodiles. This image is of the highest antiquity, and was formed probably long before the Christian æra."[*]

" Pliny notices the figures of *eagles* and *beetles* carved on emeralds, and *Marcellus Empiricus* the virtue of these *beetles*, especially for diseases of the *eye*. The most revered sort were those made according to the Samothracian mysteries. They were pieces of metal, with certain figures of stars, commonly set in rings, but not always. The Arabians in Spain spread them all over Europe, though the use

---

[*] Clarke's Commentary, 1 Sam. vi. *in fine*

of them had never become obsolete."* *Talismans* or *Telesms* have been divided into different kinds or classes, which have been thus distinguished by the indefatigable *Fosbrooke* (*Encyclop. of Antiq.*)—1. The *Astronomical*, with celestial signs and intelligible characters:—2. The *Magical*, with extraordinary figures, superstitious words, and names of unknown angels:—3. The *Mixed*, of celestial signs and barbarous words, but not superstitious, or with names of angels:—4. *Sigilla Planetarum*, composed of Hebrew numeral letters, used by astrologers and fortune-tellers:— 5. *Hebrew Names and Characters.*—Of this last kind were those formed according to the Cabalistic art. Such, for instance, appears to be the hexagonal one termed the *Shield of David* or *Seal of Solomon*, (See *Frontispiece*, fig. 5,) which was said to be a security against wounds, would extinguish fires, and perform many other wonders; and by which Solomon was said to have accomplished the most extraordinary objects. This figure had one or other of the names of God, disposed within it according to the principles and rules of the Jewish Cabala: the name most frequently inserted was the barbarous term אגלא (AGLA) contracted from the Hebrew words—אתה גבר לעלם אדני: " Thou art strong in the eternal God."†—According to R. Solomon, the *Theraphim* of the Scriptures were "images which spoke by the influence of magical art; and R. Eliezer, in *Perke Eliezer*, says, they were statues in the form of a man, constructed under certain constellations, which, from the influence they received, spoke at certain hours, giving answers to whatever questions were asked; and adds, that the reason why Rachel stole the Theraphim from her father Laban was, for fear he should learn from them the route of Jacob and his family.‡

* Fosbrooke's Encyclopedia of Antiquities, vol. i. p. 336, London, 1825, 4*to.*

† Wagenselii Sota, p. 1074 4*to*. Altdorf. Noric. 1674.—Enfield's History of Philosophy, vol. ii. p. 211, 8*vo*.—Basnage's History of the Jews.

‡ Spencer, De Legibus Hebræorum p. 354.—Gaffarel. Curiositez Inouyes, p. 53.

It is highly probable, that the prohibitory injunctions of
the *Second Commandment* were directed, not only against
idols or images actually formed in order to be venerated or
worshipped, but also against all such talismanic figures and
hieroglyphical characters as might lead the people into
idolatry in any of its varied forms.—*Michaelis* observes, that
" in order to preserve their treasures of knowledge, and their
discoveries in natural science, the Egyptian priests made use
not of common writing, but of *Hieroglyphics*. With these
they inscribed obelisks and walls, even those of subterraneous vaults and galleries ;—and also square stones which
very   much   resemble   our   grave-stones. — With   these
hieroglyphic stones, idolatry was practised.   In Egypt they
were regarded as the god *Thoth*, the god of sciences ; and,
as late as the time of Ezekiel, we find an imitation of this
species of idolatry common among the Jews, and described
in chap. viii, 8—11, of his prophecy. According, therefore,
to that fundamental principle of the Mosaic polity, which
dictated the prevention of idolatry, it became absolutely
necessary to prohibit stones with hieroglyphic inscriptions.
Besides, in an age, where so great a propensity to superstition prevailed, stones with figures upon them, which the
people could not understand, would have been a temptation
to idolatry, even although the Egyptians had not deified
them as they actually did."*—To these observations we may
add the remarks of the ingenious *Landseer* in his " Sabæan
Researches :"

" The prime cause," he observes, " of the postdiluvian
apostacies from the purer deism of Noah and of Job,
appears to have been the ignorant confounding, by a
superstitious people, of SIGNS, with CAUSES. From this
source proceeded the idolatry which is at once disclaimed
and reproved by the latter, in a sublime and often-cited
text, and which it also appears was in his time and country

* Commentaries on the Laws of Moses, vol. iv, pp. 55—59

cognisable by the magistracy. ' If, (says the venerable sufferer) I beheld the sun when it shined, or the moon progressive in brightness; and my heart hath been secretly enticed, or my mouth hath kissed my hand : this (also) were an iniquity to be punished by the Judge : for I should have denied the God that is above.' (Job xxxi. 26, 27, 28.) And on account of this prevailing heresy, Moses,— expressly prohibited their making unto themselves ' graven images,'—the likenesses of things in heaven above, &c.; and this at the very time that Cherubim were permitted, and even ordained, to be exhibited in the tabernacle, and on the ark of the covenant. Now, to have been made *to themselves;* that is, for each man to keep in his possession, whilst sojourning in the desert, these prohibited articles must have been small, to have been termed *likenesses of things in heaven above,*—objects of worship too ! they must —at least, bearing in mind the pervading astronomy of this remote period, I find it impossible to come to any other conclusion—have borne some real or fancied resemblance to planets and constellations; and to have been *graven* images, they must have been sculptured on hard and durable substances, and sculptured in intaglio : we should recollect too, that such works are, in the Bible, expressly and repeatedly distinguished from cast figures, or ' *molten* images,' as well as from such as were overlaid with beaten gold:—in short these Chaldean engravings, and the portable part of the hieroglyphical engravings of Egypt, are the only productions that have descended to our knowledge, which at all accord with what is described and prohibited in the Second Commandment."*

Divination by *Precious Stones* was likewise very extensively practised, by heathen nations, in almost every part of the world. Of this mode of Divination, Warton † offers the following conjecture as to its origin. " The nations

---

* Landseer's Sabæan Researches, pp. 36, 37.
† Warton's Hist. of English Poetry, vol. ii. 4to.

bordering upon the Jews," says he, "attributed the miraculous events of that people, to those external means and material instruments, such as symbols, ceremonies, and other visible signs or circumstances, which, by God's special appointment, under their mysterious dispensation, they were directed to use. Among the observations which the oriental Gentiles made on the history of the Jews, they found that the Divine will was to be known by certain appearances in precious stones. The Magi of the East, believing that the preternatural discoveries obtained by means of the Urim and Thummim, a contexture of gems in the breast-plate of the Mosaic priests, were owing to some virtue inherent in those stones, adopted the knowledge of the occult properties of gems, as a branch of their magical system. Hence it became the peculiar profession of one class of their sages, to investigate and interpret the various shades and coruscations, and to explain to a moral purpose, the different colours, the dews, clouds and imageries, which gems differently exposed to the sun, moon, stars, fire, or air, at particular seasons, and inspected by persons particularly qualified, were seen to exhibit. This notion being once established, a thousand extravagancies rose, of healing diseases, of procuring victory, and of seeing future events, by means of precious stones, and other lucid substances. See Plin. *Nat. Hist.* xxxvii. 9, 10.—These superstitions were soon engrafted into the Arabian philosophy, from which they were propagated all over Europe, and continued to operate, even so late as the visionary experiments of Dee and Kelly.* It is not in the mean time at all improbable, that the Druidical doctrines concerning the virtues of stones were derived from these lessons of the Magi; and they are still to be traced among the traditions of the vulgar, in those parts of Britain

---

* When king Richard I. in 1191, took the isle of Cyprus, he is said to have found the castles filled with rich furniture of gold and silver, " nec non lapidibus pretiosis, et plurimam virtutem habentibus," and precious stones which possessed great virtues.—G. Vines. *Iter. Hierosol.* cap. xli. p. 328.

aud Ireland, where Druidism retained its latest establish-ments. See Martin's *West Isles*, p. 167, 225: and Aubrey's *Miscell.* p. 128, London, 8*vo.*"

Amulets or Charms, also, were similar in nature to the oriental Telesms or Talismans, except that they were not always regarded as connected with astral influence. The term *Amulet* was probably derived either from *Amula*, a small vase for containing lustral-waters, among the ancient Romans, for purification and expiation, sometimes carried in the pocket; or from *amoliri*, to remove, from its supposed power of *removing* or *preventing* evil. The Amulets of the Persians or Greeks were small cylinders, ornamented with figures and hieroglyphics. The erudite "Sabæan Researches" of Landseer exhibit unequivocal proof, that the ancient Chaldeans and Zabian idolaters constructed and wore astrological cylinders, either as the horoscopes of their birth, or as instruments of preservation or prosperity. — The Amulets of the Greeks or Romans were gems of almost every kind, crowns of pearls, necklaces of shells, gems, coral, heads and figures of divinities, heroes, horses, dogs, rats, birds, fish, &c. and grotesque and obscene images. These they placed around the neck, especially of children, or hung them on the jambs of doors, so that, in opening them, they caused the amulets to move and ring the bells attached to them; in some cases, they were placed at the entry of shops, or even of forges. All nations, indeed, have been fond of amulets or charms: the Jews were extremely superstitious in the use of them to drive away diseases; and the Mishna forbids them, unless received from an *approved* man, who had cured, at least, three persons before by the same means.—After the Christian era, we hear of charms, made of the hair of she-bears, or toys, tied to them, as remedies against witchcraft; parts of St. John's Gospel worn round the neck; verses of the Old or New Testaments, put even upon horses; magical characters written upon slips of parchment; remedies wrapped up in scarlet cloth; ear-rings, and common rings made of ostrich's bones. Reginald Scot states, that if a Jasper be set in silver, and worn as a ring on the finger, its virtues are reported to be great and various, of which he gives the following summary, in a quaint translation from Marbodeus, by Abraham Fleming.

> Seven kinds and ten of Jasper-stones
>   Reported are to be;
> Of many colours this is known
>   Which noted is by me,
> And said in many places of
>   The world for to be seen
> Where it is bred; but yet the best
>   Is through the shining *green*,
> And that which proved is to have
>   In it more virtue plac'd;
> For being born about of such
>   As are of living chaste,
> It drives away their Ague fits,
>   The Dropsy thirsting dry,
> And put upon a woman weak
>   In travail which doth lie,
> It helps, assists, and comforts her
>   In pangs, when she doth cry.
> Again it is believ'd to be
>   A safeguard frank and free,
> To such as wear and bear the same;
>   And if it hallow'd be,
> It makes the parties gracious,
>   And mighty too that have it;
> And noisome fancies (as they write
>   That meant not to deprave it)
> It doth displace out of the mind:
>   The force thereof is stronger,
> In Silver if the same be set,
>   And will endure the longer.

In the sixteenth century, we have Amulets worn round the neck against pestilence, made of *arsenick*; and warehoused in large quantities. One item says, " A hundryth wight of amletts for the neke, xxxˢ· iiijᵈ·"—The author of the "Vulgar Errors" tells us, that hollow stones, called in the North *holy stones*, are hung up in stables to prevent the night-mare, or *ephialtes ;* and the Rev. Mr. Shaw, in his account of Elgin, &c. (See Appendix to *Pennant's Tour,*) informs us, that at the full moon in March, they cut *withes* of the misletoe, or ivy, make circles of them, keep them all the year, and pretend to cure *hectics* and other disorders by them.*—The reader who wishes to pursue the subject, may find ample opportunity in perusing old Reginald Scot's rare and curious work, entitled, *The Discovery of Witch- craft*, London, 1665, folio, in which, whilst he acknow- ledges the existence of witches and the influence of many kinds of divination, of which he gives, what he regards, incontrovertible instances, he also endeavours to expose the fallacy and fraud in the practices of many pretenders to the arts of divination, necromancy, and witchcraft, and warns the magistrates to be cautious in receiving the evi- dence preferred against persons accused of witchcraft and similar arts ; and to exercise mercy in their judicial sen- tences.—" Surely their *charms*," saith he, " can no more reach to the hurting or killing of men or women, than their imaginations can extend to the stealing and carrying away of horses and mares. Neither hath God given remedies to sickness or griefs, by words or charms, but by herbs and medicines, which He himself hath created upon earth, and given men knowledge of the same; that he might be glori- fied for that therewith He doth vouchsafe that the maladies of men and cattle should be cured : and if there be no affliction nor calamity, but is brought to pass by Him ; then let us defy the Devil, renounce all his works, and not so

* Fosbrooke's Encyclopedia of Antiquities, vol. i. pp. 207, 208, 223. London, 1825, *4to.*—Wotton's Miscellaneous Discourses, relating to the Traditions and Usages of the Scribes and Pharisees, &c. vol. ii. p. 49. London, 1718, *8vo.*—Scot's (R.) Discovery of Witchcraft, B. xiii. Chap. vii. p. 169.— Brand's Observations on Popular Antiquities, Chap. ix. p. 97, and Appendix p. 380. London, 1810, *8vo.*

I

much as once think or dream upon the supernatural power of witches.—Neither," adds he, writing at a period when persons suspected of witchcraft were frequently put to death, "let us prosecute them with such despight, whom our fancy condemneth, and our reason acquitteth: our evidence against them consisting in impossibilities, our proofs in unwritten verities, and our whole proceedings in doubts and difficulties." (Address *to the Readers.*)

DISSERTATION IX.

ON

JUDICIAL ASTROLOGY.

———

ASTROLOGY is the science of Planetary Influence, in general. NATURAL ASTROLOGY comprehends the predicting of natural effects; as the changes of weather, winds, storms, hurricanes, thunder, floods, earthquakes, &c.—JUDICIAL or JUDICIARY ASTROLOGY is that which pretends to foretel *moral events*, or such as have a dependence on the free-will and agency of man, from the aspects and positions of the heavenly bodies.

Judicial Astrology was probably invented in Chaldæa, and thence transmitted to the Egyptians, Greeks, and Romans; though some ascribe it to the Ethiopians, and others to the Arabians or Egyptians.*—The professors of it maintain, "That the heavens are one great volume or book, wherein God has written the history of the world; and in which every man may read his own fortune, and the transactions of his time.—The art, they say, had its rise from the same hands as astronomy itself. While the ancient Assyrians, whose serene unclouded sky favoured their celestial observations, were intent on tracing the paths and

---

* Stanley's History of Philosophy: *Chaldaick Philosophy*, pp. 757, 763, 774, London, 1743, 4*to*.—Bergier, Dictionnaire de Theologie, tom. i. p. 282 —*Astrologie Judiciaire*, Toulouse. 1819. 8*vo*.—Young, On Idolatrous Corruptions in Religion, vol. ii. p. 135.

I 2

periods of the heavenly bodies, they discovered a constant settled relation of analogy between them and things below ; and hence were led to conclude these were the *Parcæ*, the destinies, so much talked of, which preside at our births, and dispose of our future fate. The laws, therefore, of this relation being ascertained, by a series of observations, and the share each planet has therein ; by knowing the precise time of any person's nativity, they were enabled, from their knowledge in astronomy, to erect a scheme or horoscope of the situation of the planets, at that point of time : and hence, by considering their degree of power and influence, and how each was either strengthened or tempered by some other, to compute what must be the result thereof."*—" The way in which the Chaldeans observed the horoscope of any nativity was, that a Chaldean sat in the night-time on some high promontory, or lofty observatory, contemplating the stars : another sat by the woman till she was delivered. As soon as she was delivered, it was signinied to him who was on the promontory or observatory, which as soon as he heard, he observed the sign then rising for the horoscope ; but, in the day, he attended to the ascendants and sun's motion."†

Such is Astrology as presented to us by its advocates and apologists ; yet with all its lofty pretensions it can neither afford certainty to the enquirer, nor happiness to the adept. It is erroneous in its principles, and uncertain in its *data :* it affects a knowledge beyond the reach of human intellect, assumes positions inconsistent with Revelation, and infers conclusions contradicted by the common experience of mankind.

1. Astrological investigations proceed upon the possibility of ascertaining a knowledge of the *contingencies* of

---

* Encyc. Perth.—*Astrology.*

† Stanley's Chaldaick Philosophy, *ut sup.* p. 778.—Landseer's Sabæan Researches, p. 54.

human affairs, by the study of the aspects and positions of the various planetary bodies at certain given periods.—But nothing can be more absurd than to suppose, that a knowledge of future contingencies can be obtained by consecutive deductions from the appearances of the heavens. For, if the fates of men, and the course of mundane affairs, invariably accord with the relative positions of the stars, either the actions of men must be fixed and *necessary* and consequently *not contingent*, and the free-agency of man be destroyed; or, which is equally absurd, the planetary system must possess omniscience, and, by pretending to the fore-knowledge of contingent events, assume the prerogative of Deity itself.—" For the foretelling of things to come, which in their own nature are contingent, and in regard of us casual, is a property peculiar to God alone, and not within the power of any creature, man, or angel; a point that is plainly taught by the Prophet Isaiah, from the *fourth* chapter of his Prophecy to the *forty-eighth*: The scope whereof is to prove, that it is a prerogative appropriated to the Deity, and not communicable to the creature, to foreshew the event of things to come, which, in our understanding and reach, may either be or not be; and which, when they are, may be thus or otherwise."

2. The *Data* on which astrological calculators found their prognostications must necessarily be defective and uncertain, from the want of adequate experience and observation. The ever-varying situations of the planetary orbs, and the astonishing diversity of human characters and constitutions, added to the great mutability of secular concerns, must, for ever, prevent such a concatenated series of comparisons betwixt the aspects of the heavens and terrestrial agencies and events, as to justify decisions founded on such observations; or enable an astrological observer to state the result of his observations with axiomatic truth and precision. For although there may be the same conjunc-

tions, the same risings and settings of some of the planetary bodies; yet the influence of innumerable others which are constantly varying their positions, with the immense periods of time elapsing between important configurations of the heavens, added to the unforeseen and powerful influences of comets and other erratic bodies of eccentric movement, must render it impossible to calculate with exactness the amount and tendency of planetary influence for any given moment. The attempts to vindicate the art, by appeals to occasional instances of seeming accuracy between the predictions and the events, merely prove, that, amidst innumerable guesses and conjectural prognostications, fortuitous occurrences have sometimes happened similar to those predicted, but too infrequent and casual to establish the truth of a system founded on premises so variable and incompetent. It is even possible, that, in some cases, the predictions themselves may bring about their own fulfilment: for instance, if it be predicted that a man will die at a certain time, the very dread of the event may induce disease and render it mortal. A singular example is related by Michaelis, in which a person was cured of a dangerous illness, by Dr. Wadeln demonstrating to him the inanity of astrological predictions of death.—Many of the old divines supposed also, and not without considerable probability, that in many cases the co-incidences betwixt the prediction and the event arose from diabolical agency. —"For my own part," says Dr. Henry More, "I do not much doubt but that Astrology itself is an appendix of the the old Pagans' superstition, who were worshippers of the host of heaven, and whose priests were confederates of the Devil; and therefore it is no wonder if Dæmonolatry creep in upon Astrology, and renew their old acquaintance with one another: and assuredly it is a pleasant spectacle to those airy goblins, those haters and scorners of mankind, to see the noble faculties of men debased and entangled in so vile and wretched a mystery, which will avail nothing to Divination, unless these 'malicious deceivers' act their parts in the scene."

3. The knowledge requisite for the astrological professor, in order to enable him to form his horoscopes with infallible precision and certainty, even were we to allow the unscriptural assumption of planetary influence on human life and character, is too immense for the grasp of the human intellect in its present state of limitation and imperfection.—For who is capable of calling all the stars by name?—of marshalling the myriads of the host of heaven?—of tracing them through the infinite variety of their ever-changing positions?—of marking, without error, their separate or combined influences on secular affairs?—of investigating with invariable accuracy the capacities of inferior and terrestial objects to receive, or hinder, or change, or pervert the character and degree of astral influence, whether from the nature of the soil, the differences of climate, the kinds of aliment, the constitutions of government, the influence of education, the manners of society, or from a thousand other similar circumstances?—Must it not be affirmed?,—" Such knowledge is too wonderful for them, it is high, they cannot attain unto it."—Psalm cxxxix, 6.

4. The pretensions of astrology, far from being in accordance with the doctrines of the Holy Scriptures, are directly opposed to their dictates and injunctions.—They condemn, in severe and authoritative terms, all attempts to pry into futurity by the arts of divination, and subject those who practise them to the just judgments of God.—Thus, Levit. xix, 26, " Ye shall not use enchantment, nor observe times."—Deut. xviii. 10, 11, 12, " There shall not be found among you, any one that useth divination, or any observer of times, or an enchanter, or a witch, or a charmer, or a consulter with familiar spirits, or a wizard, or a necromancer. For all that do these things are an abomination unto the LORD : and because of these abominations the

LORD thy God doth drive them out from before thee." God denounces his judgments against Babylon, by Isaiah xlvii, 13, 14, " Let now the astrologers, the star-gazers, the monthly prognosticators stand up, and save thee from these things that shall come upon thee.—Behold, they shall be as stubble; the fire shall burn them, they shall not deliver themselves from the power of the flame."—And Jeremiah addresses his countrymen in the name of JEHOVAH, saying, " Thus saith the LORD, Learn not the way of the heathen, and be not dismayed at the signs of heaven; for the heathen are dismayed at them."—The Apostle Paul also severely reproves the Galatians for their attention to astrological practices, and regards their conduct as affording serious apprehensions of their declension in religion and apostacy from Christianity :—" When ye knew not," says the holy writer, " ye did service unto them which by nature are no gods : but now, after that ye have known God, or rather are known of God, how turn ye again to the weak and beggarly elements, whereunto ye desire again to be in bondage? Ye observe days, and months, and times, and years. I am afraid of you, lest I have bestowed upon you labour in vain." —Galatians iv. 8, 9, 10.

" The true use of the Heavens," says an excellent old writer, " consisteth in many points,—First, to declare the glory of God. ' The heavens,' saith David, (Psalm xix, 1,) ' declare the glory of God, and the firmament showeth his handy-work.'—It is an alphabet written in great letters, in which is described the majesty of God, and that by these four special points, the majesty of the work itself:—the infinite multitude of stars :—the wonderful variety of stars : —the greatness of the stars.

" Secondly, it maketh sinners and wicked men inexcusable before the judgment-seat of God. Rom. i. 20.

" Thirdly, they serve to the appointing of times, as day, night, month, year, which are both measured and described by the course of the sun and moon, and other stars ; and so the feasts of the Israelités, and the computation of the year in our church, depend thereupon, and without them there would be great confusion both in the commonwealth and church.

" Fourthly, they serve as signs :—and they are signs either of *extraordinary* things, or things which are *ordinary*. When they are signs of *extraordinary* things, then there is, and appeareth in them some extraordinary work ; as appeareth in the examples which follow : Matt. xxvii, 45. The sun was wholly eclipsed, the moon being in the full. Ezek.xxxii,7,8.—Lastly,the extraordinary going back of the sun signified the lengthening of the life of king Hezekiah.

"The stars are signs of *general* things which happen *ordinarily* every year in nature among us, as the approaching and declining of the spring, summer, harvest, winter ;— ordinary weather ;—ebbing and flowing of the sea ;—seasons of ploughing, sowing, setting, planting, cutting, felling, reaping.—I say *general*, because the particular estate and affairs of men can, in no wise, be fore-signified by the stars. I say *ordinary*, because the things which fall out seldom, and are beside the common course of nature, as plenty of all things, famine, plague, war, &c. do not depend upon the stars."

5. The futility of the conclusions drawn by astrologers from the aspects of the heavens, is proved by the contradictory occurrences of nature and the common events of civil society.—St. Augustine, in his book *De Civitate Dei*, exposes the folly of those who choose particular days for agricultural purposes, at the suggestion of astrologers, as if the positions of the stars had some special influence upon them ; and argues that the supposition is unfounded, for when a number of grains of corn are cast into the ground together, and are all ripening at one time, yet some of them are blasted, some are eaten of birds, some are trodden underfoot, and some remain untouched.—So when thousands fall in battle, or perish in the sacking of cities ; or when whole crews are lost in vessels wrecked or foundering at sea, or the

inhabitants of towns are overwhelmed by some sudden destruction, as in the case of Herculaneum or Pompeii, it cannot be supposed that all who perish were either born at the same time, or under similar configurations of the planetary system.—The testimony of other facts is also equally opposed to astrological predictions and principles. *Forty-seven* years before the nativity of Christ, there was a conjunction of the higher planets in *Scorpio*, when there was civil war between Cæsar and Pompey, and a change of empire took place in *Europe;* but according to the rules of astrology, all these troubles should have been in *Africa,* because that is said to be under the dominion of *Scorpio.* In the years of our Lord 331, and 1127, there were great conjunctions in *Virgo,* and yet the countries subject to this sign felt no baneful influences, whilst Italy and other countries not under that sign were agitated by Papal intrigues and religious contests;—so also in 1576, and 1577, two eclipses of the sun, the one in *Leo,* the other in *Capricorn,* occurred; but the countries ruled by those signs remained undisturbed by them, while Germany, though not under their influence, was the seat of trouble and commotion.—*Cardan,* the famous astrologer, tells us, (Comment. in Ptolem. et in lib. Genitur.) that he bestowed an hundred hours in calculating the nativity of our Edward VI., from which he pretended to foretel several sicknesses which would attack him in the 34th and 55th years of his age, whereas that hopeful prince did not outlive his sixteenth year. After the event, Cardan endeavoured to vindicate himself, by saying that he had omitted something in his calculation, which, if he had gone through it, as he might have done in half an hour more, would have showed him that the king would be in great danger of death in his 16th year.—The same astrologer pretended to calculate the nativity of Jesus Christ, and to deduce from thence the nature and duration of the Christian religion. Others have been guilty of the like presumption; an instance of which may be found in the *Works of the* *learned Mr. John Gregory,* where the reader is presented with a scheme of the horoscope, and the calculations of Cardan are controverted. It is even asserted, that *Cardan,* having calculated his own nativity, and in what year of his age he should die, starved himself to death to verify the prediction.*

Amongst the Romans, Astrologers were termed *Genethliaci* from calculating nativities, and *Mathematici* from erecting horoscopes and drawing mathematical diagrams : they were also called *Apotelesmatici* from their study of the secret effects and powers of the stars, or, as some have thought, from forming little figures and images designed to receive the influences of the stars, and used as helps to divination.—Severe laws were passed against them, and the practice of astrology utterly condemned, by several of the Roman emperors; and afterwards by the Christian bishops and councils, who not only censured and anathematized those who practised such arts, and forbad them to be baptized, |but also enjoined sponsors to guard the children for whom they were appointed against observing divination, or soothsaying, or wearing amulets or phylacteries (as they were frequently called) themselves, or hanging them upon others. Tertullian (De Idol. c. 9,) pointedly remarks,— " Rome and Italy cast out astrologers as the angels had been cast out of heaven : masters and scholars suffer similar punishment :" and Sozomen (lib. iii, c. 6) says, that Eusebius, bishop of Emesa, was accused of this art, and forced in consequence of it to fly from his bishopric : for all such kind of divination was looked upon as idolatry and paganism, as owing its original to wicked spirits, and as introducing an

* See Perkins's Works, vol. iii, *Discourse of Witchcraft,* ch. i, pp. 620—623. *Resolution to the Country-man ;* pp. 655—665, Cambridge, 1609, folio.— Dr. Henry More's Theological Works, B. vii, chap. 18, 19, 20, London, 1708, folio.—Long's Astronomy ; Preface, pp. 1, 6, Cambridge, 1742, 4*to.*—Works of the Reverend and Learned Mr. John Gregory, M.A. pp. 146—150, London, 1671, 4*to.*—A. Gellii Noctes Atticæ, lib. xiv, 1.

absolute fate and necessity upon human actions, and thereby taking away the freedom of the human will, and making God the author of sin.*

But unhappily neither the edicts of emperors, the decrees of councils, nor the censures of prelates and divines, have ever proved sufficient to extirpate the evil, or produce universally a merited detestation of it.—At Rome the people were so infatuated with it, that the astrologers maintained their ground in opposition to all the attempts to expel them from the city. In more modern times, the same superstition has retained considerable influence over the minds of many persons both in the higher and lower ranks of society in different countries. The French historians remark, that during the regency of *Marie de Medicis* no female undertook a journey without consulting her favourite astrologer, whom she facetiously called *son baron;* and that *Louis* XIII, was surnamed *the just* because he was born under the sign *Libra* or the Balance. They also state that at the birth of Louis XIV, his horoscope was drawn with all possible gravity and importance. In the reigns of Henry III, and IV, of France, astrological predictions were so commonly entertained and countenanced by the court, that *Barclay,*in his celebrated political satire entitled ARGENIS, successfully attacked this predominant humour, on the occasion of an astrologer undertaking to instruct the king, Henry III, in the event of a war then threatened by the faction of the *Guises;* and controverted his arguments with a point and force of reasoning, that, " if I do not greatly err," says a pious and erudite writer, " the whole sombre conclave of Star-gazers, Astrologers, and Wizards, from *Jannes* and *Jambres,* down to *Merlin, Nostrodamus, Partridge,* and *Moore,* have never yet satisfactorily answered, nor ever will

* Bingham's Antiquities of the Christian Church, vol. iv. B. xi. ch. 5, sect. 8, p. 244 ; and vol. vii. B.xvi, ch 5, pp. 269—275, London, 1715—1720, 8vo.—Bergier, Dict. de Theologie, tom. i, *Astrologie.*

be able to refute."* An extract or two from this able satirist, in which the reader will find several of the arguments which have already been urged against astrology, amplified and strengthened, shall conclude this dissertation.

"You maintain," says he, addressing the astrologer, "that the circumstances of Life and Death depend on the place and influence of the celestial bodies, at the time when the child first comes to light; and yet own that the heavens revolve with such vast rapidity, that the situation of the stars is considerably changed in the least point of time. What certainty then can there be in your art, unless you suppose the midwives constantly careful to observe the clock, that the minute of time may be conveyed to the infant, as we do his patrimony? How often must the danger of the mother distract the attention of the bystanders? And how frequently does it happen that none of them are concerned about these superstitions? Or if the child be long in the birth, how do you then determine the position of the stars? I say nothing of the errors of clocks, arising from the humidity or dryness of the atmosphere.—Again, why are we to regard the stars, only at his *nativity,* rather than at his first animation, or whilst he remained susceptible of the lightest impression!—But setting this aside, and supposing the face of the heavens accurately known: whence arises this dominion of the stars over our bodies and minds, that they must be the arbiters of our happiness, our manner of life and death? Were all those who went to battle, and died together, born under the same position of the heavens? And when a ship is to be cast away, shall it admit no passengers, but those doomed by the stars to suffer shipwreck? Or, rather, do not persons born under every planet go into battle, or on board the vessel, and, notwithstanding the disparity of their birth, perish alike. Again, all born

* Dr. Adam Clarke, in Armin. Mag. vol. xx, p. 134.—See also Bergier, Dict. Theologique, *Astres, Astrologie ;* and Encyc. Perth. *Astrology.*

under the same configuration of the stars do not live or die
in the same manner.   Are all monarchs, who were born at
the same time with the king ?   Or are they all even alive
at this day ?   Look at Cleobulus, look at yourself ; were
all who came into the world with him, as wise and virtuous
as he ; or all born under your own stars, astrologers like
you ?   If a man be slain by a robber, you will say, he was
doomed to perish by a robber's hand ; but did the same
stars, which, when the traveller was born, subjected him to
the sword of the robber ; did they likewise give the robber,
who perhaps was born long before, a power and inclination
to kill him ?   For you will allow, that it is as much owing
to the stars that the one kills, as that the other is killed ;—
and when a man is overwhelmed by the fall of a house, did
the walls become faulty, because the stars doomed him to
die thereby ; or, rather, was not his death owing to this, that
the walls were faulty ?   The same may be said with regard
to honours and employs ; because the stars which shone at
a man's nativity, promised him preferment, could those have
an influence over other persons not born under them, by
whose suffrages he was to rise?   Or, how do the stars at
one man's birth annul, or set aside, the contrary influences
of other stars which shone at the birth of another?

" The truth is, supposing the reality of all the planetary
powers : as the sun, which visits an infinity of bodies with
the same rays, has not the same effect on all ; but some
things are hardened thereby, as clay, others are softened, as
wax ; some reeds cherished, others destroyed ; the tender
herbs scorched up, the others secured by their coarser juice :
so, where many children are born together, like a field tilled
so many different ways, according to the various health,
habitude, and temperament of the parents, the same
celestial influx must operate differently.   If the genius be
suitable and towardly, it must predominate therein : if contrary, it will only correct it.   So that to foretel the life and
manners of a child, you are not only to look into the

heavens, but at the parents, the fortune which attended the pregnant mother, and a thousand other circumstances utterly inaccessible.

" Further, does the power which portends the new-born infant a life, for instance, of forty years; or perhaps a violent death at thirty; does that power, I say, continue and reside in the heavens, waiting the destined time, when, descending on earth, it may produce such an effect ? Or, is it infused into the infant itself; so that being cherished, and gradually growing up with it, it bursts forth at the appointed time, and fulfils what the stars had given it in charge? Continue in the heavens it cannot; for if the fate of the infant be derived from a certain configuration of the stars taking place at the moment of its birth, then when that is changed, the effect connected with it must cease, and a new, perhaps a contrary one take place.—What repository have you then for the former power to remain in, till the time come for its delivery? If you say, it resides in the infant, not to operate upon him till he be grown to manhood; the answer is more preposterous than the former: for this, in the instance of a shipwreck, you must suppose, is the cause why the winds rise, and the ship is leaky, or why the pilot, through ignorance of the place, runs on a shoal or rock; and in like manner that the farmer is the cause of the war that impoverishes him, or of the favourable season which brings him a plenteous harvest.

" You boast much of some predictions in which the event has answered the prediction, and which you think ought to give confidence in your art. But I deny, that, because such things have occurred, it is certain that they were the result of fate or the influence of the stars. If such coincidences have happened, I should attribute them, rather, to God himself, who, to punish you for your impious conduct, brings about those events by his own power, which you attribute to the stars. Then again, mere accident will account for many coincidences; thus dreams may sometimes give an insight into futurity; and a blind man, throwing stones at random, may sometimes hit the mark.—So whilst a million of deceptions are industriously concealed and forgotten, it need not be wondered at if a few prognostications appear, occasionally, to be correct. Out of so many conjectures, it must be preternatural if some did not hit; and it is certain, that, considering you only as *guessers*, there is no room to boast of your success. Do you know what fate awaits France in the present war, and yet are not apprehensive of what will befall yourself? Did you not foresee the opposition I should this day make to you?—If you can say whether the king shall *vanquish* his enemies; find out first whether he will *believe* you."*

* Jo. Barclaii Argenis : lib. ii, pp. 186—190, Amstel. 1664, 24*mo.*

END OF DISSERTATIONS.

REASONS

OF

THE LAWS OF MOSES,

TRANSLATED FROM THE

" MORE NEVOCHIM" OF MAIMONIDES.

K

The numerals which occur in the following pages of the text of Maimonides, severally refer to the Notes and Illustrations at the close of the Treatise.

REASONS, &c.

CHAPTER I.

Whether the Mosaic Precepts have a discoverable Design, or depend solely on the Will of God.

IT has been a dispute amongst our speculative Doctors, (1) whether the works of God be the result of his wisdom, or the mere determinations of an arbitrary will. They have also agitated a similar question, respecting the precepts of the Divine Law: Some of them resolving the cause of every precept into the sole determination of the divine will; others assuming, that every interdict and precept has its particular reason, and proceeds from divine wisdom,— and that, although we may be ignorant of many of those reasons, and of the ways of divine wisdom, yet we may rest assured that all the precepts have their causes, and are enjoined on account of their utility. This is the general sentiment of our wise men, and is favoured by our Law itself, when it says, " Just Statutes and Judgments;" and again, " The Judgments of the Lord are true and righteous altogether." (2)

Concerning what are termed " Statutes," חקים; as the precepts respecting " Garments

K 2

made of linen and woollen,"—" Seething a kid in its mother's milk,"—" The Scape-Goat,"—and of which our wise men have said,—" On the words which I have commanded thee for *Statutes,* thou art not permitted to think," that is, in order to alter or abolish them, " notwithstanding Satan may calumniate, and the nations of the world oppose them."—Concerning *these,* I say, the major part of our wise men do not suppose, that they are enjoined without cause, which would reduce them to mere words of vanity, but are satisfied that every precept has its end and use, though unknown to us from the imperfection of our knowledge, and the weakness of our minds. All the precepts then have their end and use. Of some the reason is manifest and clear, as the prohibition of Murder and Theft; but of others obscure and unknown, as the precepts noticed before, and the prohibition of " Heterogeneous Mixtures."

The Precepts, whose design and utility are understood, are commonly called " *Judgments,*" משפטים; and those whose end and design are not generally known, are denominated "*Statutes,*" חקים. Hence, it is frequently said, " That the giving of those precepts is not vain and useless, and if it appear so to us, it is because of our ignorance." The proverbial saying is also well known, that " Solomon knew all the reasons of all the precepts except that of the *Red Heifer;*" and what is sometimes said, that " God has hidden the reasons of some of the precepts, lest they should be lightly esteemed by us, as was the case with Solomon as to two of them, of which the reason was manifest."—The testimony of the Sacred Books, and the sayings of our wise men, are to the same effect.

Yet I have found one passage amongst the writings of our wise men in " Bereschith Rabba," (3) from which it would appear at first sight, as if they thought that certain precepts had no particular reason for their appointment, but were only *positive* commands. They inquire— " What does it matter to the Holy and Blessed God, whether an animal be slain by cutting its throat, or cutting off its head?" and reply, " The precepts are only given for trial צרף, that the creature may be proved or purified by them, as it is written, ' The Word of the Lord is pure or tried, צרף.' It must be acknowledged, that these words are singular, and nothing similar to them to be found in any other of their writings ; and even these may be so explained, as neither to alter their language, nor dissent from the received opinion that all the precepts have a present design and use, as they say, " The giving of these precepts is not a vain thing," &c. ; and as God has said by the Prophet, " I said not in vain to the seed of Jacob, seek ye me ; I the Lord speak righteousness, I declare things that are right." Let the unprejudiced mind, therefore, candidly receive what will now be advanced upon the subject.

Every precept, *generally* considered, must of

necessity have a cause, or reason; but the *parts*, *members*, and *circumstances* of it, are those of which it is said, " They are only *positive* pre- cepts." For instance, the Slaying of Animals for food and support, has a manifest utility; but the particular mode of slaughter, as whether it shall be by jugulation or decollation, is enjoined in order to prove and purify men by obedience, and is intimated in the very example they have proposed;—an example which I the rather notice, because the phrases of slaughtering " by the neck or by the throat," are familiar in their sayings. If, however, we strictly investigate the matter, we shall be convinced that since necessity obliges man to feed upon animals, it is right that they should be slaughtered by that means that will occasion the least pain. Now decollation can only be effected with a sword or some similar instrument, but mactation with almost any thing ;—and that death might be still more speedily produced, it was commanded that the knife should be made sharp. (4)

Oblations may also be very properly adduced as exemplifying the reasons for the particular circumstances of some of the precepts of the Law. For, that the Offering of Sacrifices has its utility I shall hereafter explain ; but, that one sacrifice should be a Lamb, and another a Ram, and that the number of animals to be offered should be fixed and definite, no reason can be assigned ; and he who should attempt, would act absurdly, and only increase difficulties by endeavouring to

remove them : for both they who believe there
are reasons for every circumstance of every precept, and they who believe there are none for
any of the precepts, are alike distant from the
truth.   Most assuredly *Wisdom*, or, if you prefer the term, *Necessity* demands the existence of
some things in the precepts for which no particular reason can be given, and without which
it would be impossible for the Law to be ordained.
The cause of the impossibility is this, that if it
should be inquired, " Wherefore ought that sacrifice to be a lamb and not a ram ?"—the same
question would still remain if a ram had been
substituted for a lamb ; for after all, some species
or other must necessarily have been appointed.
So also if any one should say, " Why must there
be *seven* lambs rather than *eight ?*"—the contrary
question might be asked, " Why ought there to be
eight, rather than seven, or ten, or twenty ?"—
for of necessity some number must be stated. It
is a point similar to the nature of possibilities,
of which this is the reason, that there must of
necessity be another possibility, and of which it
cannot be sought, " Wherefore is this possible, and
not the other ?" for the same question might be
asked if the other were in its place.   Let it
therefore be remembered, that when our wise
men any where say, that " all the precepts have
their reasons ;"—and that " Solomon knew all the
reasons of all the precepts ;"—they are to be
understood as speaking of the *general* use or

design of the precepts, and not of the *particular* parts or circumstances of them.

These things being understood, I shall proceed to distribute all the 613 Precepts (5) into certain classes, each of which will include those precepts which are of the same nature, or which have an affinity with each other ; and endeavour to point out the reasons and utility of each class in the clearest and most demonstrative manner. I shall afterwards revert to each precept of the respective classes, and explain the cause of every one of them, a few excepted, of the reasons of which I am not yet certain. I shall also note the reasons of some particular circumstances of certain of the precepts, for which there appears to have been an assignable cause. But, first, it will be necessary to premise some things in order to clear the way, and to render the explanation of those reasons more easy and better understood. With these preliminary observations I shall commence the ensuing chapter

CHAPTER II.

The Law has a two-fold Intention; the Perfection of the Mind and the Welfare of the Body.

THE general intention of the Law is two-fold, viz.—the soundness of the body, and of the mind. *Soundness of Mind,*—that the people, according to their capacities, may obtain just sentiments of religious matters. On this account some things are declared clearly and openly, but others in parables, because of the incorrect apprehension of the unskilful multitude. *Soundness of Body,*—produced by the disposition and ordering of the food which ministers to its support; and perfected, first, by the prevention of violence, so that no one may do just what he pleases, or desires, or it is possible for him to do, but that every one may regard the public good; —and, secondly, by teaching men the virtues necessary and useful for the government of the commonwealth.

It must be acknowledged, however, that one intention of the Law excels the other, for *Soundness of Mind,* which embraces matters of belief, is certainly first in dignity, though *Soundness in Body,* as referring to the government of the commonwealth and the administration of its affairs, is first in nature and time;—and being necessary first, is therefore, with all its parts, treated the most exactly and minutely in the Law; for it is impossible to arrive at the first intention without having previously secured the second. This is demonstrable, for man is capable of a *two-fold perfection*. The first perfection is of the body;—the second perfection is of the mind.

The *first Perfection* consists in health, and the best bodily dispositions. But this cannot take place unless there be at all times a supply of necessaries, as food, and other things relating to the regimen of the body, as habitations, baths, and similar conveniences. Nor can this be effected by one man alone; (for no man's capacity is sufficient for them all;) but by the political association of a whole region or city, as it has been said—" Man is, by nature, a political animal."

The *second Perfection* is mental, and comprehends the vigorous exercise of the intellectual powers, and the knowledge of every thing possible to be known by man in his most perfect state. This perfection, therefore, includes neither works, nor qualities, nor virtues, but those of science, the result of observation and diligent inquiry. To this last and noblest perfection, it is evident, none can arrive, but through the medium of the first; for no man can attain the knowledge of all that is possible to be known, even when assisted by the instructions of others, and much less by himself, whilst he is daily affected and depressed by grief, and hunger, and thirst, and heat, and cold ; but when he has gained the former perfection, he may pursue and obtain the latter :— a perfection in every way the most excellent, and especially so, because it leads to Life Eternal. The *true* Law, I mean the Law of Moses, inculcates this two-fold perfection, and even indicates that it is the design of the Law to lead men to the attainment of them. Thus it is said, " And the Lord commanded us to do all these statutes, to fear the Lord our God for our good always, that he might preserve us alive, as it is this day ;" where the latter perfection is placed first because of its dignity and excellence, which is what is intimated by the words, " For our good always," agreeably to the expressions of our wise men, who say, " That it may be well with thee in that world which is *altogether* good, and *always* lasting." So, of what is here said, " That it may be for our good always," the sense is, " That thou mayest arrive at that world, which is all goodness and all duration," subsisting for ever.— But when it is said, " That he might preserve us alive, as it is this day," it is to be understood of the first and corporeal subsistence, which is only of temporary duration, and can only be perfected by the association of a whole province or city, as we have already shown.

CHAPTER III.

The Mosaic Precepts are rational, tending either to the Well-being of the Soul or of the Body.

THE Law designs the final perfection of man, it therefore commands us to believe in the existence and unity of God, and in his knowledge, power, will and eternity, which are all final ends, and can only be attained by various previous knowledge. It also enjoins the belief of certain principles necessary to the welfare of civil and political institutions, as " that God is angry with the wicked," and therefore ought to be feared, and wickedness cautiously avoided. But of other speculations or realities, as for instance, those reasonings by which the opinions constituting the final end are verified, the Law commands nothing expressly but only generally, as when it says, " Thou shalt love the Lord."— But how strenuously this duty is enjoined, is evident from its being added, " Thou shalt love Him with all thy heart, and with all thy soul, and with all thy strength." In our Talmudical work we have shown that no love to God is rightly established, but that which is founded on a clear and extensive view of the Divine Existence and Perfections.

The sum of this reasoning is, that every precept of the Law, whether affirmative or negative is intended, first, to prevent the exercise of violence, and encourage those virtuous habits which are necessary to the existence and preservation of Political Society; and, then, to inculcate just notions of those things which are to be believed, especially such as are useful in the prevention of violence, and the promotion of virtue. Of such precepts it may be safely affirmed, that the reason and utility of them are manifest, and that there can be no doubt of their final design; for no one can doubt or inquire, why we are commanded to believe the Unity of God; or why murder, theft, or revenge are forbidden; or why we are commanded to love one another. But those which perplex the mind, and about which men dispute,—some asserting that they have no particular utility, but are mere positive commands,—and others that they have an utility, though not always discovered by us,—are those which do not appear on the face of them to have any direct relation, either to the prevention of vice, or the promotion of virtue, or the inculcation of truth, and consequently affording no assistance to the well-being of the mind, by instruction in matters of faith, nor to the well-being of the body, by instruction in the science of Political or General Economy; such are, for instance, those precepts relating to mixed garments of linen and woollen; to divers seeds; to seething a kid in its mother's milk; to cover-

ing blood ; to the decollation of the calf ; to the
redemption of the first-born of the ass ; and other
similar injunctions.   The true reasons, however,
of these and many other precepts of like nature,
I will develope, by demonstrating, that, with the
exception of some particular circumstances, and
a few precepts not understood by us at present,
they are all necessary either to the welfare of
the Soul or Body; the latter especially being
produced by the prevention of lawless violence,
and the formation of virtuous habits.   But let
not what we have already said respecting the
dogmas of faith be forgotten,—that sometimes a
precept solely regards an article of belief, and
has no other reference, as in the case of the
precepts respecting the Unity, Eternity, and
Spirituality of God ; but that at other times, the
precept is to be believed in order to banish vice
and encourage virtue ; as when it is declared,
that God is angry with the man who injures
another; as it is said, *My wrath shall wax hot,
and I will kill you with the sword;* and again,
that God will speedily hear the cry of the
oppressed and afflicted.

CHAPTER IV.

A BRAHAM, our father, was, as is well known, educated in the faith of the Zabii, (5) who maintain, that there is no God but the stars, as their books and ancient annals translated into the Arabic, and yet extant among us, undeniably prove. In them, they expressly affirm, that the stars are Divinities, (*Dii minorum Gentium,*) and the Sun, the chief Deity. They also write, that the five planets are gods, but the two great luminaries, superior ones; and add, that the sun governs both the upper and lower worlds. The before-mentioned books and annals, relate also concerning Abraham, that being educated in Cutha, (6) but dissenting from the common opinions, and affirming that there was another Creator beside the sun, they began to object first one thing and then another to him, alleging, amongst other objections, the evident and manifest influence of the sun in the world. Abraham replied, " Ye are right, and have spoken well, for the sun is like the axe in the hand of one who is felling trees." Certain arguments are then stated as having been urged by Abraham, after which it is related, that the king imprisoned him, but that even in prison he continued his opposition to their errors. The king fearing, therefore, lest his kingdom should sustain injury, and his subjects be seduced from their religion, confiscated his goods, and banished him to the most distant countries of the east. The whole relation is delivered at large in the book which is entitled, העבודה הנבטיה, (*of the worship of the Nabathæans,*) (7) but no mention whatever is made of what is written in our Canonical Books, nor of the gift of Prophecy which was conferred upon him; for they endeavoured to refute and discredit him, because he contradicted their impious opinions. (8) Nor can it be doubted, but that men who were thus involved in error, would be violently irritated by the firmness with which he combated their sentiments, and would load him with every species of contumely and reproach. But, as was his duty, he bore their injuries with patience for the glory of God, and, therefore, it was promised to him, " I will bless them that bless thee, and curse them that curse thee"—A promise, the accomplishment of which is seen, in our days, since all men admire him, and even those who are not of his seed are blessed in him. Nor are there any to be found of a different opinion respecting him, or who are ignorant of his superiority and excellence, except some descendants of the Zabii still remaining in distant parts of the world.

In the time of Abraham, the utmost to which philosophers carried their speculations, was, to esteem God to be the Spirit of the sphere, or celestial orb ; (9) supposing the celestial orbs and planets to be bodies, and the Supreme Being the soul or spirit of them. *Abubachar Alsaig* notices this opinion of theirs, in his Commentary on *Aristot. de Auditu.* The Zabii, consequently, held the eternity of the world. (10) They moreover maintained, that the first man, *Adam,* was, like others, the offspring of a man and woman, though they greatly extolled him, calling him the Prophet of the Moon, and asserting that he taught men to worship the Moon, and composed certain works on agriculture. (11) They also affirmed, that *Noah* was an husbandman, but worshipped no sort of images; on which account they censure him, and tell us that because he would worship only the Supreme Being, and for other things of a similar nature, he was thrown into prison;—and add, that Seth also dissented from Adam his father, as to the worship of the moon.—In a word, they advance so many falsehoods, that they only serve to excite ridicule, and show the imbecility of their minds, and their total ignorance of true philosophy.—Thus, they say of Adam, that when he quitted the country adjacent to India, for the confines of Babel, he carried with him many wonderful things : Amongst which were, one

L

tree whose branches, leaves, and flowers were all
of gold, and another all of stone ; and also, two
of the leaves of a third tree, so verdant that the
fire could not consume its leaves, and so large
as to cover ten thousand men of equal stature
with Adam; for that even one of the leaves he
carried with him, would have been large enough
to have covered or clothed two men. These,
and many other similar things, do they relate ; so
that I am not astonished that they should believe
the eternity of the world, when they can give
credit to such impossibilities in nature. The fact
is, that such relations are designed only to support the idea of the eternity of the world, and the
divinity of the Heavenly Bodies. But when Abraham, that Pillar of the world, had gone forth,
and learned that God is abstract and spiritual,
and that all the stars and planetary worlds are
his works, and had understood the falsehood of
those vanities in which he had been educated;
he then began to oppose and refute them publicly, and by invoking the Name of Jehovah the
Everlasting God, openly declared, that He was
God, and had created all things.

To return. The Zabii, agreeably to the sentiments adopted by them, erected images to the
stars ; to the Sun images of gold, but to the
Moon images of silver. They also distributed
the metals, and the climates of the earth amongst
the stars, adjudging a certain climate to a certain star. Afterwards they built chapels, and
placed the images in them, believing, that the

power of the stars flowed into them; that they possessed intelligence; bestowed the gift of prophecy upon men; and indicated to them what things were useful and salutary. They also affirmed the same concerning those trees that were consecrated to certain stars. When a tree was dedicated to a star, it was planted in its name, and worshipped after a prescribed form, in order that the stars might communicate spiritual powers to it, so that it might be able to prophesy according to the usual mode of prophecy, and even advise men in their sleep. —All these things may be met with in those books of the Zabii, which have been already mentioned. These are the *Prophets of Baal*, and the *Prophets of the Groves*, noticed in the Sacred Books, in whose minds these opinions were so deeply rooted, that they forsook the Lord, and cried, " O! Baal, hear us!" For through the profound ignorance and madness then reigning in the world, the Zabian errors were universally propagated, and their baneful influence diffused on every side. From them sprang Augurs, Diviners, Sorcerers, Enchanters, Magicians, Wizards, and Necromancers. (12) Concerning this people, we have already shown in our Great Talmudical Work, that Abraham our Father endeavoured by argument to refute their opinions, and by gentle and persuasive methods to draw them to the worship of the True God, until at length the Prince of Prophets arose, and completely effected the design, ordaining that such persons should be punished with death, their memory be blotted out, and extirpated from the land of the living. " Ye shall destroy their altars, and break down their images, and cut down their groves, and burn their graven images with fire." (Deut. vii. 5.) He also solemnly interdicted the imitation of their customs and practices; " Ye shall not walk in the manners of the nation which I cast out before you." (Levit. xx. 23.) For it is clearly evident from many parts of the Scriptures, that the *first intention* of our Law was, to eradicate idolatry, and to obliterate the memory of it, and of those who were addicted to it; to banish every thing that might lead men to practise it, as Pythons, Soothsayers, Passers through the fire, Diviners, Jugglers, Enchanters, Augurs, Astrologers, Necromancers, &c.; and finally, to prevent the most distant assimilation to their practices, and still more so to adopting and practising them. Hence, it is expressly declared in the Law, that as the worship paid to an idol, is an abomination to the Lord, so is the oblation offered to it; for this is what is designed when it is said, " Every abomination to the Lord, which he hateth, have they done unto their gods." (Deut. xii. 31.)

In the books of the Zabii, it will be found related, that they offered to the Sun, (their great god,) seven bats, seven mice, and seven reptiles, together with certain other matters; which is, of itself, sufficient to prove the abominable nature of their superstitions.

It is, therefore, manifest, that all those precepts and interdictions which forbid idolatry, and prohibit whatever is connected with it or might produce attachment or tendency to it, possess the highest utility; because they deliver us from those pestiferous opinions which are inimical to the perfection of both body and mind, and would throw us back into those insanities, in which our forefathers and elders were educated, as it is said, " Your fathers dwelt on the other side of the flood in old time, even Terah the father of Abraham, and the father of Nachor; and they served other gods." (Joshua xxiv. 2.) And as the Prophets truly affirmed, " They walked after vain things, which could neither profit, nor deliver." How great therefore, is the benefit of all those precepts, which thus deliver us from so great errors, and lead us to faith in the One True God ! Teaching us that God, who created all things, is ever present in the world; that he alone is to be worshipped, loved, and feared; and that to fulfil his will, nothing difficult or laborious is required, but only to love and fear him, since by these two things, his whole worship is perfected, as we shall afterwards demonstrate. Hence, it is written, "And now, Israel, what doth the LORD thy God require of thee, but to fear the LORD thy God, to walk in all his ways, and to love him, and to serve the LORD thy God with all thy heart, and with all thy soul?" (Deut. x. 12.)—But leaving this to future discussion, I return to my former proposition, and proceed to observe, that from an acquaintance with the faith, and rites, and worship of the Zabii, I have gained much insight into the reasons and causes of many of our laws, as will readily be discovered, when I come to treat of those precepts which at first seem destitute of any reason or utility.

Adverting now to those books of the Zabii, from which a more extensive knowledge may be gained of their faith and worship, and which will serve to corroborate what I advance in illustration of many of the precepts of the Law, we may first notice, as the most celebrated, העבודה הנבטיה *Of the Agriculture of the Nabatheans*, (translated into Arabic, by Aben Vachaschijah.) (13) In the following chapter, I shall explain the reason why the Zabii treated of their faith, under the name of Agriculture; and therefore shall, at present, only offer a few general remarks upon the work itself. This book is full of idolatrous ravings, and other things to which men are but too readily inclined; as of the Fabrication of Speaking Images: of Familiar Spirits: of Juggling: of Demons: of the Devil: of such as dwell in Deserts, as Satyrs; beside many other ridiculous subjects, subtilly designed to oppose and invalidate the public miracles wrought by Moses and the Prophets, by which God was universally made known to be the Judge of all men, as it is written, "That thou mayest know that the Earth is the Lord's," &c.—and again, " I am

the LORD in the midst of the earth." It is there
said of Adam, that in the book written by him,
he relates that there is a certain tree in India,
whose branches when thrown upon the ground
creep like a serpent;—that there is another tree
whose root has a human shape, and a strong
voice, uttering distinct sounds, and speaking;—
and that there also is a certain herb, which, if
taken and suspended round the neck, renders
the wearer invisible, so that none can see from
whence he comes, nor whither he goes; and
further adds, that if it be burned in the open air,
the smoke no sooner begins to ascend, than the
most tremendous noises and thunderings are
heard in the surrounding heavens. But not
only these, but many similar fooleries, do they
relate respecting the wonderful virtues of plants,
and the properties of agriculture, endeavouring
by them to overturn the true miracles, and persuade men that they were merely the effect of
skill and industry. Amongst the relations, is
that of the tree אמלוי (*Amloi*,) one of the
asheroth, i. e. groves, or trees planted in honour
of the gods, (14) which, as has been shown,
was practised among them. Of this tree, they
affirm, that it had stood in Nineveh twelve
thousand years;—that afterwards it had a dispute with the יברוח (*Jabruach*) or Mandrake,
which desired to usurp its place;—and that a
certain man who had prophesied by its influence,
but had been for a while deprived of his ability
to prophesy; being again urged by its pro-

phetic impulse, received information that it had
been engaged in the dispute with the *Jabruach*,
and was commanded to write to all Judges to
determine the dispute, and decide which of them
possessed the greater power of working wonders !—Such is the outline of this prolix fable;
but it is sufficient to teach us the opinions and
wisdom of these men.   Yet these were the wise
men of Babel, who in those days of darkness
were held in great estimation; and since the
people were educated in the belief of these
things, had it not been for the promulgation of the
knowledge of the existence of God, the Gentile
nations would even now have been involved in
the most deplorable ignorance. (15)

But to resume our former subject.   The book
already referred to, narrates a fable of a certain
idolatrous false Prophet whose name was *Thammuz*, and relates of him, that having called upon
the king to worship the seven planets, and the
twelve signs of the zodiac, he was ignominiously
put to death by him;—and that on the same night
on which he was slain, all the images from the very
ends of the earth assembled in the palace, which
had been erected for the Great Golden Image,
the Image of the Sun, which was suspended in
the air;—that the Image of the Sun dropped into
the midst of them, and weeping and mourning
the loss of Thammuz, related what had happened
to him, which caused a general lamentation and
weeping of the rest of the images during the
whole night;—but that as soon as the morning

dawned, they all flew away, and returned to their respective temples in the most distant regions. Such was the origin of the custom of weeping and mourning for Thammuz, (the false Prophet,) on the first day of the month Tham-muz, (i. e. June.) (16) Such were, therefore, the opinions entertained at that day. It is true, the history of Thammuz professes to be of the most remote antiquity ; and yet from this book much may be learned of the ravings, and practices, and festivals of the Zabii. Care, however, should be taken, to guard against their stories of Adam, of the Serpent, of the Tree of Know-ledge of good and evil, and of Vestments, lest by their novelty they should deceive the understand-ing and lead men to suppose, that such things as they relate have really occurred, when the fact is, that such things never did and never could exist. Indeed the slightest and most superficial consi-deration of the subject will be sufficient to con-vince any one, that these relations are false, and were forged after our Law was known amongst the Gentiles, and they had heard the history of the work of Creation. For receiving every thing in a literal sense, they framed these fables accordingly, and accommodated them to what was related in the Law, that they might persuade the simple and illiterate, that the world was eternal, and that what is related in the Law, was effected in the way they describe. And although some to whom I address myself may have no need of these precautions, because they are already in possession of such knowledge as will prevent the mind from adopting the reveries of the Chaldeans, Astrologers, and Zabii, who were destitute of all true wisdom; I am, nevertheless, willing to note what is necessary for the preservation of others from a belief of those fables, to which the vulgar are but too apt to give credit.

Beside the Zabian books already noticed, there are also The Book *Haistamchus,* falsely ascribed to Aristotle : The Book *Hattelesmaoth,* (i. e. of Talismans, or speaking Images:) (17) The Book *Tamtam :* The Book *Hasharab :* The Book *Maaloth haggalgal vehazzuroth haoloth becol maaleh,* (i. e. Of the Degrees of the Celestial orbs and of the figures that are ascendent in every degree:) another Book, *Concerning Talismans, or Speaking Images,* attributed to Aristotle : A Book ascribed to Hermes: A Book of *Isaac* the *Zabian,* in which he defends the Laws of the Zabii: also, a large Book, *Of the Customs and Particularities of the Law of the Zabii,* as their Feasts, Sacrifices, Prayers, and other things concerning their Faith. All these are works treating of the affairs of the idolaters, and have been translated into the Arabic tongue ; though doubtless but a small number in comparison of those that either have not been translated, or have perished through length of time. But even those which are still extant, include a considerable part of the opinions and practices of the Zabii, (some of which are known and practised at the present

day,) as the erection of temples, and sometimes
placing in them images of metal or stone; the
construction of altars, and offering sacrifices
and oblations of various kinds of food upon them;
the celebration of festivals; the assembling of
the people to prayers and other parts of worship in their temples; in which they also constructed stately monuments, calling them the
Temples of Intellectual Forms; the setting up
of images on high mountains; their reverence
for groves or trees; the erection of statues; and
various other things, of which the books already
noticed will furnish information. An intimate
knowledge of their opinions and practices, will
therefore open the door to an acquaintance
with the Reasons of the different Precepts of
the Law; for the very foundation and hinge
on which our whole Law turns, is, that it
is designed to eradicate from the heart, and
obliterate from the memory, every root and
trace of their opinions; as it is said, " That your
heart be not deceived, and turn aside, and serve
other gods, and worship them." (Deut. xi. 16.)
And also, " Lest there should be amongst you
man, or woman, or family, or tribe, whose heart
turneth away this day from the LORD our God,
to go and serve the gods of these nations." (Deut.
xxix. 18.) And again, " Ye shall overthrow
their altars, and break their pillars, and burn
their groves with fire, and you shall hew down
the graven images of their gods, and destroy the
names of them out of that place." (Deut. xii. 3.)

In short, every part of the Law presents us with the repetition and enforcement of these injunctions. Our Sages also teach us, that this is its first and principal design. Thus, in their exposition of what God hath said in those words, " Whatsoever the LORD commands you by the hand of Moses," they write, " Behold! from hence thou mayest learn, that whosoever embraces idolatry is considered as having renounced the whole Law ; and that whosoever renounces idolatry, is regarded as receiving the whole Law."

CHAPTER V.

—

*Why the ancient Idolaters united Agriculture with the Worship
of the Stars.*

THE reasons of the union of Agriculture with
the worship of the stars, are sufficiently evident from those vain and foolish opinions, which
have been avowed by the ancient idolaters themselves, since they confessedly believed that the
fruitfulness of the earth depended upon the worship of the planets and other heavenly bodies.
(18) Their Sages, Doctors, and Prophets
accordingly taught, and endeavoured to prove to
the people, that Agriculture, without which
men cannot subsist, depended upon the influence
of the Sun, and the rest of the Stars, for its
success; and that they must therefore be worshipped, since, if they were displeased, the cities
and fields would be wasted and destroyed. In
their books they write, that, by the anger of
Mars, places are rendered desert and desolate,
and become destitute of water and trees, and
inhabited by horrible dæmons;—and loudly extol
Husbandmen and Vine-dressers, who are engaged
in cultivating the earth and rendering it habi-
table, as entertaining the highest affection and
devotion for the Heavenly Bodies.

These Idolaters, also, greatly valued oxen and
cattle, and the reason they did so, was, because

of their usefulness in husbandry ; and hence they affirmed it was unlawful to slay them, since they were not only of use in cultivating the ground, but were by the influence of the stars the means of rendering it fruitful ; and that they were subjected to men, because the Deity was pleased with their being employed for agricultural purposes. Such being the opinions universally prevalent, the worship of idols was readily joined with the culture of the earth, Agriculture being necessary to both men and animals.

These sentiments gained additional strength also, from the public discourses of the Idol-Priests, (19) who, in their congregations and assemblies, impressed the minds of the people with the belief, that, by this kind of worship, rain was obtained from heaven, the trees of the field were rendered fruitful, and the earth was caused to produce plentiful harvests. Read what they themselves say in the book " *Of the Agriculture of the Egyptians;*" where, when speaking of Vines, they explicitly state their sentiments, and tell us, that their Sages and Prophets formerly commanded, that, on their Festival-Days, they should play on certain instruments in the presence of the Idols, for that the gods would confer benefits and ample remunerations on those who should act in this manner. They even point out the nature of several of these advantages, as, that they shall be favoured with long life ;—be preserved from sickness, and be shielded from misfortunes ;—that the earth shall yield its increase, and the trees bring forth fruit in abundance. Such is the language of the Zabii. When, therefore, these opinions began to be entertained and promulgated, it pleased the Ever Blessed God, in his great mercy towards us, in order to eradicate those errors from our minds, and to deliver us from those toilsome and useless services, (20) to give us his Law, by the hand of Moses, of blessed memory, who declared to us, in the name of God, that if we worshipped the stars and the other heavenly bodies, the rain would be withheld, the earth become barren and unfruitful, the trees cease to yield their fruit, various temporal evils and diseases befal us, and lastly, life itself be cut short. For all these declarations are in the Covenant which God made with us, and are to be found in every part of the Law, where it is again and again stated, that, from the worship of the stars, follows the withholding of rain ; the laying waste of the earth ; general depravity ; bodily diseases, and brevity of life ; but on the contrary, that the relinquishment of idolatry, and conversion to the true God, is succeeded by the descent of rain, the fertility of the earth, general prosperity, bodily health and long life, the very contrary to what the Idol-worshippers taught, in order to induce men to embrace idolatry. For the chief design of the Law, and what may be regarded as its foundation, is that it is intended to extirpate those opinions, and totally destroy the remembrance of them.

CHAPTER VI.

◆

*Reply to those who suppose that no Reasons can be assigned for the
Precepts of the Law.*

THERE are some men to whom it is confessedly difficult to assign a reason for any
of the Precepts, and to whom therefore it would
appear, as if no intelligible reason could be given
for any Injunction or Prohibition; whereas, the
true cause is to be found in the diseased state of
their own minds. For they suppose, that if any
arguments be advanced, which are deduced from
the advantages derivable from the Precepts in
this world, it is depreciating them as the result
of mere human reason and sagacity; but that if
no present advantage or utility be discoverable
in them, or can be assigned for them, it is a
proof that they are derived from God, since
they are incomprehensible by the human mind.
But how foolish is this mode of reasoning, which
supposes man to be more perfect than his
Creator! According to them, man acts with
design in all he does and says, but that God
commands us to do those things, from the performance of which we shall derive no benefit,
and by the neglect of which we shall sustain
no injury. Far, indeed, be this from the
Creator! who has himself intimated to us, that
the design of all the Precepts is to promote
our happiness; as is expressed in these words

already quoted : " For our good always, that he might preserve us alive, as it is at this day." (Deut. vi. 24.) In this sense also it is said, " This is your wisdom and understanding in the sight of the nations which shall hear all these things." (Deut. iv. 6.) And again, " Surely this great nation is a wise and understanding people." (Deut. iv. 6.) For these words show, that all nations will understand these statutes to be replete with the highest wisdom and intelligence. But if the causes of them were hidden, and no utility could be discovered in them, either for producing good or averting evil, wherefore should it be said of those who receive and practise them, that they are *wise*, and *intelligent* ; or that they are *great*, and the admiration of all nations? Assuredly, it must be because, as we have asserted, every one of the *six hundred and thirteen*, Precepts, (21) is in some way or other advantageous, either by inducing the belief of some salutary principle, or eradicating some pernicious notion ; by instituting some profitable regulation, or banishing some vice; or, lastly, by exciting to worthy and laudable actions, or dehorting from sinful and vicious ones ; all of which may be referred to the three divisions of FAITH, MORALS, and CIVIL POLITY. But as all the Injunctions or Prohibitions of the Law include either instructions respecting civil or political actions, or morals, or truths to be believed, there is no need at present to discuss them separately.

M

CHAPTER VII.

——◆——

As all the natural Works of God have their respective Causes and Reasons, so also have the Precepts of the Law.—The Origin of Oblations.

IF we study the works of God in nature, we shall soon discover the supreme wisdom and skill of the Creator displaying itself in the creation of inferior animals; and in the subordination and connexion of the various motions of their members. Similar wisdom and contrivance are also exhibited in the formation of the different parts of the human body; thus, for instance, the anterior portion of the brain is extremely soft, but the posterior portion somewhat more solid; the spinal marrow is still harder, and the more extended its elongation, the firmer is its consistency. The nerves are the instruments of sense and motion. (22) Of these some are only necessary for the apprehension of the senses, for which a gentle exertion is sufficient, as in the motions of the eye-lids and the jaws; which, therefore, arise from the brain: but others are required for the motion of the limbs, and therefore proceed from the spinal marrow. But because those nerves which originate in the spinal marrow, are not adequate to move the joints of the limbs, on account of their softness, the wise counsel of God has so ordered it, that fibres proceed from the nerves, and being filled with flesh, become muscles; thus, from the extremity of the nerve proceeds the muscle, which increasing in its solidity, and strengthened by the union of fibres of a finer texture, becomes a tendon, which adhering closely to the limb enables the nerves, by this means, to move the different members of the body.

I have adduced this, as one of the clearest examples noticed in the work, " On the Usefulness of the various parts ;" (i. e. of the body,) in which many admirable things are brought forward, and in which it is fully shown that every part has a manifest utility, when examined by the light of sound reason and understanding.

The same Divine Wisdom is also conspicuous in viviparous animals; for, because their young, when born, are exceedingly tender, and incapable of deriving their support from dry and solid food, the breasts of the female parent are therefore formed for the production of milk, that they may be nourished with that sort of fluid aliment, which is suited to their temperament and feebleness, until they have gradually acquired firmness and strength. A similar mode of procedure is also observable in the Divine Government, of which there are many instances in our Law, wherein the transition from one thing to its opposite is not sudden and abrupt, but gradual and easy; for it is not agreeable to the nature of man, to relinquish readily, and in a moment, that to which he has long been accustomed. Therefore when God sent Moses, our Teacher, to render us a Royal Priesthood, and a Holy Nation; he *first* taught the *knowledge* of God; as it is said, " Unto thee it was showed, that thou mightest *know* that the LORD he is God." (Deut. iv. 35.) And again, (v. 39.) " Know therefore this day, and consider it in thine heart, that the LORD he is God in heaven above, and upon the earth beneath: there is none else." And *then* instructed us in the *Worship* of God; as it is written, " To serve Him with all your heart and with all your soul." (Deut. xi. 13.) And again, " Ye shall serve the LORD your God, and he shall bless thy bread and thy water." (Exod. xxiii. 25.) And in another place, " You shall serve him and cleave unto him." (Deut. xiii. 4.) But as at that time, the universal practice, and the mode of worship in which all were educated, was, that various kinds of animals should be offered in the temples in which their idols were placed, and before whom their worshippers were to burn incense and prostrate themselves; and as there were also certain persons, set apart for the service of those temples, which, as has been already shown, were erected in honour of the sun and moon, and the rest of the planetary bodies; therefore, that divine wisdom and providence of God, which so eminently shines forth in all his creatures, did not ordain the abandonment or abolition of all such worship. For it is the well-known disposition of the human heart, to cleave to that to which it has been habituated, even in things to which it is not naturally inclined. To have decreed the entire abolition of all such worship, would therefore have been the same, as if a Prophet should come and say, " It is the command of God, that in the day of trouble, ye shall not pray, nor fast, nor publicly seek him; but your worship shall be purely mental, and shall consist in meditation, not in action."—On these accounts, the Creator retained those modes of worship, but transferred the veneration from created things and shadows, to his OWN NAME; and commanded us to direct our religious services to HIMSELF. Thus he ordained that we should build HIM a *Temple*: as it is said, " Let them make me a sanctuary." (Exod. xxv. 8.)— That an *Altar* should be consecrated to his Name : " An Altar of Earth shalt thou make unto me. (Exod. xx. 24.)—That *Sacrifices* should be offered to Him : " If any man of you bring an offering unto the Lord, ye shall bring your offering of the cattle, even of the herd and of the flock." (Lev. i. 2.)—And that we should bow down and burn incense before him. But, on the other hand, He forbade that any of these things should be done in honour of any other, as it is declared; " He that sacrificeth unto any god, save unto the Lord only, he shall be utterly destroyed :" (Exod. xxii. 20 :) and again, " Thou shalt worship no other god :" (Exod. xxxiv. 14 :)

He also separated the priests to the service of the Sanctuary, and commanded Moses concerning them; "Thou shalt anoint them, and consecrate them, and sanctify them, that they may minister unto me in the priest's office :" (Exod. xxviii. 41:) And he ordained that a sufficient provision should be made for them, because they were employed in his house, and about his offerings, by those gifts which were termed the *Gifts of the Priests and Levites.* These things did Divine Wisdom enjoin, in order to eradicate idolatry, and establish the fundamental truths of the existence and unity of God; without confounding the minds of men, by the total abolition of those modes of worship to which they had been accustomed, or by the necessity of acquiring a knowledge of new ones, with which they would have been utterly unacquainted.

I am aware, indeed, that these positions are not likely to obtain immediate assent, but will rather appear, at first sight, to be encumbered with difficulties, and lead men to enquire : How is it possible that precepts and practices, which are so clearly explained, as having their own particular reasons for their institution, should not have been independently instituted, but should have had reference to some other cause, as for instance, to lead us to the *first* intention of the Law? And what prevented the Divine Being from enjoining the *first* intention, and imparting to us the faculty of understanding it, so that there might have been no need for those things which are only *secondary* in their intention?

In order therefore to remove these doubts, and fully to explain the point in dispute; we reply, that the Law itself furnishes us with an occurrence of a similar nature, where it is said; " God led them not through the way of the land of the Philistines, although that was near ;— but—led the people about, through the way of the wilderness of the Red Sea." (Exod. xiii. 17, 18.) In like manner, therefore, as God led them out of the straight road, into another, for fear of something. which they could not bear, that they might ultimately attain their first object; so God enjoined those precepts, on account of something which our minds could not naturally bear, that we might by them be led to the knowledge of the true God, and the abandonment of idolatry, which are the first intention of the Law : For, as it would be irrational to suppose that the man who is every day working amongst bricks and mortar, or engaged in any similar employment, should, immediately, after washing his hands, go and combat with giants ; so it would be equally unnatural to expect, that those who have been trained up in the practice of those various services, and ceremonies, and modes of worship, until they have regarded them as rational, should at once renounce them all, and adopt a contrary course of action :— And as by the peculiar counsel of God, the Israelites were led about in the desert in order to acquire fortitude, to which their daily habits, and constant privations of delicacies and corporeal enjoyments, such as baths, &c. were particularly conducive; as contrary habits would have been to induce effeminacy; and yet their children were not habituated to similar humiliating and servile labours; And as all these things were done by the special command of God, according to what is said, " At the commandment of the Lord, the children of Israel journeyed, and at the commandment of the Lord, they pitched :" (Numb, ix. 18:) so also does that part of the Law proceed from the Divine Wisdom, by which it is ordained, that a kind of worship similar to what they had been accustomed, should be continued amongst them; from which they might learn those essential truths, the belief of which constitutes the *first intention* of the Law.

As to the other part of the objector's enquiry; *viz.* "Why could not the Divine Being have enjoined his *first* intention, and imparted the faculty of understanding it?," it may be answered by retorting the question; " Why could not God have led the Israelites through the land of the Philistines, and conferred valour and martial ability upon them, that there might have been no need of the pillar of cloud by day, and of fire by night ?"

The same sceptical disposition may also lead to another enquiry of the same kind, respecting the promises made to the obedient, and the threatenings denounced against the rebellious; and it may be asked, " When it was the primary intention and will of God, that we should receive his Laws, and practise the duties they inculcated ; why did he not impart the constant ability to receive and practise them, that there might have been no need to affix rewards and punishments to them, or to declare that it should be well with us if we served him, but that if we rebelled against him we should be punished, since these promises and denunciations are only designed to pursue that which is the first and chief design of the Law of God. And why did he not implant within us a disposition to embrace and practise what is agreeable to his will, and naturally to fly from every thing he abhors ?"

The answer to these and similar questions, is this, that although God sometimes miraculously changes the nature of other beings, he does not in the same way change the nature of man, and on this ground it is, that it is said, " O that there were such an heart in them, that they would fear me and keep all my commandments always, that it might be well with them, and with their children for ever." (Deut. v. 29.) This also is the cause why it has been necessary to give the precepts of the Law, and to subjoin to them promises, and to enforce them by rewards and punishments. As to the doctrine of miracles, I have elsewhere explained my sentiments on that subject; only it should be remarked, that what has just been observed, is not to be understood, as though it were impossible for God to change the nature of man, for most assuredly it is quite possible to him, and fully within the reach of his power; but the meaning is, that, according to the principles of our law, it is not his will, nor ever will be;— for if it were the will of God, thus miraculously to change the nature of man, there would be no need for the mission of the prophets, nor the promulgation of the law. (23)

Reverting to our former proposition, we proceed to observe, that as Oblations are a part of divine worship, only according to the secondary intention of the Law; but invocation, prayer, and similar duties, a part of worship approximating to the primary intention, and necessary to the attainment of it, the Divine Lawgiver has established a great distinction between these two kinds of worship. For, although oblations and sacrifices are offered in honour of the ever-blessed God, they are nevertheless not to be offered as before the giving of the Law, when every man might offer what sacrifices he pleased, at whatever time and place he chose; or if he pleased might erect a temple and assume the priestly office; for all these things are now prohibited;—a particular house has been assigned to these services, according to what is said, " Thy holy things,—thou shalt take, and go unto the place which the LORD shall choose:" (Deut. xii. 26.) And to offer sacrifices in any other place is pronounced unlawful; therefore it is written,

" Take heed to thyself, that thou offer not thy burnt-offerings in every place that thou seest." (Deut. xii. 13.) Nor are any permitted to bear the sacerdotal office, but those of a certain family; all these things being intended to check every kind of improper worship, and to· prevent the practice of every thing which the Divine Wisdom judged proper to be abolished. But prayer and deprecation are duties which every one may practise in any place, whenever he pleases; the same liberty also is allowed to every one with respect to the *Zazith*, or garments with fringes; the *Mezuzah*, or schedule affixed to the door-posts; the *Tephillin*, or phylacteries made use of in prayer, (24) and other things of a similar nature.

It is also for the reason just stated, that we find the prophets so frequently reproving men for their too great eagerness to offer sacrifices, and inculcating upon them, that they are not the first and independent object of the law, nor has the Divine Being any need of them. Thus Samuel, " Hath the LORD as great delight in burnt-offerings and sacrifices, as in obeying the voice of the LORD? Behold to obey is better than sacrifice; and to hearken, than the fat of rams." (1 Sam. xv. 22.) Isaiah also inquires, " To what purpose is the multitude of your sacrifices unto me, saith the LORD?" (Isaiah i. 11.) And Jeremiah says, " I spake not unto your fathers, nor commanded them in the day that I brought them out of the land of Egypt, concerning burnt-offerings or sacrifices; but this thing commanded I them, saying, Obey my voice, and I will be your God and ye shall be my people." (Jer. vii. 22, 23.) These words of Jeremiah have, however, given rise to a very general objection; for almost every one is ready to urge, " How could Jeremiah affirm that God did not ordain burnt-offerings, and sacrifices, when it is well known that the greater part of the precepts of the Law relate to them?" But the meaning of his words is, what has been already intimated, and is the same as if he had said, The primary intention of every part of the Law, is, that ye should know me, and forsake the service of other gods, that I may be to you a God, and that ye may be to me a people; and the precepts which enjoin oblations, and command you to worship in my house, are given to instruct and assist you in this duty; for the reason why I have transferred this mode of worship to my OWN NAME, is to efface the remembrance of idolatry, and establish the doctrine of my unity. But these designs ye have defeated, and have had regard only to the outward worship; for ye have doubted my existence, as it is said, *" They have belied the Lord, and said, It is not he."* (Jer. v. 12.) Ye have served idols, and burned incense to Baal, and have gone after other gods; and have come to my house, and have cleaved to, and had respect only to the temple of the Lord, and to the oblations, which were not the first and principal object of the law.

There is also another way of explaining these
verses of the Prophet, by which the same sentiment is maintained. For since it is clear both
from Scripture and the Cabala, that the first
precepts which were given to us, were not those
which regarded burnt-offerings and sacrifices, it
might be justly affirmed, that when God brought
up our fathers out of Egypt, he did not *command* them, i. e. *first* and principally concerning burnt-offerings and sacrifices. Nor is the
passover of Egypt any serious objection to this
explanation; for, not only did there exist a
manifest reason for its institution, but it also
took place in the land of Egypt, whilst the precepts referred to by Jeremiah, were those which
were commanded after the departure of our
fathers out of that land, as it is said, " In the day
that I brought you out of the land of Egypt."
The first precept given after the departure
from Egypt, was that which was received by
us in Marah, when it was said to us, " If thou
wilt diligently hearken to the voice of the
Lord thy God." (Exod. xv. 26.) For, " there
he made a statute and an ordinance," (or judgment,) v. 25. The words of the Cabala, are,
" In Marah, I will give the sabbath and judgments." The " statute," therefore, refers to
the *sabbath,* but the "*judgments*" or ordinances,
to the commandments for the prevention of
sin. This, as I have already shown, is the first
intention and principal object of the law, viz.
to inculcate the belief of true opinions, as for

instance, the creation of the world, to establish which, is the chief ground of the precept of the sabbath, (25) and then to banish sin from amongst men.

It is, therefore, evident, that the first precepts were not those which concerned burnt-offerings and sacrifices, which are only secondary in the intention of the law; and that what Jeremiah says, is of the very same import as what we read in the Psalms, where the people are blamed for being ignorant of the first intention of the law, and not distinguishing betwixt it and the subordinate design. " Hear, O my people, and I will speak; O Israel, and I will testify against thee: I am God, even thy God. I will not reprove thee for thy sacrifices, or thy burnt-offerings, to have been continually before me. I will take no bullock out of thy house, nor he-goats out of thy folds." Such also will be found to be the meaning of every other place, where these or similar expressions are used, and which the reader will do well constantly to recollect.

CHAPTER VIII.

———

The Prohibition of external Uncleanness and Impurity is conducive to the Purification of the Heart.

ONE general design of the law is, amongst other things, to control the appetites and restrain the passions, and to exterminate and render despicable those that are unlawful and injurious. Thus, it is well known, that the major part of men place their chief pleasure in immoderate eating and drinking, and venery;—practices, destructive of man's intellectual and highest perfection, and inimical to all good order and government. For when the depraved desires only are indulged, the mental vigour is destroyed; cares and anxieties are multiplied; hatred, malice, and envy are increased; contentions, wars, and robberies are excited, and the man suffers a premature death.

The reason of this is, that foolish men propose to themselves voluptuousness, as their chief good and ultimate aim.

To remedy this evil, God, in infinite wisdom, gave us laws calculated to banish such imaginary schemes of pleasure; to divert our thoughts

188 REASONS OF THE

from them, and to prevent every thing tending to voluptuousness, or unlawful gratifications. Such is the principal intention of our law. See, therefore, how strictly the law enjoins the punishment of death upon him who seeks enjoyment in intemperate eating and drinking ; and who, in the law, is called, "a stubborn and rebellious son,—a glutton and a drunkard." (Deut. xxi. 20.) The law commands him to be stoned, and speedily taken out of the way, before his wickedness and malice proceed to murder, and his intemperance injure and corrupt others.

In like manner, it is agreeable to the general intention of the law, that man should be kind, and gentle, and obliging to his neighbours ; not rough and crabbed, but attentive to the wishes of his friends, hearing their petitions, and granting their requests. To this effect is the divine command : " Circumcise therefore the foreskin of your heart, and be no more stiff-necked." (Deut. x. 16.) And again, " Take heed and hearken, O Israel ; this day thou art become the people of the LORD thy God." (Deut. xxvii. 9.) And, " If ye be willing and obedient, ye shall eat the good of the land." (Isaiah i. 19.) It is also said of those who are ready and prompt to receive, and obey, that which ought to be received : " We will hear and do." (Deut. v. 27.) and elsewhere, figuratively ; " Draw me, we will run after thee." (Cant. i. 4.)

Our Law also designs to inculcate purity and sanctity, or, in other words, continence and chastity, as will be hereafter explained. For when God commanded Moses to sanctify the people, to prepare them for receiving the Law, he said, " Sanctify them to-day and to-morrow." (Exod. xix. 10.) And again, Moses said to the people, " Come not at your wives;" (Exod. xix. 15.) evidently teaching, that chastity is sanctification; elsewhere teaching also the same doctrine respecting abstinence from wine; saying of the Nazarite, " He shall be holy." (Numb. vi. 5.) In the book of Leviticus also, we find it enjoined to be holy, since it is said, " Sanctify yourselves, and be ye holy." (Levit. xi. 44.) Such is the sanctity of the precepts; and as the Scripture calls the observation and fulfilment of them, *sanctification* and *purity*, so it terms the transgression of them, and the perpetration of any thing base, *impurity* and *uncleanness*.

Cleanliness of dress, ablution of the body, and the removal of all dirt and squalidness, are certainly the intention of the Law, though considered as subordinate to the purification of the heart and conduct from depraved opinions, and immoral actions. (26.) For, to suppose that exterior purity, by ablutions of the body and dress, can be sufficient, though in other respects a man indulges himself in gluttony, inchastity, and drunkenness, is the extremest folly! Hence, Isaiah says, " They that sanctify themselves, and purify themselves in the gardens, behind one (tree) in the midst, eating swine's flesh, and the abomination, and the mouse, shall be consumed

N

together, saith the LORD." (Isaiah lxvi. 17.)
For these words signify, that in public they
cleansed and purified themselves, but afterwards
in private and in their own houses defiled themselves with all manner of sin ; and ate meats that
were prohibited, such as " swine's flesh, and the
abomination, and the mouse."—As to the expression, " behind one (tree) in the midst," it most
probably refers to unchaste and forbidden
acts. From the whole, however, we learn that
they were indeed outwardly clean, but that
that inwardly they were full of evil desires, and
lusts, inconsistent with the Law ; the principal
scope and design of which is, first to check and
extinguish unholy desires ; and then to purify
the exterior, when it has purified the inward and
hidden affections of the heart. Solomon has
described those who are superstitiously attentive
to purifying the body and dress, but inwardly
inclined to evil, and addicted to impurity, when
he says, " There is a generation that are pure in
their own eyes, and yet is not washed from their
filthiness." (Prov. xxx, 12.)

Let what has now been said respecting the
designs of the Law be well considered, and it will
be found to throw light upon the causes of many
precepts which were previously involved in
obscurity.

CHAPTER IX.

The Law is accommodated to Nations, not to Individuals.

IT is necessary for the elucidation of this subject, farther to remark, that the Law is not formed for extraordinary cases, and actions of rare occurrence; but, for the common and ordinary transactions of life; and consequently that its various precepts and instructions are principally directed to the promotion of public and general good. To form, therefore, a due estimate of that Law, which is certainly Divine, regard must be had to those extensive and general benefits which result from it to the community at large; and not to the partial inconvenience or injury which here and there an individual may sustain from its authority and exercise. Just as in the operations of Nature, benefits are common and frequent; but injuries particular and seldom.

Agreeably to these views, we need not wonder, if the intention of the Law be not answered in all and every individual; but that there are some persons to be found, who, notwithstanding every legal restraint, continue irregular and imperfect· All men are not possessed of the same natural qualities; and although all proceed from the same God, and have been formed by the same power, and are committed to the same pastor, yet it would have been impossible to have constituted their natures fixed and invariable.

Besides, as the natures of men are various and mutable, Laws cannot, like medicines, be suited to every constitution at all times; for these may be accommodated to any man's temperament, at any time; but Laws must be absolute and universal, whether convenient to individuals or not; and had our Law been subjected to the inclinations and personal advantages of individuals, it could not have been free from corruption; of which, far be it from us to have any suspicion.

On this account also, it would be indecorous for those precepts of the Law, which are referable to its first intention, to be subjected to times and places, instead of being absolute and universal, according to what God hath said:— "One ordinance shall be both for you of the congregation, and also for the stranger that sojourneth with you." (Numb. xv, 15.) For, as we have elsewhere shown, the precepts are directed to general reformation.

After having made these preliminary observations, I shall now proceed to those explanations of the Law, which were at first proposed.

CHAPTER X.

The Precepts divided into Fourteen Classes.

THE Precepts of the Law, may, I conceive, be advantageously divided into fourteen classes.

The *first* class includes those precepts which contain the *Fundamental Articles of Faith.* To which are added those which relate to *Repentance* and *Fasting.*—Of the utility of precepts of this nature there can be no doubt.

The *second* class comprehends the precepts respecting *Idolatry;* to which belong also those relating to *Garments made of different materials; to Vines of different kinds;* and to the *Fruits of trees produced during the first three years after being planted.* The general reason for this class of precepts is, that they are designed to confirm and perpetuate the doctrines necessary to be believed.

The *third* class relates to the *Reformation of manners.* For morality is necessary for the due regulation of mankind, in order to promote the perfection of human society and conduct.

The *fourth* class embraces the various precepts respecting *Alms,* and *Loans,* and *Debts ;* and those which are allied to them, as those which relate to

Valuations of Property; to *Things anathematized*; and to *Judgments concerning loans and servants*. The benefit of precepts of this nature, is experienced by almost every one; for a man may be rich to day, and to-morrow he or his posterity be poor; and the man who is poor to-day may be rich to-morrow.

The *fifth* class is composed of those precepts which prohibit *injustice* and *rapine*; the utility of which is evident.

The *sixth* class is formed of the precepts respecting *Pecuniary Mulcts*; as for instance those adjudged for *Theft*, *Robbery*, and *False-witness*. The necessity and advantage of all the precepts of this nature are easily perceived; for if rogues and villains were suffered to go unpunished, there would be no end to the number of rascals of this description, nor to the depredations they would commit. Remission, or suspension of punishment in these cases, is not, as some have foolishly imagined, Clemency and Mercy; but rather Cruelty, Inclemency, and Political Ruin. True Clemency is what God has commanded; " Judges and Officers shalt thou make thee in all thy gates." (Deut. xvi, 18.)

The *seventh* class includes the precepts relating to *Pecuniary Judgments*, arising from the mutual transactions of trade and commerce; such as those of *Lending, Hiring, Depositing, Buying, Selling,* &c. The utility of precepts of this sort is very evident; for as it is necessary that men should engage in mercantile concerns, and embark their property in them; so it is equally necessary that equitable rules should be established for the direction of trade, and for a just and proportionate valuation of property.

The *eighth* class comprehends the precepts respecting *Holy Days;* as, the *Sabbath,* and various *Festival-days.* The causes and reasons of them are given in the Law itself, which, as we shall afterwards show, teaches us that they serve either for the confirmation of some article of faith, or for the recreation of the body, or for both.

The *ninth* class includes other parts of the Divine Worship, as the recital of *Prayer,* the Reading of the *Shema,* or, " Hear, O Israel," (28) and various other acts of a similar nature, which all serve to confirm the doctrines of the Love of God, and of what is to be attributed to Him, or to be believed concerning Him.

The *tenth* class contains the precepts respecting the *Sanctuary* and its *Ministers, Vessels and Instruments.* The utility of these precepts has already been noticed.

The *eleventh* class embraces the precepts concerning *Oblations.* We have also previously shown the necessity and peculiar propriety of these ordinances at the period when they were first enjoined.

The *twelfth* class comprehends those precepts which concern *Pollutions* and *Purifications;* the general design of which is to prevent persons from entering rashly into the Sanctuary; and to teach them that reverence, and honour, and fear which are due to it.

The *thirteenth* class is composed of the precepts which relate to *Prohibited Meats,* and of other precepts of a similar nature. *Vows* and the *Law of the Nazarite* belong also to this class, the general design of which is to lay restraint upon the appetite, and to check the immoderate desire of dainties and delicacies.

The *fourteenth* class is formed of the precepts relating to *Unlawful Concubinage. Circumcision,* and *the Pairing of beasts of different species,* are also included in this class. The objects of these Laws evidently is to coerce libidinous desires, to prevent their immoderate gratification and to guard men against the pursuit of them as their principal aim, which is too general a practice of foolish wordlings.

There is also another division of the precepts worthy of notice, viz :—into those which regard *God and Man;* and those which relate to *Man and Man.* In the first part will be included those precepts that are contained in the *fifth, sixth, seventh,* and part of the *third* classes; whilst the second part will embrace the rest. For all the precepts, whether affirmative or negative, the design of which is, to inculcate any article of Faith, to urge any Virtuous Action, or to reform and amend the Morals of Men, are said to be betwixt God and Man; although, it may be well to remark, that even these do, ultimately and after many intervening circumstances, lead to those occurrences which take place between man and man.

Having thus indicated the different classes of the precepts, I shall now endeavour to explain the causes and reasons of them, so far as any of them may appear useless or obscure ; except with regard to a few of them, whose design I have not hitherto been able to discover.

CHAPTER XI.

———

Of the Precepts of the First Class.

THE precepts contained in the first class, and which relate to the essential articles of faith, are evidently well founded and reasonable; and need only to be examined separately to produce the fullest conviction of their utility.

How useful, for instance, in the promotion of learning and instruction, are their various exhortations and admonitions! And yet, without wisdom and doctrine, there would be no good works, no laudable actions, no just sentiments.

Nor are those advantages obscure, which result from the reverence and honour paid to the teachers of the Law; for, unless they were great and honourable in the eyes of men, none would hearken to their words, or receive their instructions respecting the things necessary to be known or practised. The commandment which inculcates modesty and bashfulness, is designed for this end;—as it is said, " Thou shalt rise up before the hoary head." (Levit. xix. 32.)

Of this class of Precepts, is that commandment which forbids us to swear falsely or rashly by His name ; the design of which is, to impress our minds with a conviction of the greatness and glory of God, for which purpose injunctions of this nature are peculiarly suited.

The precept also, by which we are commanded to " call upon Him in the day of trouble," (Psalm l. 15.) is of the same nature, as is also the command to " blow the alarm with the trumpets." (Numb. x. 9.) For by such acts, the doctrine of a Divine Providence is confirmed, and we are taught that nothing happens by chance, and that the Most High God knows and understands our afflictions, and has power in himself to mitigate them, if we serve him ; and to exasperate and render them more severe, if we rebel against him. This is what is meant when he says, " If ye will walk by chance (Eng. Trans. *" contrary unto*") with me ;" for thereby he says, When I bring your afflictions upon you, to punish you ; if ye shall believe them to be accidental and fortuitous, then will I render them, by chance, (according to your thoughts,) more grievous and heavy. " If ye will walk by chance (Eng. trans. *" contrary unto*") with me ; then will I walk by chance (Eng. trans. *" contrary unto,*") also with you in fury." (Levit. xxvi. 27, 28.) For by supposing that those things occur by accident merely, which are really occasioned by their maintaining erroneous opinions, and practising wicked works, they are prevented from being led by them to repentance, according to what is said, " Thou

hast stricken them but they have not grieved."
(Jer. v. 3.) He has, therefore, enjoined us to
call upon Him; to offer supplications unto Him;
and to cry unto Him in the time of trouble.

The doctrine of *Repentance* clearly belongs
to the same class; that is, it is one of those
tenets necessary to be believed by those who
wish to venerate our Law. For no man can be
found who does not sin, either by being ignorant of some truth or doctrine which he ought
to believe, or by adopting a course of conduct
which is forbidden, or by yielding to the violence and predominance of anger or other passions. Were men, therefore, to believe it impossible to amend or correct their errors, they
would continue in their sins, and, seeing no
remedy remaining, would be constantly adding
to their crimes, and increasing their guilt; but
believing and embracing the doctrine of repentance, they will not only reform themselves, but
will also bring forth better fruits and more to perfection than even before they sinned grossly. On
this account those acts which confirm this true
and useful doctrine, are enjoined most frequently;
such as confessions, fastings, and oblations, both
for sins of ignorance and pride. And as the
general design of conversion from sin is, that we
may utterly forsake it, and as this too is the
intention of repentance, the utility of all these
precepts is clearly established.

CHAPTER XII.

———◆———

Of the Precepts of the Second Class; or, those which relate to Idolatry.

THE precepts of the second class were evidently enjoined, in order to preserve men from idolatry, and other false and heretical opinions of a similar tendency. Such are the precepts respecting Jugglers, Enchanters, Astrologers, and Magicians, Diviners, Pythonesses, or those who consult them, and others of the same cast. (28)

A perusal of the books already noticed will fully evince, that astrology or magic was formerly practised by the Zabii and Chaldeans, and still more frequently by the Egyptians and Canaanites; and that not only they themselves believed, but that they also endeavoured to persuade others, that, by such arts, the most admirable operations of nature might be produced, relative both to individuals and whole provinces. But how can reason comprehend, or the understanding assent to the possibility of of producing such effects by the means they adopt ?, as, for instance, when they gather a certain herb at a particular time, or take a certain and definite number of any thing; or practise any other of their many similar superstitions. These I shall class under three heads.

The *first* includes those which relate to plants, animals, and metals. The *second* refers to the time and manner in which such works are to be performed. The *third* is formed of those which consist in human actions and gestures; as, leaping, clapping the hands, shouting, laughing, lying prostrate on the earth, burning something, producing a smoke, and lastly, pronouncing certain intelligible or unintelligible words. Such are the different kinds of magical operations.

Some of their magical operations, however, partook of all these; as when they said, Pluck such a leaf of such a herb, when the moon is in such a degree and position; or, Take the horn of such a beast, or a certain quantity of his sweat, or hair, or blood, when the sun is in the meridian, or in some other part of the heavens; or, Take of such a metal, or of different metals, fuse them under such a constellation, and during a certain position of the moon; then pronounce certain words, and produce a smoke from particular leaves, and, by doing this in a certain way, such and such events will follow.

Others of their magical operations, they judged might be accomplished, by only one of the before-mentioned kinds of superstitious actions. But these were principally to be practised by women. Thus, for the *production of water*, they say, that if ten virgins shall adorn themselves, and put on red garments, leap so as to jostle each other, going forwards and backwards, and afterwards extend their fingers towards the sun, making certain signs, by this means water will be procured. They also affirm, that if four women lie down on their backs, and extending their feet upwards, strike them together, repeating certain words, accompanied by certain gestures, showers of hail will be prevented by the idolatrous and shameful action. Many other similar falsehoods and contemptible ravings may be met with in their writings, in which their operations are only to be performed by women. But in all these actions, regard and reverence must be paid, say they, to the heavenly bodies, without which it will be impossible to render them effectual ; since, according to them, every plant, as well as every animal and metal, has its proper star. They, therefore, deem these actions to be parts of the worship of the heavenly bodies, which, being pleased with certain actions, or words, or suffumigations, grant their worshippers whatever they desire. (29)

After stating these instances furnished by their own books still extant among us, I beg the reader's attention to the following remarks.

The scope of the whole Law and the very hinge on which it turns, being this, that Idolatry may be banished from among us, the very name of it be blotted out, and no power of assisting or injuring mankind attributed to the stars, it necessarily follows, that every astrologer (or magician) must be slain; because every astrologer is, doubtless, an idolater, though in a peculiar and different way from that in which the multitude are worshippers of idols; and because the greater part of such works are practised chiefly by women, therefore, the Law says, " Thou shalt not suffer a *witch* to live." (Exod. xxii. 18.) And further, because men are naturally inclined to exercise clemency to women, and to pity them, it is expressly enjoined respecting idolatry, " A man also or a *woman* shall be put to death:" (Levit. xx. 27.) To which nothing similar is to be found either with regard to the profanation of the Sabbath, or any other precept.

The magicians (or astrologers) believed themselves to be able to effect many things, by their magical arts and charms; such as expelling wild beasts and noxious animals, as lions, serpents, and such like, from the cities, and preventing all kinds of injuries to plants. Some also were found who pretended to prevent hail, and to defend vines from the injuries of worms by destroying them ; whilst others boasted of being able to prevent the falling of leaves or fruit from trees. On this account, therefore, God declared to them in the words of the Covenant, that, because of idolatry and magic, by which they thought to deliver themselves from them, those noxious creatures should be sent and con-

tinue among them, for he says, " I will also
send wild beasts among you;" (Levit. xxvi. 22 ;)
and, " I will send the teeth of beasts upon
them, with the poison of serpents of the dust."
(Deut. xxxii. 24.) And again, " The fruit of
thy land, and all thy labours, shall a nation
which thou knowest not eat up;" and, " Thou
shalt plant vineyards and dress them ; but shalt
neither drink of the wine, nor gather the grapes;
for the worms shall eat them: thou shalt have
olive-trees throughout all thy coasts, but thou
shalt not anoint thyself with the oil; for thine
olive shalt cast its fruit." (Deut. xxviii. 33,
39, 40.) The sum of which is, that by those
very actions which the idolaters adopt as the
most likely means to establish and confirm their
worship, and to persuade men that they will
thereby avert the evils that are threatened them,
and secure the opposite benefits,—by those
very practices they will draw down upon themselves the evils they dreaded, and prevent themselves obtaining the blessings they desired.
Hence the reader may perceive the design of
the special blessings and curses contained in
the words of the covenant, and observe their
great utility. And that men might be still
farther removed from every magical operation,
care was taken that nothing should be done
according to their rites and customs, and therefore all those things were forbidden, which were
asserted to produce benefit by special and occult
qualities and powers, contrary to common obser-

vation: on which account it is said, " Neither
shall ye walk in their *ordinances;*"—nor " walk
in the *manners* of the nations which I cast out
before you." (Lev. xviii, 3; xx, 53.) These
are what our Rabbins call *The ways of the
Amorites,* and consider as branches of the magical
art, because they do not originate in reason, but
arise from magical practices and astrological
observations, inducing them to worship and
venerate the heavenly bodies; and hence they
say—" That in whatever there is any thing medi-
cinal, in that there is nothing of the Ways of the
Amorites;" by which they only mean, that every
thing is lawful which is agreeable to nature and
reason, and every thing else unlawful.   Thus
when it is said,—" The tree which casts its fruit
must be loaded with stones, or anointed with
stibium; and it is asked, What reason can be
assigned for these practices?—It is evident that
the reason for loading it with stones is to weaken
its power; but that for the anointing, no sufficient
reason can be adduced, it is, therefore like every
thing similar, to be accounted as one of the ways
of the Amorites, and consequently forbidden." In
like manner, when it is inquired respecting abor-
tions of holy things, where they must be buried?
It is replied, " They must neither be suspended in
a tree, nor buried where two ways meet, because
of the *ways of the Amorites.*"   Nor ought any
doubt to arise in the mind because they freely
permitted the suspension of a key on a cross-bar,
or the use of foxes' teeth, since in those times

they placed confidence in such things as had been approved by experience, and made use of them in medicine, in the same way that we still use a certain herb as a cure for Epilepsy, by hanging it about the neck of the person afflicted; give the excrements of a dog to a scrophulous person, or for ulcerations of the throat; and prescribe a fumigation of vinegar made from saffron for imposthumes and dangerous ulcers. (30) For whatever is proved useful by experience, may be made use of in medicine, although other reasons may be wanting. Let the reader therefore attend to the important *matters* which have been unfolded to him, and keep them, for "they shall be an increase of joy on thy head."

In our great work we have shown, that it was forbidden to "round the corners of the head," (*i. e.* to shave off the hair,) or to "mar the corners of the beard," (Lev. xix, 27,) because the priests among the idolaters were accustomed thus to poll and shave themselves. (31)

The same reason also exists for the precept prohibiting the wearing "garments mingled of linen and woollen," since, as we find by their books, the priests of the idolaters clothed themselves with robes of linen and woollen mixed together, besides wearing on the finger a ring made of a certain metal.

On similar grounds it is enjoined, that "the woman shall not wear that which pertaineth unto a man, neither shall a man put on a woman's garment." (Deut. xxii, 5.) (32) For in the books of

208 REASONS OF THE

the idolaters it is commanded, that, when a man presents himself before (the image of) the *Star of Venus*, he shall wear the coloured dress of a Woman; and when a Woman adores the Star of Mars, she shall appear in armour. (33.) Another reason may also be given for this prohibition, from the tendency of such actions to excite to licentiousness and inchastity.

It is also unlawful to use, or make a gain of idols, (*i. e.* by buying or selling), and the reason is evident, lest any one, receiving an idol to break in pieces, should retain it whole, and at length fall into the snare himself; or by deriving profit from it, if broken in pieces, and melting it or selling it, should consider it as the cause of prosperity. For the vulgar are apt to take accidental things for true and substantial reasons, as we often hear men say,—From the time they dwelt in such a house; or bought that horse, or this or that thing, they have been rich, their prosperity increased, and the blessing of God has been upon them:—so that what was accidental is regarded as the true cause; and thus, by parity of reason, it might happen that from the time of selling an idol, the business of some one might prosper, his substance increase, and the sale of the image or idol thus be accounted the cause of his prosperity, and what is directly contrary to the words of the Divine Law might believed.—It is also to avoid the same error, that no gain is allowed to be made of the coverings of idols, or the oblations and instruments of idolatry: for in those times such was the confidence of men in the stars, that they believed life and death, and every kind of good and evil to be under their influence, on which account the law combats the opinion by every means, and, in order to eradicate it, directs against it the Words of the Covenant—the Testimonies—the Oaths— and the heaviest Curses, and particularly forbids us to receive or make use of any part of the price of an idol, and declares that if any one intermix it with his other property, both that and the rest of his goods shall be taken away from him, according to what is said,—(Deut. vii. 26,) —" Neither shalt thou bring an abomination into thine house, lest thou be a cursed thing like it ; but thou shalt utterly detest it, and thou shalt utterly abhor it ; for it is a cursed thing ;" So far is it from being supposed that any good can be derived from it. (34) Thus shall we find, on examination, that the reason for all the laws against idolatry, is to eradicate whatever is erroneous, and banish it from the earth.

In enumerating the things against which we are thus warned, it is important to remark that the advocates of those opinions which are destitute of foundation or utility, in order to confirm their superstitions, and to induce belief in them, artfully intimate, that those who do not perform the actions by which their superstitions are confirmed are always punished by some misfortune or other ; and therefore when any evil accidentally happens, they extol such actions or rather superstitions as they wish him to practise, hoping thereby to induce him to embrace their opinions. (35) Thus, since it is well known, from the very nature of man, that there is nothing of which men are more afraid than of the loss of their property and children, therefore the worshippers of fire declared and circulated the opinion, that, if they did not cause their sons or daughters to pass through the fire, all their children would die; there can be no doubt therefore, but that every one would hasten diligently to perform it, both from their great love to their children and fear of losing them, and because of the facility of the art, nothing more being required than to lead the child through the fire, the performance of which was rendered still more probable by the children being most generally committed to the care of the women, of whose intellectual weakness and consequent credence in such things no one is ignorant. (36) Hence the Scripture vehemently opposes the action, and uses such arguments against it as against no other kind of idolatry whatever,—" He hath given of his seed unto Moloch, to defile my Sanctuary and to profane my Holy Name." (Levit. xx, 3.) Moses therefore declares, in the name of God, that, by that very act by which they expected to preserve the life of their children, by that act they shall destroy it; because God will exterminate both him who commits the crime, and also his family: " I will set my face against that man, and against his family, and will cut him off." (Lev. xx. 5.) Nevertheless traces of this species of superstition are still existing : for we see midwives take new-born children wrapped in swaddling-clothes, and wave them to and fro in the smoke of herbs of an unpleasant odour thrown into the fire,—a relict, no doubt, of this passing through the fire, and one which ought not to be suffered. (37) From this we may discover the perverse cunning of those men who propagated and established their error with such persuasive energy, that although it has been combated by the law for more than two thousand years, yet vestiges of it are still remaining.

The idolaters acted in a similar way also respecting riches and property, for they instituted the practice of worshipping a certain tree called *Asherah*, (38) and ordered that one part of the fruit of it should be offered, and another part eaten in the idol-temple. They likewise enjoined that the same should be observed with regard to the first-fruits of every tree bearing edible fruit, adding that every tree would dry up and perish, its fruit fade or be diminished, or some other injury happen to it, if the first-fruits were not thus used, in the same manner, as we have before said, that they affirmed all children would die who were not made to pass through the fire. For fear therefore of suffering the loss of their goods, persons readily engaged to practise these things. Yet the law rose against this superstitious custom when God commanded that the fruit produced during the first three years should be burned : " When ye shall come into the land, and

shall have planted all manner of trees for food,
then ye shall count the fruit thereof as
uncircumcised : three years shall it be uncircumcised unto you : it shall not be eaten of."
(Lev. xix, 23.) For some trees bear fruit in one
year, some in two, and others in three years after
they are planted, according to the three methods
made use of in planting, by setting, by layers or
cuttings, and by grafting; no attention being paid
to the sowing of fruit-stones, or kernels with the
husks, concerning which the law enjoins nothing,
referring only to the modes of planting most
generally in use, and to the time of the first
bearing of fruit by trees in the land of Israel,
which generally was within the three years. (40)

It is, however, promised that the loss of these
first-fruits should be compensated by an increase
of fruit afterwards, as it is said, "that it may yield
unto you the increase thereof." (Lev. xix, 25.)
Nevertheless the fruits of the fourth year were
commanded to be eaten before the LORD in
his (holy) place, because the idolaters were
accustomed to eat their first-fruits in the temples
of their idols.

The ancient idolaters have also stated in their
books, that it was a practice among them to
suffer certain things, which they name, to
putrify or rot, and afterwards when the sun
was in a certain position, to sprinkle them,
accompanied with particular magical rites, about
the fruit-tree which had been planted, imagining that · if this were done by the man who

planted it, it would cause it to flower and bear fruit earlier than others usually do. (41) This strange custom they consider as being similar in its nature to the operations of the speaking images which they had, and to the other magical rites which were practised by them for the purpose of producing fruit early; but how strictly the Divine Law prohibits all magical operations, has already been shown. It is also because of this practice, that God prohibits all the fruits which trees bear for the first three years; for by this prohibition it was rendered unnecessary to endeavour to produce fruit earlier than usual; and since the trees in the land of Israel generally bore fruit in the natural way in the third year, there was no necessity for a magical rite, at that time so celebrated.

Again, among the remarkable opinions of the Zabii, are those which relate to the incision or grafting of one tree into another, affirming, that if it be done when the moon is in such or such a position;—if it be fumigated in a certain way;—and if, at the moment of incision or grafting, certain words be spoken, then that which is produced by that tree, will be exceedingly useful and salutary. (42) But the most absurd things of this nature which they have said, is at the commencement of the book, *Of grafting Olives into Citrons;* and, in my opinion, the medical work that in time past was hidden by Hezekiah, was of this kind. On this subject they say, that, when one kind is grafted into another, the cyon is to be held and inserted by a beautiful damsel during the performance of the most filthy and detestable actions:* and of the frequency of this practice, in those times, there can be no doubt, lustful gratifications being superadded to the benefits supposed to be derivable from such acts. The Law, therefore, prohibited כלאים (*Caleim,*) i. e. the grafting of one tree into another; (Levit. xix. 19;) that we might be free from this heresy of the idolaters, and detest their unnatural lusts. On account also of this mode of practising incision or grafting of trees, it was unlawful to mingle seeds of different kinds, or to sow them together; and if the reader will examine the exposition given in the *Talmud,* of this precept respecting the grafting of trees, he will find that the punishment of scourging is every where ordered to be inflicted for the transgression of it, because it is the foundation of the prohibition or the principal thing to which it refers; but the mingling of seeds is forbidden only in the land of Israel. (42)

In the before-mentioned book, it is also stated, that they were accustomed to sow barley and dried grapes together, imagining that without this union there would not be a good

---

* The words of Maimonides are,—" Oportere, ut cùm una species in aliam inseritur, surculum inserendum manu sua teneat formosa quædam Puella, quam præternaturali ratione Vir quidam vitiet et corrumpat, ipsaque congressûs hujus tempore plantulam illam arbori infigat."

vintage. The Law, therefore, *forbade the sowing of the vineyard with divers seeds;* (Deut. xxii. 9;) and enjoined that all such mixtures should be burnt. For all those rites of the Gentiles which they believed to possess particular power and influence, were forbidden by the Law, but especially those which savoured of idolatry.

Farther, if we consider their rites and ceremonies, respecting agriculture, we shall find them paying attention to the planets, especially the two great luminaries, and even regulating the time of sowing by the rising of the heavenly bodies. Smoke is also to be raised, (43) and certain circles to be made according to the number of the planets, by him who plants or sows. For they teach that all these things have a most beneficial influence upon agriculture, thereby alluring and drawing men to the worship of the stars. But on these ordinances of the Gentiles the Divine Law has pronounced the prohibition, " Ye shall not walk in the manners of the nations which I cast out before you ; for they committed all those things, and therefore I abhorred them :" (Levit. xx. 23.) And if any of these were more notorious, or common, or manifestly idolatrous than others, it has given special and particular injunctions respecting them, as of *the fruits of the first years ;—* of *divers seeds and mixed garments,* &c.—I cannot, therefore, but wonder at the saying of Rabbi Josiah, in which he teaches, that " these three, wheat, barley, and dried grapes, may be sown together by one throw of the hand," and have no doubt but that he had taken it from *the ways of the Amorites.*

It has thus, therefore, been shown by irrefragable demonstration, that *mixed garments, the fruits of the first years,* and *divers kinds of seeds,* were prohibited on account of idolatry; and lastly, that *all the ceremonies of the Gentiles* are forbidden, because, as we have already shown, they lead to idolatry.

CHAPTER XIII.

——

Of the Causes and Reasons of the Precepts of the third Class.

THE precepts comprised under the third head, are those of a *Moral and Physical nature.*

The utility of these is evident, because they include the doctrines respecting those virtues by which civil society itself is preserved; so evident indeed, as to render it unnecessary to dwell any longer upon it by attempting to demonstrate it.—Let it be remembered, however, that there are some precepts among them, which although they may appear to have no precise object, yet may be enjoined in order to acquire or produce some virtuous habit. But of the greater part of precepts of this class it is clear, that they are calculated either to create or to preserve laudable and useful habits.

CHAPTER XIV.

Of the Causes and Reasons of Precepts of the fourth Class.

THE precepts comprehended in the fourth class, are those noticed in the tracts *of Seeds, of Slaves,* and *of Pledges and Loans.*

These, when they are considered distinctly, and in order, will be found to have a manifest utility, as for instance, that we ought to be merciful to the poor and succour them in their necessities;—that we ought not to oppress the indigent, nor add affliction to the afflicted in heart, as widows, orphans, &c. *Giving alms to the poor,* being clearly a duty.

The reason for the TERUMOTH, or *Oblations voluntarily made to the Priests and Levites,* and the *Tythes,* is given in the Law when it says, " He hath no part or inheritance with thee :" (Deut. xiv. 27.) To which may be added, that the whole of the tribe of Levi were devoted to the service of God and the study of the Law, not depending upon tilling or sowing, but being set apart for sacred duties, as it is said, " They shall teach Jacob thy judgments, and Israel thy Law : they shall put incense before thee, and whole burnt sacrifice upon thine altar." (Deut. xxxiii. 10.) Thus in almost every part of the Scriptures we shall find the Levite, the Stranger, the Orphan, and the Widow, enumerated together and compared to the Poor, from having no certain possessions.

The *Second Tithes* the Law commands to be brought in kind and eaten in Jerusalem only, that the offerers might be obliged to practise almsgiving, by expending what was brought in eating and drinking, which might easily be done by gradual distribution; and also, that by assembling at one place they might be more firmly cemented together by brotherly affection and friendship.

With respect to the precepts relating to the *Fruits of the Fourth Year*, it may be remarked, that, in addition to their tendency to prevent idolatry, and partaking of the uncircumcision of the *Fruits of the three first years*, the same reason may be adduced for them, as for the Oblations (*Terumah*), Cakes, First-fruits, and First of Shearing, of all of which the first-fruits were to be consecrated to God, that men might be excited to liberality and withdrawn from avarice and gluttony. (44)

Of the same nature also is the injunction, that *the Shoulder, and the two Cheeks, and the Maw*, of the ox or the sheep which is offered, shall be given to the priest: (Deut. xviii. 3:) since the *two cheeks* may be considered as the first-fruits of the carcase of the animal; the *Right Shoulder* as the first of branch-like parts of the body; and the *Maw* (or Stomach) is the chief of all the instestines.

The law of the *First-Fruits* also promotes

Humility : for being obliged to carry their baskets on their shoulders,(Deut.xxvi,2,) and thus publicly to acknowledge God's blessings, they thereby signified that it was a part of Divine Worship, for a man to remember his former affliction and tribulation, when God should have given them rest; which is also confirmed by the law in many other places, as it is said, " Thou shalt remember that thou wast a bondman in Egypt :" (Deut. xxiv, 18 :) Since he who is in the enjoyment of riches and pleasures is in danger of forgetting his former state, when he ought to fear those evils which so readily spring from prosperity, such as pride, and haughtiness, and apostacy, and others of a like nature, agreeably to the caution, " Lest when thou hast eaten and art full, and hast built goodly houses, and dwelt therein ; and when thy herds and thy flocks multiply, and thy silver and thy gold is multiplied, and all that thou hast is multiplied ; then thine heart be lifted up, and thou forget the LORD thy God, which brought thee forth out of the land of Egypt, from the house of bondage :" (Deut. viii, 12, 13, 14, 15 :)—and again, " Jeshurum waxed fat and kicked." (Deut. xxxii, 15.) It is for fear of these evils that it is commanded in the Scriptures, to offer the first-fruits every year before the Lord and his Divine Majesty : and it is well known how forcibly they recall to mind the plagues of Egypt; as, " that thou mayest remember the day when thou camest forth out of the land of Egypt :" (Deut. xvi, 3)—and, " that thou mayest tell in the ears of thy son, and of thy son's son, what things I have wrought in Egypt :" (Exod. x. 2.) which was peculiarly proper to be done on these occasions, because they demonstrate the truth of prophecy, as well as of rewards and punishments; for every precept, which either recals to our minds the Divine Miracles, or establishes our Faith, must be of the greatest utility. This is clearly shown by what is said of the first-born of man and beast : (Exod. xii i, 14,15 :) " It shall be, when thy son asketh thee in time to come, saying, What is this? that thou shalt say unto him, By strength of hand the Lord brought us out from Egypt, from the house of bondage : and it came to pass, when Pharaoh would hardly let us go, that the Lord slew all the first-born in the land of Egypt, both the first-born of man, and the first-born of beast : therefore I sacrifice to the Lord all that openeth the matrix, being males :" which is evidently spoken of sheep, oxen, and asses, because they are domestic animals reared by men and to be found everywhere, but especially in the land of Israel and among the Israelites,—we, and our fathers, and our fathers' fathers being shepherds, as it is said, " Thy servants are shepherds, both we and also our fathers." (Gen. xlvii, 3.) On the contrary, horses and camels are not to be found in every place and among all people ; therefore when the spoiling of the Midianites is noticed, (Num. xxxi,) we find no animals mentioned, except sheep, oxen, and asses, which are the only ones necessary for

P

all men, and especially for those whose occupation is in the fields and woods: thus Jacob said, " I have oxen, asses, and flocks." (Gen. xxxii, 5.) Whereas horses and camels are confined to certain countries, and possessed only by a few distinguished persons. The neck of the firstling of an ass was to be broken, that the owner might be induced the more readily to redeem it, (Exod. xiii, 13) as it is said, " The command of redemption precedes the command of decollation."

The precepts enumerated in our tract *of the year of Redemption* (45) *and Jubilee* (46) are given *partly* in mercy to men in general, and for their comfort and rest: " Six years shalt thou sow thy land, and shalt gather in the fruits thereof: but the seventh year thou shalt let it rest and be still: that the poor of thy people may eat;" (Exod. xxiii, 10, 11;) and that the land, by being thus left untilled and suffered to rest, might become more productive :—*partly* from special kindness to the slaves and the poor by the remission of debts and the manumission of slaves :—*partly* to provide for the perpetual support and maintenance of the people; as, for instance, that the land should never be sold so as to be utterly alienated from the original owners, but remain the property of a man and his heirs for ever,—" The land shall not be sold for ever." (Exod. xxv, 23.)

Similar reasons to those already adduced for alms-giving, exist also for the precept respecting *Estimations*, (47) and *Things devoted to sacred purposes.* (Levit. xxvii.) For some of them relate to the priests, and others of them to the *repairing* and *restoring of the House of God;* and, in general, all of them have a tendency to lead men to liberality, and instead of giving place to avarice, to contemn riches for the glory of God ; the greater part of the evils and misfortunes which happen among men, arising from avarice and ambition, or too great an eagerness to amass wealth.

In like manner, if we properly consider the precepts relating to *Borrowing* and *Lending,* and examine them particularly, we shall find them all directed to the same point, that mercy, beneficence, and clemency may be exercised towards the poor, and that no one may be destitute of the necessaries of life, as, " No man shall take the nether or the upper millstone to pledge : for he taketh a man's life to pledge." (Deut. xxiv, 6.) (48)

The precepts which refer to *Servitude* and *Slaves,* have also a similar object, the promotion of piety and mercy to the poor ; of which it is no mean proof, that it was commanded *to liberate a Canaanitish slave when he had lost any member by ill usage, even if it were but a tooth;* (Exod. xxi. 26, 27 ;) that he might not be afflicted, at the same time, with both slavery and such an infirmity or defect. We have also shown in the *Mishna Thorah,* that it was not lawful to strike him with any thing but a strap or a reed, or some similar instrument ; and that if his master struck him with these so as to kill him, he himself should be punished with death, as for another murder.—But when it is said, " Thou shalt not deliver unto his master the servant, (slave) which is escaped from his master unto thee : he shall dwell with thee, even among you, in that place which he shall choose in one of thy gates, where it liketh him best, thou shalt not oppress him:" (Deut. xxiii. 15, 16 :) —There is another beneficial result beside the act of mercy, which is, that it teaches us to accustom ourselves to virtuous and praise-worthy actions, not only by succouring those who have sought our aid and protection, and not delivering them into the hands of those from whom they have fled, but also by promoting their comfort, doing them all manner of kindness, and not injuring or grieving them even in word; and if we are bound to exercise these duties towards men of the lowest condition, towards slaves, how much more must it be our duty to exercise them towards persons of superior excellence and rank who require our assistance, and receive them according to their rank and merit ? —It should, however, be remarked, that if the fugitive or run-away was a man of base and perverse character, no assistance was to be afforded him, no mercy to be shown to him, nor any part of his punishment to be remitted, (that is, not the least favour to be shown him,) although he should have sought refuge in the most sacred place, as it is said, " Thou shalt take him from mine altar that he may die." (Exod. xxi. 14.)

Where an instance is given of one who seeks protection and assistance from God, and betakes himself to that which is dedicated to Him; yet no assistance is afforded him, but he is commanded to be surrendered to his adversary:— how much less, therefore, must any private individual lend assistance to any man of such a character, or exercise mercy towards him? For such mercy, when shown to wicked men and villains, is tyranny and cruelty to others; and certainly, those actions must be the most pleasing to God, which are the most consistent with his righteous statutes and judgments; and not those merely which obtain the applause of the ignorant and foolish, by whom all are praised who indiscriminately receive and protect all that come to them without inquiry, whether oppressor or oppressed, as may be seen and known by their books and sayings. (49) The reasons of this class are, therefore, as we have shown, sufficiently clear and evident.

CHAPTER XV.

Of the Causes and Reasons of Precepts of the fifth Class.

THE precepts included in the *fifth class,* all relate to the punishment and prevention of *Damages* and *Injuries.*

The prohibitions of these are frequent in the Law, and prove that a man is considered as guilty of all those damages or injuries which are occasioned by his property or goods, so far as they might have been prevented by a proper precaution on his part; hence the blame attaches to us of all the damages done by our cattle, because we either do or may watch them carefully; and in like manner those which occur from fire, and cisterns or wells of water, because men have it in their power to guard them, and prevent the danger arising from them. (50)

There are, however, certain distinctions to be observed in relation to these precepts, agreeably to justice and equity, which shall be explained. Thus, when injury is suffered from the *teeth* or *feet,* (i. e. of cattle) in a public place, the owner is acquitted, because the *teeth* and *feet* are things which he has not power to guard, and the damage which is sustained is, in most cases, but small; to which may be added, that

he who leaves any thing in a public place,
injures himself by exposing his property to destruction; and that the owner of cattle is
accountable for damages done in the field by
the *tooth* and *foot*.—But if the damage done in
a public place be caused by a horn or any
thing similar which might have been guarded,
and from which persons travelling cannot save
themselves, the law and judgment is the same
in every place. Yet there is a difference
between a *quiet ox*, (that is, a gentle one, not
known to push with its horns,) and a *furious ox*,
(that is, one which its keeper knew was accustomed to push with its horns;) (Exod. xxi.
29, 35, 36;) for if the damage be done by the
one not used to push with its horns, then the
owner is obliged to make good only half the
damage; but if it be done by the one accustomed and known to do so, the owner is bound
to make good the whole damage. The fine
appointed in this case, for the injury done to a
slave, is thirty shekels of silver, or half the
price of a freeman; freemen being usually estimated at sixty shekels of silver, and a slave at
thirty. (51) The reason why the beast is to be
slain, is to punish the owner, and not, as the Sad-
ducees absurdly cavil, to punish the beast; and
the flesh of it was forbidden to be eaten, that he
might be induced to take particular care of it,
knowing that if it killed any one, whether great
or small, bond or free, he must lose the value of
it; and that if it had been known to be accus-

tomed to push or toss with its horns, he would, beside the loss of the beast, have to pay the estimated sum for the injury. For the same reason also it is commanded, that *the beast with which any man lieth shall be slain*, (Lev. xx, 15,) that the owner of it may watch over it with the same care and diligence as his other domestics, nor readily suffer it to be from under his eye ; for men commonly pursue riches with an ardor and attachment equal to that which they feel for their own souls, and some are more careful of their wealth than of themselves ; but with the greater part, the love of property and of life are equal, as it is said, "To take *us* for bondmen and *our asses.*" (Gen. xliii, 18.)

To this class of precepts also belongs the case of *Slaying the Pursuer*, that is, of him who *pursues* another in order to perpetrate some act of wickedness. But, the judgment that he may be put to death who intends or attempts to commit a crime without effecting his purpose, is only permitted in two cases, First, when any one pursues his neighbour with a design to murder him ; and Secondly, when any one pursues another with the intention to commit an act of impurity, since these are injuries, which, if once sustained, can never be remedied.—With respect to certain other crimes, forbidden by the House of Judgment under pain of death, as idolatry and the violation of the sabbath, by which no one is injured, the mind alone being conscious of them, the punishment of death is not inflicted on account of the intention, unless there be an actual commission of them. It may also be remarked, that concupiscence is forbidden, because it induces desire, and desire leads to rapine, as our wise men have explained it.

The reason why *things lost are commanded to be restored,* (Lev. vi, 4,) is clear; for, independently of honesty being praiseworthy, it has great reciprocal utility; for if we do not restore that which another has lost and we have found, neither will he restore to us our things; in the same way that if we honour not our fathers, neither will our sons honour us. (52)

The *Manslayer who killeth another person unawares, is commanded to flee from his own place,* [to the city of refuge,] (Numb. xxxv,11,) in order to pacify the avenger of blood, and to prevent his having *him* constantly in his sight who had committed the offence : and the return of the manslayer to his own city depended upon the death of the High Priest, the dearest and most excellent person in all Israel, that by this means also the mind of the person might be appeased whose relative had been killed; for it is natural to all men in affliction, and implanted in their very constitutions, to find comfort from seeing others in similar or greater sufferings; and no death can possibly happen more afflictive in its nature than that of the High-Priest. (53)

The utility of the precept respecting the *beheading of the heifer,* (Deut. xxi, 1—9,) is also evident : for the city bringing the heifer, is that which is nearest to the body of the man who has been murdered, and it most frequently happens that the murderer is from that place. Then the elders of the city call God to witness, that they have neglected nothing that was necessary for the security and guarding of the ways, and had diligently examined and searched all travellers, saying, as our Rabbins have expressed it ; " This man was not killed through our negligence or forgetfulness of any of our common and public constitutions; nor do we know who killed him." Now by this enquiry into the deed, by the going forth and protestation of the elders, and by the taking and striking off the heifer's head, a great deal of conversation took place about the affair and gave publicity to it, by which means either the murderer probably was found out, or was discovered by some one who had been privy to the murder, or had overheard something respecting it ; or it became known by certain signs and indications that such an one was the murderer ; but if any man or woman rose and said, Such an one committed the murder, the heifer was not beheaded ; and as it was well known that if any one knew the author of the murder and concealed it, calling upon God as a witness and avenger that he knew him not, it would be the greatest folly and sin, it was rendered highly probable that if any one knew the murderer he would be detected ; and the detection of him would be important ; for if the House of Judgment did not put him to death, the king had power to order his execution, on evidence being given against him, and if the king did not cause him to suffer, then the avenger of blood might do it by lying in wait for him.— It must therefore be acknowledged, that the beheading of the heifer was of use in the disclosure and discovery of murder. This was also farther promoted by the circumstance, that the place where the heifer was beheaded might never again be ploughed or sowed, which was done, that the owner of the land might use every effort, and neglect nothing to detect and apprehend the murderer, that the heifer might not be slain and the land be polluted for ever. (54.)

CHAPTER XVI.

Of the Causes and Reasons of Precepts of the Sixth Class.

THE sixth class of precepts treats of the *Punishments* and *Mulcts* of criminals and different delinquents.—The utility of these, in general, is well known, and has been already intimated; but the design of the present chapter is to notice the particulars of them, and show their justice and equity.

The general punishment for an injury done by one man to another, was, that what he had done to another should be done to himself; thus, if he had wounded his body, his own body must suffer;—if he had taken his money, his own money must repay him; (55)—though, in most cases, it was in the power of the injured party to pardon the offender or remit the punishment, if he thought proper. In the case, however, of murder committed from malice aforethought, the punishment could neither be remitted, nor any compensation be accepted in its stead, as it is said, (Numb. xxxv. 33.) "The land cannot be cleansed of the blood that is shed therein, but by the blood of him that shed it."—And although the man who had been mortally wounded, might live some hours or days, and retain his speech and understanding, and request that his murderer might be liberated, declaring that he had freely forgiven him; his request was not to be granted, but life was to go for life, whether small or great, bond or free, wise or foolish; for no greater crime than this can ever be committed.

In like manner also, if any one mutilated the limb of another, he was himself to be mutilated; in a word, whatever injury any man did to his neighbour, was to be retaliated on himself. As to the pecuniary mulcts now substituted for these punishments, there is no need to weary the mind by attempting to discover the cause of them, since it is not my intention, in this work, to assign reasons for the decisions of the Talmud, (though I might have somewhat to say respecting the Talmudical sentences,) but to account for the precepts of the Scriptures.

When the nature of the injuries prevented retaliation, the law enjoined recompense, and the offender was obliged to pay for the loss of time and the cure of wounds which he had occasioned. (Exod. xxi. 19.) (56)

If any one committed a trespass on the property of another, he was condemned to suffer an equal loss of his own property; as it is said, (Exod. xxii. 9.) " Whom the judges shall condemn, he shall pay double unto his neighbour;" that is, what he had purloined, and as much more. (57)

Let it also be remarked, that those crimes which are most easily effected, and of most fre-

quent occurrence, ought to be punished more
heavily and severely than those which more
rarely occur, in order more powerfully to restrain men from committing them. Hence, he
who had stolen a sheep, (Exod. xxii. 1,) was
obliged to restore twice as much as he who had
stolen any other moveable, that is, *fourfold*, and
that whether he had killed it or sold it; the
reason of which is, that being generally in the
fields, where they cannot be so readily watched
as in the city, those who steal them either hasten
to sell them that they may not be found in their
possession, or to kill them that they may be so
altered in form as not to be recognized. But if
an ox were stolen, the restitution was increased
to *fivefold*, because it was more liable to be
stolen; for sheep being fed in flocks might be
easily watched and guarded by the shepherd,
and could scarcely be carried off except during
the night, whereas, oxen being dispersed and
feeding in different places, could not be so easily
defended, and this was the reason why they
were more frequently stolen. (58)

Thus also, the law respecting " *False Witnesses*," (Deut. xix. 19,) decided that " it should
be done unto them as they had thought to have
done unto their brethren;" if they had intended
to procure their death, they themselves were to
be put to death; if they had thought to smite
them, they were to be smitten; or, if they had
designed to deprive them of money, they were to
forfeit a sum equivalent. (59)

In all these cases it is intended to proportion the punishment to the crime, and therefore these laws are called " Righteous or Just Judgments."

The reason why the robber, or he " *who took any thing from his neighbour by violence or fraud,*" (Levit. vi. 2, 5,) was obliged merely to restore the principal, (for the fifth part, which was to be added to what had been taken, was to expiate the false oath,) was, because of its infrequency; for theft was more frequent than robbery, since the former might be committed any where, but the latter not in a city without very great difficulty; besides which, theft may be committed either secretly or openly, but robbery only openly; every one, also, may guard against a robber and resist him, which he cannot do against a thief; and lastly, a robber is known and may be pursued, and exertions used to recover the things of which persons have been robbed, whilst a thief is unknown; on these accounts, therefore, a thief was fined, but a robber was not. (60)

The punishments inflicted were also greater or less, severer or lighter, in proportion to the crime, and were regulated by the four following considerations:—

First, the *Magnitude of the Crime ;* for those actions which cause the greatest injury, deserve the heaviest punishment; but where the injury is small, the punishment should be light.

Secondly, the *Frequency of the Crime ;* for

what is more frequently committed, must be restrained by severer punishment; whilst that which more rarely occurs, may be checked by more moderate infliction.

Thirdly: *The Temptation to commit the crime*; since it is certain, that no one will be deterred from that to which he is powerfully impelled, whether it be by the too great violence of his passions, or by habit and custom, or by the fear of the trouble which the omission of it would occasion, but by the fear of the severest punishment.

Fourthly; The *Facility of the Crime*; as whether it could be committed in secret and without being observed, and without being discovered or known; for such crimes can only be prevented by the infliction of heavy punishments.

After premising these things, it is further to be observed that the Law includes four degrees of punishment; the first is, *Death*, inflicted on those adjudged guilty by the House of Judgment : (61) the second, is *Excision or Cutting off* and *Scourging with the Thong*, when the sin is believed to be very great: the third is, *Scourging with the Thong*, or *Death by the hand of God*, when the crime is of a negative kind and not considered as of a very grievous nature: the fourth is, *Prohibition without scourging*, and relates to all those negative precepts in which no action is included, except those which respect him who swears rashly or falsely, who will not believe what ought to be believed of magnifying God, who refuses to offer the offerings to God, or who reproachfully curses his neighbour by the Name of God, since the common people regard curses and reproaches as greater evils than bodily injuries;—for the injuries arising from the rest of the negative precepts, unaccompanied by any action, are very small, and, consisting of words only, are not easily avoided; so that if they were prohibited under the pain of being scourged, no man's back would be free from wounds during the whole year; and therefore no punishment is assigned but admonition.

In directing the number of stripes which are to be inflicted in certain cases, wisdom and discretion must be used. For although the law is precise and definite as to the greatest number ever to be ordered, it is not so as to individuals and particular cases, because no one must have more than he can bear, and the number must never exceed forty, even though he were able to bear a hundred.

The punishment of *Death by the House of Judgment* was not annexed to *Forbidden Meats,* because no great evil arose from eating them, nor was any one so violently tempted to them, as to inchastity and similar crimes: Yet, *Excision* was denounced against some of them; as, the *Eating of Blood,* (Levit. vii. 26, 27,) because in those times men were too apt to be led into a desire and precipitancy of eating it by a certain kind of idolatry, which was the chief cause why it was so strictly forbidden.

Q

The *Eating of Fat* likewise was liable to the same punishment, (Levit. vii, 23—25,) because men are generally fond of it, and also because it was the will of God that it should be appropriated to his sacrifices on that very account.—Excision was also annexed to the *Eating of Leaven* at the *Passover*, and to the *Eating of any thing* on the day of the *Fast* or *Expiation*, which was a day of grief and sadness: because on those days the acts were performed which confirm those opinions on which the law is founded, as the Deliverance out of Egypt and the Miracles which accompanied it, and the Belief of the necessity of Conversion or Repentance, as it is said, (Levit. xxiii, 28.) " It is a day of Atonement (Expiation,) to make an atonement for you before the Lord your God." —He also was exposed *to Excision* who *ate that which was remaining of the Peace-Offering on the third day;* (Levit. xix, 5—8;) and he, who being *Unclean ate of the flesh of the sacrifice of Peace-Offerings*, (Levit. vii, 21,) was ranked with him who had eaten *Fat;* the design of these sanctions being to increase the feeling of reverence in offering up sacrifices.—But *Death by the House of Judgment* was annexed only to great and daring sins, as for instance, *Corruption of the faith* or *Heresy, Idolatry, Adultery, Incest, Murder*, or whatever might induce the commission of them; and to the *Profanation of the Sabbath*, because by the Sabbath, the belief of the creation of the world is established. Similar punishment was likewise inflicted upon the *False Prophet*, (Deut.

xiii, 1—5; xviii, 20,) and the *Despiser of the Elders*, (Deut. xvii, 12,) because of the great evils which their conduct might occasion; as it was also upon him who *smote his Father or Mother, or cursed them*, (Exod. xxi, 15; Levit. xx, 9,) since these were proofs of desperate and shameless depravity, and subversive of all domestic order, which is not an inferior but a primary part of Civil Government. It was especially denounced against the *stubborn and rebellious Son,* (Deut. xxi, 18—21,) on account of the fatal consequences that would certainly follow ; for it was more than probable, that, growing worse and worse, he would at length become a murderer. He who *kidnapped or stole a man* (Deut. xxiv, 7) was liable to the same condemnation, because it was presumed that he who was stolen was carried off to be slain ; and he who was *found breaking up,* (Exod. xxii, 2,) because, as our Rabbins explain it, he was thought to enter with an intention to murder some one. It is therefore clear, that these three, *the Rebellious Son*, the *Thief breaking up*, and *the Kidnapper*, were regarded as Murderers.—In a word, *Death by the House of Judgment* was never inflicted but for great and grievous crimes; for, even in cases of inchastity, only those instances were thus punished which were most easily effected, or were the most frequent, base and shameful, and to which there was the greatest temptation : whilst others were restrained by Excision. Neither were all kinds of Idolatry subject to this punishment, but only the more principal ones, as *the man who prayed to an idol,—who prophesied in its Name ;—or who caused his children to pass through the fire ;*—the *Augur ;*—the *Python ;*—and the *Enchanter.*

Punishments and Judgments being thus evidently necessary, it is requisite that there should be *Judges* appointed in every city ; that there should be *Witnesses* ; and that there should be a *King* who should be venerated, who should forbid and by every means restrain these things, and who should lend his aid to the Judges and afford them countenance.

We have now exhibited the causes and reasons of the precepts enumerated in our treatise entitled, שופטים (Shophetim) or " Of Judges ;" it remains for us to advert to a few things noticed in that work, connected with the precepts of this class. We observe, therefore, that since God knew the judgments of the law would be always necessary, and that at different times and in divers places and from various causes and reasons, as well as from a variety of occurrences, men would be induced to add to them or to take from them, he forbade them doing it, saying, (Deut. iv 2,) " Ye shall not add unto the word which I command you, neither shall ye diminish ought from it ;" for to do this would be greatly to the prejudice of the law, which might thereby seem not to derive its origin from God. But during the whole time and age of the *Wise-Men,* (*i. e.* of the Great Synagogue, or House of Judgment,) he permitted them to form *Hedges* whereby the judgments of the Law might be regulated in certain cases, wherein men might be inclined to alter it, that the Law itself might be confirmed, and the Hedges be rendered lasting in their obligation, as it is said, "Make a Hedge for the Law." (62) He also granted them the power of suspending certain precepts of the Law, and in some cases and with respect to some things of permitting what was forbidden, but these were only temporary in their duration.

By this means the Law may be preserved, and established, and yet be suited to all times and cases according to existing necessities; but if that special exception had been conceded to every Wise-Man, men might have perished through the diversity and multitude of opinions; God therefore forbade that any Wise-Man, except those of the Great Synagogue unitedly, should exercise this power; but commanded that whoever should oppose their united decisions should be put to death; (Deut. xvii, 12;) for the design and end of them would be lost, if every one who chose might dissent from them and disobey them.

It should also be remarked, that Criminal Actions are divided into four classes, some being involuntary and only committed by *Constraint;* others through *Error;* some through *Pride;* and others with *a High Hand,* that is frowardly and obstinately.

No punishment was inflicted on him that transgressed through *Constraint,* nor was any guilt imputed to him, as GOD himself has said, (Deut. xxii,) "Unto the damsel thou shalt do nothing; there is in the damsel nothing worthy of death." But he who transgressed through *Error* was accounted a sinner, because if he had diligently and constantly watched, he would not have fallen into error; so that although no actual punishment fell upon him, yet there was need of an atonement, and he was, therefore, obliged to offer an oblation. The Law, however, makes a distinction, betwixt a man of celebrity or a man of learning, and a private illiterate character; betwixt the King and the High-Priest, or a man who delivers a *Halacah* or Legal Decision; and declares that, whoever gives or teaches a *Halacah* or Legal decision according to his own under-standing, unless he be of the Great Synagogue or House of Judgment, or the High-Priest, is to be ranked with those who sin through Pride, and not with those who sin through Error. Hence the rebellious elder was to be punished with Death, although what he had done and taught might appear to himself to be right. But the Great Synagogue, or House of Judgment, had the right of judging according to its own views; and if the members of it erred, they were classed among those who transgressed through igno-rance, as it is said, (Lev. iv. 13,) "If the whole Congregation of Israel sin through igno-rance:————." On this ground the Rabbins have said, "Ignorance in doctrine is accounted Pride;" that is, if any one, who is deficient in knowledge, teaches and acts according to his ignorance and unskilfulness, he is considered as proud; and a different judgment will be formed of him from that which will be formed of him who eats the fat of the kidneys supposing that he is eating the fat of the tail,—or that eats the fat of the kidneys knowing it to be such, but ignorant that the fat of the kidneys is forbidden: for although the latter may be regarded as nearly allied to the proud, on account of their transgression, though it was only in the act, and they may therefore offer an oblation; no doubt whatever can exist as to him who ignorantly and daringly teaches according to his own will or understanding, since the scripture no where liberates or excuses any one for ignorance in doctrine, except the members of the Great Synagogue or House of Judgment. (63)

He who sinned through Pride was subject to the Written Judgment or Punishment written in the Law, whether it was to death by the Great Council, or to scourging, or to the chastisement of the negative precepts where scourging was not enjoined, or to a pecuniary fine; and although there were certain cases in which offences were equally punished, whether committed through ignorance or from pride, yet it was only in those instances which were of frequent occurrence, or might be committed with great facility, or which were only in word and not in act, such as the oaths of witnesses, the oaths respecting the pledges; to which may be added the violation of a betrothed bond-maid, (Lev. xx, 20,) which frequently occurs, such an one being greatly exposed, since she is neither a mere bond-woman, nor absolutely a free woman, nor really and truly the wife of any man, as the Cabala explains this precept.

Finally, he who sins with a *High Hand* (64) is the proud man who is become hardened in sin, and sins publicly and without restraint; for such an one not only transgresses the Law through concupiscence and the natural depravity of his nature, but in open violation of the Law, and with the intention of treating it with contempt: wherefore it is said, (Num. xv, 30,) "He reproacheth the LORD:" and was therefore, beyond all doubt, to be punished with death; for no one would thus sin, but he whose principles or opinions differed from the Divine law, and were directly opposed to it. Hence the common and received exposition of this law is, that the Scripture speaks of idolatry, because it is opposed to the first and principal foundations of the law, no one worshipping a star or planet but he who believes in its antiquity or eternity. In our judgment, every other transgression also, frowardly committed against the Law, originates in the same cause, and that even when an Israelite only eats flesh with milk, or clothes himself with mixed garments, or rounds the corners of his head, it is done from contempt of the law, and discovers his disbelief of it; and this we conceive is the meaning of its being said, (Num. xv, 30,) "He reproacheth the LORD."—

A criminal of this description was condemned to
suffer the death of denial, (that is, as an heretic
or apostate who had denied the faith,) not the
death of punishment, as the *citizens of a city
enticed to idolatry* (Deut. xiii, 13--17) were slain as
heretics and apostates, and their goods burned,
and not left to their heirs like those of others
who were put to death by the House of Judgment. If, therefore, any assembly or congregation of Israelites transgressed any precept
through *pride,* and with a *high hand,* the whole
of them were to be slain ; of which we have proof
in the history of the sons of Gad and Reuben,
(Joshua xxii,) where it is related, (v. 12,) *first,*
" That the whole congregation of the children of
Israel gathered themselves together—to go up to
war against them :" and then, that they solemnly
expostulated with them for having become
apostates by having unanimously consented to
an act of transgression, and thereby openly for-
saken the Law of God, which is what is intended
by saying, (v. 16,) " What trespass is this ye have
committed against the God of Israel, to turn away
this day from following the LORD ?" And *secondly,*
that the Reubenites answered and retorted upon
the accusers, (v. 22,) " The LORD God of gods,
the LORD God of gods, he knoweth, and Israel
he shall know, if it be in rebellion, or if in
transgression against the LORD." The reader
therefore may now understand, from what has
been advanced, the general principles of the

mulcts and punishments which have been mentioned.

Again, among the other precepts contained in the book concerning " Judges," is that of " *blotting out the remembrance of Amalek from under heaven.*" (Deut. xxv, 19.) For by the same reason that one man is punished separately, a whole family or nation may be punished collectively, that other families or nations, seeing or hearing of the punishment, may escape the same sins and judgments; since they will say to themselves :—" Perhaps that may befal us which befel such a family ; or perhaps that may happen to us which we are about to do to them ;" so that if any reprobate and base person should rise up amongst them, who has no concern for his own life or welfare, and is regardless of the crime he is going to commit, he may not be able easily to find in his own family any patron who will countenance his evil conduct. Thus, of Amalek, who was the first to attack the Israelites with the sword, it is said, (Exod. xvii, 14,) " I will utterly put out the remembrance of Amalek from under heaven." So also against *Ammon* and *Moab*, who were actuated by avarice in their conduct, and attempted to bring evil upon us by subtilty, judgment was denounced, by enjoining us to avoid all affinity with them, and forbidding us " to seek their peace or prosperity for ever." (Deut. xxiii, 3—6.) All these things having a divine measure and proportion of punishment, to which nothing is to be added, and from which nothing is to be taken away; but as GOD himself explains it, to be rendered to every man " according to his fault." (Deut. xxv, 2.)

To the same book (or division of the law) belongs the precept of *appointing a place and paddle without the camp*, (Deut. xxiii, 12—14,) for concealing the necessities of nature. The first intention of which was cleanliness, and the avoiding of all filth and impurity that might render man like the brute beasts ; whilst it was also further designed by these injunctions to confirm the confidence of the Israelites in the Divine Majesty dwelling among them in the time of war, as is said in the reason assigned for this precept: (Deut. xxiii, 14:) " For the LORD thy God walketh in the midst of thy camp, to deliver thee, and to give up thine enemies before thee ;" and to which this exhortation is added, " Therefore, shall thy camp be holy; that he see no unclean thing in thee, and turn away from thee." (v. 14th.) God designing thereby to deter and dehort from fornication, which is but too common and frequent among soldiers when long absent from home. In order, therefore, that we might be delivered and abstain from all such impure actions, God enjoined those acts which served to remind us that his glory dwelt in the midst of us, saying, " Thy camp shall be holy, that he see no unclean thing in thee ;" and also commanded, (v. 10, 11,) " If there be among you any man that is not clean by reason of uncleanness that chanceth him by night, then shall he go abroad out of the camp, he shall not come within the camp: but it shall be, when evening cometh on, he shall wash himself with water: and when the sun is down, he shall come into the camp again." This was done, that it might be firmly settled in the mind of every one, that their camps ought to be like the Sanctuary of God, and not like those of the Gentiles, in which every kind of corruption, transgression, rapine, theft, and wickedness, was suffered to grow freely. But my design is to direct men to the worship of God, and exhibit the reasons of it; and, as I have already stated, the causes and reasons which I shall adduce shall be such only, as may be found in the Scriptures.

In fine, to this class belongs the judgment respecting the *beautiful female captive,* (Deut. xx, 10—14,) of which our wise men say, *This Law speaks only of concupiscence.* But the reader ought, nevertheless, to be reminded, that this precept includes something relating to those virtuous and moral actions which all good men ought to practise. For, even if evil concupiscence gained such an ascendancy over a man, that he could neither conquer nor restrain it, still he was forbidden to yield to it in public, and commanded to seek privacy and retirement, since it is said, "Thou shalt bring her home to thine house." Neither was it permitted to enjoy the captive female a second time, either during the war, or before her grief and sorrow had subsided;

nor was she to be prevented from mourning, weeping, and washing, as it is enjoined, "She shall bewail her father and mother ;" for, by those who are in distress, tears are preferred to rest and recreation, until the bodily strength being evidently weakened, the person becomes incapable of sustaining an exertion of the mind, like as those who are elated with joy prefer laughter to quietness. It is therefore clear, that it is the design of the law to exercise clemency towards the captive, by allowing her to express her grief in every way, until she became languid and weary, and ceased to mourn and grieve. Let it, however, be remarked, that her captor dared not enjoy her, except during her continuance in Gentilism; and that for thirty days she might retain her own law and religion, although it were idolatry, and no one was suffered to contradict or molest her: And even if he could not induce her to embrace the rites and customs of the Law, he could neither sell her, nor use her as his slave. From all these circumstances, it is, therefore, manifest that the Law prohibited carnal access, notwithstanding she might continue in rebellion, that is, a Gentile and a Pagan, as it is said, "Thou shalt not make merchandise of her, because thou hast humbled her." (65)

CHAPTER XVII.

———

Of the Causes and Reasons of Precepts of the Seventh Class.

THE precepts of the seventh class are those which respect *Pecuniary Judgments.*

The reasons of these are evident; for they are, as it were, the measures of equitable decisions in the business and contracts usual among men; and designed to promote the mutual advantage of merchants and contractors, so that neither party may be profited solely, but each be bene-fited by the other.

The primary rule is, *that no fraud shall be committed in selling;* but that the gain shall be usual, common, and known; that the conditions of sale shall be duly observed, and that no fraud nor deception whatever shall be prac-tised, even in word.

The next precepts of the same class, are those which relate to the *four keepers:* [i. e. of goods deposited, borrowed, hired, or pledged,] (Exod. xxii. 7—15;) and of which also the reasons are evident. For he who gratuitously takes care of any thing from which he derives no advantage himself, but benefits others, is not liable to any loss, but the injury which happens must be borne by the owner of the goods; but he who requests to have goods in charge in order to derive benefit from the care of them, or to whom the owner gives a remuneration, becomes surety for all, and from his purse every loss must be made good; and when he who gives and he who receives the remuneration, mutually share the profit, they must jointly bear the loss. If the damage be occasioned by the negligence of the person intrusted, as when that which was committed to his care, is *stolen* or *lost,* then he must repay it, because he did not take proper care of what was committed to his charge; but if the injury 'sustained be such as he could not have prevented by foresight, care, or diligence, as when the limbs of sheep or cattle are *broken,* or when sheep, &c. are *carried off* or *die,* the loss must be borne by the owner himself.

The law also manifests the greatest attention to the case of *hired servants,* on account of their poverty, (Deut. xxiv. 14, 15,) enjoining their wages to be punctually and fully paid them, without any fraud or violence exercised towards them, and that their wages shall be proportioned to their labour. From the same true principle of mercy likewise proceeds the injunction, that neither *hired servants,* nor even cattle, shall be prevented from eating of the food about which they are employed. (Deut. xxv. 4.) (66)

In the class of " Pecuniary Judgments," those respecting *Inheritances* must be specially noticed; concerning which it is commanded,

(Numb. xxvii. 8—11) that no one shall deprive
another of the estate which belongs to him by
right, nor, when he dies, refuse it to his heirs,
nor dissipate, nor disperse it, but leave it to
those to whom it is most proper to bequeath it,
namely, to those who are nearest akin (to the
original proprietor.) Hence, the order to be
observed respecting it, is particularly pointed
out; for a son takes the precedency, then a
daughter, after that a brother, then, as is well
known, his father's brothers. The right of
primogeniture is also to be given to the eldest
son, because of the priority of love to him; (67)
nor must a husband indulge his affections by
transferring the right to another son by a more
beloved wife. This virtue so equitable, that
we ought to prefer those who are most nearly
related to us, and be the readiest to do them
good, is every where recommended and confirmed by the Law; hence, the Prophet says,
" He that is cruel troubleth his own flesh."
(i. e. his relatives.) (Prov. xi. 17.) Thus,
also, the Law speaks of alms-giving; " Thou
shalt open thine hand wide unto thy brother,
to thy poor, and to thy needy, in thy land:"
(Deut. xv. 11:)—and our Wise Men exceedingly commend him who does good to his
relatives, and provides for his sister's daughter; and how far we ought to go in this duty,
and how highly it ought to be commended by
us, our Law sufficiently informs us, whilst it
inculcates upon us the obligation of regarding

our relatives and kindred notwithstanding they may offend us, and not to turn away our benignant countenance from them, even if any of them should be of the vilest and most depraved character, as it is said, (Deut. xxiii. 7,) " Thou shalt not abhor an Edomite, for he is thy brother." How often soever, therefore, or whensoever we find a person to whose bounty we have been indebted, or from whom we have formerly received a favour, we are bound to remember him, because he formerly aided us, although since that time he may have done us injury; thus God hath said, (Deut. xxiii. 7,) " Thou shalt not abhor an Egyptian, because thou wast a stranger in his land ;" though, it is well known how much evil the Egyptians did to us afterwards.

We see, therefore, how many excellent and laudable actions may be learned from these precepts: the two last, indeed, do not properly belong to this place, but we have been led into the digression respecting the Edomite and Egyptian, by what was said concerning the hereditary right of relatives.

R

CHAPTER XVIII.

Of the Causes and Reasons of Precepts of the eighth Class.

THE precepts comprehended in the eighth class, are those which are enumerated in our Talmudical tract " Of Times," and the reasons of which, except in a few instances, are given in the Law itself.

The cause of the institution of the *Sabbath* is so well known, as to need no explanation; it is evidently designed to procure rest for man, by providing that a seventh part of his life shall be free from labour and fatigue, of which no one, either rich or poor shall be deprived: to which may be added, that it most powerfully confirms and perpetuates the doctrine and history of the creation of the world. (68)

The reason of the *Fast of the day of Expiation,* (Levit. xvi. 29—34,) is also clear. It excites repentance, and is likewise held on the day on which Moses, the prince of prophets, came down from the Mount with the second tables, and announced to the people the forgiveness of their great transgression: hence, it is chosen to be, for ever, a day wholly devoted to repentance and divine worship; and therefore every corporeal pleasure and all bodily labour and fatigue are forbidden on that day, and the whole of it is to be spent in confessing and forsaking sin.

The *other Festival Days* were appointed generally for purposes of joy, and because such public assemblies promote that union and affection which are necessarily required under all civil and political governments; although the peculiar and proper circumstances of those days had their distinct causes. (69)

Thus, in what relates to the *Feast of the Passover*, the reason is manifest *why it was to be celebrated for seven days*, which is, because the circumaction or revolution of seven days is the mediate circumvolution between a solar day and a lunar month, which, it is well known, is of great use, not only in natural things, but also in legal ones. (70) For the law is constantly assimilated to nature, and nature is in some sort perfected by it; for nature possesses neither reason nor understanding, but the law is, as it were, the rule and guide of the Most High God, who hath imparted understanding to those who are endued with it.—These things, however, are not within the scope of this chapter, and, therefore, we will resume our former subject.

The *Feast of Weeks*, (*i. e.* Pentecost,) was celebrated in commemoration of the day on which the Law was given (to Moses.) To honour *that day*, the days were counted from the preceding solemnity (of the *Passover*) to the present one, just as a man who is expecting his best and most faithful friend, is accustomed to count the days and hours till his arrival; and this is the true reason why the days are reckoned from the day on which the Omer or Sheaf was offered, (Levit. xxiii, 15,) and on which they were brought out of Egypt, to that of the giving of the Law, which was the chief cause and end of their coming out of Egypt, as it is said, (Exod. xix, 4,) "I brought you unto myself." And because that great and glorious manifestation continued during one day only, therefore the commemoration of it annually was peculiarly solemnized only on one day; but as the *Eating of Unleavened Bread* would have passed without any impression or distinct recollection of the reason and object of it, if it had been merely for a single day, since it frequently happens that men eat unleavened bread for two or three days together, therefore it was continued for a whole week, that the cause of it might be observed and impress the mind.

In like manner the celebration of the *Beginning of the (Civil) Year* was limited to one day, because it was intended to be a day of repentance and conversion, or awaking men out of sleep; and for the same reason *the Blowing of the Trumpets* (Levit. xxiii, 24,) was ordered to take place on that day. It was besides this, a preparation for the day of Fasting, (*i. e.* of Expiation,) as is evident from the ten days intervening betwixt the commencement of the year and the day of Expiation. (71)

The design of the *Feast of Tabernacles* was to induce joy and hilarity; and that its object might be universally spread and known, it was celebrated during seven days. The reason of its appointment at this time of the year is clearly indicated in the law, by saying, (Exod. xxiii, 16,) " When thou hast gathered in thy labours out of the field," (*i. e.* because thou hast now some rest and leisure from business.)—Aristotle in his *Ethics,* (B. viii, c. 9,) mentions a similar procedure among the Gentiles :—" The ancient sacrifices, assemblies, and conventions for sacrifices, were made at the gathering in of the fruits and productions of the earth, as the season of greatest leisure and rest."—The festival may also have been appointed at this season of the year, because the dwelling in *booths* (or tabernacles) was then most tolerable, not being much troubled either with heat or rain.

Besides this, the two feasts of the *Passover* and *Tabernacles* teach us the most beneficial Doctrines and Duties.—With regard to Doctrines, the *Passover* serves as a memorial of the miracles in Egypt, and to perpetuate the remembrance of them to future generations; and the *Feast of Tabernacles,* to preserve the memory of the *signs wrought in the desert.*—In respect to Duties, we learn from them, that in prosperity we ought to remember our former adversity with constant thanksgivings to God for our deliverance ; and that in eating unleavened bread and bitter herbs in the *Passover,* we ought to learn humility and meekness, recalling to mind the things which have happened unto us. Thus, being commanded at the *Feast of Tabernacles* to leave our houses and dwell in booths, like hermits who have their residence in deserts in the midst of great wretchedness and inconvenience, we are reminded that such was formerly our situation, as it is said, (Levit. xxiii, 42,) "That your generations may know that I made the children of Israel to dwell in booths, when I brought them out of the land of Egypt;" but are now delivered from that situation and brought to dwell in painted houses, and in the best and fattest land of the whole earth, by the peculiar favour of God, and according to the promises which were made to our fathers themselves, to Abraham, Isaac, and Jacob, because they were men perfect in knowledge and virtue. For this is one of the *foundations of the law*, or principles on which it depends, that every good which God has done or will do for us, is for the sake of Abraham, Isaac, and Jacob, because they walked in the way of the LORD, doing justice and judgment. (72)

From the *Feast of Tabernacles* we go to another Solemnity on the eighth day, (Lev. xxiii, 36, 39,) the *Feast of In-Gathering*, tending to make our joys perfect, which could not be done in tabernacles, but in large and spacious houses and palaces. (73)

As to the *four kinds of boughs or branches, which are to be carried on the day of the Feast of Tabernacles,* (Levit. xxiii, 40,) our Rabbins have, according to custom, assigned an allegorical reason for them : For they are accustomed, as those know who are acquainted with them, greatly to delight in allegories and frequently to use them, not that they consider them as conveying the mind and sense of Scripture, but in order to gratify a fondness for enigmatical writing.—To me, however, the *four kinds of boughs or branches* made use of in the *Feast of Tabernacles* appear to be intended as a sign of joy on account of deliverance from the desert, (or wilderness,) where there was neither seed, nor figs, nor vines, nor pomegranates, nor even water to drink, into a land of fruit-trees and rivers. In memory of this, He therefore commanded us to take of the best of the fruits of the land, of its most pleasant things, of its most beautiful leaves, and of the goodliest "willows of the brook;" and three reasons may be assigned why these four kinds were to be united: the *first* is, because in those times they grew in every part of the land of Israel, and might be procured by every body; the *second* is, their beauty and verdure, some of them being most sweetly and pleasantly odoriferous as the citron and myrtle, others of them not, as the palm and willow; the *third* is, because they retain their freshness and moisture for the whole of seven days, which peaches, pomegranates, and others of a similar nature do not. (74)

CHAPTER XIX.

Of the Causes and Reasons of Precepts of the ninth Class.

THE Precepts of the ninth class are those which are comprehended in our book, " Of Love."—The reason of them is clear, for the design of such *Acts of Worship* is, that we may set God continually before us, and fear and love him, and keep his commandments, and believe those things concerning him which ought to be believed by every one who professes the true religion.—These acts of worship are Prayer, Reading, [the Shema,] or, " Hear, O Israel, the Lord thy God is one Lord, &c.," (Deut. vi, 4,) blessing food, and whatever else is connected with them :—*the Benediction of the Priests*, (75) *Phylacteries, Mezuzoth, Zizith,* (76) *Purchasing the Book of the Law,* (77) and diligently *Reading* in it at certain times. (78) All these are practices so manifestly teaching many useful doctrines and opinions, that it is needless to enlarge upon them.

CHAPTER XX.

———

THE Precepts included in the tenth class are those which are noticed in the Talmudical Tracts " Of the Chosen House," " Of the Vessels and Ministers of the Sanctuary," and " Of Entering into the Sanctuary ;" the utility of which, in general, has been shown already.

It is well known that the ancient Idolaters chose high and lofty places for the scites of their Temples and Idols, and frequently erected them on mountains. (79) Our father Abraham, therefore, chose Mount Moriah, because it was the highest mountain in that region, and publicly professed the Unity of God upon it; and that towards the West, because the Holy of Holies was to be placed towards the West. From this has arisen the saying, that " the Divine Majesty is in the West," and the express declaration of our Rabbins in the *Gemara,* that " Abraham our Father pointed out the West for the Holy of Holies." But in my judgment, the reason was, that since it was the common superstition to adore the Sun and regard it as a god, men would, doubtlessly, turn themselves towards the East, and therefore our Father Abraham turned himself towards the West on Mount Moriah, that his back might be upon the Sun; for we are not ignorant of what the Israelites did when they apostatized and returned to their former errors : " They turned their backs," saith the Prophet, (Ezekiel viii. 16,) " toward the temple of the Lord, and their faces towards the east, and they worshipped the sun toward the east."—Observe this with astonishment and suitable regard !—Besides, I have no doubt, but that Moses and many others knew the place which Abraham, by a prophetic spirit, had selected and pointed out; for, Abraham had commanded, that *this* should be the place of divine worship, that is, that the temple should be erected there, as *Onkelos*, the Chaldee paraphrast, explains Gen. xxii. 13, 14, by saying, " And Abraham offered sacrifice and prayed in that place, and said before the Lord, In this place there shall be generations of worshippers." The *place* of the sanctuary was not openly and clearly indicated in the law, but only obscurely intimated in the words, " In the place which the Lord shall choose," (Deut. xii. 26,) for which, I apprehend, three important reasons may be assigned ;—*first*, lest the Gentiles should get possession of it, or involve us in war on account of it, when they knew it to be the place designated by the law :—*secondly*, lest those Gentiles who then had it in possession should exert all their power to lay it waste and destroy it :—and *thirdly*, (which is the principal reason,) lest any of the tribes should be desirous of hav-

ing it in their lot and territory, and thereby
occasion disputes about it, as was the case concerning the priesthood.—On this account also,
it was enjoined, that no one should build the
house of the sanctuary until a king should be
appointed, who should order it to be built, and
thus remove every occasion of dispute.

The ancient nations also erected temples to
the stars, and placed in them idols dedicated to
certain of the heavenly bodies which they universally worshipped ; and hence, we were commanded to build a temple to the Most High
God, (80) and to place it in the ark, (81)
enclosing the two tables of stone, in which was
written, " I am the LORD thy God,—thou shalt
have no other gods before me ;" (*i. e.* the whole
of the Decalogue.)

Further, it is acknowledged, that belief in
prophecy precedes belief in the law; (for if
there be no prophet there is no law ;) and prophecy is never communicated to a prophet, but
by the mediation of angels, as it is said, (Gen.
xxii. 15,) " The angel of the LORD called unto
Abraham," and again, (xvi. 9.) " The angel
of the LORD said unto her,"—and in innumerable other places : (82) thus, also, the first
revelation of prophecy to our teacher Moses,
was by an angel,—" The angel of the LORD
appeared unto him in a flame of fire ;" (Exod.
iii. 2 ;) consequently, belief in the existence of
angels must be prior to belief in prophecy, and
belief in prophecy prior to belief in the law.

But the Zabii being ignorant of the nature of the true God, and regarding the heavens and the heavenly bodies as that eternal Being who was free from all privation, and supposing that from thence all kinds of power flowed down into *images* and certain *trees*, called in the law *Asheroth*, (83) א, שרות, concluded that those *images* and *trees* inspired the prophets with the prophetic language which they uttered in their visions, predicting good or evil. But when the truth is made known by the Wise Men, and it is fully proved that there is a Being who is neither a body nor an attribute of body, namely, the *true God;* that he is One; (84) that besides Him there are other abstract and incorporeal Beings, (called angels,) upon whom He confers his light and goodness; and that all those beings are distinct from the spheres and their stars, they learn from thence that angels, and not *images* or *trees*, impart the words of truth to the prophets.—From what has just been said, it appears therefore clear, that belief in the existence of angels follows the belief in the existence of God, and that by them prophecy and the law are administered or confirmed.

To establish this doctrine, God commanded *the figure of two angels*, (cherubims) *to be made and placed upon the ark*, (85) that the minds of men might be confirmed in the belief of the existence of angels, since this is an article of faith next to that of the being of a God, and prior to that of prophecy and the law; for if there had only been the figure of *one* angel or cherub, it might

have led them into error, since they might
have imagined that it was an image of God
such as the idolaters made and designed to be
the object of worship, or might have been
induced to believe that there was but one angel,
and thus have fallen into different errors; but
the making of *two* cherubims, accompanied by
the declaration, " The LORD our God is one
LORD," placed these articles of belief beyond
dispute,—that angels do exist and that they are
numerous; and took away all occasion of error
in supposing they were God, by declaring that
God is one and the Creator of all of them.

After this, it was commanded to *place the
Candlestick before the ark*, (Exod. xxv. & xxvi,)
for the decoration and honour of the house of
God, (86) as it is certain that house will be
most highly venerated by men in which a light
is kept perpetually burning within a vail; (87)
and, we know how earnestly and solicitously
the law endeavours to convince us of the honour
and glory of the sanctuary, that by the view of
it we may learn humility, and gentleness and
mercy. Thus, in like manner, immediately
after enjoining the observance of the sabbath,
it is said, " Ye shall reverence my sanctuary,"
(Levit. xix. 30,) in order to increase our
veneration for it. (88)

The need of the *Altar of Incense*, of the *Altar
of Burnt-Offering*, and of their *instruments* or
utensils, is sufficiently obvious; and as to what

regards the *Table,* and the *Bread to be continually placed upon it,* I am hitherto ignorant both of the reason of them and of the objects to which they refer. (89)

The reason why God forbade *the Altar to be built of hewn stones, or to lift up any iron tool upon them,* (Deut. xxvii. 5, 6,) was, because the idolaters at that time built their altars of hewn stones, and therefore we were forbidden to act like them; and, that we might in every way avoid it, God commanded the altar to be made of earth, as it is said, (Exod. xx. 24,) " An altar of earth shalt thou make unto me ;" but where this could not be done without the use of stones, then they were to remain in their natural state unhewn and unpolished : (90) For a similar reason also he prohibited *sculptured images,* (Levit. xxvi. 1,) (91) and the *planting of trees near the altar.* (Deut. xvi. 21.) (92) The design of all these prohibitions is one and the same, namely, to prevent our worshipping Him in the manner in which the idolaters were accustomed to worship their false gods ; a practice generally and universally forbidden, when it is said, (Deut. xii. 30,) " Take heed, that thou enquire not after their gods, saying, How did these nations serve their gods ? even so will I do likewise,"— intending thereby to prohibit their acting thus towards God, and therefore subjoins this reason :—" For every abomination to the LORD which he hateth, they have done unto their gods."

It is also known, that the idolatrous worship of *Peor,* consisted formerly in *uncovering the nakedness before it;* on this account, therefore, God commanded the priests, (Exod. xxviii. 42,) to " make themselves linen breeches to cover their nakedness," when they were employed in divine worship; and also, (Exod. xx. 26.) that " they should not go up by steps unto the altar, lest their nakedness should be discovered thereon." (93.)

The precepts respecting *the custody and constant watchfulness over the Sanctuary,* were given to promote the honour and majesty of God ; (Numb. iii.) and with the same intention also it was enjoined, that no idiot or unclean person, nor even any who were mourning or unwashed, should be permitted rashly to intrude.

There were also other injunctions intended to promote reverence, veneration, and fear towards the sanctuary, among which were those who forbade any one to enter it *who was drunken and unclean, or whose hair was suffered to be long,, or whose garments were torn,* and also that which commanded that *all who ministered in it should wash their hands and feet.*

To add to the honour of God's house, and to render it more august, *he exalted the dignity of its ministers and separated the Priests and Levites from others:* — he also commanded that *the priests should be clothed with beautiful and costly vestments,* as it is said, (Exod. xxviii. 2,) " Thou shalt make holy garments for Aaron thy brother for glory and for beauty;" and ordered that *no one should be admitted into the ministry (of the sanctuary,) who had any bodily defect,* none who had any deformity being eligible to the priesthood; the reason of which was, as explained in the Talmud, because the vulgar do not judge of men according to their real perfection which is rational and intellectual, but according to their personal comeliness, and the beauty and richness of their garments: the design, therefore, of all these precepts was, that the house of God might be held, by every one, in due reverence and honour.

The *Levite* likewise, who neither offered nor sacrificed, and of whom it was not said that he might expiate sin, as was said of the priests, (Levit. iv. 26,) " The priest shall make an atonement for him," and again, (Levit. xii. 7,) " The priest shall make an atonement for her,"—but whose office was *singing,* might be rendered ineligible by his voice; for in singing the chief object is to affect the mind by the words which are sung, which can never be effected except by melodious voices, pleasant tunes, and suitable instruments of music, such as have always been in the sanctuary.

It was also to honour the sanctuary, that even *the priests themselves, the lawful ministers of the sanctuary, were forbidden to reside in it, or to enter it at pleasure;* and that *no one but the*

High-Priest was ever permitted to enter into the Holy of Holies, and that only four times annually on the day of expiation. (94)

To prevent the stench which would otherwise have been occasioned by the number of beasts which were every day slaughtered in the sanctuary, and their flesh cut to pieces and their inwards and legs washed and burnt, *God ordained that incense should be burned in it every morning and evening,* and thereby rendered the odour of the sanctuary and of the vestments of those who ministered exceedingly grateful; which has occasioned the saying of our Rabbins, that *the odour of the incense extended to Jericho.*—This, therefore, is another of the precepts conducing to the reverence and veneration which ought to be entertained for the sanctuary; for if the perfume had not been pleasant, but the contrary, it would have produced contempt instead of veneration, since a grateful odour pleases and attracts, whilst an unpleasant one disgusts and repels.

The *anointing Oil,* (Exod. xxx. 31,) produced a two-fold benefit, the *pleasantness* of what was anointed with it, and the *dignity* and *sanctity* of that which was separated by it from the rest of its kind and consecrated to a more excellent use, whether it were a man, or a garment, or any utensil. This also, as well as the other precepts, may be regarded as inducing that veneration for the sanctuary which creates reverence and fear of God; for the minds of men are peculiarly impressed with devotional feelings on entering

S

the sanctuary, and the hard heart becomes softened and humbled; and thus, by softening and humbling the hearts of men, Divine Wisdom prepares them for receiving with greater readiness the commandments of God, and leads them to fear Him, as is shown in the law, when it says, (Deut. xiv. 23,) " Thou shalt eat before the Lord thy God, in the place which he shall choose to place his name there, the tithe of thy corn, of thy wine, and of thine oil, and the firstlings of thy herds and of thy flocks : that thou mayest learn to fear the Lord thy God always." Thus the design of all the before-mentioned actions is made evident.

The cause of the prohibition that *no one else should make such oil or incense,* (Exod. xxx. 32, 33,) was, doubtless, that there might be no such perfume found elsewhere, and consequently a greater attachment be induced for the sanctuary; and also, to prevent the great evils that might arise from men esteeming themselves more excellent than others, if they were allowed to anoint themselves with a similar oil.

The reason why the *Ark was to be borne on men's shoulders,* (Numb. vii. 9,) and not on a carriage, was for the honour of the ark, and that the form and structure of it might not be injured, especially when the staves were to be drawn out of the rings, nor the Ephod or Breast-plate receive any damage.

All the Garments were to be woven throughout without seam, that the beauty of the texture might not be injured.

It was also enjoined, *that those who engaged in the service of the Sanctuary should avoid interfering with each other in their duty;* for when any business is committed to many persons, and not every one appointed to his particular office, there is the utmost danger of their becoming negligent and slothful.

Finally, *the comparative degrees (of Holiness) attributed to sacred places,* for instance, in the injunctions respecting the *Mountain of the House,* or *the Outward Court,* or *the Court of the Women,* or the *other Courts,* until we come to *the Holy of Holies,* must all be intended to increase reverence and honour for the house of God.— Thus we have shown the reasons of all this class of precepts.

CHAPTER XXI.

—

Of the Causes and Reasons of Precepts of the eleventh Class.

THE precepts of the eleventh class are enumerated by us, partly in the Talmudical treatise " Of Divine Worship," and partly in that " Of Oblations."—The general utility of them having been already explained, we shall now endeavour to give the reasons for them in particular instances, especially with reference to mankind.

The Divine Law has taught, according to the exposition of Onkelos, that the Egyptians worshipped the constellation or sign *Aries*, and, therefore, not only forbade the slaying of sheep, but held shepherds in the utmost contempt, and deemed them an abomination : hence, Moses replied to Pharaoh, (Exod. viii. 26,) " Lo! shall we sacrifice the abomination of the Egyptians before their eyes ?" (95)

Some of the Zabii also worshipped Demons, and believed that they had the form of goats, whence they called demons *Serim*, (שעירים) *Goats.* This opinion had spread throughout the world as early as the time of Moses, since we find him saying, (Levit. xvii. 7,) " They shall no more offer their sacrifices (לשערים) to *Goats*," that is, to demons thus called, and hence that class of idolaters forbade the eating of *goats*. (96)

The slaying of *Cattle* was, likewise, always regarded by the principal part of idolaters with detestation, and brute animals of that kind were held in high estimation by all of them ; and at this day there are idolaters to be met with in India, who never slay them, even in those places where they are accustomed to slaughter sheep and similar animals. (97)

To obliterate such erroneous opinions from the minds of men, it was enjoined that only these three kinds of animals, rams, goats, and cattle, should be offered in sacrifice, as it is said, (Levit. i, 2,) "Ye shall bring your offering of the cattle, even of the herd, and of the flock ;" so that by this means, that was offered to God as an atonement for our sin, which they esteemed as a crime of the greatest turpitude ; and those depraved sentiments, which are, as it were, the disease and ulcer of the human soul were cured by directly opposite measures.

On this account also God commanded us (Exod. xii.) *to slay the Lamb on the day of the Passover, and to sprinkle the blood upon the lintel and side-posts of our doors*, that we might be, thereby, not only purged from those pernicious opinions, but avow others of a contrary nature ; and that men might be convinced that the very act which they judged to be deserving of death, was actually the means of rescuing us from it, according as it is said, (Exod. xii, 23,) " The LORD will pass through to smite the Egyptians; and when he seeth the blood upon the lintel, and on the two side-posts, the LORD will pass over the door, and will not suffer the destroyer to come in unto your houses to smite you;"—thus preserving them from destruction, as the reward of that act of worship which was evidently performed in opposition to the practices of the idolaters. This, therefore, was the reason why these three kinds of animals were chosen for sacrifice in pre-ference to others; to which may be added, that they were every where to be found and obtained, which was not the case with those offered by the idolaters, who were accustomed to sacrifice lions, bears, tigers, and other wild beasts. (98)

But because there were many who were not sufficiently rich to offer *cattle*, it was commanded that such should offer sacrifices of certain *birds* which were common and in great numbers in the Land of Israel, as *turtle-doves* and young *pigeons;* and those who could not afford to offer even these might lawfully offer *bread*, baked and pre-pared in any of the ways in use at that time, whether in an oven or pan, or flat plate, or fry-ing-pan; and if any were too poor to offer even *baked-bread*, they were permitted to offer *flour* alone unbaked.

These offerings were, nevertheless, all volun-tary; for it is observed respecting them, that, although they should not be offered, no guilt should be incurred; as it is said, (Deut. xxiii, 22,)

" If thou shalt forbear to vow, it shall be no sin in thee."

It was likewise the practice of the idolaters to offer only *leavened* bread, and to choose *sweet* things for their oblations, and to anoint or besmear them with *honey;* on this account, therefore, we were forbidden to offer *leavened bread or honey;* (99) but, because they never made use of *salt* in their offerings, we were strictly commanded to use it in all our sacrifices, according to the injunction, (Levit. ii, 13,) " With all thine offerings thou shalt offer salt." (100)

In addition to this it was enjoined, that all offerings should be as *perfect* as possible, that those things which were offered to the Most High God might not be contemned, as it is said, (Malachi i, 8,) " Offer now unto thy Governor ;" it was, therefore, forbidden *to offer any animal under eight days old,* because such an one is imperfect in its kind, and similar to an abortion. Neither was it lawful to " bring the hire of a whore, or the price of a dog, into the house of the Lord ;" (Deut. xxiii, 18 ;) for both of them were vile and contemptible.—The reason already adduced was also the ground of the command *to offer the best of the bullocks and young pigeons ;* (Levit. i ;) old pigeons being neither pleasant nor tender ; and on a similar account it was ordained that the *Mincha,* or Meat-Offering, made of fine flour, should have *oil poured upon it,* (101) to render the taste of it agreeable, and *frankincense put upon it,* (102) to counteract by its excellent odour the disagreeable smell arising from the burning of flesh upon the altar; (Levit. ii, 1;) and for the same reason, to honour the Offering, and to prevent its being looked upon with con-tempt, it was commanded to "flay the Burnt-Offering," and to "wash the inwards and legs," (Levit. i, 6, 9,) (103) although the whole was to be burned: indeed, this reason will be found every where urged and inculcated, as the Prophet has noted, (Malachi i, 12,) "Ye say, The table of the LORD is polluted; and the fruit thereof, even his meat, is contemptible."

For the reasons already assigned, the eating of offerings was forbidden *to the uncircumcised and unclean ; the offering, if rendered unclean, not permitted to be eaten at all, nor the unpolluted offering itself to be eaten after a certain time,* (Levit. vii,) *nor even if it were suspected;* and when eaten, was *to be eaten in a certain place.* But the whole Burnt-Offering, being devoted to God, was not to be eaten in any way, but to be entirely consumed.

The *Sin-Offering* or Sacrifice for sin, (חטאה) (Levit. vi, 26,) and the *Trespass-Offering*, (אשם) were to be eaten in the Court on the day which they were severally offered, or during the night which followed.—The *Peace-Offerings*, (שלמים) which are inferior to the former and called by our Rabbins, (קדשים קלים,) *Minor Holy Things,* might be eaten in the city of Jerusalem, either on the same day on which they were offered or on the day following, but not afterwards, (Levit. vii, 15,) because after that time they became tainted and putrid.

For the special honour of Oblations, and all those things which were devoted to the Great and Ever-Blessed God, it was commanded, (Levit. v, 16,) that *whoever should apply any hallowed thing to his own use, should be considered as committing a trespass, and requiring atonement, and should add a fifth part and give it to the priest, even if he had committed the trespass through ignorance.* In like manner it is forbidden (Deut. xv, 19) "to do any work with the firstlings of our bullocks, or to shear the firstlings of our sheep," on account of the reverence which ought to be entertained for things consecrated to God. In the law too we are cautioned against *altering or changing Sacred Things:* for if this were suffered, a bad thing might be substituted for a good one, under a pretence of its being better, and therefore it was decreed, "It, and the exchange thereof, shall be holy."(Lev. xxvii, 10.) Nor is the reason obscure why it was enjoined (Levit. xxvii, 13,) that, he who wished to redeem any of his devoted things *should "add a fifth part to it;"* for men always regard their own advantage, and are naturally inclined to parsimony and avarice, so that they seldom accurately estimate the value of any sacred thing, or so fully exhibit it as that an adequate price may be affixed to it, and, therefore, they were ordered to make an addition to the price, to render it equal to the sum for which they would be willing to sell another. The whole of these injunctions were likewise designed to prevent any thing being despised which bore upon it the name of GOD, and was consecrated to Him. (104)

Every *Mincha, or Meat-Offering for the priest,* was commanded " to be wholly burnt, and not eaten," (Levit. vi, 23,) because every priest had to offer the oblation for himself; but if he had brought the Meat-Offering, and yet had been permitted to eat it, it would have been doing nothing, for, of the oblation of any other, who was a private man, the frankincense and a handful of flour was all that was offered; (Levit. ii, 2;) and such a diminution of the oblation would not have been sufficient, if he who brought it might have eaten the rest, nor would it have appeared to be an act of worship, and, therefore, it was ordered to be burnt.

The reason for the peculiar statutes and customs of the Passover, such as, *that it was to be eaten merely roasted with fire,—to be eaten in one house,—and not to have a bone of it broken,* (Exod. xii, 9, 46,) is evident and clear; for as *unleavened bread* was used because of haste, so for the same reason also *roasted meat* was preferred, because there was not time for food to be daintily cooked and prepared, nor could the stay to *break the bones* and *take away what, in other cases, was forbidden.* The law adduces this reason for these things, when it says, (Exod. xii. 11,) " Ye shall eat it in haste ;" for when persons are in haste there is no opportunity *for breaking bones, or for sending flesh from one house to another,* and waiting the return of the messenger, for all these things require time and leisure ; and the cause of their being " in haste," was, lest any one should be retarded so long as to be prevented from departing with the multitude, and should be intercepted and killed : they were also ordered to be always observed, that the memory of the passover might be perpetuated according to that which is said, (Exod. xii. 24,) " Ye shall observe this thing for an ordinance to thee and to thy sons for ever."

The Paschal Lamb was *to be eaten by a certain number of persons,* (Exod. xii. 4,) that every one might seriously and diligently provide it for himself, and not trust to any friend or neighbour who might neglect it.—The *uncircumcised were forbidden to eat of it,* for which our Rabbins offer the following reason : *They omitted,* say they, *the precept of Circumcision during their long sojourning in Egypt, that they might be like the Egyptians : when, therefore, the ordinance of the Passover was enjoined us, God annexed this condition to it, that no one should slay it until he had circumcised himself, and his sons and domestics, and then he might eat it. All circumcised themselves, and such was the number of the circumcised, that the blood of circumcision was mingled with the blood of the Passover ; and some vestiges of this we have in the Prophet,* (Ezek.

xvi. 6,) *saying*, " And when I passed by thee and saw thee polluted in thy own blood," *i. e. in the blood of the Circumcision and in the blood of the Passover.*

Besides, although *Blood* was in some sort considered as unclean and impure in the eyes of the *Zabii*, yet it was eaten by them, because they supposed it to be the food of demons, and that he who ate it acquired, by that means, some kind of communion with them, so that they would converse familiarly with him, and reveal to him future events, according to what is generally attributed to demons by the vulgar. There were, however, some among the Zabii, to whom the eating of blood appeared loathsome and repulsive, being what men, in general, naturally abhor. These, therefore, slew a beast and caught the blood, which they poured into a vessel or small hole in the ground, and then sitting in a circle round the blood, ate the flesh, imagining that by this action the demons drank the blood as their food, whilst they themselves were eating the flesh, and that friendship, fraternity, and familiarity were thereby contracted with them, because they had eaten at the same table and reclined on the same seat; besides which, they also believed, that demons appeared to them in their sleep, indicating many things that were to come, and discovering others. In fact, these opinions were, at that time, universally viewed and approved, and no one doubted the truth of them.

For this cause, therefore, the Divine Law, which renders those who know it perfect, was given to eradicate those inveterate diseases, *by prohibiting the eating of blood,* and, as in the case of *idolatry, enforcing the prohibition by an additional sanction;* for God says of eating blood, (Levit. xvii. 10.) " I will set my face against that soul that eateth blood, and will cut him off from among his people ;" and in the same manner he says concerning him who sacrifices his son to Moloch, (Levit. xx. 3,) " I will set my face against that man, and will cut him off from among his people; because he hath given his seed to Moloch."—A mode of expression never used but respecting idolatry and the eating of blood, and denounced against the latter because it induced and encouraged that species of idolatry which consisted in the worship of demons. (105)

But notwithstanding this, the law pronounced blood to be clean, and those who touched it, not to be polluted, as it is said, (Exod. xxix. 21,) —" Thou shalt take of the blood that is upon the altar,—and sprinkle it upon Aaron, and upon his garments, and upon his sons, and upon the garments of his sons with him; and he shall be hallowed, and his garments, and his sons, and his sons' garments with him."—It was also commanded to " sprinkle the blood upon the altar round about." (Exod. xxix. 20.) But this injunction was added, that every act of this kind of worship should be performed by *shedding* the blood, and not by *collecting* it, as it is said, (Levit. xvii. 11,) " I have given it to you upon the altar to make an atonement for your souls," *i. e.* by shedding of it, as is elsewhere observed, " He shall pour out all the blood at the bottom of the altar of the burnt-offering;" (Levit. iv. 18;) and again, " The blood of thy sacrifice shall be poured out upon the altar of the LORD thy God." (Deut. xii. 27.) (106) Even the blood of those beasts which were not designed to be offered in sacrifice, was commanded to be poured out, when they were slaughtered; for the law declares, (Deut. xii. 16,) " Ye shall not eat the blood : ye shall pour it upon the earth as water." Besides this, it was forbidden to gather themselves together round the blood, in order to feast upon it; for it is said, (Levit. xix. 26,) " Ye shall not eat any thing (על) at or upon the blood."—But because they persevered in their contumacy and rebellion, and continued to walk in the way of the nations among whom they had been educated, and yielded to be the companions of demons by eating around blood, therefore it was commanded that we should not eat the flesh of desire, in the desert, but that all our sacrifices should be " offered as Peace-offerings," (Levit. xvii. 5,) and the reason why it was the Divine will that the blood should be poured out upon the altar, and that the people should not gather round it, is indicated, by saying, (Levit. xvii. 5,) " To the end that the children of Israel may bring their sacrifices, which they offer in the open field, even that they may bring them unto the LORD, unto the door of the tabernacle of the congregation, unto the priest, and offer them for peace-offerings unto the LORD ;" and again, (v. 7.) " They shall no more offer their sacrifices unto devils." No mention is made of wild beasts or birds, because no offering was ever made of wild-beasts, and birds were offered in peace-offerings. But afterwards it was enjoined, (Levit. xvii. 13,) " Whatsoever man there be of the children of Israel, or of the strangers that sojourn among you, which hunteth and catcheth any beast or fowl that may be eaten ; he shall even pour out the blood thereof, and cover it with dust ;" so that they could not collect round it and feast together upon it, and by this means the associations of those who are in reality possessed by the devil, might be prevented, as well as communion with demons themselves :—here also, we just remark, that we may judge that this kind of belief and superstition was very generally embraced and eagerly maintained in the time of Moses our teacher, by the words of the " Song of Moses" itself, which records, that " They sacrificed unto devils, not to God;" (Deut. xxxii. 17 ;) on which our Wise Men have observed, that by the words, " Not to God," is meant, that they not only worshipped things actually existing, but mere ima-

ginary beings; the terms they use in the book
Siphri, are these, " It was not enough that they
worshipped the sun, moon, and stars, and the
celestial signs, but they worshipped even the
shadows of them."—But to return, let it be
remembered, that the flesh of desire was forbidden no where but in the wilderness, for
among the other ancient errors was also this,
that demons inhabit and are seen and conversed
with in deserts, but are never seen in cities and
populous places, so that if any one belonging
to an inhabited city wished to perform any
rite of this vain and foolish sort, it was necessary for him to withdraw from the city and go
out into the woods and desert places; therefore,
after they had entered the Promised Land, they
were permitted to eat the flesh of desire;—to
which may be added, that as the strength of the
disease weakened, the followers of it would be
diminished in number; and that it was next to
impossible for all, who were desirous of eating
the flesh of cattle, to come to Jerusalem.

Farther, let it be observed, that the *greater
the offence committed, the meaner was to be the
sacrifice which was offered;* thus, for idolatrous
error, (*i. e.* idolatry practised through ignorance,) a *she-goat* only, (Levit. iv. 27, 28,) and
for the other sins of private individuals, a *female
kid* or *lamb* was to be offered ; because in all
animals the female is accounted inferior to the
male, and as there is no sin greater than idolatry,
so there is no species of animals viler than the

she-goat : but the king or ruler, because of his dignity, was obliged to offer a *he-goat*, (Levit. iv. 22 ;) and the High-Priest and the Sanhedrim a *young bullock*, and for idolatry a *he-goat*, their error not being confined to one deed or act merely, but influencing the general opinion and having the force of doctrine on the people. Thus, also, the sins for which the *Ash am* or trespass-offering was offered, being less than those for which the *Chattaah* or sin-offering was offered, therefore, the sacrifice of the trespass-offering was to be a ram or a lamb of the flock, the nobler species of animals and the more honourable sex, as in the whole burnt-offering which was to be entirely consumed, [i. e. wholly offered to the LORD,] none but males were permitted to be offered. From a similar principle, inferior aromatics, and a smaller quantity of them, were required for the *Mincha* or meat-offering of the sin-offering, and for the Mincha or meat-offering in the case of the woman suspected of adultery, (Levit. v. 11.—Numb. v. 12,) because they were offered solely on account of the suspicion of sin, and consequently oil and frankincense were forbidden to be offered on those occasions. For God was pleased to enjoin them to be offered without the honourable additions of oil and frankincense, because the turpitude of the actions of the sinner was the cause of the oblation of the Mincha, (Numb. v. 15,) and as if, by this prohibition, he designed to bring him to sorrow and repentance, and to say to him, Because of

T

the turpitude of thy actions thy offering is
less perfect than others. In like manner, because
the conduct of the adulterous woman was
baser and more criminal than that of the man
who sinned through ignorance, so her oblation
was inferior in its nature, being of *barley-meal*
merely. Such then, is the principle on which
all these precepts are founded ;—a principle that
must be acknowledged to be admirable in its
nature.

Our Wise Men have likewise given a reason
for "a young calf" being offered "for a Sin-
Offering on the eighth day" of the consecration
of Aaron and his sons, (Levit. ix, 2,) since,
according to them, it was done to expiate the
sin of the golden calf; and that, for the same
reason, "a young bullock" was the sacrifice
offered for sin on the day of expiation or atonement. (Levit. xvi, 6.) In our opinion, a similar
reason existed for enjoining *he-goats* to be offered
as the sin-offerings at their three principal feasts,
—at the feasts of the new-moon, on the day of
expiation, and for idolatry, whether the offerings
were made for private persons or for the whole
congregation; (Numb. xxviii;) for the greatest
sin and the most grievous rebellion of that period
was sacrificing to goats, (or satyrs,) therefore
say the Scriptures, "They shall no more offer
their sacrifices *(leasseirim)* to goats." (Levit.
xvii, 7.) (108) But our Wise Men say, that the
reason why expiation was made by he-goats for

the whole congregation, was, that the whole congregation of Israel sinned about a goat, when they sold righteous Joseph into Egypt, as it is said,—" They killed a kid of the goats, and dipped the coat in the blood." (Gen. xxxvii, 31.)

Nor ought this reason to be regarded as frivolous in its nature, for the end and scope of all these actions was deeply to impress the mind of every sinner with the necessity of having his sins constantly in remembrance, like David, who said, (Psalm li, 3,) " My sin is ever before me," and to convince them that it was the duty of himself and his posterity to expiate their sins by acts of devotion analogous to the nature of their crimes : thus, if they had sinned respecting riches or property, then they ought to devote their riches with liberality to acts of Divine Worship; or if they had sinned by the actions of the body, then the body should be macerated and afflicted by fastings, and watchings, and similar mortifications; or if their dispositions had become notoriously vicious, they should endeavour to correct and amend them by the opposite virtues; or, lastly, if their sin were speculative in its nature, and they had been induced to adopt any false tenets, either through the weakness of their own understanding, or through negligence in searching and investigating Divine Truths, they might be inclined to contrary sentiments, by withdrawing their thoughts from worldly things, and restricting themselves by diligent reading and meditation to an enquiry after the Truth only. Thus Job says, (c. xxxi, 26, 27,) "If I beheld the sun when it shined, or the moon walking in brightness; and my heart hath been secretly enticed, or my mouth hath kissed my hand:" which is ˌfiguratively spoken of that caution and hesitancy which ought ever to be exercised in doubtful cases. An instance of the expiation being thus suited to the nature of the crime we have in Aaron; for when he had transgressed in the matter of the golden calf, then his oblation and that of all who sprang from him was to be a *a young bullock and a calf;* and in like manner when the sin was about the *kid,* the offering was to be a *kid.* When, therefore, these things were once firmly fixed in the mind, they would be certain to produce the effect of causing men to guard against sin, that they might not offend God, and be subjected to long and painful expiations which, during the whole of life, might perhaps never be perfected so as to procure pardon; and of inducing them studiously to avoid and flee from the principles and practices of sin. The utility of this procedure is, therefore, evident; and may serve also for the personal edification of the reader. (109)

It may be satisfactory also to explain another singular expression, though not altogether belonging to the subject of this chapter, by showing the reason, why it was said of the *Goat* offered for a sin-offering at the time of the new moon or first day of the

month, that it was " a sin-offering *unto the*
LORD:" (Numb. xxviii. 15:) and not of the
other *goats* which were offered for sin-offerings
on the principal festivals and other solemnities.
For the cause of the expression, I apprehend, is
this, that all the oblations which were offered
on the other festivals were *whole burnt-offerings,*
and that the *" kid of the goats,"* offered for a
sin-offering daily was eaten, but the whole burnt-
offerings being entirely consumed by fire, were
said to be " sacrifices made by fire *unto the*
LORD;"—therefore, it was never said of the *sin-
offerings* in general, that they were sin-offerings " *unto the* LORD," nor of the *peace-offerings* that they were " peace-offerings *unto the*
LORD," because they were commonly eaten by
the priests; and as it would have been improper
to have called those *sin-offerings,* which were
burnt " sacrifices made by fire *unto the* LORD,"
so we are not to suppose that this was the reason why it was said of the *goat* offered on the
first day of the month, that it was " a sin-offering unto the LORD," since it was not burnt but
eaten. The true reason was, that this sin-offering was peculiarly said to be *unto the* LORD, lest
this *goat* should seem to be a sacrifice unto the
moon, according to the custom of the Egyptians.
But there was no need to be afraid of this with
respect to the goats offered at the principal and
annual feasts, because they were not sacrificed
at the beginning of the month, nor distinguished
by any natural sign, but merely by the appoint-

ment of the law. The new moons, on the contrary, not originating in the law, and the Gentiles being accustomed to offer sacrifices to the moon at those times, as they did also to the sun at his rising, and when he entered into certain signs; the law, therefore, adopts a peculiar expression respecting the goat offered at the commencement of the month, and calls it " a burnt-offering unto the LORD," (Numb. xxviii. 11,) in order to extirpate such opinions from the hearts of men labouring under such a pestilential and inveterate disease.

It may further be observed, that every *Sin-Offering* which is offered to make atonement for one or more of those whose crimes are great, as in the instance of the sin-offering of the " whole congregation of Israel," when they " sin through ignorance, and the thing be hid from the eyes of the assembly," (Levit. iv. 13,) and other similar cases, the offering must be burnt *without the camp*, and not upon the altar, (v. 21,) since nothing was to be burnt upon the altar but *whole burnt-offerings* and similar oblations, which was therefore called the *Altar of Burnt-Offering*; for the *burning* of the whole burnt-offering was " an odour of sweet savour unto the LORD," (v. 31,) like every kind of incense. The design of this was most assuredly to eradicate idolatry, as we have already shown; but the *burning* of those sin-offerings was to teach us, that, as the body was burnt, so the sin was already blotted out and taken away; and as there remained no remembrance of the sacrifice consumed by fire, so there remained no remembrance of that act for which it was offered; the smoke, therefore, of such sacrifices was not an acceptable odour unto the LORD, but, on the contrary, ungrateful and abominable; and on that account, they were commanded to be burnt without the camp. For, has it not occurred to the reader, that it is said of the *Mincha* or meat-offering of the woman suspected of adultery, that " it is an offering of memorial, bringing iniquity to remembrance," (Numb. v. 15,) but that it is never said to propitiate or be pleasing? So the *Scape-Goat* being enjoined for the expiation of the sins of the whole nation which no sin-offering could expiate, and bearing all of them, as it were, at once; it was, therefore, regarded as being unfit either to be sacrificed, or burnt, or buried, and was sent to the most distant regions, or some uninhabited wilderness or island. (110) But as no one can suppose that sins are a burden of such a nature, as to be transferred from the shoulders of one man to another, so no one can doubt but that these were symbolical actions designed to impress the minds of men, and by exciting their fears to produce their conversion, so that they may say, We are free from all our transgressions; we have cast them behind our back, and banished them to the ends of the earth.

I am still in doubt as to the reason of *Wine* being offered, idolaters also offering it. There are, however, some who assign as the reason, that as the chief object of the concupiscible faculty or appetite, the cause of which is in the liver, is *Flesh*, so the object of the vital faculty, the seat of which is in the heart, is *Wine*, and the object of the animal faculty, which is situated in the brain, is *Music, and the harmonious sounds of instruments of music;* every faculty, therefore, offering unto God that which was most pleasing to it, the oblation consisted of *Flesh*, and *Wine*, and *Music* or *Singing*. (111)

The utility and cause of instituting *Festivals* are evident; for, by assembling and collecting the people together on such occasions, piety and devotion are excited, and social intercourse and brotherly love confirmed; though it is certain that the prime object of the law, in ordaining the assembling of the people together, was for the promulgation of the law itself, that by this means every one might hear and learn it.

The value of the *second Tithes*, which was to be carried to Jerusalem, (Deut. xii,) as we have already shown, (chap. xiv,) as well as the produce of the *fourth year after planting Fruit Trees*, and the tithes of *Cattle*, which, with the other tithes, were ordered to be carried thither, were all intended to increase the quantity of food at the festivals, and therefore were not permitted to be sold, nor deferred from one time to another, but brought, as is commanded Deut. xiv. 22, " year by year:"—and that *Alms* might not be forgotten at those solemnities, God himself enjoined them, saying, " Thou shalt rejoice in thy feast, thou, and thy son, and thy daughter, and thy man-servant, and thy maid-servant, and the Levite, the stranger, and the fatherless, and the widow, that are within thy gates." (Deut. xvi. 14.)— Thus we have enumerated the reasons of the injunctions of this class of precepts.

CHAPTER XXII.

———◆———

Of the Causes and Reasons of Precepts of the twelfth Class.

THE Precepts of the *twelfth* class are those which have been noticed by us in the Talmudical Treatise " Of Purifications;" and, although we have already partially indicated their utility, yet some remarks may be added, elucidating, first, the general and then the particular reasons of them.

We observe, therefore, that the Divine Law, which was given to Moses, and has received its denomination from him, was specially designed to lessen the burden and service of religious duties; and if any thing appear to us injurious and fatiguing, it is only because we are ignorant of the rites and customs of those times. For consider how vast the difference is between him who burns his own son in honour of his god, and him who, in the worship and to the honour of our God, burns only a young pigeon!; for it is written in the law, (Deut. xii. 31,) " Their sons and their daughters they have burnt in the fire to their gods."—This was the worship paid by the Gentiles to their gods, and instead of which the burning of a young pigeon or of a handful of fine flour was substituted, in our system.

In this sense, God expostulated with the people by the prophet, in the time of their rebellion, (Micah vi. 3,) " O my people, what have I done unto thee? and wherein have I wearied thee? testify against me :"—and again, (Jer. ii. 31,)—" Have I been a wilderness unto Israel? a land of darkness? wherefore say my people, We are lords; we will come no more unto thee? :"—as if he had said, What injurious or tedious precept was there in the law to cause them to wander from it?—Thus, the Most High God has elsewhere appealed to us, (Jer. ii. 5,) saying, " What iniquity have your fathers found in me, that they are gone far from me, and have walked after vanity and are become vain ?" —The intention of all these passages of Scripture is the same; and with the prefatory observations, which are of considerable moment, ought never to be dropped from recollection.

This being premised, we proceed to remark respecting the *Sanctuary*, that the chief object of the precepts respecting it was to create *devotion* and *zeal* on entering into it, and to impress the mind with *reverence* and *fear*, as it is said, (Levit. xix. 30,) " Ye shall reverence my sanctuary."—But as love and veneration for any thing, however excellent it may be, is weakened and diminished by familiarity, of which our Wise Men have admonished us, by saying, " It is well to enter into the Sanctuary when God pleases," by which they meant to convey what Solomon did when he said, (Prov. xxv. 17,)

" Withdraw thy foot from thy neighbour's house."

For this reason, therefore, God commanded that *none who were polluted should enter into the Sanctuary*, notwithstanding the numerous and various kinds of pollution rendered it almost impossible to find any who were absolutely pure : for, if any one were free from the defilement of *touching a dead body*, yet it was scarcely possible to avoid that which arose from touching one or other of *the eight creeping things* which are so frequently in our houses, or are liable to be trod upon when walking, or which may happen to fall upon our meat or into our drink ; and if he escaped defilement from these, he would be in danger of pollution from touching persons pronounced unclean by the law, (see Levit. xv,) or from involuntary defilements, (v. 16,) or from touching the couches or beds of those who were unclean ; and even when cleansed from these defilements, he was still not permitted to enter the sanctuary until the sun had gone down, and then not during the night, since some cause of pollution might occur before morning, and render him as unclean as on the preceding day. In all these cases, men were obliged to absent themselves from the sanctuary, and were prevented from entering it at pleasure ; and our Rabbins add, that " no one might enter the court to perform any act of worship, unless he previously washed himself." Consequently, by all these actions, reverence, affection, and devotion were preserved to the sanctuary; and men were excited to that humility which was principally intended by them.

The more frequent, also, any pollution was, the heavier and longer was the purification required; thus, the *touching and defilement of dead bodies*, (especially of those of neighbours and relatives,) (Numb. xix. 11—22,) being more frequent than other pollutions, no purification could be effected but by the Ashes of the Heifer, which ,were difficult to be obtained, and then not till seven days had elapsed:—again, *Issues of Blood*, (Levit. xv,) and similar pollutions, because they were more frequent and grievous than the touching of unclean persons, therefore they who laboured under them had need of *seven* days, but they who had touched such persons of *one* day only, in order to be cleansed. But purification after an *Issue of Blood*, either in man or woman, or in puerperal cases, could not be completed without an oblation, since they more rarely occurred than natural hæmorrhages.—All these causes of pollution are, in their very nature, filthy and abominable, such as *Issues, Dead Bodies, Reptiles, Lepers,* and others of a similar kind.

From these ordinances we may derive many and important benefits; as, *first,* to shun all dirt, and filth and slovenliness; *secondly,* to reverence the sanctuary; *thirdly,* carefully to study the customs of those times, because the Zabii had also their laborious rites of purification, as we shall soon show; and *fourthly*, men are thereby relieved from laborious and oppressive customs, so as not to be hindered in their usual business, on account of pollutions or purifications; for this precept respecting cleanness or uncleanness, only regarded the Sanctuary and Holy Things, as it is said, (Levit. xii, 4,) "She shall touch no hallowed thing, nor come into the Sanctuary;" leaving her at liberty to use all other things without sin, even whilst unclean, and to eat whatever kind of common food she chose. But, amongst the Zabii in some parts of the East, females were at certain times obliged to live in separate habitations, the things on which they trod were burnt, every person speaking to them was accounted polluted, and if only the wind had blown over them on to others who were pure, those persons were deemed polluted; from which we may learn how great the difference is, betwixt what they teach and what our law teaches, which allows females to perform almost every duty to their husbands even when polluted. (112) According to the customs of the Zabii, every thing also which was separated from the body, as hairs, nails, blood, &c. was considered as polluting; hence all barbers were regarded as unclean, from having to touch the hair and blood; and every one who suffered a razor to pass upon him was obliged to wash himself in pure and limpid spring-water. Many other tedious and wearisome ceremonies were also common amongst them. (113)

On the contrary, with us, the distinctions of *clean* and *unclean* refer only to the Sanctuary and Holy Things; and when the Most High God says, (Levit. xi, 44,) "Ye shall sanctify yourselves and ye shall be holy," we are not to understand this as being spoken of external cleanness or uncleanness; for as our Rabbins have said on these words, " It is the holiness of the precept;" and again when it is said in another place, " Ye shall be holy," they write, "It is the holiness of the precept" that is meant. Hence the *Transgression of the Precepts or peculiar Laws* is also called *Uncleanness or Pollution ;* and is applied particularly to the fundamental and principal precepts respecting idolatry, incest, and blood. Thus of idolatry it is said, (Levit. xx, 3,) " Because he hath given of his seed unto Moloch, to defile my Sanctuary, and to profane my Holy Name."—Of incest and other abominations, (Levit. xviii, 24,) " Defile not ye yourselves in any of these things:" and of blood, (Numb. xxxv, 33, 34,) " Ye shall not pollute the land wherein ye are." The term *Pollution* is therefore equally spoken of three things; *first*, of the dispositions of men, and of their violations of doctrinal or practical precepts; *secondly*, of external filthiness and uncleanness, as it is said, " Their filthiness is in their skirts; *thirdly*, of imaginary defilements, that is, by touching or carrying any thing unclean, of which latter species our Rabbins have said, " The words of the law suffer no pollution." The term *Holiness*, on the contrary, is made use of for the three things opposite to these. But because pollution, arising from touching a dead body, could not be purged away in less than seven days, nor without the ashes of the heifer, and the priests had continually to enter into the Sanctuary to offer sacrifices, therefore they were forbidden to pollute themselves with the dead, (Levit. xxi.) except in cases of urgent necessity, as those of the death of their parents, children, and brethren, in which natural affection would have rendered it extremely difficult to have been restrained : but as it was indispensably necessary that the High-Priest should be always in the Sanctuary, as it is said, (Exod. xxviii. 38,) " It *(i. e.* the golden plate of the mitre) shall be always upon his forehead," therefore, he was forbidden to defile himself at all, even with the dead body of his father or mother. (Levit. xxi. 11, 12.) It ought, however, to be observed, that in these prohibitions respecting the priests in general, and the High-Priest in particular, neither the wives of the sons of Aaron, nor even the daughters of Aaron, were included, since it was not incumbent on the women to offer sacrifices.

Further, because it could not be prevented from sometimes occurring, that some Israelite

or other having been defiled, though uncon-
scious of it, might enter into the Sanctuary or
eat of holy things in that state or, even act thus
presumptuously, since wicked men frequently
and daringly commit many and great transgressions; therefore, God commanded sacrifices to
be offered as expiations for the pollutions of the
Sanctuary and its holy utensils, (Levit. xvi,)
whether committed through ignorance or presumption; such, for instance, according to their
respective kinds were the goats of the feasts, the
goats of the new moons, and the scape-goat, as is
shown in their proper places. This was done,
that he who had sinned presumptuously might
not suppose that his offence, in polluting the
Sanctuary, was a light and trivial one; and yet
that he might know, that, by the offering of
the goat he was forgiven, as it is said, (Levit.
xv. 31,)—" That they die not in their uncleanness;" and again, (Exod. xxviii. 38,) " That
Aaron may bear the iniquity of the holy
things;"—and this reason is several times
repeated in different places of the law.

With respect to the pollution of the *Leprosy*,
it is our opinion, and that of our Rabbins, as
to the cause of it, that it was the punishment
of an Evil Tongue, that is, of calumny and
detraction;—that it first began in the wall of
the house;—that if the offender then repented,
it disappeared; but that if he persisted in his
rebellious conduct, it spread to his furniture;
and if he still would not desist, that it extended to

U

his garments, and at length seized upon his body. (Levit. xiii. & xiv.) This view of it was entertained by our nation equally with that which regarded the " Waters of Jealousy ;" and the utility of such a belief must be manifest to every one, especially when it is added, that the Leprosy is contagious, and that all men naturally abhor and detest it, and flee from it. (114)— But, *why was the purification of the Leper to be effected by cedar wood, and scarlet, and hyssop, and two sparrows?* (Levit. xiv. 4.)—A reason has, indeed, been assigned for it, but one which does not agree with our institutions; nor have I, to this day, met with any one that I could regard as the true one. (115) In a similar manner I have never met with any reason to which I could assent, for *the cedar-wood, and hyssop, and scarlet used in the burning of the red heifer;* (Numb. xix. 6;) nor for *the bunch of hyssop with which the blood of the passover was to be sprinkled.* (Exod. xii. 22.)

The reason why the *Red Heifer* was called *Chattah*, or sin-offering, (Numb. xix. 17,) was because it perfected the purification of the person who had been defiled by touching a dead body, so that he might enter into the Sanctuary, and eat of the holy things ; for no one, who had been defiled, would have dared to enter into the Sanctuary again, if the Red Heifer had not borne this sin, like the *golden Plate of the High-Priest's mitre*, which rendered the polluted " accepted before the LORD," (Exod. xxviii.

36, 37, 38,) and the He-goats which were burnt. (116) On this account, therefore, the garments of him who was employed about the Red Heifer were defiled, as he who touched the Scape-Goat was deemed unclean because of the multitude of sins which it bore.—We have thus stated the causes and reasons also of this class of precepts.

CHAPTER XXIII.

Of the Causes and Reasons of the Precepts of the thirteenth Class.

THE Precepts comprehended in the thirteenth class are those which we have enumerated in the Talmudical tracts, " Of forbidden meats;"— " Of the rites of slaughtering;"--" Of vows;" and " Of the Nazariteship;"—and although we have in other works largely and explicitly spoken of the utility of these precepts in general, (117) yet a more particular explanation of some of them may be added.

We commence, therefore, by remarking, that all those kinds of food which are forbidden in our law, are unwholesome; nor are there any amongst them, excepting *pork* and *fat*, concerning which a doubt can be entertained whether they be injurious to health or not.

Nor does any ground exist for hesitancy even with regard to these. For the flesh of *swine* is of too humid a nature to be wholesome; though the principal reason why the law forbade the eating of swine, (Levit. xi, 7,) was, because of their extreme filthiness and their feeding on so many foul and impure things. For it is well known how solicitously the law forbade all filthiness and dirt, even in the fields and in the camp, to say nothing of the cities. Now had swine been permitted to be eaten, the streets and houses would have become public nuisances, as we find them to be in those countries where they are nourished and eaten. It is a common saying with our Rabbins, that, " the mouth of a swine is like the most detestable filth."

The *Fat of the Intestines* (Levit. iii, 17; vii, 24) clogs the stomach too much, hinders digestion, and generates thick and cold blood, whence it is much fitter to be burnt than eaten. (118)

Blood, and that which dieth of itself, are innutritive and difficult of digestion. (Levit. vii, 26; xvii, 15.)

That which was torn with beasts, (Levit. xvii, 15; xxii, 8,) was nothing else but what was beginning to die, (or become a dead carcase,) and inclined to putrefaction.

The distinctions of *ruminating or chewing the cud* and *dividing the hoof,* among beasts; and of *fins* and *scales* among fishes, (Levit. xi,) were not the reasons why they were permitted to be eaten; nor the want of them, the causes why they were forbidden; but merely marks whereby the more noble and excellent species might be distinguished, from those that were inferior or unwholesome.

The reason why the *sinew of the thigh* was forbidden, is assigned in Scripture. (Genesis xxxii, 32.)

The *limb of a living animal,* that is, cut off whilst the animal was living, was forbidden,

(Gen. ix, 4,) because it was a proof of a cruel disposition, and because some of the Gentile kings, at that period, acting from idolatrous motives, were accustomed to take an animal, cut off one of its limbs, and afterwards eat it. (119)

Flesh eaten with milk or in milk, (Exodus xxiii, 19,) appears to me to have been prohibited, not merely because it afforded only gross nourishment, but also because it savoured of idolatry, some of the idolaters probably doing so in their worship or at their festivals: and I am the more inclined to this opinion from observing that the law, in noticing this practice, does it twice, immediately after having spoken of the three solemn annual feasts; (Exod. xxiii, 17, 19; xxxiv, 23, 26;) " Three times in the year all thy males shall appear before the Lord God.—Thou shalt not seethe a kid in his mother's milk :"—as if it had been said, When ye appear before me in your feasts, ye shall not cook your food after the manner of the idolaters who are accustomed to this practice. This reason appears to me of great weight, although, I have not yet found it in the Zabian books. (120)

The precept concerning *the slaughtering of animals* was necessary, because the natural nourishment of men consists of the fruits of the earth, and of the flesh of animals; and that the kinds of flesh allowed us were the best that could be eaten, no physician will question. Since, therefore, it was necessary, that animals should be killed, for the sake of good food and nourishment, the law enjoined that kind of death that was the easiest, and forbade them to be tortured by a cruel and lingering mode of slaughtering; or to have their nostrils slit; or to have any limb cut off, as we have already shown.—In a similar manner it was forbidden " to kill a cow or ewe, and her young, both in one day," (Levit. xxii, 28,) lest the young one should happen to be killed before the dam, which would have caused her the greatest grief, for in this case there is no difference betwixt the grief of men and that of irrational animals, the love of a mother to her infant not being the effect of reason but of instinct, which is found in most animals as well as in man. This injunction referred particularly to cattle and sheep, because these were the only domestic animals lawful to be eaten, and of which they could distinguish with certainty the mother from her young. The cause already mentioned gave rise also to the precept respecting *birds' nests,* (Deut. xxii, 6, 7,) for the eggs on which the dam is sitting, or the young ones which have need of her, are not, in general, permitted to be eaten; and when the dam is let fly, she is not distressed by seeing her young ones carried off; it, therefore, frequently happens that all are untouched, because that which might be taken may not be lawfully eaten. If the law then be thus careful to prevent beasts and birds from suffering pain and grief, how much more mankind!

The precept of *covering blood*, (Levit. xvii, 13,) we have already shown, refers to both wild beasts and clean birds.

As the law gave various precepts relative to forbidden meats, so likewise it enjoined precepts respecting lawful and unlawful *Vows.* (Num.xxx.) For persons sometimes said, " This bread is forbidden me," or " This flesh is forbidden me ;" thus rendering it unlawful for them to eat those things ; and this was done by them, in order to acquire, by this means, the virtue of contentment or continence, and to restrain an immoderate appetite : and hence, the saying, that *vows are the hedge of separation*, that is, of abstinence, or of a holy and sanctified life. But since women are apt to act too hastily, through the ardour of their minds, great inconveniences, dissensions, corruptions, and confusions might be occasioned in families, if the right of making vows rested with themselves, by one kind of food being lawful for the husband but unlawful for the wife, or lawful for the daughter but unlawful for the mother; therefore, the authority was given to the head of the family in every thing which might produce advantage or injury. There was, however, this exception, that every woman who was *in her own power*, having neither husband nor father, and who had attained the years of maturity, possessed the same right of vows as the man. (Numb. xxx, 9.)

The cause and reason of the precepts relating to the *Nazarite*, (Numb. vi,) that is, of abstinence from wine, is evident; for wine has, in many instances, both of former and latter ages, been the occasion of death to multitudes, and "many strong men have been slain by it;" (Prov. vii, 26;) the Prophet also remarks, "They have erred through wine." (Isaiah xxviii, 7.)—It was the peculiarity of the Nazarite to abstain from every kind of drink made from the vine, that he might be thereby advanced to greater honour, and learn to be content with the things that were necessary. He, therefore, who thus abstained, was accounted *holy*, and placed in equal dignity with the High-Priest as to sanctity, not daring to pollute himself for his deceased father or mother. Such was the honour arising from abstinence from wine. (121)

CHAPTER XXIV.

Of the Causes and Reasons of the Precepts of the fourteenth Class.

THE precepts included in the fourteenth class, are those which we have reviewed in the tracts " Of Women," and " Of prohibited Marriages, and Incest."—The precept of " Circumcision" also must be referred to this class.

In the preceding pages we have indicated the general scope and intention of these precepts, and now descend to the particulars of them.

It must be acknowledged by every one, that man during the whole of life stands in need of friends, as Aristotle has shown in the ninth bookof his *Ethics.* (122) In prosperity, their company and conversation are pleasant; in adversity, needful; and in old age, advantageous. It is, however, principally among children and relatives that we meet with such love and friendship; and, among them only, that brotherly affection and mutual benevolence are perfected. For when a family are connected with each other by the same parents or ancestors, we generally find friendship, benevolence, and love reigning amongst them; and to promote these is one of the primary objects of the law.

On this account *Harlots* were prohibited. (Levit. xix. 29 ;—Deut. xxiii. 17.) For, by permitting them, families would have been confounded and destroyed, and their children have been regarded by all men as aliens, and have been disowned and neglected by their kindred and neighbours : and what misfortune worse than this could possibly befal them ?—Public brothels were therefore not allowed among the Israelites, that lust and wantonness might be checked, and the evils arising from them repressed. (123) Among the benefits resulting from this prohibition, it should also be noted, that it prevented many quarrels and contentions. For if prostitution had not been forbidden, it would frequently have happened that different men, meeting at the same time and place, would have contended for the same woman, and violent quarrels, if not murder either of the men or of the prostitute, would have ensued ; for so says the Scripture, (Jer. v. 7,) " They assembled by troops in the harlots' houses." (124) To guard, therefore, against such evils, and to preserve the distinctions of families, harlots, and whoremongers were condemned, and only *public marriages* allowed ; for if even *private marriages* had been permitted, some would have been found who would have introduced women into their houses, and called them their wives. It was, therefore ordained, that if a man had *privately* espoused a woman, the marriage should afterwards be *publicly* celebrated, as it is said of Boaz, (Ruth iv. 2,) " He took ten men of the elders of the city."

But because it sometimes occurred that they did not live together in peace and concord, so that the affairs of the family were prevented from being properly conducted, the husband was therefore permitted, in such cases, to *divorce* his wife and send her away: (Deut. xxiv. 1:) and lest, if this had been done by word only, or simply dismissing her, opportunity might have been afforded to any one to quit her husband's house and live in adultery, and she and the adulterer affirm that she had been previously divorced, it was commanded that no wife should be repudiated but by a *Bill of Divorcement*, as it is said, (Deut. xxiv. 1,) " Let him write her a bill of divorcement." (125)

The precept respecting *the Woman suspected of Adultery*, (Numb. v. 12,) was given because many men were apt to be jealous of their wives; for every married woman, being afraid of the waters of jealousy, was induced to act circumspectly and guard against every thing that might distress the heart of her husband ; for even the greater part of innocent women, and those who were conscious of rectitude, strove with all their power to avoid that disgrace, preferring death to the public shame of having their heads uncovered, their hair shorn, their garments torn down to their breasts, and themselves obliged to stand bound in the sanctuary

in the sight of the multitude, and the members
of the Great Sanhedrim; so that many great
and fatal evils destructive of domestic order
were prevented, through fear of the disgrace
attendant on the trial by the Waters of Jealousy.
(126)

If a virgin were seduced, the seducer was
obliged to marry her; (Exod. xxii. 16, 17;) for
since unmarried females might be married to
any one, he who had seduced her was, assuredly,
the most proper person to marry her, being
the most likely to conceal her dishonour and
pardon her crime. But if the damsel or her
parents objected to the marriage, he was only
bound to pay her the *Dowry of Virgins.* (127)
—In the case, however, of a *Rape,* the punishment inflicted was heavier; and if marriage took
place, the violater was not suffered to put away
his wife " all his days." (Deut. xxii. 29.)

The precept of the *Levirate,* or marriage with
a brother's widow, (Deut. xxv, 5,) was founded
on an ancient custom, which was in use before
the giving of the law, but which the law
retained, and added *the loosing of the Shoe,* &c.
(v. 9,) as ignominious and disgraceful actions
that might induce the brother-in-law to fulfil
his duty to his brother's widow, even when
otherwise reluctant: as it is written in the law,
(Deut. xxix, 9,) " So shall it be done unto that
man, that will not build up his brother's house :"
and again, (v. 10.) " His name shall be
called in Israel, *the house of him that hath his*

shoe loosed." (129) Such, indeed, is the nature of that justice and equity which we have received as an inheritance from Abraham, Isaac, and Jacob, that it renders a man unalterable in his words, inviolable in his engagements, and leads him to give to every one his due :—by which there is no difference betwixt the goods of our neighbour and our own, whether placed in our possession by barter, deposit, or interest; and by which there is, lastly, the same reason for the dowry of women, as for the wages of the hireling, acknowledging no difference betwixt him who unjustly withholds the hire of the labourer, or the lawful dowry of the wife; betwixt him who oppresses or seeks for opportunity to defraud the workman of his due, and him who attempts to deprive his wife of her dowry. An illustrious example of this equity and justice, as displayed in the Divine statutes and judgments, is afforded in the sentence against him *who defames his wife.* (Deut. xxii. 13, 14.) For it is certain, that the man cannot love his wife who brands her with infamy, nor does she find favour in his eyes. Had he dismissed her according to the law of divorce, no one would have hindered him; but in that case he would have been obliged to forfeit the dowry, which was what he sought to avoid, and hoped by bringing a reproach upon her, to retain the fifty shekels which the law of God fixed as the dowry of a virgin.—The Most High God, therefore, decreed that he should be fined double, (Deut. xxii, 19,)

" They shall amerce him in an hundred shekels of silver," according to the maxim of the law, that *he whom the judges condemn shall pay double unto his neighbour*, (Exod. xxii. 9,) as in the case of false witnesses. Thus, therefore, he who defamed his wife with an intention to save the fifty shekels he ought to have allowed her, was condemned to pay a hundred for unjustly withholding the sum which he was under obligation to give her ; and because he had attempted to injure her reputation and honour by an infamous report, the judges were to endeavour to apprehend him, and punish and deprive him of his authority and dignity, by scourging him with thongs made of an ox-hide, as it is said, (Deut. xxii. 18,) " They shall scourge (or chastise) him ;"—and because, in attempting to put her away, he had sought only the indulgence of his passions, and illicit gratification, on account of his dislike to her, he was obliged, as a punishment, to retain her as his wife, and " not put her away all his days." (130)—Thus, by these means, such depraved dispositions are cured, the Divine precepts themselves being the physicians. Nor are any of the manifest ends of justice or equity either exceeded or forgotten ; for what could be more equitable than the judgment respecting the man who defamed his wife in order to deprive her of her right ; or that of the thief who obtained his neighbour's goods by false pretences ; or lastly, that touching the false witness who designed the injury of another, although he did not accomplish his object? Of every one of these the judgment is the same. The wise ordination of God is, therefore, to be admired in his *Judgments*, as well as in his *Works ;* and so saith the Scripture, (Deut. xxxii, 4,) " His work is perfect :" for as his works are most perfect, so his judgments are most righteous. But our minds are too limited to comprehend either the perfection of his works or the equity of his judgments; for whether we study the bodies of animals, or the motions of the celestial spheres, we can apprehend only parts of his works; so in like manner we can apprehend but little of his judgments; and that of which we are ignorant, far exceeds that which we know, with regard to both of them.

But to return to our former subject. Every kind of illicit Concubinage was prohibited, in order to check unlawful desires, restrain libidinous gratifications, and immoderate indulgence even in lawful pleasures ; and if temperance were enjoined in that which was according to nature and permitted by the law of God, how much more strictly ought that to be forbidden which is unnatural, detestable and filthy, and only intended to gratify the most insatiable lust, as *sodomy* and *bestiality!* (Levit. xviii, 22, 23 ; xx, 13, 15.)

Reasons of a similar nature existed also for the prohibition of *incestuous marriages ;* (Lev. xviii ;) for the persons forbidden to be married to each other, being such as usually lived together in the same house, opportunity for criminality would be easily found, and though associating with each other the judge could not have separated them from each other ; so that if such persons could have married, like others who were free and disengaged, and no punishment had been affixed to their marriage, the greater part of men would have been in danger of living in a state of constant inchastity. By the absolute prohibition, therefore, of all such marriages, under the heaviest denunciations of death by the House of Judgment and of Excision, without the least licence or permission to be hoped for, every one knew that he ought cautiously to guard against any such intention, or even suffering the thought to rest in his mind. For, that incestuous intercourse might easily take place among the persons forbidden to marry with each other, is certain ; since a man who has a wife, has very generally her mother, or grandmother, or daughter, or niece living with them, and is in their company on almost all occasions; and, on the other hand, the wife frequently converses with her husband's brothers, or father, or son. It is also as clear as the light, that a man brought up among his sisters, and aunts, and other relatives must be very generally in their company. On these accounts, therefore, all marriages betwixt near relations was forbidden. (131)

Another reason for prohibiting such marriages, I apprehend, was to recommend modesty and chastity. For such an union betwixt the *root*

X

and the *branch* is the most glaring profligacy; for instance, for a man to marry his mother or daughter; therefore, *marriage betwixt root and branch* was forbidden. Nor does it constitute any difference whether the *root* marry the *branch*, or the *branch* the *root*, or whether they meet in marriage with a third person as when any one marries *both root and branch*. On this account, a man was forbidden to marry a woman and her daughter; or, the wife of the father and the wife of the son, because these were marriages to *root* and *branch*.—*Brothers* were considered as *root* and branch; and it was, therefore, forbidden to marry a Wife's Sister and a Brother's Wife, because this was uniting two individuals to a third person, who were, as it were, root and branch.

Besides, since marriage among brothers was considered as *root* and *branch*, and even as one body, and was therefore forbidden; it was likewise forbidden to marry a *Mother's Sister*, because she was regarded as being the same as a Mother; and a *Father's Sister*, who was considered as near as a Father.—But as neither a *Father's Brother's Daughter*, nor a *Father's Sister's Daughter* were forbidden, so for the same reason neither a *Brother's Daughter* nor a *Sister's Daughter* were forbidden. But the reason why the *Father's Brother* was permitted to marry the *Wife of the Brother's Son*, and yet the *Brother's Son* forbidden to marry his *Father's Brother's Wife*, is the same as that which has already been given, namely, that the Brother's Son was usually much in the house of his Father's Brother, and his familiarity and association with his Father's Brother's Wife, equal to that which he had with his Brother's Wife; whilst the Father's Brother did not so commonly live in the house of his Brother's Son, nor was there equal intimacy betwixt the Father's Brother, and the Brother's Son's Wife: and is it not also easy to be seen, that it was because there was the same freedom and intercourse betwixt a *Father* and his *Son's Wife*, and the *Son* and the *Father's Wife*, that they were equally prohibited from marriage with each other under penalty of the same kind of death?

It is unnecessary to enter into any particular discussion respecting the prohibitory precepts relating to intercourse with a Wife *during her separation*, and with *the Wife of another Man*, (Levit. xviii, 19, 20,) since the reasons of them must be evident to every one. For, every impure imagination and thought, as well as every immodest word, or look, and action, are altogether condemned; and if we have been led unintentionally into thinking on such subjects, it becomes our duty to turn our thoughts to other objects resolutely and perseveringly, until we have succeeded in banishing the unchaste thoughts from our mind. Hence, the saying of our Wise Men:—" My son, if impurity meet thee, force it to school; if it be iron, melt it; if it be flint, break it to pieces; as it is said, " Is not my word like as a fire, saith the LORD; and like a hammer that breaketh the rock in pieces?" (Jer. xxiii, 29.)—He addresses these words to his son, by way of reproof and direction; as if he had said, " When thou art tempted to impurity and distressed by it, go into the school:— there thou mayest read, and learn, and inquire, and dispute, and thy trouble shall cease."—Nor are such admonitions as these confined to the law, but are also urged by moralists and philosophers; thus Aristotle, in his *Ethics* and *Rhetoric*, calls those who are given to appetite and lust,—" Worthless Men ;" and speaks of the " Touch" as the sense, which is the approbium of our nature, by inciting to drunkenness, gluttony, and lust.

To the same excellent and distinguished principle of purity, a virtue worthy of universal imitation, may be traced the injunctions of our Wise Men to shun the sight of any object likely to excite impure feelings.＊ This also appears to me to be the reason why God forbade " cattle to gender with a diverse kind ;" (Levit. xix, 19;) for it is certain, that no creature, generally speaking, hath a desire to mix with a creature of another kind ; and, therefore, men ought not to promote such desires, and our law guarded every

＊ " Secundum excellentem et præstantissimam hanc, omnibus meritò sectandum, virtutem præceperunt quoque nobis Sapientes nostri, ne intueamur jumenta et volucres eo momento et tempore, quo carnaliter commiscentur."

Israelite against laying aside his dignity and honour, by submitting to corrupt and immodest conduct, which was not suffered to be named, except from necessity, and assuredly no necessity existed for the heterogeneous mixtures of animals. I think it even probable, that this was the very reason for prohibiting animals of different species being yoked together in labour, as when the law says, (Deut. xxii, 10,) " Thou shalt not plough with an ox and an ass together ;" because, if thus yoked, they might at one time or other mix with each other, and these two kinds of animals were named from being in most common and frequent use, but were intended to represent all others.

In our opinion also, the principal reason for *Circumcision* was of a similar nature, and intended, not as some have conjectured, to supply a defect of nature, but a defect in morals; not to remove what was superfluous, but to restrain what was impetuous; and by a painful rite to check an evil propensity; for our father Abraham was the first who commenced the practice, of whom it is recorded how much he feared sin, and how holy and pious, and chaste he was in all his conduct. (134)

Another important reason for *Circumcision* was, that those of their own religion, that is, those who believed in *the Unity of God*, might have a certain mark to distinguish them from others, and unite them to each other; so that those who would have professed to belong to them, merely to gain some personal advantage, or to accomplish some sinister purpose te the injury of others, might be prevented by a rite, which was not like a slight scratch upon the arm, but so painful and difficult in its nature, that no one would suffer it to be performed, either on himself or his children, but on account of his faith and religion.

Besides this, we constantly see how intensely those are attached to each other, and how ready they are to aid one another, who have a common sign of being in covenant. In like manner, *Circumcision* is the covenant made by our father Abraham, upon the faith of the Unity of God; and all who are circumcised, enter by it into the covenant of Abraham, believing the Unity of God, as God hath said, (Gen. xvii, 7,) " I will be a God unto thee, and to thy seed after thee :"—and this reason is at least as strong and valid as the former, if not more so.

The reason for performing the rite of *Circumcision in Infancy* was threefold ; for, *first*, if it had been delayed until the infant had grown up, it perhaps might never have been done : *secondly*, because the operation was not so painful in an infant as in an adult, the skin more tender and the imagination less active,—an adult dreading and fearing every operation which is in prospect : and, *thirdly*, because the affection of parents for their children whilst only infants is seldom or never so strong, as when they have been longer associated with them; the faculty, which is the cause of parental affection, not being so powerfully impressed when an infant first sees the light, as when the child has been present with his parents for some years, for the impression on the mind increases by constantly seeing him, and therefore grows with its growth; but afterwards, as he advances farther into life, and attains to years of maturity, it decreases: consequently, if Circumcision had been deferred for two or three years, it would frequently happen that it would have been altogether neglected, through the affection of the parents for their children; but about the time of an infant's birth, the affection, especially of the father, to whom the precept is given, is not become strong.

Circumcision was also commanded to be performed on the *Eighth Day*, because all creatures, when recently born, are so extremely feeble, that they may be almost regarded as those that are not yet born, until the eighth day, when they begin to be numbered among those who see *the light of the world.* This is also remarked with reference to beasts, as it is said, (Exod. xxii. 30,) " Seven days it shall be with his dam ;" as if before the end of seven days it was only an abortion.—It is, therefore, clear and decisive, without any conjecture, that it was on this account that Circumcision was ordered to take place at the end of seven days. (135)

Animals which were to be offered in sacrifice, were not to be *castrated*, or similarly injured, as is expressly stated in the law, (Lev. xxii, 24,) since all things enjoined by the statutes and judgments were to be done justly and equitably. (136)—*Eunuchs,* and those who had received certain injuries, (Deut. xxiii, 1,) were forbidden to marry Israelites, because of the impropriety of and consequent sterility of such marriages. Neither was a *Bastard* suffered to marry an Israelite, that by the stigma affixed to the conduct of the parents, all inchastity might be repressed, and, the father see that, by the commission of such acts of wickedness, he brought an indelible stain upon the whole of his family. Indeed, the Seed of Israel has been honoured by every people and tongue, for holding illegitimate persons in contempt and refusing to marry them.

It was to promote the honour and dignity of the Priesthood, that the Priests were forbidden to marry a Prostitute or Profane Woman, or a woman who had been divorced from her husband. The *High-Priest* was not even permitted to marry a *Widow,* (Levit. xxi, 14,) or *one who had been espoused,* because he was the Principal and Head.

If *illegitimate persons* were forbidden to enter the congregation of the LORD, how much more Male and Female *Slaves?* (137)

The reason why it was forbidden to *contract marriages with other nations,* is assigned in the Scripture, when it says, (Deut. vii, 3; Exod. xxxiv, 16.) "Neither shalt thou make marriages with them; thy daughter thou shalt not give unto his son, nor his daughter shalt thou take unto thy son: for they will turn away thy son from following me, that they may serve other gods."

The great multitude of precepts, the special reasons of which are concealed from us, were undoubtedly given, in general, to separate us from idolatry; and the reason why in certain cases we do not discover the benefit arising from any particular precepts, is, because those things we learn from report are not as well understood as those which we know from personal observation. On this account, what we have learned concerning the rites of the Zabii from tradition and their books, is not as certain as what we have seen practised; and more especially so, as their sects and opinions have been blotted out for more than a thousand years. (138) But if, on the contrary, we had heard and known all their practices circumstantially, we should most certainly have discovered the reasons and wisdom of many of those sacrifices and purifications of which we are at present ignorant. I have, however, no doubt, but all those ordinances were enjoined in order to erase from the memory of man, those false and pernicious opinions, and to abolish those useless practices, which would have consumed our days in vanity: for those opinions prevented men from thinking upon and attending to the study and consideration of rational things, and left them no leisure for useful employments, as our Prophets have taught us. Thus Samuel (1 Sam. xii, 21,) has exhorted us, " Turn ye not aside; for then should ye go after vain things, which cannot profit or deliver, for they are vain :"—and Jeremiah, (ii, 8,) " They walked after things that do not profit :" and (xvi, 19:) " Surely our fathers have inherited lies, vanity, and things wherein there is no profit."—Consider, then, how corrupt and pernicious such a system must have been, and whether it was not necessary for every man to exert all his influence to destroy it ? —Such, therefore, was the design of the greater part of the precepts, being intended, as we have already shown, to banish those depraved opinions, and to lessen that excessive labour, and trouble, and fatigue to which those men were subjected in the worship of their gods; and even those precepts, whether negative or affirmative, the particular reasons of which are not known to us, are only so many remedies and medicines for diseases which then existed, but which, (thank God !) have not come to our knowledge, as every one will be convinced who possesses true perfection and knows the truth of what God has declared, saying, " I said not unto the seed of Jacob, seek ye me in vain." (Isaiah xlv, 19.)

We have now shown the particulars and reasons of this concluding class of precepts, and have left none of them untouched, except in a very few instances, the causes of which may be easily gathered from what we have written. —*The Reasons of the Precepts are ended.* (139)

NOTES

AND

ILLUSTRATIONS.

NOTES

AND

ILLUSTRATIONS.

NOTE I.—*Page* 143.

WHILST the Public Schools or Academies of the Jews continued to flourish in the East, the Doctors or Teachers of the Law were honoured with various distinctions and titles, and treated with the most profound respect ; but since the destruction of their schools in Mesopotamia, about the year 1040, by the Mohammedan princes, the men of learning and those who minister in the synagogues, assume only the title of *Rabbi* or *Wise-Man.*

The implicit confidence formerly placed in their Doctors, or Wise-Men, will be sufficiently demonstrated by observing that a *Wise-Man* took the precedency of the King, and that it was proverbially said of their instructions, that " The words of the Elders are weightier than the words of the Law."—See Basnage's *Hist. of the Jews*, B. iii. Chap. 29. p. 256, folio.—Lewis's *Antiquities of the Hebrew Republic*, Vol. i. B. ii. Ch. 22. p. 237, 8vo.—Lightfoot, Horæ Heb. *Works*, Vol. ii. p. 199, folio.

NOTE II.—*Page* 143.

THE judicious HOOKER expresses himself on this subject with his usual ability and learning.—" Because the point about which we strive is, the quality of our laws, our first entrance hereinto cannot better be made than with consideration of the nature of law in general, and of that law which giveth life unto all the rest which are commendable, just, and good, namely the Law whereby the Eternal himself doth work.— All things that are, have some operation not violent or casual. Neither doth any thing ever begin to exercise the same, without some fore-conceived end for which he worketh : and the end which it worketh for is not obtained, unless the work be also fit to obtain it by. For unto every end every operation will not serve. That which doth assign unto each thing the kind, that which doth moderate the force and power, that which doth appoint the form and measure of working, the same we term a *law*. So that no certain end could ever be obtained, unless the actions whereby it is attained were regular, that is to say, made suitable, fit, and correspondent unto their end, by some canon, rule or law; which thing doth first take place in the works even of God himself. All things therefore do work after a sort according to law: all other things according to a law whereof some superior unto whom they are subject is Author; only the works and operations of God have him both their Worker, and for the law whereby they are wrought. The being of God is a kind of Law to his working: for that perfection which God is, giveth perfection to that he doth. The wise and learned amongst the very Heathens themselves have all acknowledged some first cause, whereupon originally the being of all things dependeth. Neither have they otherwise spoken of that cause, than as an Agent which knowing *what* and *why* it worketh, observeth in working a most exact *Order* or *Law*. This much is signified by that which Homer mentioneth, Διος δ' ετελειἰο, 'Jupiter's counsel was accomplished :'—thus much acknowledged by Mercurius Trismegistus, τον παντα κοσμον εποιησεν ο Δημιεργος ε χερσιν αλλα λογω, 'The Creator made the whole world, not with hands, but by reason,' *(Stob. in eclog. phys.)*—thus much confest by Anaxagoras and Plato, terming the Maker of the world an *Intellectual* worker.' Finally, the Stoics, although imagining the First Cause of all things to be fire, hold, nevertheless, that the same fire, having art, did, οδω βαδιζειν επι γενεσει κοσμε, 'proceed by a certain and a set way in the making of the world.' They all confess therefore in the working of the first cause, that *Counsel* is used, *Reason* followed, a *Way* observed, that is to say, constant *Order* and *Law* is kept, whereof itself must needs be author unto itself; otherwise it should have some worthier and higher to direct it, and so could not itself be the first. Being the first, it can have no other than itself to be the author of that Law which it willingly worketh by: God, therefore, is a Law both to himself, and to all others. God worketh nothing without cause. All those things which are done by him, have some end for which they are done; and the end for which they are done, is a reason of his will to do them. His will had not inclined to create Woman, but that he saw it could not be well if she were not created, *Non est bonum,* ' It is not good man should be alone ;' (Gen. ii, 18;) therefore, let us make an helper for him. That, and nothing else, is done by God, which to leave undone were not so good. If, therefore, it be demanded, why God having power and ability infinite, the effects notwith-standing of that power are all so limited as we see they are ?, the reason hereof is, the end which he hath proposed, and the law whereby His wisdom hath stinted the effects of His power, in such sort, that it doth not infinitely, but correspondently unto that end for which it worketh, even all things, χρηςως, in most decent and comely sort, all things in *measure, number and weight.* The general end of God's external working, is the exercise of his most glorious and abundant virtue: which abundance doth show itself in variety, and for that cause this variety is often-times in Scripture exprest by the name of *riches,* (Eph. i. 7, —Phil. iv.19,—Coloss. ii. 3.)—' *The* LORD *hath made all things for his own sake.'* (Prov. xvi. 4.)—Not that any thing is made to be beneficial unto him, but all things for him to show beneficence and grace in them. The particular drift of every act proceeding externally from God, we are not able to discern, and therefore cannot always give the proper and certain reason of his works. Howbeit, undoubtedly, a proper and certain reason there is of every finite work of God, inasmuch as there is a law imposed upon it, which, if there were not, it should be infinite even as the Worker himself is. They err, therefore, who think that of the will of God to do this or that, there is no reason besides his Will. Many times no reason known to us; but that there is no reason thereof, I judge it most unreasonable to imagine, inasmuch as he worketh all things κατα τον βυλην τυ ϑελημαῖος αυτυ, not only according to his own will, but *the counsel of his own will:* (Eph. i, 2 :) and whatsoever is done with counsel or wise resolution, hath, of necessity, some reason why it should be done, albeit that reason be to us in some things so secret, that it forceth the wit of man to stand, as the Blessed Apostle himself doth, amazed thereat, *O the depth of the riches, both of the wisdom and knowledge of God ? How unsearchable are his judgments ?"* &c. (Rom. xi, 33.)—*Ecclesiasticall Politie,* pp.3—5. Lond. folio.

NOTE III.—*Page* 145.

BERESCHITH RABBA is the title of two Commentaries on the Book of GENESIS: the earlier of them composed by R. Ushaia, the disciple of R. Judah Hakkadosh, or *the holy,* who collected the *Mishna,* and was written about A. D. 210. The other was compiled by R. Bar Nachman, who flourished about A. D. 300. This has been printed in Italy, at Venice, and Constantinople; and in 1608, at Cracow, with another celebrated Commentary entitled *Mattanoth-Chehunnah.* The *Bereshith Rabba* is chiefly a collection of explanations of the Mishna, and of allegorical and historical expositions by former Rabbis. —BUXTORFII *Bibliotheca Rabbinica,* p. 43, Franeq. 1696, *8vo.*

NOTE IV.—*Page* 146.

BESIDES the Mishnical treatises, and especially the tract *Cholin* in the *Seder Kedashim,* the Jews have another small treatise on *Butchery,* in which, according to Buxtorf, the most special and important regulations are recorded. To this book they constantly refer, and if a case of difficulty occur consult some learned Rabbin. When any one has for a considerable time attended one who practises butchery, and received a certificate of his attendance and attention, and has diligently studied and become accurately acquainted with this treatise, he is promoted by the Rabbi to the office of Butcher, and a diploma or testimonial granted him, certifying that he is skilled in the art of Butchery, and granting him permission to exercise it when and where he pleases. " I have seen," says this author, " one of these Testimonials conceived in the following terms: —"THIS day [the month and year also being expressed] I have tried and examined the worthy and excellent N. son of N. and have found him expert and diligent, both in the knowledge and practice of the art of Butchery, I therefore, hereby, grant him permission to kill and inspect cattle; and allow whatsoever he kills and inspects to be freely eaten. Nevertheless, with this injunction, that for the space of one whole year from the present time he shall once in each week diligently read over the

Rites of Slaying and Inspection; that in the second year he shall read over that treatise once in each month ; and that during the rest of his life he shall read it once in every three months."
"Witness Rabbi N—."

Buxtorfii Synagoga Judaica, Cap. xxxvi, pp. 612, 613. Basil. 1661, 8vo.—See also Surenhusii Mischna. Tom, v. *Tractatus de Profanis,* pp. 114—154. Amstel. 1702, folio.—Lewis's Antiq. Heb. Rep. Vol. 3, B. 6, ch. 20, p. 216,—and Wotton's Miscellaneous Discourses, Vol. 1, p. 151.

NOTE V.—*Page* 148.

THE *written* Law, contained in the Pentateuch, is distributed by Jewish lawyers into 613 Precepts. Of these, 365 prohibit unlawful things, and are termed *negative ;* the remaining 248 enjoin things to be done, and are called *affirmative* precepts. These only have the power and authority of Law, and form the foundation of the whole Jewish jurisprudence ; but since these could not be applied to every case that might arise, so as to decide correctly in every instance, hence originated, as subsidiary aids, the Constitutions of the Prophets and Wise Men, the Decrees of the Sanhedrim, the Decisions of the Judges, and the Expositions of the Doctors, similar to the Rescripts of the Emperors, and the Responsa Prudentium or opinions of the Civilians, of the Roman Civil Law ; or the Legal Reports of British Courts of Judicature.—These subsidiary judgments constitute the Jewish *Oral Law,* pretended to have been transmitted by Moses to Joshua, and by him to the Elders, and from them conveyed by traditionary relation to the time of Judah Hakkadosh, the compiler of the Mishna. Prideaux, Præfat. in R. Moses Maimonides De Jure Pauperis, Oxon. 1679, 4to.—See also Prelim. Diss. I. of the present work, *page* 22.

NOTE V.—*Page* 155.

SEE Dissertation II, On the Zabii.—*Page* 36.

NOTE VI.—*Page* 155.

CUTH or CUTHA, afterwards called Chaldea, appears to have derived its name from the Patriarch *Cush,* and by an

Y

interchange of letters, frequent in the Babylonish dialect, to have been denominated *Cûth* or *Cûtha*. Hence the Samaritans were called *Cuthites* by the Jews, because, when Shalmaneser, King of Assyria, had besieged and carried captive the inhabitants of the city of Samaria, he re-peopled the city with people from various countries, among whom were the *Cuthites*. From the hatred subsisting between the Jews and Samaritans, the Jews not unfrequently applied the term, by way of contempt, to the Gentiles in general.—Hyde, De Vet. Pers. C. ii. pp. 36–40.

NOTE VII.—*Page* 156.

THE *Nabathæans* were a people of Arabia Petræa, strongly addicted to the Zabian idolatries and superstitions. The learned HAMMER, Secretary to the Imperial Legation at Constantinople, has translated into English from the Arabic, a curious work on " *Ancient Alphabets and Hieroglyphic Characters*," written by Ahmad Bin Abubekr Bin Wahshih, by birth a Nabathæan, but by profession a Mohammedan, who flourished in the ninth century, and translated several of the books of the ancient Nabathæans into Arabic. In the work already mentioned, he has presented the reader with the old Nabathæan hieroglyphic, secret, or magical alphabet, as well as several other hieroglyphical alphabets made use of by the ancient Chaldeans, Sabæans, or Zabii, &c.—See Hammer's Ancient Alphabets and Hieroglyphic Characters explained. London, 1806, 4*to.*

NOTE VIII.—*Page* 156.

THE following legendary story taken from the *Bereshith Rabba*, is translated by the animated pen of Hyman Hurwitz in his " Hebrew Tales:"

ABRAHAM being brought before *Nimrod*, was urged by the tyrant to worship the fire. " Great King," said the Father of the Faithful, " would it not be better to worship *water*? It is mightier than fire, having the power to extinguish it."— " Worship the water then," said Nimrod. — " Methinks," rejoined Abraham, " it would be more reasonable to worship the *clouds*, since they carry the waters, and throw them down upon the earth."—" Well, then," said the impatient king, " worship the clouds, which, by thine own confession, possess great power."—" Nay," continued Abraham, " if power is to be the object of adoration, the preference ought to be given to the *wind*, which, by its greater force, scatters the clouds and drives them before it."—" I see," said Nimrod, " we shall never have done with this prattler. Worship the wind, then, and we will pardon thy former profanations."—" Be not angry, great King," said Abraham, " I cannot worship the fire, nor the water, nor the clouds, nor the wind, nor any of the things thou callest *gods:* The power they possess is derived from a Being, not only most powerful, but full of *Mercy* and *Love*. The Creator of heaven and earth. Him alone will I worship." —" Well then," said the tyrant, " since thou refusest to adore the fire, thou shalt speedily be made sensible of its mighty force."—He ordered Abraham to be thrown into a fiery furnace. But God delivered him from the raging flames, and made him a source of blessing to many nations.—Hurwitz's Hebrew Tales, p. 142.

NOTE IX.—*Page* 157.

THE doctrine of an *Anima Mundi*, or soul of the world, was maintained also by the Stoics and other ancient sects: *Manilius*, who flourished in the reign of Augustus, in his astronomical poem on the *Sphere*, thus states their sentiments :

——————GOD, the World's Almighty Soul,
By secret methods rules and guides the whole;
By unseen passes, he himself conveys
Through all the mass, and every part obeys.
To proper patients he kind agents brings :
In various leagues binds disagreeing things.
Makes some powers act, and some receive their force ;
And thus whilst Nature keeps her vital course,
Though different powers the several things divide,
The world seems one, and all its parts allied.

MANILIUS. B. I. vi.

In a curious work on " Ancient Alphabets and Hiero-glyphics," written in Arabic by IBN WAHSHIH, and translated by M. JOSEPH HAMMER, there is the subjoined singularly formed Hieroplyphic symbol, called by Kircher, *Anima Mundi.*

Of this symbol, the author says, " This figure is expressive of the most sublime secret, called originally, *Bahumed* and *Kharuf,* (or Calf,) viz. *The Secret of the Nature of the World,* or *The Secret of Secrets,* or *The Beginning and Return of every thing.*"—On which, M. Hammer remarks: " It is superfluous to recall here to the memory of the reader the great antiquity and mysterious sense of the idolatrous veneration in which the *Calf* has been continually held ;—or to repeat any thing that has been said on the worship of *Apis* in Egypt, renewed by the Israelites in the worship of the *Calf,* and preserved, at this moment, in the mysterious rites of the Druses. Let us remember only a circumstance which shows wonderfully the concordance and relation of the name of *Bahúmíd* and its translation.—*Bahumed* or *Bahumet* is related, in the History of the Templars, to have been one of their secret and mysterious formulas, with which they addressed the idol of a *Calf* in their secret assemblies. Different etymological explanations and descriptions of this word have been brought forward, but none surely so satisfactory as this, which proves that the Templars had some acquaintance with the hieroglyphics, probably acquired in Syria."—Hammer's Ancient Alphabets and Hieroglyphic Characters explained. London, 1806, 4to. Pref. p. xiii. and pp. 22, 23.

NOTE X.—*Page* 157.

In subsequent ages, Aristotle, and other Philosophers, defended the erroneous position, and believed that "the world was eternal, without beginning or end."—Enfield's History of Philosophy, vol. i. B. ii. Ch. ix. Sect. 1.

NOTE XI.—*Page* 157.

Ibn Wahshih says, "The Chaldeans were the wisest men of their times, being well acquainted with every science and art. Their first equals and rivals were the *Curds*. But, however, there is as great a difference between these two nations, as between a glow-worm and a fixed star. The first superiority the *Curds* had over them, was in agriculture and botany. They pretended to descend from the sons of *Bineshad*, and to have got possession of the books of ADAM on *Agriculture*, and of the books of *Safrith* and *Coothami*. They pretended to have all the seven antediluvian books inspired by heaven.—They pretended to possess the art of magic and talismans, but this is not so; for all these sciences were handed down to them from the Chaldeans, who first cultivated them. This pretension to the antiquity of their learning, is the reason of the inveterate hatred between the *Chaldeans* and *Curds*."—Hammer's Ancient Alphabets, &c. p. 52.

NOTE XII.—*Page* 159.

The remarks of Dr. Boothroyd on the different terms applied to those who practised divination in some or other of its forms, deserve attention.—"Connected with the worship of Idols," he observes, "were the various practices of augury, divination, soothsaying, &c.—The most general expression for *Divining* is קסם (*Kasas.*) It denotes either to attempt to foretel events by some kind of arts, or to conjecture by prudence and experience. (Comp. Deut. xviii. 10. with Prov. xvi.

10, and Isai. iii. 2.)—*Michaelis* thought it denoted the Harus-
pex, one who divined by inspecting the liver and other viscera
of sacrificed animals; *Dathe*, divining by the lot; and *Rosen-
müller*, divining by arrows. (Ezek. xxi. 26.) I am satisfied
that it denotes rather the Act of Divination in general, some
of the various kinds being afterwards mentioned; as,—
1. *Observer of the Clouds.*—By the appearance of the clouds
and of the sky, the state of the weather may often be conjectured; and from this, perhaps, arose the practice of pretending to foretell other events.—2. *Enchanter,* one who divined
by serpents; probably, having tamed them, he divined by
their motions. *Bates* renders ' Juggler.'—3. *Sorcerer,* one
who divined by using some kind of drugs.—4. *Charmer,* one
who composed magical spells, to guide and protect. It is
probable that they were composed in verse; which the people
repeated. (Psalm lviii. 6.)—5. *Ventriloquist* or *Pythonist.*—
6. *Wizard.*—7. *Necromancer.*—The Greek Translators uniformly render the first term as I have done: and, I suspect,
that those who possessed this art, were also denominated
Wizards, or the Knowing Ones, and Necromancers, as pretending to consult the dead. (1 Sam. xxiii. 7, &c.)—That
persons possessing this art would be regarded as under some
kind of Divine influence, by an ignorant race, is very natural;
and it is not improbable, that they might believe themselves
to be so. Similar superstitious arts obtained among all the
heathen nations, and still exist among them, and even among
ignorant men in Christian countries."—Boothroyd's New
Family Bible and Improved Version, Introd. Part iii, Ch. vi,
p. 52, vol. i. Pontefract, 1818, 4*to.*

NOTE XIII.—*Page* 162.

THIS is the same author whose work on *Ancient
Alphabets and Hieroglyphic Characters* has been translated from
the Arabic by the learned *Hammer*, Secretary to the Imperial
Legation at Constantinople.—By Hammer, his name is given
as, AHMAD BIN ABUBEKR BIN WAHSHIH, and by abbreviations,
IBN WAHSHIH. Kircher calls him *Aben Vaschia* and *Aben
Wahschia.*—He was a Nabathæan by birth, and though a
Mohammedan, translated several works from his native tongue
into Arabic, amongst which are enumerated, one on Scientific

Instruction, entitled, *The Tree of Paradise,* another on Natural Magic, treating of the knowledge of the particular properties of plants, metals, animals, &c. entitled *Taufinút, that is, Putrefactions :* and the one referred to by Maimonides, deemed the most classical of their Agricultural works, called, *The Agriculture of the Nabathœans.* Besides these, he also translated two works from the *Curdic* language into Arabic, one of them, *On the Culture of the Vine and the Palm tree;* the other, *On Water, and the Means of finding it out in unknown Ground.* But that which we are inclined to regard as his most important work is the treatise on *Ancient Alphabets and Hieroglyphic Characters,* in which he has furnished the reader with much curious and recondite information on these subjects; and which completely proves the astonishing influence and extent of the Zabian astrological and idolatrous superstitions.—This laborious performance, which occupied him twenty-one years, he deposited in the treasury of the Calif *Abd-ul-malik bin Marwân,* in the 241st year of the *Hijrah,* about A. D. 863.—The translation by M. Hammer is beautifully printed, with the Arabic text, at the press of Bulmer and Co. in 4*to.*

NOTE XIV.—*Page 163.*

Landseer, in his *Sabœan Researches,* has attempted to show that the word *Ashre,* rendered " Groves" in our translation of the Scriptures, means a kind of Orrery or Armillary Machine used for purposes of divination; and supposes them to have been probably about the height of a man, with small balls branching off curvedly from the sustaining rod or axis; and referring to 2 Kings xxi, he says, " The Sabæan Ashre appears to have been erected within the precincts of the temple, where the altars also were built; but besides this—perhaps immoveable—armillary machines, which, for the purpose of divination, Manasseh had constructed in the courts of the temple, he had also a small copy, or 'graven image' of the Ashre within ;—doubtless to assist in the celebration of those Sabæan rites, which were performed in the interior during his idolatrous reign, and which are described by Ezekiel : For there can be no reasonable doubt, that the idolatries which the Prophet saw in vision on the banks of the Chebar, were those with which the temple at Jerusalem had really been polluted."— Landseer's Sabæan Researches, pp. 262—307.

It is certain that the word translated " Groves," cannot always be interpreted to mean a *Grove of Trees*, since we read of "setting up Groves under every green tree;" (2 Kings xvii. 8. &c.;) nor always strictly designated an *Image*, for we also read that the people " made them molten images,—and made a *grove*, and worshipped all the host of heaven,—and used divination!" (v. 16.)—See also Judges vi. 25, 26, 28, 30 ; 2 Kings xxiii. 4, &c. &c.—Hence, Selden supposes the term was used for the Images worshipped in the Groves, especially *Astarte* or *Venus:* Others have conjectured that as by *Baal* was meant the *sun*, so by *Asherah* or " Groves" was meant the *moon*, worshipped as the "Queen of Heaven".—Selden, De Diis Syris, edit. Bayer Syntag. 2, p. 160. Additamenta ad cap. 2, p. 286, Amstel. 1680, 8*vo.*—See also Dr. A. Clarke's Commentary on 2 Kings xxi. at the end.

It must, however, be admitted, that in some places the word is justly translated " Grove," as in Deut. xxi, 21. " Thou shalt not plant thee a grove of any trees near unto the altar of the Lord thy God."—" Trees," says, Dr. Gloster Ridley, " were the original temples of the gods ;—they were also the symbols or images of them ;—and their several attributes were expressed by several trees, which were perpetually appropriated to their respective deities, and called by their names ; and therefore addressed and appealed to, as if they had themselves the attributes and powers of their Prototypes, to hear the covenants made in their presence, and to punish the violaters of them."— MELAMPUS, Notes on, Canto iii, p. 259, Lond. 1781, 4*to.*

NOTE XV.—*Page* 164.

OF the truth of this assertion, and of the true origin of knowledge, especially that which relates to God and Divine things, I conceive every one must be satisfied who will read with candour and attention Gale's *Court of the Gentiles*, a work of immense learning and research ; Dr. Ellis's *Knowledge of Divine Things from Revelation, not from Reason or Nature*, a valuable work, though consequently imperfect from the Author dying before he had completed his design ; and the Analysis of Ellis's work and of Meiner's *Historia Doctrinæ de Vero Deo*, or History of Opinions relative to the True God, with the writer's own *Remarks*, given by Christie in his *Miscellanies: Philosophical, Medical and Moral*, London, 1789, 8vo. Of which it is to be regretted only one volume of this work was published, the dissertations in that volume affording ample proof of the great learning and talents of its author.

On the great difficulty of discovering the one true God by the efforts of reason, it has been well observed, that it is the most difficult of all truths, and that which the human mind will last of all be able to attain. For, unless a man had found out the magnitude, order, and motions of the celestial bodies, and the revolutions of time;—unless, by the continual study of nature he had discovered that the forms and qualities of plants, and animals, and men, were all exactly such as they ought to be, so that nothing could have been more proper for use, or more beautiful and excellent in its kind;—unless he clearly perceived that this glorious frame of nature could not exist without a cause, nor be caused by fortune, chance, necessity, or the blind efforts of some unintelligent nature;— unless, in short, he saw that there was nothing in the whole universe that could, with any reason, be censured or blamed, and was convinced that all those things which terrify the vulgar, tempests, snow, hailstones, earthquakes, fires, diseases, yea, and the vices of men themselves, all tended to the perfection of the universe, and the good of the whole, so that nature could not exist without these very things, which are regarded as evils;—unless human nature had attained the knowledge of all these high and difficult truths, it could not have discovered the One supremely Excellent Mind, the wise and good Creator of universal nature.—But, " Who is sufficient for these things?" Can we conceive that any nation, or any philosopher, by the mere efforts of feeble erring reason, ever attained this perfect knowledge of the universe—this power of explaining every phenomenon, solving every doubt, and answering every objection?—As nothing is absolutely perfect but God himself, none of his works can give a complete idea of him; and as they are all imperfect in themselves, so they are still more imperfectly comprehended by our narrow minds. The works of nature are, indeed, a path that leads to God; but what is a path, unless there be a light from heaven, to show the traveller how to keep it? Without this directing beam, man would never arrive at the end of his journey, but be for ever bewildered amidst the intricacies of the way, and "find no end, in wandering mazes lost."

The difficulty of discovering the one true God, appears also most remarkably from this circumstance, that even the Jews and Christians to whom he was revealed, and to whom his existence was confirmed by innumerable testimonies, were not able to retain this high knowledge, but have been continually deviating into idolatry and the worshipping of false deities and inferior gods. What was so difficult for men to preserve, when communicated to them, could scarcely have been within their power to find out. If Jehovah be exalted so *high* above our feeble grasp, where is the man who will say, that he first stretched his arm to heaven, and brought him down to earth and comprehended him? Surely we may ask with the sacred writer—" Canst thou by searching find out God?—canst thou find out the Almighty to perfection? It is as high as heaven; what canst thou do? deeper than hell, what canst thou know? The measure thereof is longer than the earth, and broader than the sea." (Job xi, 7—9.)

Two testimonies shall conclude this long note, the former of an heathen, the latter of an infidel.—PLATO says, (Epinom.) " This is established most clearly, and on the firmest grounds, that when men first began to think concerning the gods—what they were, and how they existed and employed themselves— their opinions on these subjects were not taken up from the ideas and reasoning of learned *men*."—And the historian HUME remarks,—" It appears to me, that if we consider the improvements of human society, from rude beginnings to a state of greater perfection, polytheism or idolatry was, and *necessarily must have been*, the first and most ancient religion of mankind. —'Tis a matter of fact incontestible, that, about 1700 years ago, all mankind were idolaters. The doubtful and sceptical principles of a few philosophers, or the theism, and that too not entirely pure, of one or two nations, form no objection worth regarding."—Essays, Nat. Hist. of Religion, vol. ii. p, 417.

See CHRISTEE's MISCELLANIES pp. 343—348, 377 ;—and an ingenious and ably written pamphlet by George Redford, A.M., entitled, *The True Age of Reason; or A Fair Challenge to Deists.* Lond. 1821.

NOTE XVI.—*Page 165.*

THIS may be regarded as a curious illustration of Ezek. viii, 14, and certainly more accordant as a legendary tradition with the superstitions of the Zabii, than the more modern explanation of the "Women weeping for Tammuz," which refers it to the festival held in commemoration of the death of *Adonis,* who was slain by a boar.—ADONIS is fabled to have been a beautiful youth beloved by Venus, and killed by a wild boar in Mount Lebanon, from whence sprang, according to the story, the river *Adonis* said to run with *blood* at the time of the year when his festival was held, a story probably occasioned by a *red ochre,* over which the river ran with violence by its usual increase at this season of the year. The women of Phœnicia, Assyria, and Judea, mourned for Adonis at that period, as being dead, wearing the most obscene images, and prostituting themselves in honour of him, paying the price to the temples of Venus. After mourning his loss for a certain time, his return to life was announced, and the mourners indulged in the most extravagant joy.—It is not improbable, but that this was frequently connected with the mourning of the Egyptians for Osiris, who was said to have been slain by Typhon, and whose death was mourned by the Egyptian women in a similar manner, and the mourning followed by a festival of joy.—*Milton* has wrought up the story of Adonis with great effect in the following lines;—

————THAMMUZ came next behind,
Whose annual wound in Lebanon allur'd
The Syrian damsels to lament his fate,
In am'rous ditties all a summer's day;
While smooth Adonis, from his native rock,
Ran purple to the sea, suffused with blood
Of Thammuz yearly wounded. The love tale
Infected Sion's daughters with like heat:
Whose wanton passions in the sacred porch
Ezekiel saw, when, by the vision led,
His eye surveyed the dark idolatries
Of alienated Judah.

PAR. LOST, B. i, p. 446.

Godwyn's Moses and Aaron, Lib. 4. c. 2.—Lewis's Antiq. Heb. Repub. vol. iii, B. v. ch. 20, p. 90—Dr. A. Clarke's Comment on Ezek. viii, 14.—Jahn's Biblical Archæology, translated by T. C. Upham, pp. 525, 526, Andover, (America,) 1823, *8vo.*

NOTE XVIII.—*Page* 166.

SEE the Dissertation VI., "On Talismans and Talismanic Figures."—*Page* 112.

NOTE XVIII.—*Page* 169.

MANILIUS, in his Poem on the Sphere, maintains this opinion, in the following lines,

THE God, or reason, which the orbs doth move,
Makes things below depend on signs above;
Though far removed, though hid in shades of night,
And scarce to be descried by their own light,
Yet nations own, and men their influence feel;
They rule the public, and the private will:
The proofs are plain.   Thus from a different star
We find a fruitful or a barren year;
Now grains increase, and now refuse to grow;
Now quickly ripen, now their growth is slow.
The moon commands the seas, she drives the main
To pass the shores, then drives it back again.
                                                    B. II.

NOTE XIX.—*Page* 170.

THESE public discourses of the Zabian priests, and their object, strongly remind us of the practices of the idolatrous priests of CEYLON, as related by *Harvard* in his interesting "Narrative of the Establishment and Progress of the Mission to Ceylon and India," &c. &c.—" The Man-doos, or temporary buildings of leaves, which are frequently erected in the country for Budhuist preaching, are termed *Banna-Mandooas,* or *Bible-Houses.* These buildings are in the form of Chinese pagodas, and tastefully ornamented. They contain two raised pulpits, from one of which the principal priest recites, sitting, from the Banas, in the Pali language; a subordinate priest occupies the other, who interprets the sentences to the people, as delivered, in the vernacular tongue.—As many priests are in attendance the services are continued for several successive nights; the congregations assembling after sun-set. The people sit during the service on their heels; and, with admirable patience, will continue in that posture several hours; occasionally expressing by a kind of chorus (which may be heard at a considerable distance) their admiration of the doctrines. The priests are carried to and from the pulpits on the shoulders of their disciples. The expense of erecting the Mando, and making the necessary preparations, is defrayed by the inhabitants of the neighbourhood. Great quantities of food are cooked and sent to the priests at their lodging-rooms, which are built expressly for their reception. Instead of stands for their lamps, at the public services, the natives will frequently undertake, as an act of merit, to bear them on their heads (each lamp weighing four or five pounds) during the whole night, and to supply it with oil from a bottle in the right hand, as occasion requires."

NOTE XX.—*Page 171.*

THE reason adduced by our author for the Mosaic Institutions, from their being intended to deliver the Israelites from the burdensome ceremonies of other rituals, may not, at first, appear of much force, to those who have been accustomed to the simplicity of the Christian system, but to those who have studied the rituals of many of the Pagan nations, and will compare them with that instituted by Moses, the argument will be found to be forcible and correct. See for instance, the *Essays, On the religious ceremonies of the Hindus,* by H. T. Colebrooke, Esq. inserted in vols. vi and vii of the *Asiatic Researches.*—From these essays it appears, that the *Vedas,* or sacred books, from which he extracted his account of the Hindu ceremonies, were composed more than a thousand years before the Christian era; and it may, therefore, be reasonably conjectured, that many of them would be similar to those in use among the still more ancient Zabian idolaters.

NOTE XXI.—*Page 173.*

SEE Note 4. p. 333, *ante.*

NOTE XXII.—*Page* 174.

On the Anatomical observations of Maimonides, I have been favoured with the following remarks by a medical friend, and am happy in being permitted to present them to the reader :—

"Maimonides is incorrect in supposing the Muscles are formed from fibres proceeding from the nerves.—Muscles constitute what is called the flesh of animals, and are composed of masses of fibres lying parallel with each other, and intermixed with a quantity of membranous matter. The muscles terminate in tendons, which connect them with the bones.—The tendons consist of longitudinal fibres of a very firm texture and closely united together. It is supposed that no nerves are sent to them. The nerves sent to the muscles are very considerable, especially to those which are under the control of the will, being greater in proportion to their size than to any other part of the body, except the organs of sense. Haller remarks, the nerves going to the thumb are more in quantity than those that supply the whole substance of the liver. It has been thought that each muscular fibre, or at least each of the smallest bundles into which the fibres are arranged, contains one of the ultimate branches of a nerve and artery.

"In opposition to the received opinion, Stuart thought that the muscular fibre was composed of a string of vesicles immediately formed from the substance of the nerves, which he conceived was similar to that of the tendons, and that these vesicles were covered by a net-work of blood-vessels.

"We have no proof that the Cerebellum and Spinal Cord are of firmer consistence than the Cerebrum. If we cut into the interior of the brain, we find it to be composed of two substances that differ in their colour and consistence—these have obtained the names of the cortical or cineritious, and the medullary matter. The cortical is on the outside, and is of a reddish brown colour: it is obviously of a softer consistence than the medullary part. Like the brain, the Spinal Cord posseses both medullary and cineritious matter, though their respective position is reversed.

" To the lower portion of the brain is attached a number of small white cords, called nerves,—bodies of a similar kind pass from the Spinal Cord,—the former (the Cerebral) generally supply the organs of Sense,—the latter are received by the Muscles:—both are disposed in pairs, and proceed in corresponding directions to the two sides of the body.

" The office of the nervous system is to produce sensation. The two specific powers that distinguish living from dead matter, are spontaneous motion and sensation,—the first confined to the muscles,—the latter to the brain and nerves. When a nerve is acted upon in such a manner that its appropriate power is incited, motion is not necessarily incited, but the animal feels. On the other hand, motion may be produced when unattended with sensation.—The two powers, therefore, motion and sensation, although in a great number of instances they are connected together, being reciprocally the cause of each other, may exist separately."

NOTE XXIII.—*Page* 182.

" THE history subsequent to the Exodus," says, Dr. D. G. Wait, " as well as the various legends preserved by the ecclesiastical writers, incline us to believe that the Israelites, during their residence in Egypt, had declined, to a certain extent, from their primitive faith; that the pomps, processions, and imposing ordinances of the country had usurped an influence over their minds, and had incapacitated them from wholly returning to the plain and unsophisticated system of their ancestors. The Epistle to the Galatians (iii, 19) assigns the origin of the Law to some defection of this nature. Yet, it seems, that at first they were again to be tried by a simple moral code; for those who retrace the Ten Commands to the vestiges of the patriarchal laws in Genesis, are supported by no inconsequential arguments ;—and had the Israelites not proved themselves, by their homage to the golden calf, to have been unworthy of these plain and intelligible requisitions, it is probable that the ceremonial parts, which were afterwards annexed to them, would have been less obscure and complicated ; but this early prepossession in favor of the Egyptians, signalized as their deliverance had been by manifest displays of Almighty power, and the watchful superintendence of the God of their ancestors, showed that their minds were not sufficiently elevated to receive moral precepts and religious doctrines, divested of those symbolical appendages in which the greater part of the world had enveloped them. But those ceremonies which God saw fit to accommodate to their preconceptions of religion, and to their recently acquired habits, at the time they obviated their prejudices, were directly contrasted with those by which the apostates had been diverted from the service of their Creator, and were eminently calculated to render the Israelites a distinct people; and as they became wearied of the yoke of their exactions, and warned by the consequences attending the violation of them, as well as enlightened by the calamities which they afterwards suffered from the votaries of these superstitions, many were, according to the Divine purpose, gradually prepared to adopt that more rational and intellectual system, which, in the fulness of time the Messiah was ordained to make known."—Dr. D. G. Wait's *Course of Sermons Preached before the University of Cambridge, in the year MDCCCXXV*, pp. 5—8, Lond. 1826, 8vo.

The opinion of Maimonides, that certain rites and ceremonies were copied from the Egyptians, in the formation of the Hebrew Ritual, has been maintained with great learning by Sir John Marsham, in his *Canon Chronicus*; and by Spencer in his celebrated work, *De Legibus Hebræorum*. This notion has, however, been successfully combated by Herman Witsius in his *Ægyptiaca;* and by J. Meyer in his *Tractatus de Temporibus et Festis Diebus Hebræorum.*—Dr. Woodward's *Discourse of the Wisdom of the Ancient Egyptians*, is justly characterised by Bishop Watson as "a short and able refutation of the notion maintained and defended by Spencer;"—and the recent *Course of Sermons* by Dr. Wait, from which the preceding extract has been made, presents the reader with several irrefutable arguments against the same opinion.

Without entering into any discussion on the subject, the writer may be allowed to express his conviction, that it is much more probable, that, whatever ceremonies were practised by the Egyptians similar to those existing among the Israelites, were originally derived either from patriarchal tradition and usage, or from the influence and religious services of "Joseph and his Brethren," during the period of their power and popularity; than that the Israelites adopted any of their sacred institutions from a nation whose chief deity was an *ox* and their inferior deities, cats, and beetles, and onions ;—who, notwithstanding all the eulogiums passed upon them, never attained in Literature to the use of *simple Alphabetical characters* ;* nor in Architecture, to the use of the *Arch* in any of their buildings, sacred or domestic;—and whose existing monuments are distinguished by massiveness and Cyclopean magnitude, and not by taste and elegance, either of form or sculpture.

NOTE XXIV.—*Page* 183.

WHEN the Jews repeat their prayers in the morning they make use of the garments with fringes called *Zizith,* and also the *Tephilin* or Phylacteries.—"As to the former," says David Levi, "it is to be observed, that every male of the Jewish nation is obliged to have a garment with fringes at the four corners thereof, as it is commanded in Numb. xv, 37, "And the Lord spake unto Moses, saying, Speak unto the children of Israel, and bid them that they make them fringes in the borders of their garments, throughout their generations, and that they put on the fringe of the borders a ribband † of blue, and it shall be unto you for a fringe, that ye may look upon it, and remember all the commandments af the Lord and do them."—"And every morning when they put on the said garments, they must take the fringes thereof in their hands and say the following grace : ' Blessed art thou, O Lord our God! King of the universe, who hath sanctified us with his commandments, and commanded us the commandment of the fringes !'

* I am not ignorant of the persevering and recondite labours of Dr. Young, and M. Champollion, in attempting to decypher the obscure symbols of Egyptian inscriptions, nor unwilling to grant them the praise so justly earned ; but, with every acknowledgment of the importance of their discoveries, it still remains the fact, that what is regarded, even by those learned men, as a species of alphabetical character, is too symbolical and complex for purposes of general learning.

† The Hebrew words mean a *thread* of blue, and not a ribband.—"Maimonides (in Hilcoth Zitzzis) says, that in making the Zizith, four threads are put through the eyelet hole at each corner, which being doubled make eight, one of which is to be blue, if it can be got."

Z

"This garment (the Zizith) is made of two square pieces, with two long pieces like straps joined to them, in order that one of the said square pieces may hang down before upon the breast, and the other behind; at the extremity of the four corners are fastened the fringes, [or tassels] by the means of five knots; which knots, with the eight threads of each finger are thirteen; and the numerical letters of the Hebrew word ציצת (Zizith) amount to 600, which added together make the number 613, which is exactly the number of precepts contained in the law."—LEVI's Ceremonies of the Jews, p. 183—185.

The *Tephilin* or Phylacteries are small slips of parchment or vellum, on which certain portions of the Law are written, inclosed in cases of parchment, or *black calf skin,* and tied about the forehead and left arm. The Jews consider them as a divine ordinance, and found their opinion on Exod. xiii, 9, and similar passages. The design of them is believed to have been, *first,* to put them in mind of those precepts which they should constantly observe; and *secondly,* to procure them reverence and respect in the sight of the Heathen. The *Phylacteries* or *Tephilin, for the head,* had four cavities, in every one of which is put a section of the law, written with great exactness, upon very fine vellum. These four sections are Deut. vi, 4—9; xi, 13—21; Exod. xiii, 1—10; and Exod. xiii, 11—16.—The *Tephilin,* or *Phylacteries for the arm,* have only one cavity. The same passages are inclosed in it, as in the head-phylactery, but written on one piece of vellum instead of four.— Dr. Lightfoot thinks it not unlikely, that our Saviour himself wore the Jewish *Tephilin* or Phylacteries, and the *Zizith* or Fringes, according to the custom of the nation; and that he did not condemn the *wearing* of them, but the pride and hypocrisy of the Pharisees in making them *broad* and visible, to obtain fame and esteem for their devotion and piety.

The *Mezuzoth* are portions of Scripture written with great care upon slips of vellum, and inclosed in cylindrical tubes of lead, or cane, or wood, and nailed to the door-posts of the Jewish houses. The portions of Scripture written on the slips of parchment are Deut. vi, 4—9; and Deut. xi, 13—21.— When these are rolled up, the name שדי, *Shaddai,* or *Almighty,* is inscribed upon them; and, being inclosed in the tube, are fastened to the door-posts.—See Levi's Ceremonies of the Jews, pp. 185—192, 213.—Leo of Modena's History of the Rites, &c. of the present Jews, &c. translated by E. Chilmead, P. i, c. 2, p. 5; c. 5, pp. 15, 16. Lond. 1650, 16mo.—For Engravings of the *Phylacteries* and *Mezuzah*, see the *Frontispiece* of this volume.

NOTE XXV.—*Page* 186.

" This is the specific reason assigned for its adoption into the Mosaic polity. ' In six days the Lord made heaven and earth, the sea, and all that in them is, and rested the seventh day: WHEREFORE the Lord blessed the Sabbath day, and hallowed it.' (Exod. xx. 11.) Great must have been the efficacy of this ordinance in restraining the Israelites from idol worship, the besetting sin of that stubborn people. Being instituted in memory of the work of creation, every act of compliance with the command was a virtual acknowledgment of the one Jehovah, in opposition to the numerous false deities of surrounding nations. The remission of their worldly employments on the seventh day, naturally called to remembrance God's creating the world in six days, and resting on the seventh. In the constant renewal of this recollection, their minds must have been as constantly impressed with the first and fundamental truth of all religion, the unity and omnipotence of the Deity. With every returning Sabbath, their thoughts were directed to the Supreme Being, who, existing eternally, infinite in his perfections, and the Creator of the universe, was alone deserving their praise, their reverence and worship."—To which we may add, that, " as such a memorial, the Sabbath is of equal utility to all mankind, and will continue so to the latest posterities : but it was likewise in an especial manner useful to the Jews as commemorative of their deliverance from Egyptian bondage. In the repetition of the Sinaitic law in the book of Deuteronomy, this is declared to be one object of its institution. (Deut. v, 15.)—That the Sabbath was also instituted, partly with the view of being a SIGN, is asserted by the inspired writers: (Exod. xxxi, 16, 17 :)—whereby it was asserted, that Jehovah was the only God whom the Israelites worshipped, and that they were his peculiar people:"—and " the Jewish Sabbath, being in some respects ceremonial, has been considered as having a TYPICAL meaning, and it derives a degree of proba- bility from the general typical nature of the Mosaic ordinances." —Holden's Christian Sabbath: Sect. i. Chap. iii. pp. 135—139. Lond. 1825, 8vo.

NOTE XXVI.—Page 189.

ABLUTIONS appear to have been amongst the oldest cere- monies practised by different nations. Moses enjoined them ; the Heathen adopted them ; and Mohammed and his followers have continued them : thus they have become established in the world, and associated with nearly all religions. The Egyptian priests had their diurnal and nocturnal ablutions ; the Greeks their sprinklings ; the Romans their lustrations and lavations; the Jews their frequent washings and purifications. The ancient Christians had their ablutions before communion ; which the Romish church still retains sometimes before, sometimes after mass: the Syrians, Copts, &c. have their washings on Good Friday: the Turks their greater and less ablutions; their Ghost and Wodou, &c.—So far do the Mohammedans carry their views of religious ablutions, that their writers assert, that " Purity or Cleanliness is the foundation of religion ;" and that " Purity or Cleanliness is the half of Faith," similar to the old English proverb, " Cleanliness is next to Godliness."

The superstitious character of the Jewish ablutions practised in the time of our Saviour, will be found discussed at length in *Cap.* ix. of the *Notæ Miscellaneæ*, appended to Pocockii *Porta Mosis.*—In vol. V. of the " Asiatic Researches," the Hindoo ablutions are described by H. T. Colebrooke, esq. in an Essay, " *On the religious ceremonies of the Hindus, and of the Brahmins especially :*"—and the subject of Mohammedan ablutions is investigated by the learned Pocock in *Specimen Historiæ Arabum*, Oxon. 1650. 4*to.* pp. 302—304 ; and by Sale, in *The Preliminary Discourse*, prefixed to his translation of the " Koran," Sect. iv. p. 138. Lond. 1801, 8vo.

NOTE XXVII.—Page 195.

ONE of the parts of the liturgy of the Jews, and which they regard as one of the most solemn, is called KIRIATH SHEMA.

It consists, "in reading, of three portions of Scripture. The first is from the beginning of the 4th verse of the 6th chapter of Deutoronomy, to the end of the 9th verse : the second, from the beginning of the 13th verse of the 12th chapter of Deutoronomy, to the end of the 21st verse: and the third, from the beginning of the 37th verse of the 15th chapter of Numbers, to the end of the chapter: and because the first of these portions, in the Hebrew Bible, begins with the word שמע Shema, i. e. "Hear;" all these three portions together are called the SHEMA, and the reading of them Kiriath Shema ; that is, the *reading of the Shema*. The reading of the *Shema* twice a day, that is, Morning and Night, is what they are expressly bound to do, because of the words of the Law, in Deut vi. 7; and xi. 19. "And thou shalt talk of them when thou liest down, and when thou risest up ;" i. e. at the usual time of mankind lying down, which is at night, and the usual time of rising, which is the morning."—Levi's Ceremonies of the Jews, p. 178.—See also Wotton's Miscellaneous Discourses, vol. i. pp. 171—193: and vol. ii. p. 10.

NOTE XXVIII.—*Page* 201.

SEE Dissertation IX. "On Judicial Astrology," page 127 ; and Note 12. p. 337.

NOTE XXIX.—*Page* 203.

REGINALD SCOT, or his Continuator, observes, "That which is most remarkable in the infernal proceedings is this, that there is not any nation under the sun, but the Devil hath introduced himself amongst them, through their ceremonies and worship, though quite opposite to one another. For in the kingdom of China,—he is conjured and exorcised through the repetition of several superstitious invocations to the sun and moon. In Tartary the magicians go quite another way to work, with offerings to the ocean, to the mountains, and the rivers, fuming incense and divers sorts of feathers, by which means the devils are compelled to appear. So that we see how this Proteus can dispose himself in the divers kingdoms of this world ; being called by other names in Tartary, China, the East and West Indies, &c. than amongst the

European conjurers. Likewise, the Greeks and Romans could invocate spirits by prayers to the moon, and divers sacrifices of milk, honey, vervain, and blood: and those that are addicted to conjurations in Christianity, have attained to a more lofty and ample manner of incantation and conjuring with magical garments, fire, candles, circles, astrological observations, invocations, and holy names of God, according to the Cabala of the Jews; so that every distinct nation hath conformed its conjuration unto the ceremonies of that religion which it professeth."

These observations are fully confirmed by the details of more modern writers on the customs and practices of various nations. To instance only in the *Hindoos*, Mr. Ward informs us in his elaborate and valuable " View of the History, Literature, and Mythology of the Hindoos," that " The Hindoos are enveloped in the greatest superstition, not only as idolaters, but in their dread of a great variety of supernatural beings, and in attaching unfortunate consequences to the most innocent actions.—They consult astrologers on many occasions, and have the strongest faith in the power of incantations to remove all manner of evils.—Many Hindoo married women, who are not blessed with children, wear incantations written with lac on the bark of the bhōōhrjjŭ, in order to obtain this blessing. They wear these charms on the arm, or round the neck, or in the hair, inclosed in small gold or brass boxes. The Hindoos repeat incantations when they retire to rest— when they rise—when they first set their foot on the ground— when they clean their teeth—when they eat—when they have done eating—when it thunders—when they enter on a journey—when they want to kill or injure a supposed enemy— when they wish to cure the scab in sheep," &c.

We may, therefore, add, in the words of the old writer, already quoted, that " notwithstanding the coming of Christ hath prevented the Devil's force in general; yet, such nations as have never embraced the Christian faith, are still deluded and bewitched by him; because the centre hath never been actually awakened in any of them; so that the Devil's power prevails over them mightily, to seduce them to worship things visible, and not the true God: for where the most darkness is in religion and worship, or in natural understanding, there his

power is most predominant."—Reginald Scot's Discovery of
Witchcraft:—*Discourse concerning Devils and Spirits*, B. ii, pp.
58, 59, Lond. 1665, folio.—Ward's View of the History,
Literature, and Mythology of the Hindoos, vol. iii, pt. ii, pp.
209—212, Lond. 1820, 8vo. Third edit.

NOTE XXX.—*Page* 207.

REGINALD SCOT, in the work quoted in the preceding note,
B. xii, gives many of the forms of incantation used i the
pretended cure of diseases, as well as of the amulets worn on
similar occasions. He also relates the following curious story
strongly marking the folly of such conduct: "An old woman
that healed (or rather pretended to heal) all diseases of cattle,
for which she never took any reward but a penny and a loaf,
being seriously examined by what means she brought these
things to pass, confessed, that, after she had touched the sick
creature, she always departed immediately, saying,—

> MY loaf in my lap,
> My penny in my purse ;
> Thou art never the better,
> And I am never the worse."

Scot's Discovery of Witchcraft, B. xii, ch xiv, p. 138.

NOTE XXXI.—*Page* 207.

THE Hebrew word which we translate " corners," (Lev. xix,
27,) signifies also the *ends* or *extremities* of any thing : and the
meaning is, they were not to cut their hair equal, behind and
before, as the worshippers of the stars and the planets, particularly the Arabians, did ; for this made their head have the
form of an hemisphere.—Bochart notes, (lib. i, Canaan, c. 6,)
Idumæans, Ammonites, Moabites, and the rest of the inhabitants of *Arabia Deserta*, are called " circumcised in the corners,
i. e. of the head. Jer. ix, 26."—Patrick in Levit. xix, 27.

" *Herodotus* observes, that the Arabs shave or cut their hair
round, in honour of Bacchus, who, they say, had his hair cut
in this way. (Lib. iii, c. 8.)—He says also, that the Macians, a
people of Lybia, cut their hair round, so as to leave a tuft on
the top of the head. (Lib. iv, c, 175.) In this manner the
Chinese cut their hair in the present day.—The *hair* was much

used in divination among the Greeks; and particularly about the time of the giving of the Law, as this is supposed to have been the era of the Trojan war. We learn from Homer, that it was customary for parents to dedicate the hair of their children to some god; which, when they came to manhood, they cut off and consecrated to the deity. Achilles, at the funeral of Patroclus, cut off his golden locks, which his father had dedicated to the river god Sperchius, and threw them into the flood.—Στας απαν ευθε πυρης.—κ. τ. λ.—Iliad, l. xxiii, x. 142, &c.

> But great Achilles stands apart in prayer,
> And from his head divides the yellow hair,
> Those curling locks which from his youth he vow'd,
> And sacred grew to Sperchius' honoured flood.
> Then sighing, to the deep his locks he cast,
> And roll'd his eyes around the watery waste.
> Sperchius! whose waves, in mazy errors lost,
> Delightful roll along my native coast!
> To whom we vainly vow'd, at our return,
> These locks to fall, and hecatombs to burn—
> So vow'd my father, but he vow'd in vain;
> No more Achilles sees his native plain;
> In that vain hope, these hairs no longer grow;
> Patroclus bears them to the shades below.
>
> POPE.

" From Virgil we learn that the *topmost lock* of hair was dedicated to the infernal gods.—Æneid, l. iv, v. 698.

> The sisters had not cut the topmost hair,
> Which Proserpine and they can only know,
> Nor made her sacred to the shades below—
> .... ,
> This offering to the infernal gods I bear;
> Thus while she spoke, she cut the fatal hair."
>
> DRYDEN.

Dr. Adam Clarke's Commentary in Lev. xix, 27.

NOTE XXXII.—*Page* 207.

These heterogeneous mixtures whether of garments, seeds, or animals, were evidently forbidden to prevent idolatry. Thomas Aquinas (Prim. secund. qu. 102, art. 6,) says, " All these mixtures were forbidden out of hatred to idolatry, because the Egyptians made mixtures of this nature in seeds, animals, and garments, to represent the different conjunctions of the planets;" and William of Paris remarks more at large, that "The idolaters by these intermixtures and conjunctions intended to intimate that it would be wise in husbandmen and shepherds to worship the stars; since they believed that by their favour and influence, the sheep would produce abundance of wool, and the fields copious harvests of grain. They therefore mixed linen and woollen together in their garments, that their worship might be successful, and that the stars might produce abundance of both. This practice was, therefore, on this account forbidden; and the more strenuously so, because these mixtures of woollen and linen were made according to certain positions of the stars."—Spencer, De Legibus Hebræorum, lib. ii, c. 21. p. 402, Hagæ-Comit. 1686, 4to.

Maimonides (in *Halach. Kelaim.*) observes, that if a man saw an Israelite wear such a garment, it was lawful for him to fall upon him openly, and tear his garment in pieces, even if he were his master who taught him wisdom.—The reasons alleged for this abhorrence were the same as for many other precepts, being designed to preserve them from the horrid confusion, which was among the Gentiles, by incestuous and unnatural mixtures.—See Patrick's Commentary, Levit. xix, 19.

NOTE XXXIII.—*Page* 208.

"As the heathens made such a multiplicity of gods out of one and the same person; so likewise did they confound their sexes, making the same deity sometimes a god, sometimes a goddess, or rather all of them of both sexes. Hence it is, that the Greeks used the word Θεος, both for gods and goddesses: and after the same manner was the word *Deus* used by the Romans.—Hence it was, that the Cyprians represented their Venus with a beard, having a sceptre in her hand, dressed as a woman, but masculine in her stature and name Ἀφροδιτος;—and the statue the Syrians worshipped in the temple of Heliopolis, was that of a woman clothed like a man. So at Rome they had a *Fortuna Mascula* and *Virilis*, and a *Fortuna Barbata.* They had likewise, as Servius and Lactantius tell us, an *armed* Venus. The Gentiles, to signify this mystery of community of sexes in their deities, counter-

feited themselves to be masculine-feminine in their worshipping them. They thought to please their gods by presenting
themselves before them, as like them as they could ; and by
wearing a habit different from their sex, to recommend themselves to such deities as they supposed of doubtful, or rather
of both sexes, This was preatised especially in the worship
of Venus.—Their women thought they could not appear more
acceptably in the presence of the god of war, than dressed in
arms ; and their men, in the presence of the goddess of love,
than in the habit proper to the soft and tender sex ; and so
Philocorus, (apud Macrob. l. iii, c. 8,) an old Greek author,
tells us of the Asiatics, that when they sacrificed to their
Venus, 'the men were dressed in women's apparel, and the
women in men's, to denote that she was esteemed by them both
male and female.'—Julius Firmicus describes this manner of
worship as common amongst the Assyrians and Africans.
From them it passed into Europe. The Phœnicians carried it
with them into Cyprus, (Servius ad Æn. l. ii,) where we find
it practised ; and we meet at Coos with the high-priest of
Hercules sacrificing in women's apparel ; and the Argives
performing their *Hybristica,* or sacred rites of incivility, 'the
women clothed with men's coats and breeches, and the men
with women's veils and petticoats ;'—Plutarch, 'Of the
Virtues of Women,' 4 :—and the same thing was practised
by the *Ithyphalli* in the rites of Bacchus ; and by the Athenians in their *Ascophoria.*"—Young, On Idolatrous Corruptions in Religion, vol. i, pp, 97—105.

NOTE XXXIV.—*Page* 209.

"THE Jews were so sensible of all this, after they had
severely smarted for their idolatry, that they thought it
unlawful to use any vessel that had been employed in sacrificing to a false god : nay, to warm themselves with the wood
of a grove that was cut down ; or to sit under the shadow of
it for coolness sake, while it was standing ; or so much as to
use the ashes of the wood, that were left after the grove was
burnt."—Selden, Lib. ii, *De Jure Nat. et Gent. juxta Discipl.
Hebr.* cap. vii.—Patrick's Commentary, Deut. vii. 26.

NOTE XXXV.—*Page* 210.

THE combined influence of hope and fear in producing the most powerful effects upon mankind, is strongly evinced in the superstitious practices of India. " The widow who ascends the funeral pile," says Mr. Ward, " is promised by the shastrŭ that, by the merit of this act, she shall take her deceased husband and seven generations of his family, and seven generations of her family, with her to the heaven of Indru, the King of the gods, where they shall reside during 30,000,000 of years. Seduced by these promises, and having the prospect, should she not burn, of nothing but domestic slavery and perpetual widowhood, multitudes annually perish on these funeral piles."—He also informs us, that the "Dowugnu Bramhuns go from house to house, proposing to cast nativities : sometimes they stop a person in the street, and tell him some melancholy news, as, that he will not live long ; and the poor superstitious Hindoo firmly believing that these people can read his fate in the palm of his hand, or in the motions of the stars, and that they can avert disasters by certain ceremonies, gives them his money."—Ward's View of the History, Literature, and Mythology of the Hindoos, vol. iii, Pref. p. xxiii; Part ii, p. 206.

NOTE XXXVI.—*Page* 210.

WHEN we recollect the degraded state of females in the East, we need not wonder that Maimonides has expressed himself so contemptuously respecting the intellectual character of women.—For, is it possible to read the statements of those who have resided in those countries, relative to the oppressed and destitute situation of females of every rank, without feeling a burst of indignation against a conduct so unjust and baneful.—" There are no female schools among the Hindoos," says a benevolent and competent writer in 1820, " every ray of mental improvement is carefully kept from the sex* As they are always confined to domestic duties, and

---

* An old adage is always present with the Hindoos, that if a woman learn to read, she will become a widow.—Ward's View of the History, &c. of the Hindoos, vol. iii, P. ii, p. 168.

carefully excluded from the company of the other sex; a Hindoo sees no necessity for the education of females, and the shastrŭs themselves declare, that a *woman has nothing to do with the text of the védŭ:* all her duties are comprized in pleasing her husband, and cherishing her children."

It is, however, pleasing, to learn that, since Mr. Ward wrote, Native Female Schools have been established in several parts of India, under the patronage of the most distinguished European residents, and are gradually removing the native prejudices against the education of females of all classes.

NOTE XXXVII.—*Page* 211.

" That it was the practice of the ancient heathens to pass through fire, as a rite of initiation or lustration is certain, from what Suidas tells us of the mysteries of Mithra, that they who were to be initiated were, δια πυρος παρελθειν: and it is plain from Virgil, that it was used in the worship of Apollo by the Etrurians on Mount Soracte, [now San Areste,] Æn. xi, v. 786.—It may be, the Canaanitish custom was much the same with what the Romans did annually at their *Palilia*, which were feasts kept on the 12th of May, which was the birth-day of their city, to the honour of their goddess Pales, who, as Gyraldus tells us, was the same as the *Mother of the gods* or *Astarte*, and that some took her to be of the feminine, others of the masculine gender. Varro, as he is quoted by the scholiast on Horace says, " The country people have private as well as public feasts of *Pales*, when they jump over a great fire, made of stubble and hay, imagining themselves to be purified by the *Palilia*." Ovid describes this usage, Fast. l. iv. This practice continued a long while in Persia; and if we believe some authors, it is even still practised by the worshippers of fire. Theodoret, on 2 Kings xvi, mentions it as continuing in his time; and St. Chrysostom blames, amongst other heathenish customs then remaining, the lighting two great fires, and passing between them; and the 65th canon of the Council of Trullo, [held A.D. 692] condemns the observing the new moon, with making fires before their doors, and leaping on them."—Young, *ut sup.* p. 117.

The *Scholiast* upon this canon of the Council of Trullo, observes:—The *new-moon* was always the first day of the month, and it was customary among the Jews and Greeks, to hold a feast at that time, and to pray that they might be lucky during the continuance of the month. Of these it was that God spake by the Prophet, " My soul hateth your *New-Moons* and your Sabbaths." They also kindled fires before their shops and houses, and leaped over them, imagining that all the evils which had befallen them formerly, would be burnt away, and that they should be more successful and lucky afterwards. Now about the period of the sitting of the Synod, there were some of the Christians who observed this custom upon the same accounts that the Heathen did, which occasioned its being forbidden by the Council; and that if a Clergyman was guilty of it, he should be deposed: if a Layman, excommunicated. He also tells us, that on *St. John Baptist's eve,* the vulgar were wont to make fires for the whole night, and leap over them, and draw lots, and divine about their good and evil fortune.

There was a feast at Athens kept by private families, called *Amphidromia,* on the fifth day after the birth of a child, when it was the custom for the gossips to *run round the fire* with the infant *in their arms;* and then having delivered it to the nurse, they were entertained with feasting and dancing.

Dr. Moresin, in a learned work written in Latin, and dedicated to James I, entitled, " The Origin and Increase of Depravity in Religion," states that he himself was an eye-witness of a remarkable custom, which then existed in Scotland. " They take," says he, " the new-baptized infant, and vibrate it three or four times over a flame, saying and repeating thrice, ' Let the flame consume thee now, or never.' "

Mr. Borlase, in his account of Cornwall, says, " The Cornish make bonfires in every village on the eve of St. John Baptist's and St. Peter's days, which I take to be the remains of part of the Druid superstition."—Brand's Observations on Popular Antiquities, Chap. xxvii; and Observations on Ch. xxvii, pp. 273, 274—278.

NOTE XXXVIII.—*Page 211.*

THE particular species of tree indicated by the term אשרה, *(Ashreh)* is not certain, though it is most probable the oak is intended. (See Ezek. vi, 13.) But whatever may have been

its original and special designation, it is conjectured that, from
the veneration in which this tree was held, originated the appli-
cation of the term to an *idol*, or to *idols :*—(Judges iii, 7 ; 1 Kings
xiv, 23; xv, 13; 2 Kings xvii, 10, 16; xxi, 7 ; xxiii, 4, 6, 7 ;
2 Chron. xxxiii, 19 ; Isaiah xvii, 8, *et al. :*)—to *groves* planted for
idolatrous purposes:—and that the name of the Sidonian
Venus, ASARAH or ASTARTE, as well as the terms ASHEROTH
and ASHTAROTH, were derived from the same source.—See
Judges ii. 13 ; 1 Sam. vii. 3, 4, *et al.*—See Selden De Diis Syris,
Syntag. 2. Cap. 2, et Additamenta Beyeri: pp. 294—296; and Parkhurst Heb. Lex. sub voce, אשר—See also Note 14, page 340.

NOTE XL.—*Page* 212.

" THE use and end of their FIRST-FRUITS, was, that the
after-fruits might be consecrated *in them.* For this purpose,
they were enjoined to offer the First-Fruits of their *Trees,*
which served for food : (Levit. xix. 23, 24:) in which this
order was observed ; the three first years after the tree had
been planted, the fruits were accounted ' uncircumcised' and
' unclean.' It was unlawful to eat them, sell them, or make any
benefit of them. On the fourth year they were accounted
' holy ;' that is, either they were given to the priests; (Numb.
xviii. 12, 13 ;) or the owners ate them before ' the Lord at
Jerusalem,' as they did their *second tythe :* and this latter is the
common opinion of the Hebrews. After the *fourth* year they
returned to the use of the owner. We may call these simply
The First-Fruits.

" Secondly : they were enjoined to pay yearly the First-
Fruits *of every year's increase ;*—and of them there were many
sorts; first, *First-Fruits in the Sheaf :* (Levit. xxiii. 10:)
secondly, *First-Fruits in two wave-loaves.* (Levit. xxiii. 17.)
These two bounded the harvest: that *in the sheaf* was offered
in the *beginning* of harvest, upon the fifteenth of Nisan ; the
other, of the *loaves* at the *end*, upon their Pentecost: and
(Levit. xxiii.) they are both called תנופה, *Tenuphoh,*
that is, *Shake-offerings.*—Thirdly : there was a first of the
Dough, (Numb. xv. 20,) namely the four-and-twentieth part
thereof, given unto the Priests ; which kind of offering was
observed, even when they were returned out of Babylon.
(Nehem. x, 37.)—Fourthly, they were to pay unto the Priests

the First-Fruits *of the threshing-floor.* (Numb. xv, 10.) These two last are called תרומה *Terumoth,* that is, '*heave-offerings ;*" this, 'the heave-offering of the threshing-floor ;' the other, 'the heave-offering of the dough.'—*Tenuphoth* and *Terumoth,* both signify *shake-offering, heave-offering,* or *wave-offering,* but with this difference; that *Terumoth* was by a waving of elevation, lifting the oblation *upward* and *downward,* to signify that God was Lord both of heaven and earth. The *Tenuphoth* was by a waving of agitation, waving it *to* and *fro,* from the right hand to the left, from the East to the West, from the North to the South ; by which kind of agitation, they acknowledged God to be the Lord of the whole world."—Godwyn's Moses and Aaron, lib. 6, Chap. 2, pp. 214, 215.

The oblation of the First-Fruits of the *threshing-floor,* " was distinguished by the Rabbis into two sorts : the first of these was, the First-fruits of *seven* things only, Wheat, Barley, Grapes, Figs, Pomegranates, Olives, and Dates. These the Talmudists call by the name of *Biccurim,* which signifies ' the choicest part,' or what was first ripe. The owner might bring in what measure he pleased ; but in gathering, he always bound the portions he designed for the Priests about with rushes, and said, ' Let this be for the First-Fruits.'—The second was paid of Corn, Wine, and Oil, and whatever else was for the support of human life.—Under this kind of First-Fruits is included the first of the *Fleece.*—By this means the Priests were provided with Clothes, as by other offerings with food. The wool also of Goats, which were shorn in those countries, is included under the Fleece of Sheep.

" When the people brought up their First-Fruits to Jerusalem, it was done with great pomp and ceremony. All the cities that were of one station, that is, out of which one course of priests proceeded, were gathered together into a stationary city, and lodged in the streets. In the morning, he who was the first among them, said, ' Arise, let us go up to Zion, to the house of the Lord our God.' An ox went before them with gilded horns, and an olive crown upon his head, for a peace-offering, and the pipe played before them, until they approached near to Jerusalem. When they came to Jerusalem, they crowned their First-Fruits, that is, they exposed them to sight in as much glory as they could, and the chief men, and

the high-officers, and treasurers of the temple, came to meet
them, to do them the more honour that they were coming;
and all the workmen in Jerusalem rose up to them, and
saluted them, in this manner:—' O our brethren, inhabitants
of the City N—. ye are welcome.'—The pipe played before
them, till they came to the Mount of the Temple. Every one,
even the King himself, took his basket upon his shoulder, and
went forward till he came to the Court. The Levites then
sang, ' I will extol thee, O Lord, because thou hast exalted
me, and hast not made mine enemies to rejoice over me.'—
While the basket is yet upon his shoulders, he recites that
passage, ' I profess this day to the Lord my God:'—when he
speaks these words:—'A Syrian ready to perish was my
father,' (Deut. xxvi. 3, 5,) he casts down the basket from his
shoulders, and holds his lips, while the priest waves it hither
and thither. The whole passage being recited to the 10th
verse, he places the basket before the altar, worships, and
goes out. They used to hang turtles or pigeons about their
baskets, which were adorned with flowers; and these they
designed as an offering. The fruits themselves belonged to
the priests of the course that were then in service; and the
party who brought them was obliged to lodge in Jerusalem all
the night after he had presented them ; and the next morning
he was allowed to return home."—Lewis's Antiquities of the
Hebrew Republick, vol. i. b. 2, Chap. 8, pp. 145, 146. Lond.
1724, 8vo.

" The Heathen, in all probability, from hence derived the
custom of carrying their First-Fruits, as a tithe every year,
unto the Island *Delos*, where Apollo was supposed to have his
special residence : and this, not only from the islands there-
abouts, and the neighbouring countries, but from all parts of
of the world ; as the Jews we find every where sent from the
countries where they dwelt, a sum of money every year, instead
of First-Fruits and Tithes, unto Jerusalem ; which privilege
the Romans allowed them after they had conquered them, as
Josephus tells us, Lib. vii. *De Bello Jud.* Cap. xiii.—So we
read in several authors, that they were solemn embassies sent
from several people, by chosen persons unto Delos, to celebrate there the feast of Apollo, with music and dancing, &c.
particularly the Athenians, Peloponnesians, and Messenians,

&c. of whom see Ezek. Spanhemius in his ' Observations on Callimachus,' p. 487 : and, which is most strange, the Hyperboreans, a very northerly people sent *frugum primitias* to this island, as Pliny, and I know not how many other authors, testify.—Which was done to testify their honour to this god, and for the maintenance of his priests and other ministers, who attended upon him there. For Delos, of itself, was but a barren isle, the soil being dry and stony."—" There are other footsteps of this among the Heathen ; the *Mystica vannus Iacchi* mentioned by Virgil in his ' Georgicks,' being nothing else (according to Servius) but *vas vimineum,* a wicker-basket, in which their First-Fruits were carried. See the same Spanheim, p. 495."—Patrick on Deut. xxvi, 2 ; see also on v. 14 ; and Spencer, De Leg. Heb. Lib. 2, C. 24, Sect. 1.

An interesting anecdote, illustrative of this practice, is given in Mr. Buckingham's recent *Travels in Mesopotamia.*—" In pursuing our way across the plain, [one of the plains of the Turcomans,] we passed a party of husbandmen gathering in the harvest, the greater portion of the grain being now fully ripe. They plucked up the corn by the roots, instead of reaping it, a practice often spoken of in the Scriptures, though reaping seems to be made the earliest and most frequent mention of. On seeing the caravan, one of the labourers ran from his companions and approached us, danced, stood on his hands, with his feet aloft in the air, and gave other demonstrations of joy, when he presented us with an *ear of corn* and a *flower,* as an offering of the First-Fruits of the year ; another remnant of a very ancient usage in the ' wave-offering' of the sheaf and the ear of corn, commanded to the Israelites by Moses. We returned for it a handful of paras, or small tin-coin, and answered the shout of joy which echoed from the field, by acclamations from the caravan."—Buckingham's Travels in Mesopotamia, quoted in New Month. Mag. p. 203. March, 1827.

NOTE XLI.—*Page 213.*

Dr. Cudworth in his valuable " Discourse concerning the true Notion of the Lord's Supper," p. 36, gives the following extract from an ancient Karaite Comment on the Pentateuch,

A A

which at once illustrates these magical sprinklings, and explains one of the Mosaic Precepts. (Exod. xxiii. 19.) " It was a custom of the ancient Heathens, when they had gathered in all their fruits, to take a kid, and boil it in the dam's milk, and then, in a magical way, to go about and besprinkle with it all their trees, and fields, and gardens, and orchards ; thinking by this means they should mᴀke them fructify and bring forth fruit again more abundantly the following year :"-" wherefore," adds Dr. Cudworth, " God forbad his people the Jews at the time of their ingathering, to use any such superstitious or idolatrous rite."

NOTE XLII.—*Page* 213.

SUPERSTITIOUS notions relative to the Moon's influence, have universally obtained, and until very recently prevailed in our own country. One of our old writers, of no mean account, amongst other "points" of "good husbandry," observes,

> IN March is good *graffing*, the skilful do know,
> So long as the wind in the East do not blow :
> From *moon* being chang'd till past be the prime,
> For graffing and cropping is very good time.
>
> TUSSER.

NOTE XLII.—*Page* 214.

THE prohibition of sowing a field with mixed seed, was probably intended not only to prevent the Israelites from *mingling* with other nations and adopting their idolatrous prac-tices, but also to promote the interests of agriculture, by preventing those heterogeneous mixtures which would have lessened the quantity or injured the excellency of their crops. " The law," says Michaelis, "meant nothing more than that care was to be taken to have the seed as pure as possible, and that it was to be selected and dressed with the greatest atten-tion, to prevent two different kinds of grain from coming up together.—It was a general prohibition, not to sow two sorts of corn together. For both sorts will not ripen at the same time ; and the consequence is, that in reaping there must be a

loss on one of them. Nor yet are both of the same height; so
that the higher of the two will deprive the other of sun-shine,
free air, and wind."—Michaelis's Commentaries on the Laws of
Moses, translated by Dr. A. Smith, vol. iii, Art. 268, pp. 342,
358. London, 1814, 8vo.

"It was a further rite taught by idolatry, that barley and
dried grapes should be sowed together, supposing such a mix-
ture made their vineyards better. By such actions, as Dr.
Spencer rightly observes, they signified that their vineyards
were consecrated to Ceres and Bacchus, and were recommended
to their protection, and expressed, in effect, a dependance on
their influence for their fruitfulness. Such rites as these were
a sort of renunciation of the protection and blessing of the true
God, and a declaration of their hope in favour of other gods
besides Him, to whom they recommended themselves, rather
than to Jehovah, for the fruitfulness of their vineyards; therefore the Hebrew ritual directs, "Thou shalt not sow thy vineyard with different seeds, lest the fruit of the seed thou hast
sown, and the fruit of thy vineyard, be defiled."—Lowman's
Rational of the Ritual of the Hebrew Worship, p. 242. Lond.
1816, 8vo. See also Spencer, De Leg. Heb. lib. 2, c. 18, sect.
1, 2, 3, pp. 379—385. Hagæ Comitum, 1686, 4to.

Bishop Patrick also justly remarks, (Comment. Deut. xxii. 9,)
"If the Israelites had followed this custom, it would have made
both the Corn and the Grapes that sprang up from such seed
impure, because polluted by idolatry; the very smell of
which God would not have to remain among the Israelites, as
Maimonides speaks in his *More Nevochim*, P. 3, C. 37. Every
one also knows that it was unlawful for the Israelites to eat
any of the fruits of the earth, till the First-Fruits of the earth
had been offered unto God; which would not have been
accepted by him of such things as these, that were expressly
forbidden by his law; and consequently the whole crop
became unclean to them, and might not be used by them."

NOTE XLIII.—*Page* 215.

A SOMEWHAT similar practice obtains even in our own
country in the present day, in the Wolds of Yorkshire, where
it is customary to raise *smoke* in the fields, when they finish

ploughing. This they call, " Burning out the witch."—See also
Asiatic Researches, vol. iv, p. 342.

NOTE XLIV.—*Page* 219.

SEE note 40, p. 364, on the " First-Fruits."

NOTE XLV.—*Page* 222.

As a period of seven days was completed by the Sabbath, so
was a period of seven years by the *Sabbatick Year*. During
this year, nothing was sown and nothing reaped; the vines
and the olives were not pruned: there was no vintage and no
gathering of fruits, even of what grew wild: but whatever
spontaneous productions there were, were left to the poor, the
traveller, and the wild beast. (Levit. xxv. 1–7; Deut. xv.
1—10) Extraordinary fruitfulness was promised on the sixth
year, but in such a way as not to exclude care and foresight.
(Levit. xxv. 20—24.) We are not to suppose, however, that
the Hebrews spent the seventh year in absolute idleness. They
could fish, hunt, take care of their bees and flocks, repair their
buildings and furniture, manufacture cloths of wool, linen,
and of the hair of goats and camels, and carry on commerce.
Finally, they were obliged to remain longer in the tabernacle
or temple this year, during which, the whole Mosaic law was
read, in order to be instructed in religious and moral duties,
and the history of their nation, and the wonderful works and
blessings of God. (Deut. xxxi. 10—13).—On account of there
being no income from the soil, debts were not collected.
(Deut. xv. 1, 2.) Some have supposed that they were not,
however, cancelled, as was imagined by the Talmudists; and
have considered Deuteronomy xv, 9, as showing that the
Hebrews were admonished not to deny money to the poor on
account of the approach of the Sabbatical Year, during which
it could not be exacted; but that nothing further than this
could be educed from that passage.—Jahn's Biblical Archæology, by T. Upham, A. M. sect. 79, 350, pp. 86, 444.
Andover, (America,) 1823, 8*vo*.

Calmet gives the following reasons for this ordinance :—
(1.) To maintain, as far as possible, an equality of condition

among the people, in setting the slaves at liberty, and in permitting all, as children of one family, to have the free and indiscriminate use of whatever the earth produced.—(2.) To inspire the people with sentiments of humanity, by making it their duty to give rest, proper and sufficient nourishment to the poor, the *slave*, and the *stranger*, and even to the *cattle.*—(3.) To accustom the people to submit to, and depend on, the Divine providence, and expect their support from that in the *seventh* year, by an extraordinary provision on the *sixth.*—(4.) To detach their affections from earthly and perishable things, and to make them disinterested and heavenly-minded.—(5.) To show them God's dominion over the country, and that HE, not *they,* was lord of the soil; and that they held it merely from his bounty.—(6.) To recall to mind the memory of the Creation, by the weekly Sabbath, the seventh year, and the Jubilee or week of years.

"That God intended to teach them the doctrine of Providence, by this ordinance, there can be no doubt: and this is marked very distinctly: (Levit. xxv, 20, 21:) 'And if ye shall say, What shall we eat the seventh year? Behold, we shall not sow nor gather-in our increase: Then I will command my blessing upon you, in the sixth year, and it shall bring forth fruit for three years.' That is, there shall be, not three crops in one year, but one crop, equal in its abundance to three, because it must supply the wants of three years. (1.) For the *sixth* year, supplying fruit for its own consumption. (2.) For the *seventh* year, in which they were neither to sow nor reap. And, (3.) For the *eighth* year, for though they ploughed, sowed, &c. that year, yet a whole course of its seasons was requisite to bring all these fruits to perfection, so that they could not have the fruits of the *eighth* year till the *ninth,* (see v. 22,) till which time God promised that they should eat of 'the old store.' What an amazing proof did this give of the being, power, providence, mercy, and goodness of God! Could there be an infidel in such a land, or a sinner against God and his own soul, with such proofs before his eyes, of God and his attributes, as one Sabbatical year afforded?"—Dr. A. Clarke's Comment. Exod. xxiii. 11; Calmet, Dictionnaire de la Bible; *Année Sabbatique.*

NOTE XLVI.—*Page 222.*

THE JUBILEE was celebrated every *fiftieth* year, that is, after seven times seven years. (Levit. xxv, 8.) The return of the year of Jubilee was announced on the tenth day of the seventh month, Tisri, (September,) being the *day of expiation* or *atonement*, by the sound of trumpets or rams' horns. The Rabbins say, that every private man was bound to blow with a trumpet, and make this sound nine times, that every one might be the more inclined to hearken to the general proclamation, and fulfil the obligations of the festival. The uses of th Jubilee are thus enumerated by Dr. Godwyn:—" There were five main uses of this feast. First, for the general release of servants. Secondly, for the restoring of lands and tenements to their first owners who formerly sold them. Thirdly, thereby a true distinction of their tribes was preserved; because lands returned unto their owners in their proper tribe, and servants to their own families. Fourthly, some are of opinion, that, as the Grecians computed their times by the number of *Olympiads;* the Romans by their *Lustra;* the Christians by their *Indictions;* so the Jews by their *Jubilees.* Lastly, it mystically shadowed forth that spiritual Jubilee which Christians enjoy under Christ, by whose blood we have, not only a re-entry into the ' kingdom of heaven,' which we had formerly forfeited by our sins, (and this was aptly signified by the Israelites' re-entry upon their lands formerly sold,) but also the ' sound of the Gospel," which was in this feast typified unto us by the noise of trumpets, is gone throughout the world; and thus the ' Lord God hath blown the trumpet,' as Zechariah's phrase is. (Zech. ix, 14.) But neither this release of servants, nor restoring of lands, was until the tenth day of the month Tisri, [the day of expiation or atonement,] at which time it was proclaimed by the sound of trumpets or rams' horns. The nine first days of this month, the servants feasted and made merry, and wore garlands in token of their liberty approaching." —Godwyn's Moses and Aaron, lib. 3, c. 10, p. 134—136.— Jahn's Biblical Archæology, sect. 351.—Patrick's Comment. Levit. xxv. 8, 9, 10, 11.

NOTE XLVII.—*Page* 222.

" MAIMONIDES, in his treatise on this subject, *(c. ult.)* says, He that gave us the Law, knows the most intimate sense of all men's souls, and penetrates into the most secret recesses, and lurking places of human desires ; and He seeing that their love of riches would make them very saving; so that, if out of a religious motion, they had consecrated any thing to Him, they would be prone to repent of it; He therefore ordained, that if any man had a mind to redeem what he had consecrated, he ' should add a fifth part to its just value:' that is, pay well for it."—Patrick's Comment. Levit. xxvii, 15.

NOTE XLVIII.—*Page* 223.

AMONG the Israelites in the time of Moses, it must have been very common to *lend on pledge*. But while pledges are under no judicial regulation, much extortion and villainy may be practised, when the poor man who wishes to borrow is in straits, and must of course submit to all the terms imposed by the opulent lender. Moses, therefore, to guard against some of the chief abuses of pledging, prohibited the taking or keeping in pledge certain indispensable articles, such as the *Upper Garment of the poor*, which, like the *hyke* of the Arab, served him for clothing by day, and for a covering or blanket by night, (Exod. xxiii, 25, 26; Deut. xxiv, 12, 13,) and the *Upper and Nether Millstones* which were necessary to provide him with food; for as the Israelites had no public water or wind-mills, every one was obliged to grind his corn in his own house, and for that purpose had either a hand-mill, or one somewhat larger turned by asses, so that if he had been deprived of the mill-stones, however abundant his corn might have been, he and his family must have wanted bread. (Deut. xxiv, 6.) These instances are evidently given as examples, to shew, that, in general, no pledge was to be exacted from the needy, the want of which might expose him to an inconvenience or hardship; more especially as we find the law-giver declaring, that God would regard the restoration of such pledges as alms-giving or righteousness. Nor was this attended with loss to the creditor; since he had it in his power, ultimately, to seize the whole property of the debtor;

---

and if he had none, his person; and in the event of non-payment, to take him for a bond-slave. The law gave him sufficient security, but prevented him from exercising unauthorized severity.—See Michaelis's Commentaries on the Laws of Moses, vol ii, Art. 150.

NOTE XLIX.—*Page 225.*

THE following remarks on SLAVERY as permitted by the Jewish laws, are worthy the author and translator of those elegant apologues, the " Hebrew Tales."

" SLAVERY.—The limited and qualified toleration of slaves as the less of two evils, by a law, which, in its own scheme and spirit, supplied a constant antidote, affords no justification of slavery under different circumstances ; and much less, of its abuses.

" ' If I did despise the cause of my man-servant or my maid-servant, when they contended with me; what then shall I do when GOD riseth up ? and, when He ariseth, what shall I answer him ? Did not He that made me in the womb make him ? and did not one fashion us in the womb ?' (Job. xxxi, 13—15.)

" That slavery is an evil, and an evil of great magnitude, no one possessed of common sense will for a moment deny. The Divine legislator has himself acknowledged it as such, by numbering it among the heavy maledictions which would befal the Israelites, should they ever forsake the religion of their ancestors ; and by the various laws which he instituted for its amelioration. That he did not entirely interdict it, we must attribute to the then state of society, which would not admit of its total abolition, without introducing still greater evils.

" For let it be recollected, that the period when the Divine law was first promulgated, this system of human misery had already existed for ages. The noxious weed had grown up and flourished in its full vigour, it overspread the fairest part of the globe, and was too deeply rooted to be at once eradicated.

" But although he did not entirely abolish slavery, he broke asunder some of its most tremendous shackles, and so limited, circumscribed, and ameliorated it, that it hardly merited that odious name.

"There were only two extreme cases in which a Hebrew could be reduced to a state of bondage. First: when an individual guilty of theft could not make the restitution which the law adjudged, in which case the proper authorities might sell him * in order to make the required compensation. Secondly, when an individual was reduced to such extreme indigence, as to prefer slavery to an actual state of starvation,† when the law allowed him to dispose of his person.—In both cases, the period, as well as the nature of the service, was limited by law. The master was enjoined still to look upon the wretched man, as on a poor unfortunate brother whose miserable condition ought to excite compassion. He dared not employ him in any very laborious or degrading work, was obliged to maintain his wife and children, though not entitled to the produce of their labour; in short, he was required to treat him with such mildness and forbearance ‡ that the Hebrew writers have justly observed, 'that he who purchases a Hebrew slave purchases a master instead of a servant.' The Heathen slave purchased by a Hebrew, was, it is true, not so well off; as neither the period nor the nature of his service was limited; nor could he acquire property, for whatever the slave possessed belonged to his master.

"But even over him the law spread its protecting shield; for though it suspended his civil, it protected his moral and personal rights. It provided him with many opportunities by

* They could only sell him for the term of six years, at the expiration of which, or at the commencement of the Jubilee, as either of them chanced to happen first, he regained his freedom.

† In such a case, the individual might dispose of himself for any period; but still, when the Jubilee arrived, he regained his freedom, though the term agreed upon had not then expired. In either of the above cases, the slave might redeem himself at any time, by paying the master a proportionate part of the purchase-money which the law compelled the purchaser to accept.

‡ "Thou must not," says the traditional law, "eat fine bread, and give him (the slave) coarse bread, drink fine wine, and give him an inferior sort, sleep on a bed and let him lie on straw, but thou must in every respect treat him as thou dost thyself."

which he could gain his freedom :* it secured his life by making the killing of a slave, or even the causing his death by immoderate correction, a capital crime punishable with death ; it protected him against cruelty, by obliging the master to give him his freedom in case he wantonly injured any of his limbs, or even knocked out any of his teeth; and it sheltered him against unprovoked insults, and insured him good treatment, by that benign mildness and benevolence which its Divine precepts were so well calculated to inspire. That savage cruelty and remorseless barbarity, which the Heathen exercised towards their slaves, could never exist under the Hebrew laws ; the followers of which were strictly enjoined to extend kindness even to brute animals, much more to human beings. Accordingly, we find that the Israelites treated even their Heathen slaves with the greatest forbearance and mildness ;†

* The Heathen slave might, before he had performed an act of servitude to the purchaser, become a proselyte, and thus acquire his freedom at once. All that the purchaser could then require of him was the repayment of the purchase-money, The master might, at any time, give him his freedom, or it might be purchased for him by any of his friends.

Lastly, the master was compelled to give it him, in case he deliberately maimed his limbs, or knocked out any of his teeth.

† " Though the law," says Maimonides, " did not expressly enjoin us not to treat the Heathen slaves with rigour, yet piety and justice require us to be merciful and kind to them.—We ought, therefore, not to oppress them nor lay heavy burdens upon them : nay, we ought to let them partake of the same food with which we indulge ourselves. Our pious ancestors made it a rule to give their slaves a portion of every dish prepared for their own use; nor would they sit down to their meals before they had seen that their servants were properly provided for ; considering themselves their natural protectors ; remembering what King David said, ' Behold, as the eyes of slaves are directed towards their masters, and as the eyes of the handmaid towards her mistress,' &c.

" Equally improper is it to insult them either by words or blows. The law has delivered them over to *subjection* but not to *insult*. Nor must we bawl at them, or be in a great *passion* with them, but speak to them mildly and attend to their reasonable complaints. Such conduct Job considered as very meritorious, as he said, "If I ever did despise the cause of my slave or handmaid when they contended with me, what then shall I do when the Almighty rises up ?," &c.

" Cruelty and violence characterize Heathen idolaters; but the sons of Abraham, the Israelites, whom the *Holy* (blessed be his name !) has so emi-

and, indeed, many of them carried their humanity so far, as never unnecessarily to rebuke them, nor to speak harshly to them, nay, they would even let them partake of the same food on which they themselves subsisted, well knowing that a slave has feelings as well as the master, and ever bearing in mind the words of Job, 'that the same Maker that formed the master, formed the slave, and that they were both fashioned in the same mould.'"—Hurwitz's (Hyman) Hebrew Tales, No. LV. pp. 153—158. Lond. 1826, 12mo.

——

ON THE subject of SLAVERY, it is pleasing to mark the influence of Christianity in repressing its cruelties and gradually inducing its entire abolition. The following historical observations and extracts will elucidate the progress of emancipation from slavery, and exhibit the powerful, but ultimately successful, struggle of the Gospel with the barbarous and idolatrous prejudices of the inhabitants of the Northern countries of Europe.

At an early period Slave-Markets were regularly established in various parts of Europe, especially at Rome, Bristol, and other places; but when the Christian religion was at length received by the different nations of this part of the world, it totally changed the ancient trade. On one side the precepts of Christianity were spread among barbarians, and the doctrine of equal rights, to which nature and a future life entitle all human beings, without the least exception, made the slave-trade gradually to cease. On the other hand, the importation of slaves, and all traffic of this nature, were severely prohibited. "There is no council held," says Hildebrand, in his "Historia Conciliorum," "where the abolition of the slave-trade has not been a serious object." Besides, a doctrine was established by the clergy, that eternal salvation would be the surest reward for the emancipation of slaves; nay, the Christian priests and confessors obliged their penitents, who had no slaves in their possession, to buy some and manumit them in the presence of the people assembled in the church. The

nently distinguished by wise and just laws, ought to be kind and compassionate, and as merciful as *He* of whom it is said, ' He is good to all, and his mercy extends over all his works.' "—Maimonides Yad Hachzakah, B. 4.

Norwegian Law, called "Gulething's Law," says,—"The slave shall be brought into the church, and the Holy Bible laid on his head, which being done, he shall be free." The priests themselves set good examples, they purchased slaves, particularly youths of a good and promising appearance, received them into orders, and thus made them entirely free.

St. Bonifacius tells us, that the newly converted Germans sold their slaves to their infidel neighbours for human sacrifices, which, at length, was stopped by Gregory the second, who made the offender guilty of a capital offence. Charloman ordered the synod of Leptin, in the year 743, that a man who sold his slave to an infidel should be infamous, and excommunicated in the same manner as a murderer, if the slave, thus sold, was intended to fall a victim to the gods: And in Norway, it was absolutely forbidden to sell a slave out of the kingdom, unless he had committed an enormous crime.—With a view to promote the abolition of this savage custom, which proved to be fatal to persons of the most exquisite beauty, and the most exalted character, it was enacted, that the ceremonies of emancipation among the Christians should resemble the form of the heathen sacrifices, and engage in the same way the imagination both of Christians and Heathens. By this means the slaves obtained a chance of liberty ; and were often brought to the church, placed on the altar, and symbolically sacrificed to the true God.

The national assemblies of the Heathens commenced with the bloody worship, and the Christians passed a law, that on such occasions a slave should be made free, and the expense of the feast at which he obtained his liberty defrayed by the public. The ancient Norwegian law before the year 1222, (Part 1, c. 3,) says, "We shall manumit a slave in our annual assembly at Gula; each member shall emancipate his slave by turn, and the whole assembly shall pay six ounces of silver, in order to defray the expenses of the feast of liberty. Whoever neglects to procure a slave in his turn, shall be fined in twelve ounces of silver to the bishop, and the assembly shall be obliged to buy a slave at their own expense, for the above mentioned purpose."

The liberty of a man's selling into slavery his own children, was restrained to certain rules. They begun by enacting, that the child which was sold for a slave, should recover its liberty by paying the sixth part of the purchase-money to the master. And it was further ordered, that no such slave should be exported out of his native country.

At length the duration of this kind of slavery was reduced to the certain term of seven years, or, as the Icelandic law called Geagas, which prevailed from the year 928 till the year 1267, more equitably ordered it, till the purchase-money and expenses made on the slave were re-imbursed.

It is difficult to fix the certain æra when the emancipation of slaves was universally introduced in Europe; for though Boden points out the year 1250, in his book *De Republica*, yet we know that slavery lasted much longer in some countries. The abolition of the slave-trade was a very serious object of the legislative power, through more than four centuries, for we find no council of the middle age without one canon at least relative to this business.

The civil government gave every support they could afford to so pious and so benevolent endeavours of the Church; and both agreed, that the undertaking could only be accomplished by slow degrees. The steps adopted for this purpose were on one side to forbid the exportation of slaves, to throw the slave-trade into the hands of Christians, who ought to know their common duties, and to make some regulations concerning a humane treatment of the slaves. On the other hand, laws were passed that opposed the home-traffic, and rendered it as difficult as possible.

In the year 779, Charles the Great passed a law that no slave should be exported out of his dominions ; and in the council at Rheims, it was enacted, that the slave-trade should only be carried on by Christians, and that a man who sold his slaves either to a Jew or a Heathen, should be excommunicated, and that the contract should be void. Kidnapping was, however, very frequent among the Christians, particularly in Nordalbingia, (the present Dukedoms of Schleswick and Holstein,) who used to force those Christians who had fled to them from their Heathen neighbours, to re-enter the slavery, and suffer themselves to be re-sold to their former masters ; till at length, St. Anschar, archbishop of Hamburgh, prevailed on them to abolish this disgraceful custom, and to issue a law, " that whoever should be accused of kidnapping, should clear himself by the judgment of God, (so the ordeal was then called,) and should be excluded from the rights of of producing witnesses, or taking the oath prescribed by common law ;" a law which bordered very near upon that of the Jews : (Exod. chap. 21 :) " And he that stealeth a man, or if he be found in his hand, he shall surely be put to death." What Charles the Great and the synods, in different parts of Germany, France, and Italy, had enacted, with respect to the slave-trade, was followed by other princes.

For Canute the Great, king of England, passed a law, " That no Christian should be sold for exportation." This same law had been enacted before, viz. in the synod of Enham, in the year 1009,—" Ne Christiani et innocentes extra Patriam vendantur."

By such means the foreign slave-trade decreased, and could only be carried on by fraudulent means, and by a description of persons who were carefully watched by the bishops, whom a synod had authorised to inquire throughout their respective dioceses, " whether slaves were exported; whether a Christian were ever sold to a Jew or Heathen ; or, whether a Jew dealt in slaves who professed to be Christians ?" The famous market at Bristol, where the slaves were imported from all parts of England, and there sold to Irish merchants, who continued to buy slaves from England during the reign of King John, was much depressed and diminished by St. Wulfstan, whose example was imitated by the second synod of London, which enacted, " Nequis illud nefarium negotium, quod hactenus in Anglia solebant homines sicut bruta animalia venundari, deinceps ullatenus facere præsumat."

In Norway, few steps were taken towards the abolition of the slave-trade before the year 1270. The law, which, till that time, guided all civil business, was passed by King Hacon, who began his reign in the year 1222, and died in the year 1263. In this law much is spoken of the slaves, who seem to have been happier in Norway than in any other part of Europe ; for the slave could obtain his liberty by a prescription of twenty years, and the law guarded his life against the master, who, for having killed his slave, was liable to be punished as a murderer. The slave who destroyed his infant child, was considered as one of the greatest offenders; but as they had no capital punishments in Norway at that time, the punishment was being sold for exportation. The slave had some property accruing from his own industry, when not employed in his master's service; a property which sometimes enabled a skilful slave to recover his liberty. Snorro Sturleson, in Historia Rer. Norvegicar. Havn., 1777, vol. ii, in the life of King Oluf, remarks, that, the King, dissatisfied with some great men in the county of Thundhem, which then laboured under scarcity, forbade the inhabitants of the southern parts of Norway, to give even the least relief to their brethren in the North. A near relation of the famous Einar Thambaskielfer came to him and asked for corn; Einar, having fully explained the impropriety of complying with desires contrary to the proclamation of their royal master, said, " My slaves, for whose actions I am by no means legally bound, possess corn in plenty, it is their property, and they can dispose of it according to their own pleasure." The slaves in Denmark appear to have enjoyed the same privilege. The master of a slave could not refuse him his liberty, when offered the purchase-money: nay, it was sufficient if half the sum was delivered. The manumission prescribed in the same law, (Frostathing's Law of Hacon Haconson, part i,) is particularly curious:—" If a slave takes land and settles, then shall he give an entertainment, called the *Feast of Liberty*, the expenses of which shall be nine bushels of malt and a ram. A free-born man shall cut off the head of the ram, and the master shall unlock the collar * surrounding the slave's neck. If the master refuses to grant the slave leave to give the Feast of Liberty, then shall the slave request it before two witnesses, and in their presence invite his master with five friends of his. The slave then shall prepare the entertainment, and let the uppermost seat be ready to receive his master and mistress. Thus the slave shall recover his liberty, which recovery he shall prove

---

* In the museum of the Antiquarian Society at Edinburgh, is a metal collar, constructed with a ring for receiving a padlock, with the following inscription:--" Alexander Stewart found guilty of death, for theft at Perth, the 5th of December, 1701, and gifted by the Justiciary as a perpetual servant to Sir John Erskine, of Alva."—This collar was found in the grave of the deceased, in the burial ground at Alva.

by those who were present at the feast, against all attempts which his master may pursue for the future." Such was the state of the law in Norway when it was totally abolished, in the year 1270, by King Magnus, called the " Reformer of the Law."

During the existence of slavery in Denmark, it much resembled the Roman ; and it is uncertain how or when the Danish slaves were emancipated.—In Sweden, the state of slavery fell and rose in the same degree as it did among her neighbours. In Upland, the servitude was abrogated by King Byrger, in the year 1295, and King Erie Magnusen spread the blessing of liberty over the rest of that kingdom in the year 1335, for the purpose, as he said, of following God, who has rescued the whole of mankind from slavery.

From these extracts and observations it appears, that slavery is an evil characterizing nations in a state of barbarism, and must serve to convince us that Europe would never have attempted, much less have effected, the happy alterations which have taken place within her own limits and dominion, had she not first received the humane doctrines of Christianity.—See Professor Thorklyn's Essay on the Slave Trade, *passim*. London, 1788, *8vo*.

NOTE L.—*Page 226.*

" THESE different regulations are as remarkable for their justice and prudence, as for their humanity. Their great tendency is to shew the valuableness of human life, and the necessity of having peace and good understanding in every neighbourhood ; and they possess that quality which should be the object of all good and wholesome laws—the *prevention of crimes*. Most criminal codes of jurisprudence seem more intent on the punishment of crimes, than on *preventing* the commission of them. The law of God always *teaches* and *warns*—that his creatures may not fall into condemnation; for judgment is his strange work, *i. e.* one reluctantly and seldom executed, as this text is frequently understood."— Dr. A. Clarke's Comment. Lev. xxii, at the end.

NOTE LI.—*Page 233.*

A SHEKEL was worth about *three shillings* of our money; so that a slave was valued at 4*l.* 10*s.*, and a freeman at double, or 9*l.*

The price or estimated value of *slaves* and *captives* has generally fluctuated with existing circumstances; and in many places, at different periods, they have been regarded as articles of barter, and frequently exchanged for horses, arms, and loaves of bread, and meat. Lullus, archbishop of Mentz, asserts, that he saw a horse exchanged for a male-slave. St. Rembert, archbishop of Hamburgh, received from the heathen Danes, a great number of their slaves for the horse upon which he rode, and whom he purchased in order to instruct in Christianity, and then liberate. Jornandes tells us, that the Goths exchanged their slaves for a piece of bread and meat. Among the Franks, the price of a skilful slave was ten shillings of gold; but in Denmark, Norway, and Sweden, the regular price never exceeded one mark of silver, or one pound twelve shillings sterling; and in Wales, a slave was equal to a head of cattle. A slave was, everywhere in the northern parts of Europe, sold with the same forms and solemnities as a horse or any other beast; except in Denmark, where a proclamation before a court of law was ordered to precede the sale; and the same custom was paid for an imported slave as for an ox, viz. a saiga or penny, if the slave was to be sold. The slaves being chained together, were brought to market and sold in lots, each lot containing a number of slaves. Thus, St. Eligius, bishop of Noyons, often bought twenty, thirty, fifty, nay, whole ship-loads in such lots, consisting of men, women, and children, from Germany, Britain, Italy, and the Levant. Helmold beheld at one time, in the market at Mecklenburgh, seven thousand Danes exposed to sale. At that time, certain merchants engaged only in this branch of trade, principally Jews, especially in France, and acquired considerable property by this nefarious traffick. But none of these European slave-dealers were more savage than the inhabitants of Verdun, who, having emasculated the boys, sold them at an immense price to the Arabs, who were then settled in Spain. On the other hand, the Saracens raised an incredible number of slaves for the Venetians, who sold them publicly at Rome. In Iceland, a singular law existed relative to the poor, and which deserves to be noticed for the reverence to parents which it exhibits; it is found in the law of the republic of Iceland, called " Gragaas," in the book relative to the Poor, c. i.—It is as follows :—

B b

" 1. Be it enacted, That the son maintain his mother, in preference to his other relations.

" 2. That he support his kindred, as long as he can afford it, in the following order; first his father, then his own children, and next after them his cousins.

" That the claims of his other kindred be relative to his right of coming to the inheritance of them. If the son have no fortune, then shall he sell himself into slavery for the support of his father; who, on the mother's situation being more aggravated, shall give up his place to her, and he shall be supported by his nearest relations.

" The father has the alternative of selling himself and his children into slavery, on account of their education.

" If a person aforesaid be found to beg, then shall he who ought and could support that person, pay a fine to the public."

This servitude or slavery was, however, to last no longer than the urgent necessity continued.—See an " Essay on the Slave Trade," pp. 7—10, 17.

NOTE LII.—*Page 229.*

" The Roman lawyers laid it down as a sound maxim in jurisprudence, ' That he who found any property, and applied it to his own use, should be considered as a thief, whether he knew the owner or not; for, in their view, the crime was not lessened, suppose the finder was totally ignorant of the right owner.'—Qui alienum quid jacens, lucri faciendi causâ sustulit, furti obstringitur, sive scit, cujus sit, sive ignoravit; nihil enim ad furtum minuendum facit, quod cujus sit, ignoret.—DIGESTOR. lib. xlvii; tit. ii; leg. xliii, sect. 4. On this subject, every honest man must say, that the man who finds any lost property, and does not make all the inquiry to find out the owner, should, in sound policy, be treated as a thief. It is said of the Dyrbœans, a people who inhabited the tract between Bactria and India, that if they met with any lost property, even on the public road, they never touched it. This was actually the case in *this* kingdom, in the time of Alfred the Great, about A.D. 888; so that golden bracelets hung up on the public roads were untouched by the finger of rapine. One of Solon's laws was, *Take not up what you laid not down.* How easy to act by this principle in case of finding lost property : ' This is not mine, and it would be criminal to convert it to my use, unless the owner be dead, and his family extinct.' When all due inquiry is made, if no owner can be found, the lost property may be legally considered to be the property of the finder."—Dr. A. Clarke's Comment. on Levit. vi. 4.

NOTE LIII.—*Page* 229.

Six of the cities given to the Levites, were appointed as *cities of refuge,* to which the *manslayer,* or he who had accidentally occasioned the death of another, without " malice aforethought," might flee, as to an asylum, and be protected from the *goel* or avenger of blood. (Numb. xxxv. 11.) To give the unhappy individual every possible advantage in his flight, it became the duty of the Sanhedrim, to make the roads that led to those cities convenient and wide, and remove every thing out of the way that could possibly obstruct his flight. No river was to remain without a bridge, the road was to be everywhere levelled, and be, at least, thirty-two cubits broad. At every turning, posts were erected with the inscription, " REFUGE—REFUGE," in order to guide him in the way ; and two students in the law were appointed to accompany him, that if the avenger (who was always the next heir to him that had been killed) should overtake him before he reached the city, they might endeavour to pacify him, and induce him to suspend his revenge till the fugitive was either condemned or acquitted in a court of justice. When the manslayer arrived at the city gates, he was examined by proper persons, who were to determine whether he deserved protection. If the inquiry was satisfactorily answered, he was received into the city, until he could be brought before the court of judgment in the city where the fatal occurrence had happened. If the court decided, that the death of the deceased had been casually occasioned, the unfortunate manslayer was sent back to the city of refuge, to remain there till the death of the high-priest. A convenient habitation was assigned him ; and, according to the declarations of the Jews, the inhabitants were obliged to teach him some trade, by which he might be able to support himself. To render their situation more comfortable, the mothers of the high-priests used to feed and clothe these refugees, that they might not pray for the death of their sons, upon whose decease they were all restored to liberty. No person, however, had the benefit of refuge but the ignorant and involuntary manslayer ; but no money or interest could purchase his liberty before the time appointed. If he died before his release, his bones were delivered to his relations, after the death of the high-priest, to be buried in the sepulchre of his fathers.—Lewis's Antiquities of the Hebrew Republick, vol. i. b. 2, c. 13, pp. 184—187.—See also Jahn's Biblical Archæology, sect. 264, p. 326.—Horne's Introduction to the Critical Study of the Scriptures, vol. iii. p. ii. c. 3, sect. 4, p. 145 ; and Carpenter's Popular Introduction to the Study of the Holy Scriptures, p. ii. c. 2, sect. 4, p. 296.

NOTE LIV.—*Page* 231.

IN order to increase the abhorrence of murder and homicide among the Israelites, and to represent it as polluting both the land and the people ; or in other words, in order, not only to deter them from murder, but to make every man, who knew any thing of a murder, disposed to give every information concerning it, there was, in the case of a murdered person being found in the fields, and his murderer remaining unknown, a certain ceremonial ordained by way of expiation. The statute relative to it is recorded in Deut. xxi, 1—9.—The reason for bringing the heifer into a valley, through which ran a stream of water, is said by Abendana, to be, that the inhabitants of each city might be the more careful to prevent such murders, being otherwise in danger of losing the best ground that belonged to their inheritance ; for the land where the body was found was never to be sown any more. In this valley, one of the elders or magistrates coming behind the heifer struck off her head ; for so the murderer was supposed to have treacherously surprized the slain man. If the murdered man was found before the heifer's head was struck off, it was suffered to return to the pasture amongst the other cattle ; but the murderer was to be cut off by the sword. Such a ceremonial was peculiarly necessary to give publicity to such an event, at a period when the modern means of communicating intelligence by the press did not exist ; and it was, therefore, useful in contributing to place men's lives in greater security. Hence it has been well observed by a learned prelate, that, " no (other) ancient law made such provision for the discovery and expiation of secret murders as this of Moses. For the very best of them, which is that of Plato, enacts no more than this, That if a man was found dead, and he that killed him, after a diligent search, could not be heard of, public proclamation should be made, that he who was guilty of the fact should not come into any holy place, nor any part of the whole country ; for if he were discovered and apprehended, he should be put to death, and be thrown out of the bounds of the country, and have no burial."—Lib. ix, *de Legibus*, p. 874; Michaelis's Commentaries on the Laws of Moses, vol. iv, art. 278, p. 253 ; Lewis's Antiq. of the Hebrew Republic, b. vi, c. 8, p. 170; Bishop Patrick's Comment. on Deut. xxi, 9.

NOTE LV.—*Page 232.*

THE earliest notice we have of the *Lex Talionis*, or returning *like for like*, is Exod. xxi, 24, 25. It constituted one of the celebrated Roman laws of the XII Tables, but was afterwards changed to a pecuniary fine to be levied at the discretion of the Prætor. It is still continued in the *Canon Law*, in the case of the *Calumniator*, who is adjudged to the punishment he intended to have inflicted upon another. The arguments for and against this peculiar mode of judgment, by the *Lex Talionis*, may be found at length in Michaelis's "Commentaries on the Laws of Moses," vol. iii, art. 240, 241, 242. Distinguishing betwixt the exercise of justice by civil authority in the state, and the extension of mercy by individuals to those who have injured them, he defends the principle, when regulated by law, as in the case of the Israelites, and modified by limitations according to the character and degree of civilization of the respective nations among whom it is exercised ; and considers the *Lex Talionis* under the direction of the magistrate, as guarding the nation against the infliction of infuriated revenge, by exasperated individuals.

NOTE LVI.—*Page 233.*

THE substitution of pecuniary mulcts for such injuries as those described Exod. xxi, 18, 19, were wise and excellent institutions; and most courts of justice still regulate their decisions, in similar cases, by these precepts.—The Jews say that satisfaction was to be made to the injured person for the loss he had sustained in five particulars ;—for the hurt in his body ;—the loss of his time ;—the pain he had endured ;—the charge of physician or surgeon ;—and the disgrace. Upon which the Hebrew doctors observe that, some men being able to earn more by their labour than others ; and the disability occasioned by the stroke, being greater or less, of longer or shorter continuance, a proportionate compensation must be made to the person injured, regulated by these considerations and others of a like nature.—See Patrick in *loc.*

NOTE LVII.—*Page 233.*

THE meaning of the precept, in Exod. xxii, 9, appears to be, that when a man had affirmed he had either deposited certain things with another, or had lent them to him, or that the accused person was charged with having taken them ; that, in such cases, both parties should be brought before the judges, and a legal examination should take place. If it appeared that the accusation was unjust, then he who pretended to have deposited the goods was adjudged to pay double the value of the things pretended to have been dishonestly retained ; but if the accusation proved to be true, then the fraudulent person was ordered to pay that amount to the man whom he had defrauded. —It is added by the Hebrew lawyers, that, if the goods had been lost by mere chance, nothing was to be paid ; and if a man brought an action against another, about such things as those mentioned already, and the defendant acknowledged part of the charge but denied the rest, he was to restore to the extent of the confession he had made, and to be put upon his oath as to the part which he denied ; or if he denied the whole, and he that brought the accusation had but one witness against him, he was allowed to clear himself by an oath.—See Patrick *in loc.*

NOTE LVIII.—*Page 234.*

THE true reasons of the difference between the fines of restitution for oxen, and those for sheep, seem to be, not only that, as Maimonides supposes, an ox might be more easily stolen than a sheep, but because it was of greater value, and also of more use in husbandry.—Lewis's Antiq. of the Heb. Republick, vol. iii, B. 6, c. 10, p. 177.—Pastoret, Moyse considéré comme Legislateur et comme Moraliste, chap. 5 § 5. p. 445, Paris, 1788. 8vo.

NOTE LIX.—*Page* 234.

A *false witness*, according to the *law of retaliation*, (JUS TALIONIS,) was to be punished with the same punishment which was decreed against the crime, in reference to which he had falsely testified. (Deut. xix, 16—21.) Some of our excellent English laws have been made on this very ground. In the 37th of Edw. III, ch. 18, it is ordained, that all those who make suggestion shall incur the same pain which the other should have had, if he were attainted, in case his suggestions be found evil. A similar law was made the 38th of the same reign, c. 9. By a law of the Twelve Tables, a false witness among the Romans was thrown down the Tarpeian rock; and among the Athenians an action lay not only against a false witness, but also against the person who produced him: a fine was laid upon them, and they were declared infamous; and if they were found thrice guilty of this crime, they, and their posterity were declared infamous to the latest generation. —Clarke and Patrick in Deut. xix, 19.

In the time of Christ, the JUS TALIONIS, (see Note 55,) was confounded with moral principles, *i. e.* it was taught, that the law of Moses, which was merely civil or penal, rendered it perfectly justifiable, in a moral point of view, for a person to inflict on another the same injury, whatever it might be, which he himself had received. (Matt. v, 38—40.) The persons who expounded the law to this effect, do not appear to have recollected its true character, as a civil or penal law, nor to have remembered that the literal retaliation could not take place until after the decision of a judge on a suit, brought by the person injured, and then was never to exceed the original injury.—Jahn's Biblical Archæology, by T. C. Upham, sect. 256, p. 315.

NOTE LX.—*Page 235.*

BISHOP PATRICK renders Levit. vi, 4,—" When he hath sinned and *acknowledges* his guilt." By this translation he recon-
ciles the contradiction which appears betwixt this law and that
in Exod. xxii, 1, 7, 9, where a *five-fold* restitution is required;
and adds, " that the reason of the difference betwixt these
laws is, because in Exodus he speaks of those thieves who were
convicted by witnesses in a court of law, and then condemned to make such great restitution; but here, of such as,
touched with a sense of their sin, came voluntarily and acknowledged their theft, or other crime, of which nobody convicted
them, or at least confessed it freely when they were adjured;
and, therefore, were condemned to suffer a less punishment, and
to expiate their guilt by a sacrifice."—This interpretation, he
thinks, is confirmed by Numbers v, 7, where the first words
may be translated, " If they shall confess their sin that they
have done," &c. and deems this explanation preferable to the
one given by Maimonides.—See Patrick *in loc.* and Lewis's
Antiq. of Heb. Rep. vol. ii, b. 4, c. 10, p. 536; vol. iii,
b. 6, c. 10, p. 177.

NOTE LXI.—*Page 236.*

THE CAPITAL PUNISHMENTS among the Jews, inflicted by
the Sanhedrim, or house of Judgment, were—*Stoning, Burning,
Slaying with the sword* or *Beheading,* and *Strangling* or *Hanging.*
Of these, *Stoning* was accounted the most severe. *Burning*
was regarded as worse than the sword, the *Sword* worse
than strangling, and *Strangling* or *Hanging* the easiest.

STONING was practised among many other nations beside the
Jews. By the laws of Moses, the witnesses were to throw the
first stone against the criminal, and after the witnesses, the
people. (Deut. xiii, 10, xvii, 7; Joshua vii, 25; John
viii. 7.)

BURNING was a punishment variously executed; sometimes
by a fire made of faggots, and which was probably the mode
practised in the cases mentioned in Levit. xx, 14;—xxi, 9.—
R. Elieser Ben Zadok says, he saw a priest's daughter thus

burnt for fornication; (Patrick *in loc.*)—sometimes, if the Rabbins are to be believed, by pouring melted lead down the throat of the living criminal; sometimes the body was consumed by fire, after the condemned person had been stoned. (Joshua vii. 25.)

SLAYING WITH THE SWORD OR DECAPITATION.—Decapitation, or beheading, was a method of taking away life that was known and practised among the Egyptians, (Gen. xl. 17—19,) and was also in use among the Jews, as is clear from 2 Kings x. 7; Matt. xiv. 10; but it may be doubted, whether this was the usual method of putting to death, designated by the expresssion, "slaying with the sword," which was most probably effected by plunging the sword into the bowels of the criminals, though used for destroying them in any way by that weapon.

STRANGLING or HANGING.—The Jews say that the malefactor was placed up to the loins in dung, a napkin put round his neck, which was drawn tight by two of the witnesses, who acted as executioners, until he was strangled to death. Of this, however, there is no proof in the Scriptures. The *hanging*, or suspension on a tree, which is there spoken of, was a posthumous disgrace inflicted on the body of one who had been previously executed. (Joshua viii. 29, x. 25; Numb. xxv. 4, 5.)

The other punishments mentioned by Maimonides are, DEATH BY THE HAND OF GOD; EXCISION or CUTTING OFF; SCOURGING; and REPROOF or ADMONITION.

DEATH BY THE HAND OF GOD, or BY THE HAND OF HEAVEN, is understood by the Jewish writers to mean, a sudden and signal punishment inflicted by the immediate power of God, and not by the authority of any human magistrate. This death was supposed to be merely personal, and not to affect children or posterity. The words, *lest they die*, so frequently used in the Law, in relation to Aaron and his sons, or the affairs of the sanctuary, are interpreted by them, as referring to this punishment.

EXCISION OR CUTTING OFF, was understood to be a deeper degree of indignation, and a more awful stroke, than *Death by the hand of Heaven;* and was thought to signify a premature death, to die without children, and to forfeit the happiness of the other world.—" Cut off," as the meaning evidently is, from all the blessings and privileges of that Covenant which God had made with Israel.—On the precept respecting the Sabbath, (Exod. xxxi. 14,) it has been excellently remarked, by the learned Selden, (De Synedriis,) from Eliah ben Moseh, a Karaite writer, that, he who violates a negative precept, either does it secretly, which is the most frequent, or openly, which but seldom happens, unless he be an apostate, and profligate wretch. Now, the Scriptures threaten him that secretly breaks the Sabbath with " cutting off," by the hand of God, according to what is written in this place. Incestuous and unlawful conjunctions are similarly threatened, (Levit. xviii. 29,) because they are committed secretly.—But if any one did any work openly on the Sabbath, so that there were witnesses of it, he was to be stoned, according to what is said, Numb. xv. 25 ; though if he did it by mistake, either secretly or openly, he was only to bring a sacrifice for his error ; and if he offended against any of the decrees of the Wise-Men about the Sabbath, he was to be beaten. Or, if there were no Court of Judgment in the place, (as now, in their present condition,) then all such transgressors were left to God to punish them, whatever was their crime.

SCOURGING was twofold, either with *rods*, or with *thongs*. The former was in use among the Romans, as well as the latter ; but the latter only amongst the Jews. The person who was convicted of a crime, and was sentenced to be scourged, was extended upon the ground, and the stripes, which were never to exceed forty, were inflicted on his back, in the presence of the judge. (Deut. xxv, 2, 3.)—Afterwards, the Jews, for fear of exceeding the number prescribed by the Law, fixed it at thirty-nine, which were inflicted in their synagogues. (Matt. x, 17.) They employed for the purpose a whip or scourge, with three lashes made of thongs from an ox's hide. Thirteen blows consequently inflicted thirty-nine stripes. (2 Cor. xi, 24.) When the sentence was to be executed, the prisoner was tied by his hands to a low post or pillar, a cubit and a half high, (according to the Rabbins,) so that his body "bowed down" upon it. (Deut. xxv, 2.) He was then stripped down to his waist, and the executioner standing behind him, on a stone, performed his office, whilst the chief judge repeated all or part of certain passages of scripture, viz. Deut. xxviii, 58 ; xxix, 9 ; and Psalm lxxiii, 38.—After having suffered the sentence of the law, no person was to be reproached for the punishment he had undergone, nor upbraided with the crime for which he had been punished. Sometimes, in atrocious cases, they fastened small bones, or pieces of lead to the scourges, or tied thorns to the thongs, (called, say the Jews, *Scorpions*, in 1 Kings xii, 12,) in order to render the punishment more terrible.

REPROOF, or ADMONITION, was an ecclesiastical censure, the same perhaps with St. Paul's *Rebuke*, 1 Tim. v, i. The person who lay under it, was to keep himself within doors, as one who ought to be ashamed of his conduct. He was not to appear in public, nor in the presence of him who pronounced the sentence, though others were not bound to avoid his company, but might resort to his house. The occasions on which this censure was exercised were two, *Money* and *Epicurism :* On account of *Money*, when any one owing money to another did not pay it, and on being summoned before the Court, refused to pay it ; on account of *Epicurism*, when any one, by his disregard of the Divine law, proved himself to be a presumptuous person, governed by no rule, and circumscribed by no law.—Godwyn's Moses and Aaron, lib. 5, chap. vii ; viii.—Lewis's Antiq. of the Heb. Repub. vol. i, c. 8, 9.— Jahn's Biblical Archæology, sect. 257, 258, 259.—Leusden, Philologus Hebræo-Mixtus, Dissert. xlvii, xlviii. Ultraject. 1682, 4to.

NOTE LXII.—*Page* 241.

THE "Hedges of the Law," as they were termed, were the injunctions and decisions of the Wise-Men of the Sanhedrim, designed to secure obedience to the Law.—"After the Captivity of Babylon iniquity abounded ; men's defects in what is good were innumerable, and their practices of what is ill incorrigible.—To find out a proper remedy against this universal corruption, and to bring about a true reformation, it is said the men of the Great Synagogue recommended to the judges, to be slow in judging ; to the priests, to instruct a great number of disciples ; and to the scribes, to make *a Hedge* to the Law, in order to terrify the people from breaking through it. Actions indifferent in themselves were then prohibited or commanded, to the end that bad actions might be more carefully avoided, and good ones promoted and practised. The design was certainly innocent and good, but by these means, human inventions were substituted for the Law of God; mere external forms and precepts took place of the eternal and unchangeable duties of religion and piety ; the real practice of true virtue was neglected, the most eminent men for learning and holiness of life, pharisees, scribes, doctors, and expounders of the Law, became very strict and jealous, even to superstition, in observing the rites and ceremonies of the Law, in outward purifications, in the washing of pots, and cups, and the like; whilst they took no care at all to purify their own minds from all unrighteousness, and to practise those great duties which are briefly summed up in the love of God and our neighbour."

The decree of the members of the Great Synagogue or Sanhedrim, as given in the *Pirke Avoth* or Chapters of the Fathers, (supposed to be originally written by R. Juda, but afterwards added to the Mishna) is, "Be slow in judgment; instruct a great many disciples; and make a Hedge to the Law."—It is also a proverbial saying of the Jews, that "The Masorah is the Hedge of the Law."— Stehelin's Rabbinical Literature, or the Traditions of the Jews, vol. i, Prelim. Pref. p. 24, Lond. 1748, 8*vo.*—Buxtorf. Lex. Talmud. סיג.

NOTE LXIII.—*Page 243.*

The exculpation of the members of the Sanhedrim was not granted them individually and personally, but collectively and officially; for this being the highest and most sacred tribunal, the punishment of its errors rested with God, the Supreme Head of the Theocratical Government.

NOTE LXIV.—*Page 244.*

"None were guilty of this crime," of sinning presumptuously, or as it is literally in the Hebrew *with a High*

Hand, "but those who, as the words immediately following express, 'reproached the Lord:' (Numb. xv, 30 :) nor was any one considered as reproaching the Lord, but such as openly cast contempt upon his commands. Abarbinel restricts the crime of sinning ' with a high hand,' to those who deny the Law to be of divine origin, and that 'publicly, perversely, and deliberately.'—Abarbinel is followed by Grotius, (Numb. xv,) who contends that the phrase, "he that doeth aught presumptuously," is to be understood of one " who obstinately denies the being of a God, or the divine inspiration of the Law."—Outram, On Sacrifices, Diss. i, c, 13, p. 156.

NOTE LXV.—*Page* 249.

THIS view of the Mosaic precept is maintained also by our author, in his YAD HACHAZAKAH, tom. iv, tit. 20, c. 8, Amstel. 1702, folio.—Dr. Prideaux has published this, and the two succeeding chapters with a Latin translation, and notes, in his *Tractatus de Proselytis,* c. iii, p, 137—appended to *R. Moses Maimonides De Jura Pauperis, et Peregrini apud Judæos,* Oxon. 1689, 4*to.*—But after comparing what Maimonides and other Jewish writers, as well as more modern Commentators, have said, and comparing their arguments with the sacred text, I am persuaded, that our author's judgment has been warped by the decisions of the Talmudists, who " have made the word of God of none effect by their traditions ;" and that the great objects of the Jewish legislator were, *to check the licentiousness of the soldiery,* and inculcate *chastity* and *humanity;* and not to give countenance to illicit gratifications or impure desires. If a soldier was attracted by the beauty of a female captive, he was permitted to marry her, though she was not one of his own nation, after he had allowed her sufficient time to mourn her separation from her relatives and to reconcile her to her situation ; but if, after having married her, he became dissatisfied with her, though he might divorce her and " put her away," yet he was not suffered either to sell her or retain her as a slave, but was obliged to liberate her, and let her go whither she pleased, because, having cohabited with her as his wife, he had, to use the Scripture phraseology, " humbled her."—The sentiments of R. Bechai and Philo, both of them

Jewish writers of eminence, accord with this representation. R. Bechai, says, "God would have the camp of Israel holy, and not defiled with fornication and other abominations, as the camps of the Gentiles:" And Philo observes, "Moses ordered every thing most excellently in this law: first, in not letting the reins loose to men's desires, but restraining them for thirty days; in which time, secondly, a trial was made of his love, whether it was a furious ungovernable passion, or had something of reason in it, which advises us to do nothing suddenly, but after serious and long deliberation. And, thirdly, this was a merciful law to the captive; that if she were a virgin, she might bewail her unhappiness in not being disposed of in marriage by her parents; if a widow, that she had lost her first love, and was now to be married to one, who would be her lord, as well as her husband."—See Patrick on Deut. xxi, 11—13.

NOTE LXVI.—*Page* 251.

THE process of *Threshing*, "is, in the East, more properly termed *heading out* the grain. It is performed by five or six oxen travelling round upon the same floor: when employed in this labour, the 'muzzling' of them is expressly forbidden by the Hindoo laws."—Tennant's Indian Recreations, vol. 2, p. 278. This kindness extended to oxen, by the Hindoo legislators, was probably derived from the far earlier precepts of the Mosaic code. It would also seem, that it was not merely the intention of the Jewish precept to provide for the welfare of "oxen," but to enjoin, with the greater force and effect, that a similar right should be allowed to human labourers, whether hirelings or slaves. Moses specified the ox, as the lowest example; and what held good in reference to it, was to be considered as so much the more obligatory in reference to man. It would appear, therefore, that not only servants, but also day-labourers, might eat of the fruits they gathered, and drink of the *must* which they pressed. The wages of the latter appear to have been given them over and above their meat, and, in consideration of this privilege, to have been so much the less, as is the practice in our agricultural districts in England at present. The following decision of the Jewish doctors, is given in the *Raba Mezia,* fol. 83. "The workman may lawfully eat of what he works among; in the vintage, he may eat of the grapes; when gathering figs, he may partake of them; and in harvest, he may eat of the ears of corn. Of gourds and dates he may eat the value of a denarius."— Michaelis's Commentaries on the Laws of Moses, vol. ii, art. 130, pp. 190, 191.

How very differently humane, even towards the brute creation, is the ordinance of the Jewish legislator, to the practice of other nations; for, although the Egyptians, Greeks, and Romans used oxen in "treading out their corn," either with their feet, or by drawing a cart or other machine over it; yet, they were accustomed to prevent their eating the corn, some by muzzling them; others, by daubing their mouths with dung; others, by hanging a wooden instrument about their necks, which hindered them from stooping down; and others, by putting sharp pricks into their mouths; or keeping them without drink; or covering the corn with skins.—See Bocharti Hierozoicon, p. i. lib. 2. cap. 40, referred to by Patrick on Deut. xxv. 4.

NOTE LXVII.—*Page 252.*

PRIOR to the time of Moses, the father exercised the right of declaring the first son of the most beloved wife as the FIRST-BORN with regard to the right of inheritance, though not actually so in point of age; we may instance the cases of Isaac preferred to Ishmael, and Joseph to the older sons of Jacob. (Gen. xxi. 10—14; xxiv, 36; xlviii, 5—7, compared with 1 Chron. v, 2.) This right, which could not fail to occasion much secret ill-will, jealousy, and hatred, where polygamy was usual, was suspended by the Mosaic statute, which enjoined, that he should be recognized as the *first-born,* who first made his appearance in the world, without any difference to the wife who was the most beloved; and consequently assigned to him the double portion of the inheritance. (Deut. xxi, 15—17.)

" The right of PRIMOGENITURE in males," says Blackstone, " seems to have only obtained among the Jews, in whose constitution the eldest son had a double portion of the inheritance, in the same manner as with us, by the laws of King Henry the First, the eldest son had the capital fee or principal feud of his father's possessions, and no other pre-eminence; and as the eldest daughter had afterwards the principal mansion, when the estate descended in coparcenary. The Greeks, the Romans, the Britons, the Saxons, and even originally the feudists, divided the lands equally; some, among all the children at large; some, among the males only. But when the emperors began to create honorary feuds, or titles of nobility, it was found necessary (in order to preserve their dignity) to make them impartible, or as they stiled them, *feuda individua*, and in consequence descendible to the eldest son alone. This example was farther enforced by the inconvenience that attended the splitting of estates; namely, the division of the military services, the multitude of infant tenants incapable of performing any duty, the consequential weakening of the strength of the kingdom, and the inducing younger sons to take up with the business and idleness of a country life, instead of being serviceable to themselves and the public, by engaging in mercantile, in military, in civil, or in ecclesiastical employments. These reasons occasioned an almost total change in the method of feudal inheritances abroad; so that the eldest male began universally to succeed to the whole of the lands in all military tenures: and in this condition the feodal constitution was established in England by William the Conqueror. Yet we find that socage* estates frequently descended to all the sons equally, so lately as the reign of Henry the Second; and it is mentioned as a part of our ancient constitution, that knights' fees should descend to the eldest son, and socage fees should be partible among the male children. However, in Henry the Third's time, we find that socage lands, in imitation of lands in chivalry, had almost entirely fallen into the right of succession by primogeniture, as the law now stands; except in Kent, where they gloried in the preservation of their ancient gavelkind tenure, of which a principal branch was the joint inheritance of all the sons; and except in some particular

---

* SOCAGE or SOCCAGE, in its most general and extensive signification, seems to denote a tenure by any certain and determinate service; and in this sense it is by our ancient writers constantly put in opposition to chivalry, or knight-service, where the render was precarious and uncertain.

manors and townships, where their local customs continued
the descent, sometimes to all, sometimes to the youngest son
only, or in other more singular methods of succession."

Amongst the Jews, various rights were attached to the
Primogeniture : for (1.) they were peculiarly consecrated to
God ; (Exod. xxii, 29 ;)—(2.) they were next in honour to their
parents; (Gen. xlix, 3 ;)—(3.) they had a double portion of
their father's goods ; (Deut. xxi, 17 ;)—(4.) they succeeded
them in the government of the family, or kingdom ; (2 Chron.
xxi, 3 ;)—(5.) they had the sole right of conducting the service of God, both at the tabernacle and temple; and hence
the tribe of Levi, which was taken in lieu of the first-born,
had the sole right of administration in the Divine service.
(Numb. viii, 14—17.)—See Michaelis's Commentaries on the
Laws of Moses, vol. i, Art. 79, pp. 427—429 ; Blackstone,
B. ii, c. 14, sect. iii; Dr. A. Clarke's Commentary on Gen.,
xxv, 31.

NOTE LXVIII.—*Page* 254.

" FROM various passages of the Sacred Writings, it appears
that the Sabbath was in part designed to afford a weekly rest
and refreshment from the toil of worldly occupations. (Exod.
xxiii, 12.) Of this rest, not only servants and labourers, but
beasts of burden were to partake: a wise and merciful law,
which extended the repose so needful for man to the brute
animals subjected to his domination. Being also appointed to
be kept holy to the Lord, it afforded a frequent opportunity
for sacred meditation, and for such pious exercises as
administer to the spiritual welfare of the soul. Time was thus
allowed for the performance of many rites, and ceremonies, and
obligations enjoined in the Levitical law.

" Much as it contributed to the support of religion in general,
it was specially designed to keep in memory the Creation of
all things by Jehovah Elohim. This is the specific reason
assigned for its adoption into the Mosaic polity. (Exod. xxi,
11 ; xxxi, 17.) Great must have been the efficacy of this
ordinance in restraining the Israelites from idol-worship, the
besetting sin of that stubborn people. Being instituted in
memory of the work of creation, every act of compliance with

C c

the command was a virtual acknowledgment of the one Jehovah, in opposition to the numerous false deities of surrounding nations. The remission of their worldly employments on the seventh day, naturally called to remembrance God's creating the world in six days, and resting on the seventh. In the constant renewal of this recollection, their minds must have been as constantly impressed with the first and fundamental truth of all religion, the unity and omnipotence of the Deity. With every returning Sabbath, their thoughts were directed to the Supreme Being, who, existing eternally, infinite in his perfections, and the Creator of the universe, was alone deserving their praise, their reverence, and worship."—See Holden's Christian Sabbath, ch. iii, sect. i, pp. 133—140. London, 1825, 8vo.

NOTE LXIX.—*Page 255.*

THE fifth day before the Feast of Tabernacles, viz. the tenth day of the seventh month or Tisri, [September,] was the day of atonement or expiation. (Levit. xvi, 1—34; Exod. xxiii, 26—30; Numb. xxix, 1—11.) It was a day of fasting, and the only one during the whole year, on which food was interdicted from evening to evening. (Levit. xxiii, 27—29; xxv, 9.)—It was called the Feast, (or sometimes the Fast) of *Expiation* or *Propitiation,* because the High Priest then made confession unto God of his own sins and of the sins of the people; and performed certain rites and ceremonies in order to expiate them, and make an atonement unto God for them.—Upon this day, the high-priest was permitted to enter the holy of holies; and, according to the later Jews, had the privilege, on this day, to pronounce the word JEHOVAH or peculiar name of God, which was never allowed to be spoken by any one but by the high-priest, and by him only on this day.

The institution of this solemn day was first occasioned by Moses, on that day, coming down from the mount, after three several fasts of forty days, having obtained the reconciliation of God to Israel, bringing with him the renewed *Tables,* and a full commission to build the Tabernacle, and to set up divine worship amongst them.—See Jahn's Biblical Archæology, chap. iii, sect. 357, p. 452; Godwyn's Moses and Aaron, lib. 3, c. 8, p. 129; Lewis's Antiq. of the Heb. Rep. vol ii, c. 15, p. 571.

NOTE LXX.—*Page 255.*

THE subjoined solution of the reason adduced by Maimonides, for celebrating the Passover for seven days, is from the pen of a learned friend.

" Festum enim Paschatis quod attinet, cur septem diebus celebrandum sit, manifestum est ; quia nempe circumactio vel revolutio septum dierum est circumvolutio media inter diem Solarem et mensem Lunarem, quæ ut magnum habet (sicuti nosti) usum in rebus naturalibus, ita quoque in legalibus. Lex etenim perpetuo assimilatur naturæ, et res naturales aliquo modo perficit."

" The Paschal Lamb was always killed at the time of the Full Moon. If we suppose Saturday or the Jewish Sabbath to be the time of the Full Moon, and consequently the time of killing the Paschal Lamb, unleavened bread would be eaten from the fourteenth day of the Lunar month, until Saturday the 21st day, which being the ' Terminus,' or ' Circumactio,' or ' Revolutio,' of the seven days, would actually be the middle period, between the 14th day, the mean of the Lunar month and the following Sunday, the period signified by the terms ' solarem, vel naturalem diem,' by which we may consider the Saturday to be signified, independently of the time computed by the Moon. This will appear still more evident if we consider further the words of our learned author, ' Lex etenim,' &c. For as the Full Moon is a mean between the ' luna dimidiata' and the ' luna gibbosa,' so the ' terminus' of the week, in which the Passover is celebrated, is assimilated to nature, who, by her unerring law, makes the Full Moon, or the time from the Change to the Full, the mean of the Lunar month."

NOTE LXXI.—*Page 256.*

MAIMONIDES explains his views more fully in his " YAD," in the treatise on *Repentance,* (c. 3,) where he says : " The sound of the Trumpet at this time, did in effect say, Shake off your drowsiness, ye that sleep ; and, being awaked, watch to your duty : Search and try your ways : Remember your Creator and repent. You, whom the vanity of the times hath led into a forgetfulness of the Truth ; who spend your days, wandering after empty things which profit nothing, bethink yourselves, and take care of your souls. Let every one forsake his evil way, and his thoughts which are not good."

Bonfrerius supposes that God put honour upon this month, because it was the *seventh;* that as every *seventh day* was a Sabbath, and in every *seventh year* the land rested, &c., so every *seventh month* of every year was a kind of *sabbatical* month; there being more feasts in this month than in any other month of the year.—See Bishop Patrick on Levit. xxiii, 24,—who adds, that the "Blowing of Trumpets" at this time was most probably designed as a memorial of the Creation of the world, which took place in Autumn, and was the reason why they anciently began their year at this time, as they still do in the East.

NOTE LXXII.—*Page* 258.

Pococke, in his Miscellaneæ, p. 170, 227, has shown, that the Jews believed that the fire of hell had no effect on any of their nation, because Abraham, Isaac, and Jacob came down to deliver them. This superstitious notion has been adopted from the Jews by the Mohammedans, who, although in contradiction to the Koran, believe, that, at the day of judgment, Christ, David, and Moses, will, by their intercession, deliver those from hell who have believed in their doctrine, even after it had been opposed by Mohammed. One of the principal maxims of the Jews is, that "all Israel partakes of eternal life." Another of their doctrines is, "God promised to Abraham, that if his children were wicked, he would consider them as righteous, on account of the sweet odour of his circumcision." To confute this, and other erroneous principles of the Jews, appears to have been the chief object of St. Paul, in his Epistle to the Romans.—See Marsh's Michaelis's Introduction to the New Testament, vol. iv. p. 95; London, 1802, 8vo.

NOTE LXXIII.—*Page* 258.

The feast of *In-Gathering*, noticed Levit. xxiii, 36, 39, was a distinct solemnity; though, from its immediately following the Feast of Tabernacles, it was usually regarded as the *last* or *great day* of that feast, and celebrated with still greater festivity. No

servile work was to be done upon it, and praises were sung to
God at the temple, with trumpets and instruments of music.
Upon this day they read the last section of the Law, and
likewise began the first, lest they should seem more joyful in
ending their Sections or Parashioth than willing to begin
them.—Lewis's Antiquities of the Hebrew Republic, vol. ii,
b. iv, c. 21, p. 605.

NOTE LXXIV.—Page 259.

The Jews say, that the *Booths* or *Tabernacles* were to be
made in the open air, or under the shelter of a tree, and
neither to be covered with cloth, nor made too close with
the boughs of which they were constructed; but to be
left sufficiently open for the sun and stars to be seen,
and the rain to descend through them. They were to
remain in them as in their houses; and, consequently, to
place household furniture in them, and regularly to sleep in
them, except in rainy weather, when they were permitted to
sleep in their houses, till the rain had ceased. In Nehemiah's
time, some made their booths upon the flat roofs of their
houses, others in their courts, and others in the streets.
(Nehemiah viii, 15; Deut xxii, 8.)—The Rabbins also teach us,
that every man brought his burden of boughs every morning,
or otherwise fasted that day; and this burden they termed
Hosanna. It appears to have been in allusion to this, that,
when our Saviour rode into Jerusalem, the people cut down
branches from the trees, and strewed them in the way, crying,
" Hosanna to the Son of David." (Matt. xxi. 9.)

On the first day of the feast, they prepared branches of
palm, willow, and myrtle, and tied them together with gold or
silver twist, or with other strings or twigs; and these they
carried in their hands every day of the feast. This practice
probably gave rise to the calumny cast upon the Jews by
Plutarch, who compares this feast to the drunken festival
of Bacchus, in which the Bacchides ran up and down with
certain javelins in their hands wrapped round with ivy, termed
Thyrsi, and which, therefore, leads him to call the Jewish feast,
Θυρσοφοριαν *the bearing about of the Thyrsi.*

At the close of the last day of the feast, the ceremony of *drawing and pouring out water* took place; which was regarded with so much pleasure, that the Talmudists have a saying, that, " He who never saw the rejoicing of drawing water, never saw rejoicing in all his life."—The manner in which it was conducted, was this;—when the parts of the sacrifice were laid upon the altar, one of the priests with a golden tankard went to the fountain of Siloam, and there filled it with water. He then returned back into the court through the water-gate, and as soon as he arrived, the trumpets were sounded. Afterwards he went up to the ascent of the altar, where two basins were placed, one of them having wine in it, and the other having the water poured into it; after which the wine was poured into the water, or the water into the wine, and both poured out by way of libation. This custom is supposed to be referred to by our Lord, John viii, 37, 38; and by Isaiah xii, 3.—Godwyn's Moses and Aaron, lib. 3, c. vii, p. 116.— Lewis's Antiquities of the Hebrew Republic, vol. ii, b. iv, ch. xx, xxi, pp. 594—603, 605.

NOTE LXXV.—*Page 260.*

" It was the proper office of the priests to *bless the people.* The Benediction was to be pronounced by the priest standing, so that he might be seen with his hands lifted up, and spread, and speaking with a loud voice, with his face towards the assembly. This was the form of the blessing—' The Lord bless thee, and keep thee: the Lord make his face shine upon thee, and be gracious unto thee; the Lord lift up his countenance upon thee, and give thee peace.' (Numb. vi, 24, 25, 26.) There is nothing performed among the Jews with such solemnity, and in which they place so much sanctity, as in this solemn Benediction: and at this day, they that are of the family of Aaron, go up to the steps which lead to the place where the Book of the Law is kept, and lifting up their hands as high as their heads, pronounce the Blessing in their synagogues upon the assembly."— Lewis's Antiquities of the Hebrew Republic, vol. i, b. ii. c. 7, p. 138.

NOTE LXXVI.—*Page* 260.

FOR an explanation of the Phylacteries, Mezuzoth and Zizith, see the preceding note 24, *page* 349.

NOTE LXVII.—*Page* 260.

THE " Purchasing the Book of the Law," refers to an annual practice among the Jews. On the 9th day of the Feast of Tabernacles, or 23d day of the month Tisri, (September,) a festival is celebrated called the FEAST OF THE JOY OF THE LAW, instituted, we are told, as a day of thanksgiving and joy, that they have been permitted to hear and study the Law another year. The last and first sections of the Law having been read, the books or MSS. of the Law contained in the ark or cupboard of the synagogue were taken out and carried round the synagogue; lighted wax candles being usually placed in the ark during the ceremony, that it may not appear empty. " I have seen," says Leusden, " in the synagogue at Amsterdam, about sixty manuscripts, ornamented with gold and silver, and wrapped in the most costly coverings, borne by an equal number of persons, with the greatest pomp." Afterwards apples, pears, nuts, and other fruits, were thrown amongst the boys who were present, that they might partake the general joy.

The reading of the sections of the Law being completed on this day, several offices connected with it became vacant, which being highly valued, on account of the honour they were supposed to confer upon those who sustained them, were put up to auction and assigned to the highest bidder after the third proclamation. The principal of these offices were,—(1.) The lighting of the candles for the ensuing year:—(2.) The office of giving and carrying the wine to be consecrated on the Sabbath and other festival days:—(3.) Rolling and unrolling the manuscripts of the Law:—(4.) Elevating the Law, in the sight of the congregation, after having been read:—(5.) Assisting in unrolling and rolling up the manuscript of the Law, by holding and turning the ornamented rollers on which it was mounted, and supporting the cloth in which it was to be wrapped.

The money arising from the sale of these and similar offices, was applied to the repairs of the synagogue and the relief of the poor.—Buxtorfii Synagoga Judaica, cap. xxvii, pp. 543—545. Basil. 1661, 8vo.—Leusdeni Philologus Hebræo-mixtus. Dissert. xxxix, pp. 279—281. Ultraject. 1682, 4to.

NOTE LXXVIII.—*Page* 260.

THE diligent study of the Law was strenuously enjoined by the Jewish doctors. Maimonides, in his tract *De studio legis,* says, " Every Israelite, whether poor or rich, healthy or sick, old or young, is obliged to study the Law ; and even if so poor as to be maintained by charity, or beg his bread from door to door, and have wife and children, he must devote some time to the daily and nocturnal meditation of it ; for it is said, ' Thou shalt meditate therein day and night.' " (Joshua i. 8.) He further enquires, " How long ought a man to pursue the study of the Law ?" and replies, " Till death, as it is said, ' Lest they depart from thy heart all the days of thy life.' (Deut. iv, 9.) For when any one neglects to learn the Law, he forgets it. The time devoted to the study of the Law should be divided into three parts, the first of which should be dedicated to the reading of the Scripture, the second to the Oral Law, and the third to learning the dependence of things on their principles, eliciting one thing from another, comparing things together, and acquiring the knowledge of the various modes of interpretation by which Scripture is explained, until he understands the chief heads of moral duties, and how to distinguish what is lawful or unlawful, and other similar matters drawn from tradition." So far indeed does our author carry his views on this subject, that he affirms, even " an artificer ought to devote nine hours a day to studying the Law, namely, three to reading the Scriptures, three to learning the traditions, and three to obtaining a knowledge of what may justly be deduced from them, or of the *Gemara.*"—Maimonides, De Studio Legis, a Clavering, pp. 4, 5, Oxon. 1705. 4to.

NOTE LXXIX.—*Page* 261.

IT is a strange oversight in our great author, to attribute the selection of Mount Moriah, as the scene of Abraham's offering up Isaac, to a compliance with the customs of the Heathen, when Moses has so expressly declared the displeasure of God against the practice of idolatrous sacrifices on Mountains and " High-Places." " These," says he, " are the statutes and judgments, which ye shall observe to do in the land, which the LORD God of thy fathers giveth thee to possess it, all the days that ye live upon the earth. Ye shall utterly destroy all the places, wherein the nations which ye shall possess served their gods, upon the high mountains, and upon the hills, and under every green tree: and ye shall overthrow their altars, and break their pillars, and burn their groves with fire; and ye shall hew down the graven images of their gods, and destroy the names of them out of that place. Ye shall not do so unto the LORD your God ;" that is, Ye shall not imitate them by choosing "high mountains and hills," &c. as the chief places of worship. (Deut. xii, 1—4.)

If any reason were to be given for the preference of Mount Moriah, as the place of the trial of Abraham's faith in the offering up of his son Isaac, a plausible one is offered by those commentators who suppose that this Mount Moriah, and the Mount Calvary on which the Redeemer was crucified, were the same ; and that the sacrifice offered by Abraham being a representative one, the place was called " Jehovah-Jireh" by Abraham, and a tradition kept up that " Jehovah should be seen in a sacrificial way on this mount, which was accomplished in the fulness of time, when Jesus was offered on that very mountain, for the sins of mankind."

The reader who wishes to pursue the subject of Heathen worship on *Mountains* and *High-Places*, may find ample opportunity by consulting Young, *On Idolatrous Corruptions in Religion*, vol. i, pp. 214—230.

NOTE LXXX.—*Page* 263.

" CONCERNING the origin of TEMPLES, as well as of almost all other things, there is variety of opinions. If we believe Herodotus, the Egyptians were the first that made altars, statues, and temples ; nevertheless, it does not appear there were any in Egypt in the time of Moses ; at least, he makes no mention of them, though he had frequent occasion to do it.

Lucian says also, that the Egyptians were the first that built temples, and the Assyrians took the custom from them ; but all this is uncertain: nor have we any thing more to be depended on, than what we find in Holy Scripture. The first mention that is there made, is of the Tabernacle, built by the order of God ; which was truly a portable Temple, and which had within it a more secret and sacred place than others, called the *Sancta Sanctorum*, to which the sacred and secret places in the Pagan temples, called *Adyta*, answered.—The first temple of the Heathens which the Scripture takes notice of, is that of Dagon, the god of the Philistines, in which was a statue of a human form. The Greeks, who were taught many things of the Phœnicians, may well be supposed to have learnt to build temples of them. But be that as it will, it is certain that the Romans borrowed from the Greeks both the Worship of the gods, and the form of their Temples."— Montfaucon's Antiquity Explained, vol. ii, b. ii, ch. i, p. 29. London, 1721, fol. edit. Humphreys.

" Moses—only made an altar surrounded with twelve pillars, what we should call a Cromlech and Stone-Circle, in the construction of which, all hewn stones and iron tools were prohibited. Thus Stonehenge is of the most ancient form of Temples.

" The proportions of the Temple of Solomon, a fine oblong square, (like Grecian temples, not like a college or inn of court, as in the editions of Josephus,) may be considered, says Mr. Wilkins, (Magna Græcia, Intr. viii, ix, xv,) the standard by which the early Greeks were directed in the construction of their temples."—Fosbrooke's Encyclopædia of Antiquities, vol. i, c. iv, pp. 30, 31. London, 1825, 4*to.*

NOTE LXXXI.—*Page 263.*

The Ark was sometimes called the *Ark of God,* and the *Ark of the Lord,* because upon it God was pleased to manifest himself by the *Shechinah* or visible symbol of the Divine Presence ; and sometimes the *Ark of the Testimony,* and the *Ark of the Covenant,* because the tables of stone, called the Tables of the Testimony, which were Witnesses of the Covenant between God and the Israelites, were placed in it. It was a small chest or coffer, made of Shittim-wood, overlaid on the inside and on the outside with thin plates of gold. A border or wreathing of gold went round the top of it, which was called the *crown ;* and a cover of gold beaten or founded to the exact length and breadth of the ark, was then laid on, and preserved in its position by the golden border into which it was fitted. This cover, which had at each end a cherub of gold, beaten out of the same piece as the cover or lid itself, was denominated the *Mercy-seat* or *Propitiatory.* On or before this, the high-priest sprinkled the blood of the expiatory sacrifices on the great day of atonement; and here God promised to meet the people. From the glorious symbol of the Divine Presence resting on the Cover or Mercy-seat, between the two cherubs, it is frequently said, in Scripture, that " He dwelleth between the Cherubim." (Exod. xxv, 10—22 ; xxxvii, 1—9.)

It has been remarked in former notes, that the Heathen borrowed many of their rites and practices from the Hebrews, as appears to have been the case in the present instance, contrary to the conjecture of Maimonides, who supposes that the Jews derived the formation of the ark from their Pagan neighbours. —For it has been justly observed by a learned commentator, that " in many cases, they (the Heathens) seem to have studied the closest imitation possible, consistent with the adaptation of all to their preposterous and idolatrous worship. They had their JAO or JOVE, in imitation of the true JEHOVAH; and from the different attributes of the Divine Nature, they formed an innumerable groupe of gods and goddesses. They had also their temples, in imitation of the temple of God ; and in these they had their holy and more holy places, in imitation of the courts of the Lord's house ; and as there is no evidence, whatever, that there was any temple among the Heathens, prior to the tabernacle, it is reasonable to conclude, that it served as a model for all they afterwards builded. They had even their portable temples, to imitate the Tabernacle ; and the shrines for Diana, mentioned Acts xix, 24, were of this kind. They had also their *Arks,* or sacred *coffers,* where they kept their most holy things, and the mysterious emblems of their religion; together with candlesticks or lamps to illuminate their temples, (which had few windows,) to imitate the golden candlestick in the Mosaic tabernacle. They had even their processions, in imitation of the carrying about of the Ark in the wilderness; accompanied by such ceremonies, as sufficiently shew, to an unprejudiced mind, that they borrowed them from this sacred original."·

Apuleius, describing a solemn idolatrous procession, *De Aur. Asin. lib.* ii, after the Egyptian mode, says, " A *chest* or *ark* was carried by another, containing their secret things, entirely concealing the mysteries of religion."

Plutarch, in his treatise, *De Iside, &c.* describing the rites of Osiris, says, "On the 10th day of the month, at night, they go down to the sea ; and the stolists, together with the priest, carry forth the sacred *chest,* in which is a small boat or vessel of gold."

Pausanias likewise testifies, (lib. vii, c. 19,) that the ancient Trojans had a *sacred ark,* wherein was the image of Bacchus, made by Vulcan, which had been given to Dardanus by Jupiter.—See Dr. A. Clarke's Commentary on Exod. xxv.

NOTE LXXXII.—*Page 263.*

THAT the Ministry of Angels was frequent in the Patriarchal age, is evident, from the passages referred to by Maimonides. It must also be granted, that the LAW was "ordained by angels, in the hand of a mediator," (Gal. iii. 19,) by their being the agents employed by the Divine Being, in transmitting the Law to Moses, who was, in that case, the mediator between God and the people ; (Deut. v. 5 ;) but it may justly be questioned, whether our author be correct in supposing, that prophecy is never communicated but by the ministry of angels, since many passages of the Holy Scriptures speak of the Prophetic influence, as being imparted directly, and without any intermediate agent, to the person prophesying or foretelling future events.—See amongst others, 1 Sam. x. 6, 10 ; Ezek. ii. 2 ; xi. 4, 5 ; 2 Chron. xv. i.

NOTE LXXXIII.—*Page 264.*

ON the terms ASHERAH and ASHEROTH, see Note 38, pp. 361, 362.

NOTE LXXXIV.—*Page* 264.

THE following curious anecdote is related in the Mishna, under the title "Avoda Zara," or "Strange or Idolatrous Worship."

"Some Roman Senators examined the Jews in this manner, 'If God had no delight in the worship of idols, why did He not destroy them?' The Jews made answer, 'If men had worshipped only the things of which the world had no need, He would have destroyed the objects of their worship; whereas now, they worship the Sun, and Moon, and Stars, and Planets; and then He must have destroyed His world for the sake of these deluded men.' 'But still,' said the Romans, 'why does not God destroy the things which the world does not want, and leave those things which the world cannot do without?' 'Because,' replied the Jews, 'this would strengthen the hands of such as worship these necessary things; who would then say, Ye allow now that these are gods, since they are not destroyed.'"—Wotton's Miscellaneous Discourses, vol. i, p. 145.

NOTE LXXXV.—*Page* 264.

IT is probable that the two *Cherubims* placed on the ark of the covenant, were emblematical representations of beings of an angelical nature. The shape or form of them, any further than that they were winged creatures, is not certainly known; for the opinion of those writers, who suppose that they were similar in form to those which Ezekiel saw in his vision, is unsupported by any decisive proof, and can be regarded only as a conjecture. Be this as it may, we know they were two in number, one at each end of the mercy-seat, with their wings stretched out, so that one wing of each cherub touched the side of the tabernacle on which it was respectively placed, and the other wings met together over the middle of the ark and the propitiatory. Their faces turned inward, one toward another, added to their other positions, gave to the whole work of the ark, mercy-seat, and cherubim, the form of a seat which represented the throne of God.

These Cherubim have been considered, by some, as designed to be emblems of Jehovah himself, or rather of the Trinity of persons in the Godhead. " But that God, who is a pure spirit, without parts or passions, perfectly separate and remote from all matter, should command Moses to make material and visible images or emblematical representations of himself, seems highly improbable; especially considering that he had repeatedly, expressly, and solemnly forbidden every thing of this kind, in the second commandment of the moral law, delivered from Sinai, amidst thunder and lightning, burning fire, blackness, darkness, and tempest, pronouncing with an audible and awful voice, while the whole mountain quaked greatly, and the sound of the trumpet waxed louder and louder, 'Thou shalt not make unto thyself any graven image, or any likeness of any thing that is in heaven above, or in the earth beneath, or in the water under the earth: thou shalt not bow down,'" &c· Hence God's demand by his Prophet, "To what will liken me, or shall I be equal, saith the Holy One?" Add to this, that in most or all of the places "where the Cherubim are mentioned in the Scriptures, God is expressly distinguished from them. (Gen. iii. 24; Psalm xviii, 10; xcix, i; Ezek. ix, 3; x, 4, 18)—It seems, therefore, much more probable, as Dr. Owen, Dr. Macknight, Mr. Pierce, and many other eminent Divines, have supposed, that they represented the angels who surrounded the Divine Presence in heaven. Accordingly they had their faces turned towards the mercy-seat, where God was supposed to dwell, whose face the angels in heaven always behold, and upon whom their eyes are continually fixed to observe and receive his commands; as they are also upon Christ, the true Propitiatory, which mystery of redemption *they desire*, St. Peter tells us, *to look into*." (1 Pet.i. 12.)—Martindale's Dictionary of the Holy Bible, vol. i, art. *Cherub*. London, 1818, 8vo.

NOTE LXXXVI.—*Page 265.*

"TITUS, after the overthrow of Jerusalem, A.D. 70, had the GOLDEN CANDLESTICK, and the golden *Table of the shew-bread*, the *silver Trumpets*, and the Book of the *Law* taken out of the temple, and carried in triumph to Rome; and Vespasian lodged them in the temple which he had consecrated to the goddess of Peace! Some plants, also, of the *balm* of Jericho, are said to have been carried in the procession. At the foot of Mount Palatine there are the ruins of an arch, on which the triumph of Titus for his conquest of the Jews is represented; and on which, the several monuments, which were carried in the procession, are sculptured, and particularly the *golden candlestick*, the *table of shew-bread*, and the two *silver trumpets*. A correct model of this arch, taken on the spot, now stands before me; and the spoils of the temple, the *candlestick*, the *golden table*, and the two *trumpets*, are represented on the pannel, on the left hand, in the inside of the arch, in *basso-relievo*. The *candlestick* is not so ornamented as it appears in many prints; at the same time, it looks much better than it does in the engraving of this arch given by Montfaucon, Antiq. Explic. vol. iv, pl. 32. It is likely, that on the real arch, this candlestick is less in size than the original, as it scarcely measures three feet in height.—See the *Diarium Italicum*, p. 122."—Dr. A. Clarke's Commentary on Exod. xxv, 31.

NOTE LXXXVII.—*Page 265.*

LIGHTED LAMPS were used in religious ceremonies, both by the Greeks and Romans. This, it is probable, as Montfaucon observes, was derived to the Gentiles from the Hebrews. The Athenians lighted lamps chiefly on the feasts of Minerva, Vulcan, and Prometheus. The Romans also used lamps in their temples, and on their solemn days. The square temples, in general, admitted no light but at the door; and the *Cella*, *Penetrale*, *Sacrarium*, or *Adytum*, as it was variously called, was a dark, interior, walled building, similarly situated to the choirs of our churches, into which the people were not permitted to enter. These, therefore, must necessarily have been lighted by artificial lights.

Lamps were also introduced into Sepulchres, some of which are said to have burned perpetually, and hence the fictions of lamps having been found burning, after the lapse of several ages. It is also a singular connection, that as many of the Gentile gods were deified heroes or patriots, sacrifices were offered at their tombs, and their sepulchres were the first temples dedicated to them.

In the early ages, some Christians imitated the Heathen, by placing lamps in their sepulchres. Some lamps in the cabinet of

Genevieve have the monogram of Christ.—Montfaucon's Antiquity Explained, vol. v, pt. ii, b. 2, ch. 2, p. 138 ; ch. 3, p. 140—142. London, 1722, fol. edit. Humphreys.—Foosbrooke's Encyclopedia of Antiquities, vol. i, ch. 4, pp. 30, 82, 33; ch. 9, pp. 281, 282. London, 1825, 4*to*.

NOTE LXXXVIII.—*Page* 265.

" This Reverence consisted principally in coming to it so prepared as the Law required ; in such purity and cleanlinesss as was there prescribed; and then behaving themselves there with an awful humility. But the better to secure this reverence, the masters in Israel ordained that no man should come into the ' Mountain of the House' with a staff, or a sword, or a girdle with a purse, or with shoes on his feet ; and that no man should spit there, nor make it a thoroughfare, nor go out of it with his back towards the sanctuary, but go backward leisurely, with his face towards it, till he was out of the gate."—Patrick's Comentary on Levit. xix, 30, P. Cunæus, De Repub. Heb. lib. ii, cap. 12, 13, pp. 245—256. Lugd. 1617, 8*vo*.

NOTE LXXXIX.—*Page* 266.

Rabbi Shem Tob, in his commentary on this chapter of the More Nevochim, has the following judicious observations on the design of the Tabernacle and its Furniture :—

" God, to whom be praise, commanded a house to be erected for Him, resembling a royal palace. In a royal palace are to be found all those things which we have mentioned. There are some persons who guard the palace ; others, who execute offices belonging to the royal dignity, who furnish the banquets, and do other things necessary for the monarch : others, who daily entertain him with music, both vocal and instrumental. In a royal palace there is a place appointed for preparation of the victuals, and another where perfumes are burned.

" In the palace of a king, there is also a table, and an apartment exclusively appropriated to himself, which no one ever enters, except him who is next in authority, or those whom he regards with the greatest affection. In like manner it was the will of God to have all these in his house, that he might not in any thing give place to the kings of the earth. For He is a great king; not indeed in any want of these things : but, hence it is easy to see the reason of the daily provisions given to the priests and Levites, being what every monarch is accustomed to allow to his servants. And all these things were intended to instruct the people, that the Lord of Hosts was present among us. ' For he is a great king, and to be feared by all the nations.' "—Outram, On Sacrifices, Diss. i. c. 3, p. 48, edit. Allen.

NOTE XC.—*Page* 266.

These Altars were designed to be occasional and temporary only, the stated ones. being at the Tabernacle ; they were therefore ordered to be formed of earth, or unhewn or unpolished stones, which might easily be thrown down, and neither draw the people from the Tabernacle, nor give occasion to idolatry by artificial workmanship or imagery. By these injunctions also, they were prevented from lavishing unnecessary expenses or time, on altars, which, during their journeying in the wilderness, and prior to the erection of the Tabernacle, they could not carry with them, and must be very frequently leaving behind them. (Exod. xx. 24 ; Deut. xxvii. 5, 6.)

NOTE XCI.—*Page* 266.

The terms used by the Sacred Writer, and translated, "Graven, or Sculptured Images," are אבן משכית (*aben maschith.*) Michaelis supposes, that these were stones with *hieroglyphic* figures engraven upon them, and that they w er connected with the Egyptian idolatries. The Egyptian god of learning, whom foreign nations called *Hermes* or *Mercurius*, was denominated *Thoth*, whom Jablonski (in *Pantheon Egypt.*) has shewn, to mean nothing more than stones, inscribed with hieroglyphic figures. An imitation of this species of idolatry appears to have been common among the Jews, so late as the time of Ezekiel, who in his prophecy, (Ezek. viii. 8—11,) describes a subterraneous vault, the walls of which were covered with hieroglyphic figures of quadrupeds and creeping things, exactly like those in Egypt. According, therefore, to that fundamental principle of the Jewish polity, which dictated the prevention of idolatry, it became absolutely necessary to prohibit stones with hieroglyphic inscriptions; besides, in an age where so great a propensity to superstition prevailed, stones with figures upon them, which the people could not understand, would have been a temptation to idolatry, even though the Egyptians had not deified them, as they actually did. —The very learned Bishop Patrick has a similar suggestion:— " Possibly," says he, " this may signify such images as were common among the Egyptians in after times ; which were not representations of their gods, but were full of *symbols* and *hieroglyphics*, expressing some of the perfections of their gods. These God would as'little allow among his people, as any of the former."—Michaelis's Commentaries on the Laws of Moses, vol. iv. art. 250, p. 55 ; Patrick's Comment. on Levit. xxvi, 1.

NOTE XCII.—*Page* 266.

HERODOTUS tells us, the way to the Temple of Mercury had, on both sides, trees that reached up to heaven ; (Euterpe, p. 91 ;) and Homer sings,

> And build an altar in the woody grove,
> Near the clear flowing spring.
>   HYMN IN APOLL.

The very term by which a *grove* was designated in Latin, derived its name, *Lucus*, from the *light* arising from the sacrifices and offerings of incense.—" A *luce* sacrificiorum *Lucus* appellatum."—Nic. Perot. in Cornucop. Col. 165. 30.

The Groves thus planted about idol temples and altars, became the resort of the lewd and profligate of all descriptions. " On this account, God would have no groves or thickets about his altar ; that there might be no room for suspicion, that any thing contrary to the strictest purity, was transacted there. Every part of the Divine worship was *publicly* performed, for the purpose of general edification."—Ridley's MELAMPUS, Notes, pp. 176, 232, 233, 259. 4to. 1781 ; Dr. A. Clarke on Deut. xvi. 21 ; see also Bishop Patrick, *in loc.*

NOTE XCIII.—*Page* 267.

THE worship of Baal-Peor was the most obscene that can be imagined. Rabbi Solomon Jarchi says,—" Eo quod distendebant coram illo foramen podicis, et stercus offerebant."—See Selden, De Diis Syriis, Syntag. i. cap. 5 ; Beyeri Additamenta, ad c. 5. See also for proof of the derivation from this worship, the Phallic and other similar rites of the Egyytians, Greeks, and Romans, and other nations, Schedius *De Diis Germanis*, Syntag. i. c. iv. Amsterod. 1648, *8vo.*

NOTE XCIV.—*Page* 269.

THE Christian will find the true reason, a figurative one, of the High-Priest entering only a stated number of times into the Holy of Holies, in the EPISTLE TO THE HEBREWS, ch. ix, that Epistle forming the most accurate and complete developement of the symbolical character of the Mosaic Ritual.

NOTE XCV.—*Page* 272.

ANOTHER reason also may be assigned for the hatred of the Egyptians to Shepherds, arising out of their national history. Egypt had long been governed by its native princes, when certain strangers, called *Hycsos*, or *Pastor*, or *Shepherd-Kings*, from Arabia, or Phœnicia, invaded and seized a great part of Lower Egypt, and Memphis itself. These foreign princes governed about 260 years. Under one of them, Abraham visited Egypt, and was placed in critical circumstances by the beauty of his wife Sarah. This was about the year 1920 before Christ ; and 95 years afterwards, Thethmosis or Amosis, having expelled the Shepherd-Kings, began to reign in Lower Egypt. About the year B. C. 1728, Joseph was sold into Egypt, and by an extraordinary chain of providences was raised to the chief dignity of the kingdom under Pharoah. Even at that period, the same prejudice was entertained against *Shepherds*, as in after ages ; for we find that the Egyptians would not eat at the same table with the Hebrews. (Gen. xliii. 32.)—See also Young, *On Idolatrous Corruptions in Religion*, vol. i. pp. 267—272.

NOTE XCVI.—*Page 273.*

THE Hebrew word שְׂעִירִים, which is used Levit. xvii. 7, literally means *Goats*, but is generally considered as intended to designate *Dæmons* or *Devils*, which are supposed to have been worshipped under the form of Goats, or to have appeared under that or a similar form to their worshippers. Parkhurst's explanation of the term in his Lexion is, "Certain idols, representing the power of the heavens, in storms, tempests, rains. Most probably they were in the form of wild goats, or of other rough, shaggy animals."—See also Schedius, *De Diis Germanis*, Syntag. iv. c. 1, p. 489.

The *Satyrs, Sileni, Fauni, Pans,* and *Sylvani* of the Romans were similar deities. There is not one of these several kinds to whom different authors do not give the horns and ears of a *goat,* the tail, thighs, feet, and legs of the same animal.— Montfaucon (*Antiq. Explained,* vol, i.) has given many representations of these figures.

NOTE XCVII.—*Page 273.*

DR. F. BUCHANAN informs us, that amongst the JAINS, or A'RHATAS, a sect in India, it is considered, " that to kill an animal of the cow kind is equally sinful with the murder of one of the human species. The death of any other animal, although a crime, is not of so atrocious a nature.—The *Gurus* (or Teachers) excommunicate all those who eat animal food."— Asiatic Researches, vol. ix, pp. 283, 284, London, 1809. 8vo. —Mr. Ward, speaking of the Hindoos generally, observes, "Nothing can exceed the abhorrence expressed by the Hindoos at the idea of killing cows, and eating beef, and yet the Védŭ itself commands the slaughter of cows for sacrifice, and several Pooranŭs relate, that at a sacrifice offered by Vishwamitrŭ, the Bramhŭns devoured ten thousand cows which had been offered in sacrifice."—Ward's View of the History, Literature and Mythology of the Hindoos, vol. iii, p. 105, note; London, 1820, 8vo.

NOTE XCVIII.—*Page 274.*

"AMONG the Israelites it was provided by the Divine Law, that no species of animals should be used for sacrifices, except such as were chosen from bullocks, goats, sheep, turtle-doves, or pigeons. These were the species most distinguished for gentleness; they most abounded in Canaan, and were principally in use for common food: and besides, it was a received opinion, among some nations at least, that some of these animals were proper objects of religious worship, but that they could not be slain without incurring the greatest guilt."—Outram, On Sacrifices, Diss. i, ch. 9, p. 113.

NOTE XCIX.—*Page* 275.

" WHEN any one went to consult the Oracle of Trophonius, he carried with him into the den, cakes in his hands:"—and, "the learned Spanheim (in Nubes Aristoph.) has produced several instances of persons going into Trophonius's cave, and carrying with them always, cakes kneaded with *Honey*."— " Pure *Honey* was likewise burnt upon the altars to the Heathen gods; nay, there were scarce any of the gods, if any at all, who had not *Honey* burnt to them in sacrifice."—Sykes's Essay on the Nature, Design, and Origin of Sacrifices, pp. 95, 97, 116; London, 1784, 8vo.

NOTE C.—*Page* 275.

SALT was the symbol of friendship and covenant; it was also of an agreeable savour, and possessed the quality of preserving food from putrefaction; and hence it is that a durable covenant is called, " a Covenant of Salt." (Numb. xviii, 19, *et al.*)—On these accounts, salt was to be used with all the meat-offerings duly presented, and sprinkled on the offerings when laid upon the altar.—Maimonides, however, is not correct, in supposing that the Heathen did not use salt in their sacrifices, unless, as might possibly be the case, the idolaters in the time of Moses did not make use of it in their rites, but afterwards adopted it from the practice of the Israelites.—See Cudworth On the true Notion of the Lord's Supper, pp. 94—97:—and Sykes's Essay on the Nature, &c. of Sacrifices, pp. 84—89.

NOTE CI.—*Page* 275.

IT was customary in the East, to make bread of flour and oil mixed together. The Persian *Maza* was barley-flour, mixed

with oil and water, and was the daily diet of the Romans.   It
is still commonly used in India as an ingredient in the food of
the natives.—Sykes's Essay on Sacrifices, p. 92.—Tennant's
Indian Recreations, vol. ii, p. 125.

NOTE CII.—*Page 275.*

A TWO-FOLD reason may be given for the frequent burning
of *Frankincense;* for *first,* it was a gum which on being burnt
produced a strong and grateful odour, and was, therefore,
peculiarly proper to prevent the offerers of oblations from
being annoyed by the unpleasant effluvia arising from the
slaughtering and burning of animal sacrifices;—an advantage
powerfully aided by the other suffumigations of a similar
nature;—and *secondly,* the Frankincense thus offered was
emblematical of the acceptableness of the prayers which
accompanied the offering.—See Rev. v, 8; viii, 3, 4.—Sykes
also adds, that "in the case of the Meat-Offering, the Frankincense was to be burnt, the better to consume the offering;"
—and that, "it was found too in experience, that Frankincense
had a peculiar efficacy in driving away or in destroying *flies;*
and by that means was of signal use, where there was much
burning of flesh."—Sykes's Essay, On Sacrifices, pp. 95, 99.

NOTE CIII.—*Page 276.*

OF this rite, Maimonides (in *Maase Korban,* c. 6,) says, "In
the room allotted for that purpose, they wash the fat of the breast
as much as is necessary; but the entrails, three times at the
least: and these they wash on marble tables placed between
the pillars."—But, to preserve the court from being polluted
with filth, they were first washed privately in the washing-room;
and the operation afterwards repeated on the marble tables,
from a belief that the coldness of the marble would check the
tendency to putrefaction.—Cleanliness and purity were evidently the first objects of this repeated washing; but Philo
(De Animal. ad Sacrif.) supposes, the washing of the legs or
feet, and entrails, to have conveyed important instruction.—
"Nor is it without mystery that we are commanded to wash
the feet and entrails. The washing of the entrails symbolically

inculcates the necessity of being freed from unruly appetites, and purified from the stains contracted by drunkenness and gluttony, vices exceedingly pernicious to human life. The washing of the feet signifies that henceforth we ought to walk not on the ground, but through the skies."—Outram, On Sacrifices, Diss. i, c. xvi, p. 200.

NOTE CIV.—*Page* 278.

DR. OUTRAM in the conclusion of chap. ix. Diss. I. of his excellent work, "On Sacrifices," thus briefly sums up the arguments which he has advanced in it, to prove that "the efficacy of all the Sacrifices primarily and properly had respect, not to men, but to God."

" In the *first* place, we have shown, that God appointed the Jewish sacrifices to be offered to himself with certain solemnities.—*Secondly*, that those rites were designed and contrived to signify God's power over life and death, his authority to punish and pardon, and his supreme dominion over the universe.—*Thirdly*, that those rites by which any thing was thus offered or presented to God, partook of the true nature of Divine worship, though only of an external kind; and had respect to God, as much as bowing the knee, bending the head or body, or any other similar ceremonies which are employed in sacred services as acts of Divine worship.—*Lastly*, that the sacrificial rites, whether performed by the offerer himself, or by the priest, were required to be performed in such a manner, that the external and symbolical worship should be accompanied by the worship of the mind; by that faith in the providence, justice, and goodness of God, that reverence for his holy laws, that repentance for sins, and those purposes of future obedience, which become all sincere and pious men; and whoever offered sacrifices with this state of mind, was accepted of God."

NOTE CV.—*Page* 281.

AMONGST the inhabitants of the hills near Rájamahall in India, when a *Demauno* or *Dewassy*, who seems to partake of the twofold character of priest and conjurer, is to be initiated;

after having gone through several preceding ceremonies, " he approaches the door of his chief, and makes signs to have a cock, and a hen's egg brought to him ; the latter he immediately eats, and wringing off the head of the cock, *sucks the reeking blood,* and throws away the body."—" A Demauno *drinks of the reeking blood* of all offerings sacrificed while he is present." —" The *Maungy* of every village sacrifices a buffalo annually." On the day appointed, the Maungy sits on a sacred stool, with the Demauno on the ground on his left hand, who gives the Maungy a handful of unboiled rice, which he scatters, and prays for protection for himself and his dependants. Those who suppose themselves possessed of devils, run and pick up the rice ; and are then seized and bound, until the buffalo has been hamstrung, and his head cut off, when they " are set at liberty, and immediately rush forward *to take up the buffalo's blood, and lick it while reeking.*"—Asiatic Researches, vol. iv, pp. 39, 41, 42. London, 1801, 8vo. See also Dissertation V. on Blood, page 76.

NOTE CVI.—*Page 282.*

The " pouring out" of the blood of the victims offered in sacrifice, (Levit. iv. 18 ; Deut. xii, 27,) was regarded by Jews as *expiatory :* thus R. Moses Ben Nachman *(ad Levit. i,)* says, " It was just that his blood should be shed, and that his body should be burned. But the Creator, of his mercy, accepted this victim from him, as his substitute and ransom ; that the blood of the animal might be shed instead of his blood ; that is, that the life of the animal might be given for his life."— See this, and other similar quotations, in Dr. Outram's excellent work on Sacrifices, Diss. i, c. 22, p. 285, &c.

The Pagans, also, in subsequent ages, at least, entertained the idea of the expiatory and cleansing influence of *blood.* The Taurobolium affords an extraordinary instance of the influence of this opinion. I quote an animated account of it, from Maurice's *Indian Antiquities,* vol. 5, c. 4, pp. 957—959. " They had sacrifices, denominated those of *Regeneration ;* and those sacrifices were always profusely stained with blood. The Taurobolium of the Ancients, a ceremony in which the high priest of Cybele was consecrated, was a ceremony of this kind, and might be called a Baptism of Blood, which they conceived imparted a spiritual new birth to the liberated spirit. In this dreadful and sanguinary ceremony, according to the poet Prudentius, (cited at length by Banier, "On the Ancient Sacrifices,") the high-priest about to be inaugurated, was led into a dark excavated apartment, adorned with a long silken robe and a crown of gold. Above this apartment, was a floor perforated in a thousand places with holes, like a sieve, through which the blood of a sacred bull, slaughtered for the purpose, descended in a copious torrent upon the inclosed priest, who received the purifying stream upon every part of his dress, rejoicing to bathe with the bloody shower his hands, his cheeks, and even to bedew his lips and his tongue with it. When all the blood had run from the throat of the immolated bull, the carcase of the victim was removed, and the priest issued forth from the cavity, a spectacle, ghastly and horrible, his head and vestments being covered with blood, and clotted drops of it adhering to his venerable beard. As soon as the Pontifex appeared before the assembled multitude, the air was rent with congratulatory shouts ; so pure, and so sanctified, however, was he now esteemed, that they dared not approach his person, but beheld him at a distance with awe and veneration."

It has been before observed, that, by these initiations or baptisms of blood, the ancients conceived that they had obtained an eternal regeneration or new-birth: nor were they confined to the priests alone; for persons, not invested with a sacred function, were sometimes initiated by the ceremony of the Taurobolium; and one invariable rule on the initiations was, to wear the stained garments as long as possible, in token of their having been thus regenerated. The sacrifice of regeneration was also sometimes performed, for the purification of a whole nation, on the monarch that governed it. The animal sacrificed was not obliged to be always of one species; instead of a bull, a ram was frequently sacrificed, when the ceremony was called CREOBOLIUM, and sometimes a she-goat, when it obtained the name of ÆGEBOLIUM."—See also Montfaucon's Antiquity Explained, vol. ii, pt. 1, b. 3, p. 106.

NOTE CVIII.—*Page* 286.

SEE Note 96, p. 416.

NOTE CIX.—*Page* 288.

IF Maimonides intends, by this mode of reasoning, to suggest that human actions can become actually meritorious and expiatory in the sight of God, his system is certainly unscriptural. But, if he only meant to intimate, (as we are inclined to think,) how virtuous *habits* are to be acquired, so far as human effort is concerned, the following passages from his favourite author will illustrate his theory:

"The *habit* of Moral Virtue, like all other practical arts, can be acquired or preserved by practice only. By building we become architects; by harping, musicians; and in the same manner, by acts of justice, we become just; and by acts of courage, courageous;—and in proportion as we indulge or restrain the excitements to anger and pleasure, we become adorned with the habits of meekness and temperance, or deformed by those of passionateness and profligacy. In one word, such as our actions are, such will our *habits* become. Actions therefore ought to be most diligently attended to; and it is not a matter of small moment how we are trained from our youth.

"We ought to consider to what extremes or faults we are most prone; for different men are more or less easily beset by different faults or vices; and what these are by which each is most liable to be entangled, he will best discover by attending to the pleasure which he has in indulging, or the pain in restraining them. In order to correct his character, he must bend it, in a contrary direction, as we straighten a crooked stick; but, above all, he must beware of the blandishments of pleasure, of which we are seldom impartial or uncorrupt judges; treating this fair enchantress, as the aged senators in Homer did the beautiful Helen, whose words on this occasion cannot be too often repeated, nor their example too strictly imitated.

> They cry'd, No wonder, such celestial charms
> For nine long years have set the world in arms;

What winning graces! what majestic mein!
She moves a goddess, and she looks a queen!
Yet hence, Oh Heaven! convey that fatal face,
And from destruction save the Trojan race!

Il. iii, v. 203, &c.

By thus banishing pleasure, we shall be less liable to error."—
ARISTOTLE's ETHICS, vol i, B. ii, pp. 176, 190, London,
1797, 4*to.* edit. Gillies.

NOTE CX.—*Page* 291.

MAIMONIDES, in his treatise on "Repentance," says, "The
Scape-goat expiates all the sins mentioned in the Law,
whether light or heavy, whether committed through contumacy or error, whether done ignorantly or knowingly. Every
one who *repents* is thus atoned for by the Scape-Goat; but if
any one do *not* repent, then only his lighter transgressions are
expiated by the Scape-Goat."—Maimonides *De Pœnitentia,*
à Clavering, c. i, sect. v, p. 44. Oxon. 1705, 4*to.*

The sacrificing of the one goat, and the liberating of the
other, was, in later ages at least, accompanied with numerous
ceremonies, which the reader may find detailed in Lewis's
Origines Hebrææ: Antiquities of the Hebrew Republic, B. iv,
vol. 2. ch. 14, pp. 559—570; Spencer, *De Legibus Hebræorum,*
tom. ii, lib. iii, Dissert. viii, p. 450; and other writers on
Jewish Antiquities.—Leo, of Modena, says, speaking of the
later Jews, "The vigil or evening before this Fast, they were
wont heretofore to use a certain ceremony with a *Cock,* swing-
ing it about their head, and giving it up *in exchange of themselves:* and this they called *Caparah* or *Reconciliation.*"—Buxtorf
adds, that the men took a *white* cock, and the women a *hen,*
and swung the cock three times round the priest's head,
saying, "This cock shall be a propitiation for me;" and then
killed it, confessing themselves to be worthy of death.—Leo
of Modena's History of the present Jews. London, 1650.—
Buxtorfii Synagog. Judaic. c. 20.

The ASWAMEDHA JUG, or Horse-sacrifice of the Hindoos,
seems to have been derived from the *Azazel* or Scape-Goat of
the Jews: for Mr. Halhed tells us, from a Hindoo commentary
upon the Vedas, that "the *Horse* so sacrificed (or offered) is

in the place of the sacrificer, bears his sins with him into the wilderness, into which he is turned adrift, and becomes the expiatory victim of those sins."—Maurice's *Indian Antiquities* vol, 2, p. 173.—See also Dr. A. Clarke's and Bishop Patrick's Commentaries on Levit. xvi, in which the subject is pursued at length.

BRUCE, the Abyssinian traveller, relates the following occurrence, which took place at the time of his arrival at Yambo.— "We found, that, upon some discussion, the garrison and townsmen had been fighting for several days; in which disorders the greatest part of the ammunition in the town had been expended; but it since had been agreed on, by the old men of both parties, that nobody had been to blame on either side, but the whole wrong was the work of a *Camel*. A Camel therefore was seized, and brought without the town; and there a number on both sides having met, they upbraided the Camel with every thing that had been either said or done.— After having spent great part of the afternoon in upbraiding the Camel,—each man thrust him through with a lance, devoting him *Diis manibus et Diris* by a kind of prayer, and with a thousand curses upon his head. After which every man retired, fully satisfied as to the wrongs he had received from the Camel. The reader," adds Mr. Bruce, " will easily observe in this some traces of the Azazel or Scape-Goat of the Jews."—Bruce's Travels, vol. i, pp. 252, 253. 4to.

NOTE CXI.—*Page* 292.

" THE true reason why Meat-Offerings and *Drink-Offerings* were required to attend upon the Burnt-Offerings and Peace-Offerings, was, because these sacrifices were a *Feast*, and are called the " bread" or food of God, (ch. xxviii, 2,) and therefore as *Bread* and *Wine*, as well as flesh, are our refection, so God required them at his table."—Patrick's Commentary on Numb. xv, 5,—See also Sykes's Essay on Sacrifices, pp. 102—110.

" The Egyptians regarded *Wine* as a poison that sprang from the blood of dæmons; while Moses commanded it to be offered unto God, and to be drunken during the sacrifice-feasts."

In the greatest part of Egypt no *Olives* were cultivated, and therefore no *Oil* was made. The oil of Palestine was most abundant and peculiarly excellent.—The use of it therefore insensibly attached the Israelites to Palestine in preference to Egypt, which was of great importance to their national comfort, especially as they had formerly longed to return to Egypt, merely to eat of its productions.—Michaelis's Commentaries on the Laws of Moses, vol. iii, Art. 190, 191.

NOTE CXII.—*Page* 298.

AMONGST the JAINS, a Hindoo sect in India, "When a woman is unclean, she must stay at a distance from her rela-tions, in unchanged clothes, for four days. On the morning of the fifth day she is permitted to mix with her family after ablution."—Asiatic Researches, vol. ix, p. 251, 8vo.—And among the *Inhabitants of the hills near Rájamahall*, "Women at certain times are considered impure: should one in such a condition touch a man by accident, even with her garment, he is defiled; and for this offence she is fined a fowl, which is sacrificed, and the blood is sprinkled on the man to purify him."—Asiatic Researches, vol. iv. p. 79, 8vo.

NOTE CXIII.—*Page* 299.

THE reader who wishes to pursue the enquiry respecting the *Pollutions* and frivolous and tedious *Ceremonies* of the Heathens, may consult Montfaucon's *Antiquity Explained*, Ward's *View of the History, Literature and Mythology of the Hindoos*, and the *Asiatic Researches,* especially the Essays *On the Religious Cere-monies of the Hindus* by H. T. Colebrook, Esq. commencing in vol. v.—A short extract or two from one of them may elucidate the subject:

"If he happen to sneeze, or spit, he must not immediately sip water, but first touch his right ear in compliance with the maxim, 'After sneezing, spitting, blowing his nose, sleeping, putting on apparel, or dropping tears, a man should not immediately sip water, but first touch his right ear.'

"I omit the very tedious detail respecting sins expiated by a set number of repetitions; but in one instance, as an atone-ment for unwarily eating or drinking what is forbidden, it is directed that eight hundred repetitions of the *Gáyatri* should be preceded by three suppressions of breath, touching water during the recital of the following text :—' The bull roars ; he has four horns, three feet, two heads, seven hands, and is bound by a threefold ligature : he is the mighty resplendent being, and pervades mortal men.' The bull is justice personified."—Asiatic Researches, vol. v, p. 348, and p. 356, Note.

NOTE CXIV.—*Page 302.*

SEE the preliminary Dissertation, " On Leprosy", p. 102.

NOTE CXV.—*Page 302.*

ACCORDING to R. Abarbanel, " the *living bird* signified that the *dead flesh* of the leper was restored to soundness ; the *cedar wood* which is not easily corrupted, that he was healed of his *putrefaction ;* the *scarlet-thread,* or *wool,* or *fillet,* that he was restored to a healthy *complexion,* his blood being purified ; and the *hyssop* which was purgative and odoriferous, that the disease was completely removed, and the bad scent that accompanied it, entirely gone."—Patrick's, and Clarke's Commentaries on Levit. xiv. 4.

NOTE CXVI.—*Page 303.*

" *TYPHO* was looked upon by the Egyptians as a dæmoniac power ; and because they were of opinion that Typho was born of a *red* complexion, they were therefore used to devote to him, such of the Neat kind, as they found to be of a *red colour.* —Their hatred to Typho carried them so far, that they had certain solemnities, wherein, to abuse and affront him, they mishandled and abused such men as they found to have *red* hair. Nay, Diodorus tells us, (l. .i.) that they anciently sacrificed such persons as had red hair like Typho, at the sepulchre of Osiris—In opposition to this idolatry, and to preserve the Israelites from being infected with it, God commands the *Water of Expiation* (Numb. xix.) to be made of the *Ashes of a red heifer, without spot,* that is, perfectly *red.*—The *Heifer* was to be *red,* that God's people might receive the benefit of being purged from their uncleannesses by a beast of that colour which was most abominable and abhorred by their idolatrous neighbours.—As the Egyptians adored the *Heifer* with the most enthusiastical veneration, the Jews were to use it with the greatest contempt, as a polluted creature, not fit to appear in the presence of their God; to carry it without the camp, to the place where they put malefactors to death; and there to slay and burn it, the smoke and odour of it not being acceptable, but abominable to the Lord. This they were to do in the presence of God's priest, who was to see that all was performed agreeably to the rites and ceremonies observed in the worship of JEHOVAH, and not according to the superstitions of Egypt. And, to inspire them with a farther detestation,— the Priest and all who were concerned in killing and burning, were to be ' unclean until the evening,' &c. (Numb. xix. 3 :) and, in opposition to the Heathens' fanatical practice of *scattering* the ashes of the sacrifices of their *red* oxen contumeliously in the air, ' a man who was clean was to *gather up* the ashes of the heifer, and lay them up without the camp, in a clean place.' "—Young, On Idolatrous Corruptions in Religion, vol. i, pp. 208—213. See also Spencer, De Leg. Heb. tom. i, lib. ii, c. xv. p. 338.

NOTE CXVII.—*Page 304.*

SEE Maimonides's Talmudical work, entitled YAD ; and his *Notes* on the Mishna, in Surenhusii MISHNA.

NOTE CXVIII.—*Page 305.*

THAT *Fat* which was a part of the flesh might be eaten, (as appears from many places, particularly Deut. xxxii. 14,) but not that which only lay upon it, and might be separated from it; which was burnt upon the altar, when they sacrificed either bullock, sheep, or goat : and when they killed any of these, or other clean creatures, for their food at home, still they were to forbear to eat the *Suet ;* particularly out of reverence to God, whose portion it was at the altar; and partly because it was heavy and too strong a food: and it seems to have been offered upon the altar, because it was so unctuous, that it would easily burn, aud make the flesh also consume the sooner. But from its being God's part, it came thence to signify, the best and most excellent of any kind of thing. (Numb. xviii, 17; Psalm lxxxi, 16; Psalm xxii, 29.)—Bishop Patrick's Commentary on Levit. iii, 16.

NOTE CXIX.—*Page* 306.

See Dissertation V, p. 81.

NOTE CXX.—*Page* 306.

See Note 41, p. 365.

NOTE CXXI.—*Page* 309.

Bishop Patrick has explained, and defended the Vow of the Nazarite against Dr. Spencer, with great learning and ability, in his Commentary on Levit. vi, from which the following is an extract :—" The directions which God here gives about it, (*i. e.* the *hair,*) are manifestly opposite to the way of the Gentiles. For the Nazarites are here directed to cut their Hair, (when the time of their separation was completed,) at the door of the Tabernacle; when it was also to be burnt; whereas, the Gentiles hung their hair, when they had cut it, upon trees, or consecrated to rivers, or laid it up in their temples, there to be preserved. The Hebrew *Nazarites* also are required to offer various sorts of sacrifices, when they cut their hair, of which we scarcely or rarely read any thing among the Gentiles; and all the time of their separation were to drink no *wine,* nor eat *grapes,* &c. which was not known among the Heathen. From whence it is, one may think, that they are so often put in mind of the Lord, in this Law of the Nazarites,—to put them in mind, that, though they used this rite which was common to other nations, yet, it was in honour of the Lord only, whom they acknowledged to be the Author of health, and strength, and growth.

NOTE CXXII.—*Page* 310.

The reader will find the subject of Friendship excellently treated in the 8th and 9th Books of *Aristotle's Ethics.* In the commencement of the 8th Book, he has a sentiment very similar to what is expressed by our author:—"Friendship is necessary in youth, as the preservative against irreparable errors; it is necessary in old age, as the consolation amidst unavoidable infirmities; it is necessary in the vigour of man-hood, as the best auxiliary in the execution of illustrious enter-prises."—Aristotle's Ethics and Politics, by Gillies, b. 8, p. 330, vol. i. London, 1797, 4to.

NOTE CXXIII.—*Page* 311.

THE words of Maimonides are, " Magnâ autem ex parte ob hanc quoque rationem Scorta publica sunt prohibita, ut hoc pacto libido et lascivia cohibeatur. Nam per varietatem prostibulorum illorum non parùm augetur libido hominis. Nunquam etenim tam vehementer accenditur homo erga corpus illud, cui est assuetus, sicut accenditur erga corpora nova, formis et proprietatibus discrepantia."

NOTE CXXIV.—*Page* 311.

IT is probable, that the prohibitions of harlotry, and the denunciations against public prostitutions, had reference also to those detestable rites of Paganism, practised by the wor-shippers of Baal-Peor, Ashteroth, and others of their deities. Similar impurities are still practised in India. Mr. Ward, in the Preface to the third vol. of his "View of the History, &c. of the Hindoos," pp. 37, 38, says, " The author has witnessed scenes of impurity in Hindoo worship, which he can never commit to writing.—The songs and dances witnessed in the Hindoo temples at the time of the Doorga festival, at mid-night, would disgrace a house of ill-fame."

NOTE CXXV.—*Page* 312.

THE reader will find the subject of DIVORCES fully treated in Selden's " Uxor Hebraica," lib. iii, in which he has given the *Form of a Jewish Bill of Divorcement*, cap. xxiv, p. 369; and in cap. xxx, p. 34, a copy of a curious document by which *John de Cameys* divorced his wife, *Margaret*, in the reign of

E e

King Edward, and transferred her and her property to *William Paynel.*—Copies of the Jewish *Bill of Divorcement,* are also given in Levi's "Ceremonies of the Jews," p. 146; Dr. A. Clarke's Commentary on Deut. xxiv, 2; Buxtorf's Synagoga Judaica, p. 644, and other similar works.

NOTE CXXVI.—*Page* 313.

THE learned Wagenseil has compiled a ponderous quarto volume on the subject of the trial by the *Waters of Jealousy,* entitled, "SOTA," in which he affords every information to the inquirer. The reader may also consult *Lewis's Antiquities of the Hebrew Republic,* vol. iii, ch. xxxiv, in which he will find a compendious detail of this Jewish practice.

NOTE CXXVII.—*Page* 313.

" ACCORDING to the *Targumist* and to Deut. xii, 29, the dowry was fifty shekels of silver, which the seducer was to pay to her father, and he was obliged to take her to wife; nor had he authority, according to the Jewish canons, *ever to put her away by a bill of divorce.* This one consideration was a powerful curb on disorderly passions, and must tend greatly to render marriage respectable, and prevent all crimes of this nature."—Dr. A. Clarke's Commentary on Exod. xxii, 16. See also Patrick *in loc.*

NOTE CXXVIII.—*Page* 313.

BY the *Gentoo code of Laws* :—" If a man by force commits adultery with a woman of an equal or inferior caste, against her consent, the magistrate shall confiscate all his possessions, castrate him, and cause him to be led round the city, mounted on ass."—See other similar laws, in Stuart's *View of Society in Europe,* b. i, sect. 3, note 13, p. 191; Edinburgh, 1792, 8vo.

NOTE CXXIX.—*Page* 314.

THE term *Levirate,* is from the old Latin word *Levir,* signifying a *husband's brother.* " The *Mongols,* who inhabit quite a different region of Asia, and give themselves very little concern about their genealogies and descendants, have a law, which, in like manner, enjoins the marriage of a brother's widow." Michaelis supposes the practice to have arisen at a period much more early than Moses, from the difficulty of obtaining wives, where polygamy was practised: the rich collecting great numbers of females, as concubines, and thereby rendering the remaining number of marriageable females extremely small.—See Michaelis's Commentaries on the Laws of Moses, vol. ii, article 98 ; and Lewis's Antiquities of the Hebrew Republic, vol. iii, ch. 29.

NOTE CXXX.—*Page* 315.

In the defamation of a wife by her husband, regard was had, on the one hand, to the gross reproach cast upon the woman herself, her parents, her brothers and sisters, and her whole family ; and on the other, to the two following circumstances ; *first,* that the woman, being defenceless, and in the power of her accuser, neither could nor would avenge herself, and of course required the more ample protection from the laws ; and *secondly,* that a wife can never have the means of exculpating herself to the world, from the disgrace of such charges, unless a court of justice inquire into the case, and award her satisfaction, proportioned to the greatness of the injury she has sustained.—Michaelis's Commentaries on the Laws of Moses, vol. iv. art. 291, p. 295.

NOTE CXXXI.—*Page* 317.

" The real reason," says Michaelis, " for which a people, that would avoid being overwhelmed with the greatest profligacy, must prohibit incestuous marriages, absolutely, and without the slightest prospect of dispensation is this ; that, considering the free intercourse that such persons have one with another, some of whom, besides, live from their infancy in the same house, it would be impossible to prevent the prevalence of whoredom in families, or guard against the effects of very early corruption among young persons, if they could entertain the least hope of throwing a veil over past impurity, by subsequent marriage."—Commentaries on the Laws of Moses, vol. ii, art. 108, p. 68. See also art. 102—111.

NOTE CXXXIII.—*Page* 321.

SPENCER, *Legibus Hebrœorum*, lib. ii, c. 20, supposes, with great plausibility, that these inhibitory laws were given in opposition to certain practices of the Zabian idolaters, and quotes *Gulielmus Parisiensis*, who refers to certain books written expressly on that subject. He also suggests, that these unlawful mixtures of cattle were prohibited, lest they should lead on to incestuous and unlawful acts amongst the Israelites themselves.

NOTE CXXXIV.—*Page* 321.

MAIMONIDES words are— *" Circumcisio*, meo judicio, propter hanc rationem instituta est, ut libido Hominum diminuatur, et membrum hoc, quantum fieri potest, ad actum istum debilitetur.

NOTE CXXXV.—*Page* 323.

CIRCUMCISION was designed to be a *sign*, and a *seal*. (Romans iv, 11.)

1. As a *sign*, it *distinguished* the Israelites from all other people as God's peculiar people; it was *commemorative* of the Divine covenant, and perpetually reminded them of it: it was *figurative* of that purity of heart, which God promised to bestow on those who truly desired it: and it was *initiatory*, all who embraced Judaism being subjected to it.

2 As a *seal*, it was a *mark* impressed by order of Jehovah, as a token of his covenant with Abraham and his posterity; and the Jews, by submitting to it, acknowledged their obligations to fulfil the conditions of the covenant, whether the rite was personally and voluntarily suffered, or whether it was performed by parental and federal authority in childhood.— See Spencer, De Leg. Heb. vol. i, lib. i, c. 4, sect. 2.

Other reasons have also been adduced of a *Physical* nature for this rite. For, (1.) It has been said to be preventive of certain diseases, peculiarly dangerous in hot climates, particularly the *anthrax* or *carbuncle*. (2.) It is asserted to be conducive to population.—See Michaelis's Commentaries on the Laws of Moses, vol. iii, art. 186; Jahn's Biblical Archæology, ch. 10, sect. 162, p. 171; Blumenbach's Institutions of Physiology, sect. xxxvi, p. 283, note. London, 1817, 8vo.

The question, whether the Jews derived circumcission from the Egyptians, or the Egyptians from the Jews?, is perhaps impossible to be decided. It is, however, certain that Herodotus wrote too long after Moses to prove that the Jews derived it from the Egyptians; though there are some reasons for supposing it in existence before Abraham.—See Spencer, De Leg. Heb. lib. i, c. iv. sect. 4; Michaelis *ut supra*, article 185; Jahn *ut sup.*

NOTE CXXXVI.—*Page* 324.

" Non multiplicabit homo coitum, sicut diximus, neque etiam omninò eum tollet, cùm dictum sit; *Crescite et multiplicamini.* Sic debilitatur quidem istud membrum aliquo módo in circumcisione, sed non prorsus abscinditur, verùm remanet in suâ constitutione naturali, et cavetur ne aliquid addatur.

NOTE CXXXVII.—*Page* 324.

Maimonides evidently adopts the prejudices of the Eastern nations relative to the lower orders of society, nearly approaching to the Hindoo abhorrence of inferior *castes.*—See Ward's View, &c. vol. iii, pt. i, ch. 2.

NOTE CXXXVIII.—*Page* 325.

Maimonides does not appear to have had any knowledge of the descendants of the Zabii existing in his day, or for a thousand years previous; and, therefore, could not derive his views of the Zabii from any works, considered by him as modern, as has been conjectured by some late writers.

NOTE CXXXIX.—*Page* 326.

In conclusion, we may remark, that the more the Mosaic code of Laws is studied, the more fully shall we be convinced of its Divine origin, and of the wisdom, prudence, and mercy pervading every part of it. The Jews had been in bondage to a cruel and idolatrous nation; their minds were debased, and their habits were sensualized; yet they were to become the depositaries of the Divine Law, and the harbingers of the

MESSIAH. Some of the precepts guarded them against idolatrous practices, and inculcated hatred of them; others directed them to the unity, purity, justice, and mercy of JEHOVAH. Some institutions prefigured the blessings of Messiah's reign; others symbolized the necessity of atonement; and others impressed the conviction of personal sinfulness; whilst, as a whole, they induced humility, elevated the mind to God, promoted holiness, and directed to the great REDEEMER: fully justifying the appeal of Moses:—" WHAT NATION IS THERE SO GREAT, THAT HATH STATUTES AND JUDGMENTS SO RIGHTEOUS AS ALL THIS LAW, WHICH I SET BEFORE YOU THIS DAY?" (Deut. iv, 8.)

END OF NOTES AND ILLUSTRATIONS.

INDEX.

A

F f

438 INDEX.

G

J

K

L

G G

U

H H

V

W

Y

Z

THE END.

JAMES NICHOLS, PRINTER,
2, Warwick Square, Newgate Street, London.

REPRINTS OF LEGAL CLASSICS
PUBLISHED BY
THE LAWBOOK EXCHANGE, LTD.

A'Beckett, Gilbert Abbott. *The Comic Blackstone* **[bound with] [Anstey, John].** *The Pleader's Guide, A Didactic Poem by John Surrebutter; American edition by James L. High.* With illustrations by George Cruikshank. Chicago: Callaghan & Cockcroft, 1870. xii, 376, 57, 65 pp. Reprinted 2001 by The Lawbook Exchange, Ltd. ISBN 1-58477-104-6. Cloth. $95.

Adams, John. *A Defence of the Constitutions of Government of the United States of America.* Philadelphia: Printed by Budd and Bartram, for William Corbett, 1797. Three volumes. Reprint available August 2001 by The Lawbook Exchange, Ltd. LCCN 00-067586. ISBN 1-58477-140-2. Cloth. $250.

Anderson, William C. *A Dictionary of Law, Consisting of Judicial Definitions and Explanations of Words, Phrases, and Maxims, and an Exposition of the Principles of Law: Comprising a Dictionary and Compendium of American and English Jurisprudence.* Chicago: T.H. Flood and Company, 1889. viii, 1140pp. Reprinted 1996 by The Lawbook Exchange, Ltd. LCCN 96-35844. ISBN 1-886363-23-4. Cloth. $125.

Ashburner, Walter. *The Rhodian Sea-Laws. Edited from the Manuscripts.* Oxford: Clarendon Press, 1909. ccxciii, 132 pp. Reprinted 2001 by The Lawbook Exchange, Ltd. LCCN 00-065551. ISBN 1-58477-173-9. Cloth. $75.

Austin, John. *The Province of Jurisprudence Determined.* London: John Murray, 1832. xx, 392, lxxvi pp. Reprinted 2000 by The Lawbook Exchange, Ltd. LCCN 99-33457. ISBN 1-58477-023-6. Cloth. $75.

Baldwin, Henry. *A General View of the Origin and Nature of the Constitution and Government of the United States, Deduced from the Political History and Condition of the Colonies and States, from 1774 until 1788. And the Decisions of the Supreme Court of the United States. Together with Opinions in the Cases Decided at January Term, 1837, Arising on the Restraints on the Powers of the States.* Philadelphia, Printed by J. C. Clark, 1837. v, [1], 197 p. Reprinted 2000 by The Lawbook Exchange, Ltd. LCCN 00-026728. ISBN 1-58477-098-8. Cloth. $60.

Bancroft, George. *History of the Formation of the Constitution of the United States of America. Second Edition.* New York: D. Appleton and Company, 1882. Two volumes. xxiv, 520; xiv, 501 pp. Reprinted 2000 by The Lawbook Exchange, Ltd. LCCN 99-23946. ISBN 1-58477-002-3. Cloth. $175.

Bar, Carl Ludwig von. *A History of Continental Criminal Law.* Boston: Little, Brown, and Company, 1916. lvi, 561 pp. Reprinted 1999 by The Lawbook Exchange, Ltd. LCCN 99-32341. ISBN 1-58477-013-9. Cloth. $90.

Barton, Dunbar Plunket. *Shakespeare and the Law.* With a foreword by James M. Beck. Boston: Houghton Mifflin Company, 1929. xl, 167 pp. Reprinted 1999 by The Lawbook Exchange, Ltd. LCCN 99-26602. ISBN 1-58477-000-7. Cloth. $60.

Bauer, Elizabeth Kelley. *Commentaries on the Constitution 1790-1860.* New York: Columbia University Press, 1952. 400 pp. Reprinted 1999 by The Lawbook Exchange, Ltd. LCCN 98-45409. ISBN 1-886363-66-8. Cloth. $75.

Beard, Charles Austin. *The Office of the Justice of the Peace in England, in its Origin and Development.* New York: Columbia University Press, 1904. 184, [1] pp. Reprinted 2001 by The Lawbook Exchange, Ltd. ISBN 1-58477-102-X. Cloth. $60.

Beard, Charles. *An Economic Interpretation of the Constitution of the United States.* New York: The Macmillan Company, 1952. xxi, 330 pp. Reprinted 2001 by The Lawbook Exchange, Ltd. LCCN 00-036834. ISBN 1-58477-111-9. Cloth. $80.

Beard, Charles A. *The Supreme Court and the Constitution.* New York: The Macmillan Company, 1912. vii, 127 pp. Reprinted 1999 by The Lawbook Exchange, Ltd. LCCN 98-50368. ISBN 1-886363-78-1. Cloth. $45.

Beck, Theodric Romeyn. *Elements of Medical Jurisprudence.* Albany: Websters and Skinners, 1823. Two volumes. xxxiv, 418; viii, [9]-471 pp. Reprinted 1997 by The Lawbook Exchange, Ltd. LCCN 96-35845. ISBN 1-886363-24-2. Cloth. $125.

Benedict, Russell. *Acts and Laws of the Thirteen Original Colonies and States: Constituting the extraordinary collection of Hon. Russell Benedict.* New York: American Art Association, 1922. [272]pp. Reprinted 1998 The Lawbook Exchange, Ltd. LC 98-20196 ISBN 1-886363-56-0. Cloth. $85.

Bentham, Jeremy. *A Fragment on Government. Edited with an Introduction by F.C. Montague.* Oxford: The Clarendon Press, 1891. xii, 241 pp. Reprint available December 2001 by The Lawbook Exchange, Ltd. ISBN 1-58477-166-6. Cloth. $65.

Bentham, Jeremy. *Plan of Parliamentary Reform, in the Form of a Catechism, with Reasons for each Article. With an Introduction, Shewing the Necessity of Radical, and the Inadequacy of Moderate, Reform.* London: T.J. Wooler, 1818. 156 pp. Reprint available December 2001 by The Lawbook Exchange, Ltd. LCCN 00-058816. ISBN 1-58477-121-6. Cloth. $65.

Black, Henry Campbell. *A Dictionary of Law. Containing Definitions of the Terms and Phrases of American and English Jurisprudence, Ancient and Modern. Including the Principal Terms of International, Constitutional, and Commercial Law; with a Collection of Legal Maxims and Numerous Select Titles from the Civil Law and Other Foreign Systems.* St. Paul, Minn.: West Publishing, 1891. x, 1253 pp. Reprinted 1991 by the Lawbook Exchange, Ltd. LCCN 91-62383. ISBN 0-9630106-0-3. $150.

Black, Henry Campbell. *A Law Dictionary. Containing Definitions of the Terms and Phrases of American and English Jurisprudence, Ancient and Modern. And Including the Principal Terms of International, Constitutional, Ecclesiastical and Commercial Law, and Medical Jurisprudence, with a Collection of Legal Maxims, Numerous Select Titles from the Roman, Modern Civil, Scotch, French, Spanish, and Mexican Law, and Other Foreign Systems, and a Table of Abbreviations.* St. Paul, Minn.: West Publishing, 1910. 1314 pp. Reprinted 1995 by the Lawbook Exchange, Ltd. LCCN 97-10320. ISBN 1-886363-10-2. Cloth. $150.

[Blackstone, William]. Eller, Catherine Spicer. *The William Blackstone Collection in the Yale Law Library. A Bibliographical Catalogue.* New Haven: Yale University Press, 1938. xvii, 113 pp. Reprinted 1993 by The Lawbook Exchange, Ltd. LCCN 99-38826. ISBN 0-9630106-5-4. Cloth. $50.

Bondy, William. *Separation of Governmental Powers in History, in Theory, and in the Constitutions.* New York: Columbia College, 1896. Reprinted 1999 by The Lawbook Exchange, Ltd. vi,[7]-185, [1] pp. LCCN 98-44994. ISBN 1-886363-65-X. Cloth. $65.

Bonner, Robert J. and Gertrude Smith. *The Administration of Justice from Homer to Aristotle.* Chicago: The University of Chicago Press, [1930]. Two volumes. ix, 390; vii, [320] pp. Reprinted 2001 by The Lawbook Exchange, Ltd. ISBN 1-58477-117-8. Cloth. $160.

Botsford, George Willis. *The Roman Assemblies from their Origin to the End of the Republic.* New York: The Macmillan Company, 1909. x, 521 pp. Reprint available December 2001 by The Lawbook Exchange, Ltd. ISBN 1-58477-165-8. Cloth. $85.

Bouvier, John. *Institutes of American Law. New Edition by Daniel A. Gleason. In Two Volumes.* Boston: Little, Brown, & Company, 1880. lxviii, 651; iv, 798pp. Reprinted 1999 by The Lawbook Exchange, Ltd. LCCN 98-54288. ISBN 1-886363-80-3. Cloth. $250.

Bouvier, John. *A Law Dictionary Adapted to the Constitution and Laws of the United States of America, and of the Several States of the American Union; with References to the Civil and Other Systems of Foreign Law.* Philadelphia: T. & J.W. Johnson, 1839. Two volumes. 559; 628 pp. Reprinted 1993 by The Lawbook Exchange, Ltd. LCCN 99-047231. ISBN 0-9630106-7-0. Cloth. $130.

Brackenridge, Hugh. *Law Miscellanies: Containing an Introduction to the Study of Law; notes on Blackstone's Commentaries, Shewing the Variations of the Law of Pennsylvania from the Law of England, and what Acts of Assembly Might Require to be Repealed or Modifies; Observations on Smith's Edition of the Laws of Pennsylvania; Strictures on Decisions of the Supreme Court of the United States, and on Certain Acts of Congress, with Some Law Cases, and a Variety of Other Matters, Chiefly Original.* Philadelphia: P. Byrne, 1814. 588 pp. Reprint available October 2001 by The Lawbook Exchange, Ltd. LCCN 00-059548. ISBN 1-58477-161-5. Cloth. $100.

[Brandeis, Louis D.]. *Brandeis on Zionism. A Collection of Addresses and Statements by Louis D. Brandeis with a Foreword by Mr. Justice Felix Frankfurter.* Washington, D.C.: Zionist Organization of America, [1942]. viii, 156 pp. Reprinted 1999 by The Lawbook Exchange, Ltd. LCCN 98-49331. ISBN 1-886363-60-9. Cloth. $65.

Broom, Herbert. *A Selection of Legal Maxims, Classified and Illustrated. Eighth American, from the Fifth London Edition, with References to American Cases.* Philadelphia: T. & J.W. Johnson & Co., 1882. lxxviii, 993 [i.e. 779] pp. Reprinted 2000 by The Lawbook Exchange, Ltd. LCCN 99-049329. ISBN 1-58477-052-X. Cloth. $125.

Brown, Basil. *Law Sports at Gray's Inn (1594) Including Shakespeare's connection with the Inns of Court, the origin of the Capias Utlegatum re Coke and Bacon, Francis Bacon's connection with Warwickshire, together with a reprint of the Gesta Grayorum.* New York: [Privately Printed by the Author], 1921. xciv, 188, 88, [9] pp. LCCN 99-049829. ISBN 1-58477-056-2. Reprint available September 2001 by The Lawbook Exchange, Ltd. Cloth. $85.

Brown, Everett S. *The Constitutional History of the Louisiana Purchase 1803-1812.* Berkeley: University of California Press, 1920. xi, 248 pp. Reprinted 2001 by The Lawbook Exchange, Ltd. ISBN 1-58477-151-8. Cloth. $75.

Browne, Arthur. *A Compendious View of the Civil Law and of the Law of the Admiralty: being the substance of a course of lectures read in the University of Dublin.* New York: Halstead and Voorhies, 1840. Two volumes. xvi, 536; xi, 567 pp. Reprinted 2000 by The Lawbook Exchange, Ltd. LCCN 99-18284. ISBN 1-886363-88-9. Cloth. $175.

Buckland, W.W. *The Roman Law of Slavery: The Condition of the Slave in Private Law from Augustus to Justinian.* Cambridge: Cambridge University Press, 1908. xii, [2], 735 pp. Reprinted 2001 by The Lawbook Exchange, Ltd. LCCN 99-056922. ISBN 1-58477-068-6. Cloth. $175.

Burrill, Alexander M. *A New Law Dictionary and Glossary: Containing Full Definitions of the Principal Terms of the Common and Civil Law, Together with Translations and Explanations of the Various Technical Phrases in Different Languages, Occurring in the Ancient and Modern Reports, and Standard Treatises; Embracing Also All the Principal Common and Civil Law Maxims. Compiled on the Basis of Spelman's Glossary, and Adapted to the Jurisprudence of the United States; with Copious Illustrations, Critical and Historical.* New York: John S. Voorhies, 1850. Two volumes. xviii, 1099 pp. Reprinted 1998 by The Lawbook Exchange, Ltd. LCCN 97-38481. ISBN 1-886363-32-3. Cloth. $195.

Bussell, F.W. *The Roman Empire. Essays on the Constitutional History from the Accession of Domitian (81 A.D.) to the Retirement of Nicephorus III. (1081 A.D.)* London: Longmans, Green, and Co., 1910. Two volumes. xiv, 402; xxiii, 521 pp. Reprinted 2000 by The Lawbook Exchange, Ltd. LCCN 99-087026. ISBN 1-58477-082-1. Cloth. $175.

Calabresi, Guido. *A Common Law for the Age of Statutes.* Cambridge: Harvard University Press, 1982. xi, 319 pp. Reprinted 2000 by The Lawbook Exchange, Ltd. LCCN 99-44889. ISBN 1-58477-040-6. Cloth. $85.

Calhoun, George M. *The Growth of Criminal Law in Ancient Greece.* Berkeley: University of California Press, 1927. x, 149 pp. LCCN 99-43192. ISBN 1-58477-037-6. Reprinted 2000 by The Lawbook Exchange, Ltd. Cloth. $50.

Cameron, James R. *Frederick William Maitland and the History of English Law.* Norman: University of Oklahoma Press, [1961]. xvi, 214 pp. Portrait frontis. Illustrations. Reprinted 2001 by The Lawbook Exchange, Ltd. LCCN 00-067585. ISBN 1-58477-135-6. Cloth. $85.

Campbell, John, Baron. *Shakespeare's Legal Acquirements Considered.* London: John Murray, 1859. vi, 117 pp. Reprint available October 2001 by The Lawbook Exchange, Ltd. ISBN 1-58477-126-7. Cloth. $60.

[Cardozo, Benjamin]. *Law is Justice. Notable Opinions of Mr. Justice Cardozo.* Foreword by Robert F. Wagner. Edited by A.L. Sainer. New York: Ad Press Ltd., [1938]. xvii, 441 pp. Frontis. Reprinted 1999 by The Lawbook Exchange, Ltd. LCCN 99-34154. ISBN 1-58477-010-4. Cloth. $75.

Cardozo, Benjamin. *The Paradoxes of Legal Science.* New York: Columbia University Press, 1928. v, 142 pp. Reprinted 2000 by The Lawbook Exchange, Ltd. LCCN 00-024469. ISBN 1-58477-097-X. Cloth. $75.

Chafee, Zechariah. *Free Speech in the United States.* Cambridge, Massachusetts: Harvard University Press, 1967. xviii, 634 pp. Reprinted 2001 by The Lawbook Exchange, Ltd. LCCN 99-087317. ISBN 1-58477-085-6. Cloth. $125.

[Cherokee Laws]. *Compiled Laws of the Cherokee Nation.* Tahlequah, I.T.:National Advocate Print, 1881. 370pp. Reprinted September 1998 by The Lawbook Exchange, Ltd. With a new introduction by Michael Weber. LCCN 98-12741. ISBN 1-886363-42-0. Cloth. $60.

Cherry, Richard R. *Lectures on the Growth of Criminal Law in Ancient Communities.* London: Macmillan and Co., 1890. xi, 123 pp. Reprint available October 2001 by The Lawbook Exchange, Ltd. LCCN 00-067010. ISBN 1-58477-167-4. Cloth. $65.

Chipman, Nathaniel. *Principles of Government. A Treatise on Free Institutions Including the Constitution of the United States.* Burlington: Edward Smith, 1833. viii, 144, 145a-188a, [145]-330 pp. Reprinted 2001 by The Lawbook Exchange, Ltd. LCCN 99-048863. ISBN 1-58477-046-5. Cloth. $80.

Chitwood, Oliver Perry. *Justice in Colonial Virginia.* Baltimore: Johns Hopkins Press, 1905. 123, [1] pp. Reprinted 2001 by The Lawbook Exchange, Ltd. ISBN 1-58477-114-3. Cloth. $65.

Clark, H.B. *Biblical Law: Being a text of the statutes, ordinances, and judgments established in the Holy Bible-with many allusions to secular laws-ancient, medieval, and modern-Laws of documented to the Scriptures, judicial decisions, and legal literature.* Portland, Ore.: Binfords & Mort, [1943]. xxiv, 304 pp. Reprinted 2000 by The Lawbook Exchange, Ltd. LCCN 99-053316. ISBN 1-58477-062-7. Cloth. $75.

Cohn, Morris M. *An Introduction to the Study of the Constitution; A Study showing the Play of Physical and Social Factors in the Creation of Institutional Law.* Baltimore: The Johns Hopkins Press, 1892. xi, 235 pp. Reprinted 2000 by The Lawbook Exchange, Ltd. LCCN 99-38730. ISBN 1-58477-032-5. Cloth. $50.

Coke, Edward Sir. *The First Part of the Institute of the England, or, A commentary upon Littleton. Not the name of the Author only, but of the Law Itself. Revised and Corrected With Additions of Notes, References, and Proper Tables, by Francis Hargrave and Charles Butler, Esqrs. Of Lincoln's Inn, Including also The Notes of Lord Chief Justice Hale and Lord Chancellor Nottingham; and An Analysis of Littleton, written by an unknown Hand in 1658-9.* By Charles Butler, Esq. The Eighteenth Edition, Corrected. London, J. & W.T. Clarke, 1823. Two volumes. ccxvi,[606]; iv, [772] pp. Reprinted 2000 by The Lawbook Exchange, Ltd. LCCN 99-41675. ISBN 1-58477-033-3. Cloth. $195.

Coke, Sir Edward. *The Second Part of the Institutes of the Laws of England; Containing the Exposition of Many Ancient and Other Statutes.* London: Printed for W. Clarke and Sons, 1817. Star-paged. [18], 746, [49] pp. Reprint available November 2001 by The Lawbook Exchange, Ltd. ISBN 1-58477-200-X. Cloth. $125.

Coke, Sir Edward. *The Third Part of the Institutes of the Laws of England; Concerning High Treason, and Other Pleas of the Crown and Criminal Causes.* London: Printed for W. Clarke and Sons, 1817. Star-paged. [10], [244], [20] pp. Reprint available November 2001 by The Lawbook Exchange, Ltd. ISBN 1-58477-201-8. Cloth. $75.

Coke, Sir Edward. *The Fourth Part of the Institutes of the Laws of England; Concerning The Jurisdiction of the Courts.* London: Printed for W. Clarke and Sons, 1817. Star-paged. [12], 364, [49] pp. Reprint available November 2001 by The Lawbook Exchange, Ltd. ISBN 1-58477-202-6. Cloth. $85.

[Continental Legal History]. *A General Survey of Events, Sources, Persons & Movements in Continental Legal History. By Various European Authors.* With an introduction by Albert Kocourek. Boston: Little, Brown, 1912. liii, 754pp. Reprinted 1998 by The Lawbook Exchange, Ltd. LCCN 98-11159. ISBN 1-886363-47-1. Cloth. $110.

Cooley, Thomas M. *The General Principles of Constitutional Law in the United States* of America. Boston: Little, Brown, and Company, 1880. xxxix, 376 pp. Reprinted 2001 by The Lawbook Exchange, Ltd. LCCN 00-056301. ISBN 1-58477-120-8. Cloth. $85.

Cooley, Thomas M. *A Treatise on the Constitutional Limitations which Rest Upon the Legislative Power of the States of the American Union. Fifth edition.* Boston: Little, Brown, and Co., 1883. lxxxi, 886pp. Reprinted 1998 by The Lawbook Exchange, Ltd. LCCN 98-12730. ISBN 1-886363-53-6. Cloth. $120.

Cooley, Thomas McIntyre. *A Treatise on the Constitutional Limitations Which Rest Upon the Legislative Power of the States of the American Union. [1st edition].* Boston: Little, Brown, and Co., 1868. xlvii, 720pp. Reprinted 1999 by The Lawbook Exchange, Ltd. LCCN 99-20589. ISBN 1-886363-92-7. Cloth. $95.

Cooper, Thomas. *A Treatise on the Law of Libel and the Liberty of the Press; Showing the Origin, Use, and Abuse of the Law of Libel: With Copious Notes and References to Authorities in Great Britain and the United States: As Applicable to Individuals and to Political and Ecclesiastical Bodies and Principles.* New York: G.F. Hopkins & Son, 1830. xxxviii, 184 pp. Reprint available December 2001 by The Lawbook Exchange, Ltd. ISBN 1-58477-134-8. Cloth. $75.

Corwin, Edward. *The Doctrine of Judicial Review: Its Legal and Historical Basis and Other Essays.* Princeton: Princeton University Press, 1914. ix, 178 pp. Reprinted 2000 by The Lawbook Exchange, Ltd. LCCN 99-32362. ISBN 1-58477-011-2. Cloth. $60.

Curtis, George Ticknor and Joseph Culbertson Clayton. *Constitutional History of the United States from their Declaration of Independence to the Close of the Civil War.* New York: Harper & Brothers, 1889, 1896. Two volumes. xiii, 774; x, 780 pp. Reprint available October 2001 by The Lawbook Exchange, Ltd. LCCN 00-065554. ISBN 1-58477-129-1. Cloth. $250.

Darrow, Clarence and William J. Bryan. *The World's Most Famous Court Trial. Tennessee Evolution Case. A Complete Stenographic Report of the Famous Court Test of the Anti-Evolution Act, at Dayton July 10 to 21, 1925, Including Speeches and Arguments of Attorneys.* Cincinnati: National Book Company, [1925]. [4], 339 pp. Reprinted 1997 by The Lawbook Exchange, Ltd. LCCN 97-38485. ISBN 1-886363-31-5. Cloth. $75.

Darrow, Clarence. *A Persian Pearl. And Other Essays.* East Aurora, NY: The Roycroft Shop, 1899. 175 pp. Reprinted 1997 by The Lawbook Exchange, Ltd. LCCN 97-5174. ISBN 1-886363-27-7. Cloth. $50.

Darrow, Clarence S. *An Eye for an Eye.* New York: Fox Duffield & Company, 1905. 213 pp. Reprinted 1996 by The Lawbook Exchange, Ltd. LCCN 99-047232. ISBN 1-886363-07-2. Cloth. $55.

Davis, C.K. *The Law in Shakespeare*. Washington, D.C.: Washington Law Book Co., [1883]. 303 pp. Reprinted 1999 by The Lawbook Exchange, Ltd. LCCN 98-32333. ISBN 1-886363-75-7. Cloth. $60.

Dawson, John P. *A History of Lay Judges*. Cambridge, Mass.: Harvard University Press, 1960. viii, [2], 310 pp. Reprinted 1999 by The Lawbook Exchange, Ltd. LCCN 98-50812. ISBN 1-886363-69-2. Cloth. $75.

DePuy, Henry F. *A Bibliography of the English Colonial Treaties with the American Indians*. New York: the Lenox Club, 1917. [108] pp. Reprinted 2001 by The Lawbook Exchange, Ltd. ISBN 1-58477-163-1. Cloth. $50.

Dodd, Walter Fairleigh. *The Revision and Amendment of State Constitutions*. Baltimore: The Johns Hopkins Press, 1910. xvii, 350 pp. Reprinted 1999 by The Lawbook Exchange, Ltd. LCCN 98-50815. ISBN 1-886363-73-0. Cloth. $65.

Duer, William Alexander. *A Course of Lectures on the Constitutional Jurisprudence of the United States; Delivered Annually in Columbia College, New York. The Second Edition, Revised, Enlarged, and Adapted to Professional as well as General Use.* Boston: Little, Brown & Co., 1856. xxiv, 545 pp. Reprinted 2000 by The Lawbook Exchange, Ltd. LCCN 99-16385. ISBN 1-58477-020-1. Cloth. $85.

Elias, Gbolahan. *Explaining Constructive Trusts*. Oxford: Clarendon Press; Oxford University Press, 1990. xxii, 177 pp. Reprint available October 2001 by The Lawbook Exchange, Ltd. ISBN 1-58477-208-5. Cloth. $75.

Esmein, A[dhemar]. *A History of Continental Criminal Procedure with Special Reference to France. Translated by John Simpson; with an editorial preface by William E. Mikell and introductions by Norman M. Trenholme and by William Renwick Riddell.* Boston: Little, Brown and Company, 1913. xlv, 640 pp. Reprinted 2000 by The Lawbook Exchange, Ltd. LCCN 99-045906. ISBN 1-58477-042-2. Cloth. $100.

Evans, E.P. *The Criminal Prosecution and Capital Punishment of Animals*. New York: E.P. Dutton, 1906. x, 384pp. Reprinted 1998 by The Lawbook Exchange, Ltd. LCCN 98-12801. ISBN 1-886363-52-8. Cloth. $65.

Farnam, Henry W. *Chapters in the History of Social Legislation in the United States to 1860*. Washington: Carnegie Institution of Washington, 1938. xx, 496 pp. Reprinted 2000 by The Lawbook Exchange, Ltd. LCCN 99-049362. ISBN 1-58477-054-6. Cloth. $100.

[Field Codes]. [New York 1850-1865]. New York Field Codes. 1850-1865.
Vol. I. *The Code of Civil Procedure of the State of New-York, Reported Complete by the Commissioners on Practice and Pleadings. 1850.*
Vol. II. *The Code of Criminal Procedure of the State of New York, Reported Complete by the Commissioners on Practice and Pleadings. 1850.*
Vol. III. *The Civil Code of the State of New York, Reported Complete by the Commissioners of the Code. 1865.*
Vol. IV. *The Penal Code of the State of New York, Reported Complete by the Commissioners of the Code. 1865.*
Vol. V. *The Political Code of the State of New York. 1860.*
With a new introduction by Michael Weber. Reprinted 1998 by The Lawbook Exchange, Ltd. Five volume series. [8], xcvi, 791; liii, [1], 486; cxii, 776; lxiv, 406, clxvii; xlvii, 607 pp. ISBN 1-886363-40-4 (set). Cloth. $495.

Field, Stephen J[ohnson]. *Personal Reminiscences of Early Days in California, with Other Sketches... To Which is added the Story of his Attempted Assassination by a Former Associate on the Supreme Bench of the State by Hon. George C. Gorman.* [Washington, D.C.]: Printed for a Few Friends. Not Published, [1893]. vi, 406pp. Reprint available September 2001 by The Lawbook Exchange, Ltd. LCCN 00-067118. ISBN 1-58477-133-X. Cloth. $85.

Freeman, A.C. *A Treatise of the Law of Judgments. Including All Final Determinations of the Rights of Parties in Actions or Proceedings at Law or in Equity. Revised, and Greatly Enlarged by Edward W. Tuttle.* San Francisco: Bancroft-Whitney, 1925. Three volumes. 1216; 1280; 1264 pp. Reprinted 1993 by The Lawbook Exchange, Ltd. LCCN 99-047228. ISBN 0-9630106-6-2. Cloth. $295.

Finkelman, Paul, editor. *A Brief Narrative of the Case and Tryal of John Peter Zenger Printer of the New York Weekly Journal.* New York: Brandywine Press, [1997]. vii, 175 pp. Reprinted 2000 by The Lawbook Exchange, Ltd. LCCN 99-049431. ISBN 1-58477-051-1. Cloth. $50.

Finkelman, Paul. *An Imperfect Union: Slavery, Federalism and Comity.* Chapel Hill: The University of North Carolina Press, 1981. xii, 378 pp. Reprinted 2000 by The Lawbook Exchange, Ltd. LCCN 00-021509. ISBN 1-58477-092-9. Cloth. $85.

Finkelman, Paul. *Slavery in the Courtroom. An Annotated Bibliography of American Cases.* Washington: Library of Congress, 1985. Illustrated. xxvii, 312pp. Reprinted 1998 by The Lawbook Exchange, Ltd. LCCN 98-11284. ISBN 1-886363-48-X. Cloth. $85.

Fisher, Sydney George. *The Evolution of the Constitution of the United States. Showing That It Is a Development of Progressive History and Not an Isolated Document Struck Off at a Given Time or an Imitation of English or Dutch Forms of Government.* Philadelphia: J.B. Lippincott, 1897. 398 pp. Reprinted 1996 by The Lawbook Exchange, Ltd. LCCN 97-41054. ISBN 1-886363-08-0. Cloth. $65.

Flanders, Henry. *An Exposition of the Constitution of the United States. Designed as a Manual of Instruction.* Philadelphia: E.H. Butler & Co., 1860. xii, 311 pp. Reprinted 1999 by The Lawbook Exchange, Ltd. LCCN 99-31594. ISBN 1-58477-014-7. Cloth. $60.

Flanders, Henry. *A Treatise on Maritime Law.* Boston: Little, Brown and Company, 1852. xvi, 444 pp. Reprinted 1999 by The Lawbook Exchange, Ltd. ISBN 1-886363-72-2. Cloth. $75.

Ford, Paul Leicester. *Pamphlets on the Constitution of the United States, Published During Its Discussion by the People 1787-1788.* Brooklyn, N.Y., 1888. viii, 451 pp. Reprinted 2000 by The Lawbook Exchange, Ltd. LCCN 99-25089. ISBN 1-886363-95-1. Cloth. $75.

Forsyth, William. *The History of Lawyers. Ancient and Modern.* Boston: Estes & Lauriat, 1875. Illustrated. xvii, 404 pp. Reprinted 1996 by the Lawbook Exchange, Ltd. LCCN 95-51103. ISBN 1-886363-14-5. Cloth. $60.

Forsyth, William. *History of Trial by Jury [Second edition].* Jersey City: Frederick D. Linn, [1875]. x, 388 pp. Reprinted 1994 by The Lawbook Exchange, Ltd. LCCN 96-14505. ISBN 0-9630106-8-9. Cloth. $65.

Fortescue, Sir John. *The Governance of England: Otherwise Called The Difference between an Absolute and a Limited Monarchy. A Revised Text edited with Introduction, Notes, and Appendices by Charles Plummer.* London: Oxford University Press, 1885. xxiii, 387pp. Reprinted 1999 by The Lawbook Exchange, Ltd. ISBN 1-886363-79-X. Cloth. $65.

Fortescue, Sir John. *DeLaudibus Legum Angliae. A Treatise in Commendation of the Laws of England.* With Translation by Francis Gregor. Notes by Andrew Amos and a Life of the Author by Thomas (Fortescue) Lord Clermont. Cincinnati: Robert Clarke & Co., 1874. lxiv, 302 pp. Reprinted 1999 by The Lawbook Exchange, Ltd. LCCN 99-16485. ISBN 1-58477-019-8. Cloth. $65.

Foss, Edward. *A Biographical Dictionary of the Judges of England From the Conquest to the Present Time 1066-1870.* London: John Murray, 1870. xv, 792 pp. Reprinted 2000 by The Lawbook Exchange, Ltd. LCCN 99-12577. ISBN 10886363-86-2. Cloth. $100.

Friedberg, Emil Albert and Aemilius Ludwig Richter. *Corpus iuris canonici.-Editio Lipsiensis secunda / post Aemilii Ludouici Richteri curas ad librorum manu scriptorum et editionis Romanae fidem recognouit et adnotatione critica instruxit Aemilius Friedberg.* Liepzig : Tauchnitz, 1879-1881. Two volumes. civ, 1472 columns (736 pp.); lxxxii, 1340 columns (670 pp.) LCCN 99-088231. Reprinted 2000 by The Lawbook Exchange, Ltd. LCCN 99-088231. ISBN 1-58477-088-0. Cloth. $300.

Friend, Willam L. *Anglo-American Legal Bibliographies. An Annotated Guide.* Washington, D.C.: United States Government Printing Office, 1944. xii, 166 pp. Reprinted 1996 by The Lawbook Exchange, Ltd. LCCN 96-11002. ISBN 1-886363-21-8. Cloth. $65.

Fuller, Lon L. *The Law in Quest of Itself.* Boston: Beacon Press, 1966. [vi], 150 pp. Reprinted 1999 by The Lawbook Exchange, Ltd. LCCN 99-32863. ISBN 1-58477-016-3. Cloth. $45.

Futrell, William H. *The History of American Customs Jurisprudence.* New York: Published privately, 1941. 314pp. Reprinted 1998 by The Lawbook Exchange, Ltd. LCCN 98-11342. ISBN 1-886363-51-X. Cloth. $60.

Gest, John Marshall. *The Lawyer in Literature.* London: Sweet & Maxwell, Limited, 1913. xii, 249 pp. Reprinted 1999 by The Lawbook Exchange, Ltd. LCCN 99-18365. ISBN 1-886363-90-0. Cloth. $60.

Gierke, Otto. *Natural Law and the Theory of Society 1500 to 1800.* With a Lecture on the Ideas of Natural Law and Humanity by Ernst Troeltsch. Translated with an Introduction by Ernest Barker. Complete in one volume. Cambridge: The University Press, 1950. Reprint available October 2001 by The Lawbook Exchange, Ltd. LCCN 2001016483. ISBN 1-58477-1490-6. Cloth. $110.

Giesecke, Albert Anthony. *American Commercial Legislation Before 1789.* New York: University of Pennsylvania: D. Appleton and Company, agents, 1910. 167 pp. Reprint available October 2001 by The Lawbook Exchange, Ltd. LCCN 00-058813. ISBN 1-58477-153-4. Cloth. $65.

Gilmore, Grant. *Security Interests in Personal Property.* Boston: Little, Brown & Company, 1965. Two volumes. xxxiv, 651; xiii, 653-1508 pp. Reprinted 1999 by The Lawbook Exchange, Ltd. LCCN 99-10258. ISBN 1-886363-81-1. Cloth. $195.

Girard, Paul F. *A Short History of Roman Law. Being the First Part of his Manuel Elementaire De Droit Romain. Translated by Augustus Henry Frazer and John Home Cameron.* Toronto: Canada Law Book Company, 1906, v, 220 pp. Reprinted 2000 by The Lawbook Exchange, Ltd. LCCN 99-087383. ISBN 1-58477-078-3. Cloth. $55.

Goodenough, Edwin R. *The Jurisprudence of the Jewish Courts in Egypt: Legal Administration by the Jews under the Early Roman Empire as Described by Philo Judaeus.* New Haven: Yale University Press, 1929. vii, 268 pp. Reprint available December 2001 by The Lawbook Exchange, Ltd. ISBN 1-58477-152-6. Cloth. $75.

Goodhart, Arthur L. *Five Jewish Lawyers of the Common Law.* London: Oxford University Press, 1949. [4], 74 pp. Reprinted 2000 by The Lawbook Exchange, Ltd. LCCN 99-049934. ISBN 1-58477-045-7. Cloth. $60.

Gould, James. *A Treatise on the Principles of Pleading in Civil Action.* Boston: Lilly and Wait, 1832. x, 536 pp. Reprint available November 2001 by The Lawbook Exchange, Ltd. LCCN 00-059549. ISBN 1-58477-158-5. Cloth. $95.

Greenidge, A.H.J. *The Legal Procedure of Cicero's Time.* Oxford: The Clarendon Press, 1901. xiii, 599 pp. Reprinted 2000 by The Lawbook Exchange, Ltd. LCCN 99-26771. ISBN 1-886363-99-4. Cloth. $85.

Greenleaf, Simon. *The Testimony of the Evangelists Examined by the Rules of Evidence Administered in Courts of Justice with an Appendix Containing a History of the Most Ancient Manuscript Copies of the New Testament, and a Comparison of their Text with that of the King James' Bible by Constantine Tischendorff. Also a Review of the Trial of Jesus.* New York: James Cockcroft & Company, 1874. Reprint available September 2001 by The Lawbook Exchange, Ltd.xxiii, 613 pp. LCCN 00-021510. ISBN 1-58477-020-1. Cloth. $95.

Greenleaf, Simon. *A Treatise on the Law of Evidence.* Boston: Little, Brown, and Company, 1899. Three volumes. Reprint available September 2001 by The Lawbook Exchange, Ltd. LCCN 00-065554. ISBN 1-58477-116-X. Cloth. $350.

Grotius, Hugo. *The Freedom of the Seas or The Right which Belongs to the Dutch to Take Part in the East Indian Trade.* Translated with a Revision of the Latin Text of 1633 by Ralph van Deman Magoffin. Edited with an Introductory Note by James Brown Scott. Originally published: New York: Oxford University Press, 1916. xv, 83pp., paged in duplicate. Reprint available September 2001 by

The Lawbook Exchange, Ltd. LCCN 2001022509. ISBN 1-58477-182-8. Cloth. $65.

Haines, Charles Grove. *The Conflict over Judicial Powers in the United States to 1870.* New York: Columbia University Press, 1909. 180 pp. Reprinted 2001 by The Lawbook Exchange, Ltd. LCCN 99-088241. ISBN 1-58477-080-5. Cloth. $60.

Haines, Charles Grove. *The Role of the Supreme Court in American Government and Politics 1789-1835.* Berkeley: University of California Press, 1944. xiii, 679 pp. Reprint available October 2001 by The Lawbook Exchange, Ltd. ISBN 1-58477-207-7. Cloth. $120.

Haines, Charles Grove and Foster Sherwood. *The Role of the Supreme Court in American Government and Politics 1835-1869.* Berkeley: University of California Press, 1957. x, 533 pp. Reprint available October 2001 by The Lawbook Exchange, Ltd. ISBN 1-58477-197-6. Cloth. $95.

Hale, Matthew. *The History and Analysis of the Common Law of England.* Stafford: J. Nutt, 1713. [x], 264, [28], 176 pp. Reprinted 2000 by The Lawbook Exchange, Ltd. LCCN 99-33739. ISBN 1-58477-024-4. Cloth. $85.

Harper, Robert Francis. *The Code of Hammurabi King of Babylon. About 2250 B.C. Autographed Text transliteration...* Chicago: The University of Chicago Press, 1904. xxviii, 194, ciii (plates) pp. Illus. Reprinted 2000 The Lawbook Exchange, Ltd. LCCN 99-23953. ISBN 1-58477-003-1. Cloth. $75.

Harris, Virgil M. *Ancient, Curious, and Famous Wills.* Boston: Little, Brown, and Company, 1911. xiv, 472 pp. Reprinted 1999 by The Lawbook Exchange, Ltd. LCCN 99-20588. ISBN 1-886363-93-5. Cloth. $75.

Hearn, William Edward. *The Aryan Household Its Structure and its Development. An Introduction to Comparative Jurisprudence.* London and New York: Longmans, Green, and Co., 1891. viii, 494 pp. Reprint available December 2001 by The Lawbook Exchange, Ltd. ISBN 1-58477-124-0. Cloth. $90.

Henderson, Gerard Carl. *The Position of Foreign Corporations in American Constitutional Law. A Contribution to the History and Theory of Juristic Persons in Anglo-American Law.* Cambridge: Harvard University Press, 1918. xix, 199 pp. Reprinted 1999 by The Lawbook Exchange, Ltd. LCCN 99-18233. ISBN 1-886363-89-7. Cloth. $50.

Hicks, Frederick C. *History of the Yale Law School to 1915.* With a new introduction by Morris L. Cohen and a new index. New Haven: Yale University Press, 1935-1938. 301 pp. Illustrated. Reprinted 2001 by The Lawbook Exchange, Ltd. LCCN 2001016436. ISBN 1-58477-175-5. Cloth. $75.

Hicks, Frederick. *Men and Books Famous in the Law. With an introduction by Harlan F. Stone.* Rochester, New York: Lawyers Co-operative Publishing, 1921. 259 pp. Reprinted 1992 by The Lawbook Exchange, Ltd. LCCN 92-070809. ISBN 0-9630106-2-X. Cloth. $50.

Hohfeld, Wesley. *Fundamental Legal Conceptions as Applied in Judicial Reasoning.* Edited by Walter Wheeler Cook, with a New Foreword by Arthur L. Corbin. New Haven: Yale University Press, 1964. xv, 114 pp. Reprinted 2000 by The Lawbook Exchange, Ltd. LCCN 00-064108. ISBN 1-58477-162-3. Cloth. $55.

Holdsworth, William S. *Charles Dickens as a Legal Historian.* New Haven: Yale University Press, 1929. 157 pp. Reprinted 1995 by The Lawbook Exchange, Ltd. LCCN 96-46579. ISBN 1-886363-06-4. Cloth. $40.

Holdsworth, William S. *Essays in Law and History.* Edited by A.L. Goodhart and H.G. Hanbury. Oxford: At the Clarendon Press, 1946. xv, 302 pp. Reprinted 1995 by The Lawbook Exchange, Ltd. LCCN 99-047234. ISBN 1-886363-13-7. Cloth. $65.

Holdsworth, W.S. *The Historians of Anglo-American Law.* New York: Columbia University Press, 1928. 175 pp. Reprinted 1994 by The Lawbook Exchange, Ltd. ISBN 0-9630106-9-7. Cloth. $50.

Holt, W. Stull. *Treaties Defeated by the Senate. A Study of the Struggle Between President and Senate Over the Conduct of Foreign Relations.* Baltimore: The Johns Hopkins Press, 1933. vi, [1],328 pp. Reprinted 2000 by The Lawbook Exchange, Ltd. LCCN 99-39606. ISBN 1-58477-029-5. Cloth. $65.

Holthouse, Henry James. *A New Law Dictionary, Containing Explanations of Such Technical Terms and Phrases As Defined in the Works of Legal Authors, in the Practice of the Courts, and in the Parliamentary Proceedings of the Houses of Lords and Commons, To Which Is Added An Outline of An Action at Law and of A Suit in Equity. Edited, from the Second and Enlarged London Edition, With Numerous Additions, by Henry Penington.* Philadelphia: Lea and Blanchard, 1847. viii, [17]-495 pp. Reprinted 1999 by The Lawbook Exchange, Ltd. LCCN 98-49350. ISBN 1-886363-67-6. Cloth. $75.

Horton, John Theodore. *James Kent: A Study in Conservatism, 1763-1847.* New York: D. Appleton-Century Co., [1939]. xi, 354 pp. Reprinted 2000 by The Lawbook Exchange, Ltd. LCCN 99-056927. ISBN 1-58477-069-4. Cloth. $80.

Huebner, Rudolf. *A History of Germanic Private Law.* Translated by Francis S. Philbrick; with an editorial preface by Ernest G. Lorenzen and introductions by Paul Vinogradoff and by William E. Walz. Boston: Little, Brown and Company, 1818. lix, 788 pp. Reprinted 2000 by The Lawbook Exchange, Ltd. LCCN 99-055138. ISBN 1-58477-065-1. Cloth. $120.

Hurst, James Willard. *The Growth of American Law: The Law Makers.* Boston: Little, Brown and Company, 1950. xiii, 502 pp. Reprinted July 2001 by The Lawbook Exchange, Ltd. ISBN 1-58477-194-1. Cloth. $90.

Hurst, James Willard. *Law and Markets in United States History: Different Modes of Bargaining among Interests.* [Madison]: The University of Wisconsin Press, [1982]. vii, 207 pp. Reprinted 2001 by The Lawbook Exchange, Ltd. LCCN 00-067116. ISBN 1-58477-136-4. Cloth. $80.

Hurst, James Willard. *Law and Social Order in the United States.* Ithaca: Cornell University Press, 1977. 318 pp. Reprinted 2000 by The Lawbook Exchange, Ltd. ISBN 1-58477-113-5. Cloth. $85.

Ilbert, Courtenay. *The Mechanics of Law Making.* New York: Columbia University Press, 1914. viii, 209 pp. Reprinted 2001 by The Lawbook Exchange, Ltd. LCCN 99-047156. ISBN 1-58477-044-9. Cloth. $70.

Jackson, E. Hilton. *Latin for Lawyers. Containing I: A Course in Latin, with Legal Maxims and Phrases As a Basis of Instruction. II. A Collection of Over One Thousand Latin Maxims, with English Translations, Explanatory Notes, and Cross-References. III. A Vocabulary of Latin Words.* London: Sweet & Maxwell, 1915. viii, 300 pp. Reprinted 1992 by The Lawbook Exchange, Ltd. LCCN 92-074408. ISBN 0-9630106-4-6. Cloth. $50.

Jacobs, Clyde E. *Law Writers and the Courts. The Influence of Thomas M. Cooley, Christopher G. Tiedeman, and John F. Dillon upon American Constitutional Law.* Berkeley: University of California Press, 1954. x, 223 pp. Reprint available October 2001 by The Lawbook Exchange, Ltd. ISBN 1-58477-207-7. Cloth. $85.

Jacob, Giles. *The Law-Dictionary: Explaining the Rise, Progress, and Present State of the English Law; Defining and Interpreting the Terms or Words of Art; and Comprising Copious Information on the Subjects of Law, Trade, and Government. Corrected and Greatly Enlarged by T[homas] E[dlyne] Tomlins.* New York: Printed for, and Published by I. Riley, 1811. Six volumes. viii, 531; [2], 543; [2],618; [2], 472; [2], 553; [2], 471pp. Reprinted 2000 by The Lawbook Exchange, Ltd. LCCN 98-49349. ISBN 1-886363-68-4. Cloth. $495.

Jaques, E.T. *Charles Dickens in Chancery: Being an Account of his Proceedings in Respect of the "Christmas Carol" with Some Gossip in Relation to the Old Law Courts at Westminster.* London: Longmans, Green & Company, 1914. 95 pp. Reprint available November 2001 by The Lawbook Exchange, Ltd. ISBN 1-58477-106-2. Cloth. $60.

Jhering, Rudolf Von. *Law as a Means to an End.* Translated from the German by Isaac Husik with an Editorial Preface by Joseph H. Drake and with Introductions by Henry Lamm and W.M. Geldart. Boston: The Boston Book Company, 1913. lxi, 483 pp. Reprinted 1999 by The Lawbook Exchange, Ltd. LCCN 99-23754. ISBN 1-58477-009-0. Cloth. $80.

Jhering, Rudolph von. *The Struggle for Law. Translated from the Fifth German Edition by John J. Lalor. Second Edition, with an Introduction by Albert Kocourek.* Chicago: Callaghan and Company, 1915. lii, 138 pp. Reprinted 1997 by The Lawbook Exchange, Ltd. LCCN 97-6826. ISBN 1-886363-25-0. Cloth. $60.

Johns, C.H.W. *Babylonian and Assyrian Laws, Contracts and Letters.* Edinburgh: T. & T. Clark, 1904. xxii, 424 pp. Reprinted 2000 by The Lawbook Exchange, Ltd. LCCN 99-32862. ISBN 1-58477-022-8. Cloth. $75.

Johns, C.H.W. , translator. *The Oldest Code of Laws in the World: The Code of Laws Promulgated by Hammurabi, King of Babylon, B.C. 2285-2242.* Edinburgh: T. & T. Clark, 1926. xii, 88 pp. Reprinted 2000 by The Lawbook Exchange, Ltd. LCCN 99-053070. ISBN 1-58477-061-9. Cloth. $60.

Kalman, Laura. *Legal Realism at Yale, 1927-1960.* Chapel Hill: University of North Carolina Press, 1986. xii, 314 pp. Reprint available September 2001 by The Lawbook Exchange, Ltd. ISBN 1-58477-203-4. Cloth. $85.

Kames, Henry Home, Lord. *Historical Law-Tracts. The Second Edition.* Edinburgh: A. Kincaid, 1761. xv, 463 pp. LCCN 99-43133. ISBN 1-58477-038-4. Reprinted 2000 by The Lawbook Exchange, Ltd. Cloth. $95.

Keller, Morton. *Affairs of State: Public Life in Late Nineteenth Century America.* Cambridge: Harvard University Press, 1977. ix, 631 pp. Reprinted 2000 by The Lawbook Exchange, Ltd. LCCN 99-087921. ISBN 1-58477-086-4. Cloth. $95.

Kelsen, Hans. *Collective Security under International Law.* Washington, D.C.: United States Government Printing Office, 1957. Reprint available September 2001 by The Lawbook Exchange, Ltd. LCCN 00-053507. ISBN 1-58477-144-5. Cloth. $70.

Kelsen, Hans. *General Theory of Law and State.* Translated by Anders Wedberg. Cambridge: Harvard University Press, 1945. xxxiii, 516pp. Reprinted 1999 by The Lawbook Exchange, Ltd. LCCN 98-32334. ISBN 1-886363-74-9. Cloth. $75.

Kelsen, Hans. *The Law of the United Nations. A Critical Analysis of Its Fundamental Problems.* New York: Frederick A. Praeger, [1964]. xvii, 994 pp. Reprinted 2000 by The Lawbook Exchange, Ltd. ISBN 1-58477-077-5. Cloth. $125.

Kelsen, Hans. *Peace Through Law.* Chapel Hill: The University of North Carolina Press, 1944. xii, 155 pp. Reprinted 2001 by The Lawbook Exchange, Ltd. ISBN 1-58477-103-8. Cloth. $60.

Kelsen, Hans. *The Pure Theory of Law.* Translation from the Second German Edition by Max Knight. Berkeley: University of California Press, 1967. x, 356pp. Reprint available October 2001 by The Lawbook Exchange, Ltd. ISBN 1-58477-206-9. Cloth. $95.

Kelsen, Hans. *Society and Nature: A Sociological Inquiry.* London: K. Kegan Paul, Trench, Trubner & Co., Ltd., [1946]. viii, 391 pp. Reprinted 2000 by The Lawbook Exchange, Ltd. LCCN 99-054869. ISBN 1-58477-064-3. Cloth. $85.

Kelsen, Hans. *What is Justice? Justice, Law and Politics in the Mirror of Science.* Berkeley: University of California Press, 1957. [vi], 397 pp. Reprinted 2000 by The Lawbook Exchange, Ltd. ISBN 1-58477-101-1. Cloth. $95.

Kent, William. *Memoirs and Letters of James Kent, L.L.D.* Boston: Little, Brown, and Company, 1898. x, 341 pp. Reprinted 2001 by The Lawbook Exchange, Ltd. LCCN 00-026688. ISBN 1-58477-100-3. Cloth. $75.

Kovalevsky, Maxime. *Modern Customs and Ancient Laws of Russia. Being the Ilchester Lectures for 1889-90.* London: David Nutt, 1891. x, 260 pp. Reprinted 2000 by The Lawbook Exchange, Ltd. LCCN 99-16487. ISBN 1-58477-017-1. Cloth. $65.

Kulsrud, Carl J. *Maritime Neutrality to 1780. A History of the Main Principles Governing Neutrality and Belligerency to 1780.* Boston: Little, Brown, and Company, 1936. x, 351 pp. Reprinted 2000 by The Lawbook Exchange, Ltd. LCCN 99-38825. ISBN 1-58477-027-9. Cloth. $65.

Langdell, C.C. *A Selection of Cases on the Law of Contracts. With References and Citations. Prepared for Use as a Text-book in Harvard Law School.* Boston: Little, Brown & Co., 1871. xvi, 1022 pp. Reprinted 1999 by The Lawbook Exchange, Ltd. LCCN 99-28293. ISBN 1-58477-001-5. Cloth. $120.

Lauterpacht, H[ersch]. *The Function of Law in the International Community.* Oxford: Clarendon Press, 1933. xxvi, 470 pp. Reprinted 2000 by The Lawbook Exchange, Ltd. LCCN 00-022124. ISBN 1-58477-090-2. Cloth. $90.

[Legal History]. *Select Essays in Anglo-American Legal History. By Maitland, Pollock, Holmes, Beale, Holdsworth and Others.* Boston: Little, Brown, and Company, 1907. Three volumes. 847; 823; 862 pp. Reprinted 1992 by The Lawbook Exchange, Ltd. LCCN 91-77977. ISBN 0-9630106-1-1. Cloth. $195.

Lieber, Francis. *On Civil Liberty and Self-government. Enlarged edition in one volume.* Philadelphia: J.B. Lippincott & Co.. 1859. xix, [15]-629 pp. Reprinted 2001 by The Lawbook Exchange, Ltd. LCCN 99-056928. ISBN 1-58477-070-8. Cloth. $100.

Livingston, Edward. *A System of Penal Law, for the State of Louisiana: Consisting of A Code of Crimes and Punishments, A Code of Procedure, A Code of Evidence, A Code of Reform and Prison Discipline, A Book of Definitions. Prepared Under the Authority of a Law of the Said State. To Which are Prefixed a Preliminary Report on the Plan of a Penal Code, and Introductory Reports to the Several Codes Embraced in the System of Penal Law.* Philadelphia: James Kay, Jun. & Brother, 1833. v, 745 pp. Reprinted 1999 by The Lawbook Exchange, Ltd. LCCN 99-11403. ISBN 1-886363-83-8. Cloth. $95.

Llewellyn, Karl N. *Jurisprudence. Realism in Theory and Practice.* [Chicago]: The University of Chicago Press, 1962. viii, 531 pp. Reprinted 2000 by The

Lawbook Exchange, Ltd. LCCN 99-056923. ISBN 1-58477-067-8. Cloth. $95.

[Macaulay, Thomas Babington]. *A Penal Code Prepared by the Indian Law Commissioners, and published by Command of the Governor General of India in Council.* London: Pelham Richardson, Cornhill, 1838. viii, 138 pp. Reprint available November 2001 by The Lawbook Exchange, Ltd. LCCN 99-16486. ISBN 1-58477-018-X. Cloth. $65.

[MacDonell, Sir John and Edward Manson]. *Great Jurists of the World.* Edited by Sir John MacDonell and Edward Manson. With an Introduction by Van Vechten Veeder. Boston: Little, Brown, and Company, 1914. Illustrated. xxxii, 607 pp. Reprinted 1997 by The Lawbook Exchange, Ltd. LCCN 97-8298. ISBN 1-886363-28-5. Cloth. $95.

[Madison, James]. Hunt, Gaillard, Scott, James Brown. *The Debates in The Federal Convention of 1787 Which Framed the Constitution of the United States of America.* New York: Oxford University Press, 1920. xcvii, [1], 731 pp. Reprinted 1999 by The Lawbook Exchange, Ltd. LCCN 98-51911. ISBN 1-886363-77-3. Cloth. $110.

Maitland, Frederic William. *Roman Canon Law in the Church of England: Six Essays.* London: Methuen & Co., 1898. vii, 184 pp. Reprinted 1998 by The Lawbook Exchange, Ltd. LCCN 98-22357. ISBN 1-886363-57-9. Cloth. $65.

Maitland, Frederick W., Montague, Francis C., *A Sketch of English Legal History.* Edited with Notes and Appendices by James F. Colby. New York: G.P. Putnam's Sons, 1915. x, 234pp. Reprinted 1998 by The Lawbook Exchange, Ltd. LCCN 98-11337. ISBN 1-886363-50-1. Cloth. $50.

Maitland, Frederick William. *English Law and the Renaissance (The Rede Lecture for 1901) with Some Notes.* Cambridge: at the University Press, 1901. 98 pp. Reprinted 2000 by The Lawbook Exchange, Ltd. LCCN 99-41654. ISBN 1-58477-034-1. Cloth. $60.

Maitland, F.W. *The Constitutional History of England. A Course of Lectures Delivered.* Cambridge: Cambridge University Press, 1908. xxviii, 547 pp. Reprinted 2001 by The Lawbook Exchange, Ltd. LCCN 00-068895. ISBN 1-58477-148-8. Cloth. $95.

Mangum, Charles. *The Legal Status of the Negro.* New York: D. Appleton-Century Co., [1939]. xi, 354 pp. Reprinted 2000 by The Lawbook

Exchange, Ltd. LCCN 99-056927. ISBN 1-58477-081-3. Cloth. $80.

Marke, Julius J., editor. *A Catalogue of the Law Collection at New York University With Selected Annotations.* New York: The Law Center of New York University, 1953. xxxi, 1372 pp. Reprinted 1999 by The Lawbook Exchange, Ltd. LCCN 99-19939. ISBN 1-886363-91-9. Cloth. $185.

Marsden. R.[eginald]. G.[odfrey], ed. *Documents Relating to Law and Custom of the Sea.* [n.p.]: The Navy Record Society, 1915-6. Two volumes. xxxiii, 561; xl, 457, [5] pp. Reprinted 1999 by The Lawbook Exchange, Ltd. LCCN 99-24138. ISBN 1-886363-96-X. Cloth. $175.

Marshall, John. *The Constitutional Decisions of John Marshall,* Edited, with an introductory essay by Joseph P. Cotton, Jr. New York: G.P. Putnam, 1905. Two volumes. viii, 144, 145a-188a, [145]-330 pp. Reprinted 2001 by The Lawbook Exchange, Ltd. LCCN 99-048862. ISBN 1-58477-050-3. Cloth. $175.

[Marshall, John]. Servies, James Albert. *A Bibliography of John Marshall.* Washington: United States Commission for the Celebration of the Two Hundredth Anniversary of the Birth of John Marshall, 1956. xix, 182 pp. Reprinted 2000 by The Lawbook Exchange, Ltd. LCCN 99-088239. ISBN 1-58477-083-X. Cloth. $65.

Mathews, John. *Legislative and Judicial History of the Fifteenth Amendment.* Originally published Baltimore: The Johns Hopkins Press, 1909. x, 11-126 pp. Reprinted 2001 by The Lawbook Exchange, Ltd. ISBN 1-58477-176-3. Cloth. $60.

Maxwell, W. Harold and C.R. Brown. *A Complete List of British and Colonial Law Reports and Legal Periodicals. Arranged in Alphabetical and in Chronological Order with Bibliographical Notes.* **[With]:** *Check List of Canadian and Newfoundland Statutes.*[Third Edition]. Toronto: The Carswell Company, Limited, 1937. viii, 141, 49 pp. Reprinted 1995 by The Lawbook 0. Cloth. $80.

McCulloch, J.R. *The Works of David Ricardo, Esq., M.P. with a Notice of the Life and Writings of the Author.* London: John Murray, 1846. xxxiii, 584 pp. Reprinted 2000 by The Lawbook Exchange, Ltd. LCCN 99-39612. ISBN 1-58477-028-7. Cloth. $90.

McKechnie, William Sharp. *Magna Carta. A Commentary on the Great Charter of King John. With an Historical Introduction. Second Edition, Revised and in part Re-written.* Glasgow: James Maclehose and Sons, 1914. xvii,530, [2] pp. Reprinted 2000 by The Lawbook Exchange, Ltd. LCCN 99-38731. ISBN 1-58477-031-7. Cloth. $95.

McLaughlin, Andrew C. *The Courts, The Constitution and Parties. Studies in Constitutional History and Politics.* Chicago: University of Chicago Press, 1912. vii, 299 pp. Reprint available August 2001 by The Lawbook Exchange, Ltd. LCCN 00-058812. ISBN 1-58477-155-*Seventh Exclusive: With Explanatory Notes and a Glossary.* London: J. Nichols, 1780. x, 434 pp. Reprinted 1999 by The Lawbook Exchange, Ltd. LCCN 99-17114. ISBN 1-886363-87-0. Cloth. $75.

McNamara, M. Frances. *Ragbag of Legal Quotations.* Albany: Matthew Bender & Company, 1960. xi, 334 pp. Reprinted 1992 by The Lawbook Exchange, Ltd. LCCN 92-074141. ISBN 0-9630106-3-8. Cloth. $50.

Meiklejohn, Alexander. *Free Speech and Its Relation to Self Government.* New York: Harper Brothers Publishers, [1948]. xiv, 107pp. Reprint available September 2001 by The Lawbook Exchange, Ltd. LCCN 99-87204. ISBN 1-58477-087-2. Cloth. $80.

Mendelsohn, S. *The Criminal Jurisprudence of the Ancient Hebrews. Compiled from the Talmud and other Rabbinical Writings, and Compared with Roman and English Penal Jurisprudence.* Baltimore: M. Curlander, 1891. 270 pp. Reprint available October 2001 by The Lawbook Exchange, Ltd. ISBN 1-58477-150-X. Cloth. $80.

Merriam, C.E., Jr. *History of the Theory of Sovereignty Since Rousseau.* New York: Columbia University Press, [1900]. x, [11]-233 pp. Reprinted 1999 by The Lawbook Exchange, Ltd. LCCN 98-32385. ISBN 1-886363-76-5. Cloth. $65.

Minor, Raleigh C. *Notes on the Science of Government and the Relations of the States to the United States.* [Charlottesville]: University of Virginia, 1913. x, 171 pp. Reprinted 1995 by The Lawbook Exchange, Ltd. LCCN 99-047233. ISBN 1-886363-09-9. Cloth. $40.

Moore, Blaine Free. *The Supreme Court and Unconstitutional Legislation.* New York: Columbia University Press, 1913. 158 pp. Reprint available November 2001 by The Lawbook Exchange, Ltd. ISBN 1-58477-099-6. Cloth. $60.

Morris, Robert C. *International Arbitration and Procedure.* New Haven: Yale University Press, 1911. x, 238 pp. Reprinted 2001 by The Lawbook Exchange, Ltd. LCCN 00-059547. ISBN 1-58477-160-7. Cloth. $70.

Morris, Thomas D. *Free Men All: The Personal Liberty Laws of the North 1780-1861.* Baltimore: The Johns Hopkins University Press, 1974. xii, 253 pp. Reprinted 2001 by The Lawbook Exchange, Ltd. ISBN 1-58477-107-0. Cloth. $75.

Neely, Robert D. *The Lawyers of Dickens and Their Clerks.* Boston: The Christopher Publishing House, [1936]. 67pp. Reprint available October 2001 by The Lawbook Exchange, Ltd. LCCN 00-021520. ISBN 1-58477-091-0. Cloth. $60.

Neilson, George. *Trial by Combat.* Glasgow: William Hodge & Co., 1890. xiv, 348 pp. Reprinted 2000 by The Lawbook Exchange, Ltd. LCCN 99-059101. ISBN 1-58477-075-9. Cloth. $75.

[Nichols, J.]. *A Collection of all the Wills, Now Known to Be Extant, of the Kings and Queens of England, Princes and Princesses of Wales, and every Branch of the Blood Royal, from the Reign of William the Conqueror, to that of Henry the Seventh Exclusive: With Explanatory Notes and a Glossary.* London: J. Nichols, 1780. x, 434 pp. Reprinted 1999 by The Lawbook Exchange, Ltd. LCCN 99-17114. ISBN 1-886363-87-0. Cloth. $75.

Ogle, Arthur. *The Canon Law in Mediaeval England. An Examination of William Lyndwood's "Provinciale," in Reply to the Late Professor F.W. Maitland.* London: John Murray, 1912. xv, 220 pp. Reprinted 2000 by The Lawbook Exchange, Ltd. LCCN 99-33827. ISBN 1-58477-026-0. Cloth. $65.

Oldroyd, Osborn H. *The Assassination of Abraham Lincoln. The Flight, Pursuit, Capture and Punishment of the Conspirators.* Washington, D.C.: O.H. Oldroyd, 1901. xviii, 305pp. Illustrated. Reprint available September 2001 by The Lawbook Exchange, Ltd. ISBN 1-58477-125-9. Cloth. $75.

[Parker, James]. [Legal Manual]. *Conductor Generalis, or The Office, Duty and Authority of Justices of the Peace, High Sheriffs, Under-Sheriffs, Goalers, Coroners, Constables, Jury Men, Over-seers of the Poor, and also The Office of Clerks of Assiza And of the Peace &c. Collected out of all the Books hitherto written on those Subjects, whether of Common or Statute Law. To which is added, A Collection out of Sir Matthew Hales concerning The Descent of Lands. The Whole Alphabetically Digested Under the Several Titles, With a Table Directing to the*

Ready finding out Proper Matter under those Titles. Philadelphia: Printed and Sold by Andrew Bradford, 1722. [8], xii, 232pp. **[with]** *The Office, Duty and Authority of Sheriffs, How and in what Manner to execute the same, according to the Common and Statute Laws of Great-Britain, which are now in Force and Use. Likewise, Of Under-Sheriffs and their Deputies; and where the High-Sheriff shall be answerable for their Defaults, and where not, &.* Philadelphia: Andrew Bradford, 1721. [233]-299, [1] pp. Reprint available October 2001 by The Lawbook Exchange, Ltd. LCCN 00-058810. ISBN 1-58477-123-2. Cloth. $80.

Perry, Ross R. *Common-law Pleading: Its History and Principles. Including Dicey's Rules Concerning Parties to Action and Stephen's Rules of Pleading.* Boston, Little, Brown and Company, 1897. xxvi, 494 pp. Reprinted 2001 by The Lawbook Exchange, Ltd. ISBN 1-58477-105-4. Cloth. $95.

Pharr, Clyde. *The Theodosian Code and Novels and the Sirmondian Constitutions. A Translation with Commentary, Glossary, and Bibliography.* [Princeton]: Princeton University Press, 1952. Quarto. Book measures 9"x12." xxvi, 643pp. Reprinted 2001 by The Lawbook Exchange, Ltd. ISBN 1-58477-146-1. Cloth. $150.

Phillimore, John George. *Principles and Maxims of Jurisprudence.* Originally published London: John W. Parker and Son, 1856. xxiv, 408 pp. Reprint available September 2001 by The Lawbook Exchange, Ltd. ISBN 1-58477-177-1. Cloth. $85.

Plucknett, Theodore F.T. *A Concise History of the Common Law. Fifth Edition.* Originally published Boston: Little, Brown and Company, 1956. Reprinted 2001 by The Lawbook Exchange, Ltd. LCCN 00-067821. ISBN 1-58477-137-2. Cloth. $125.

Pollock, Frederick and Frederic William Maitland. *The History of English Law before the Time of Edward I.* Cambridge: Cambridge University Press, 1898. Two volumes. xxxviii, 688; xiv, 691 pp. Reprinted 1996 by The Lawbook Exchange, Ltd. LCCN 96-16003. ISBN 1-886363-22-6. Cloth. $165.

Pollock, Sir Frederick. *The Expansion of the Common Law.* London: Stevens and Sons, Limited, 1904. vii, 164pp. Reprint available September 2001 by The Lawbook Exchange, Ltd. LCCN 00-067015. ISBN 1-58477-169-0. Cloth. $65.

Pollock, Sir Frederick. *The Genius of the Common Law.* New York: The Columbia University Press, 1912. vii, 141 pp. Reprinted 2000 by The Lawbook Exchange, Ltd. LCCN 99-047160. ISBN 1-58477-043-0-1. Cloth. $55.

Pomeroy, John N. *A Treatise on Equity Jurisprudence As Administered in the United States of America. Adapted for All the States and to the Union of Legal and Equitable Remedies under the Reformed Procedure.* San Francisco and New York: Bancroft-Whitney and Lawyers Cooperative, 1941. Five volumes. 914; 1134; 1063; 1104; 716 pp. Reprinted 1995 by The Lawbook Exchange, Ltd. ISBN 1-886363-05-6. Cloth. $450.

Poore, Ben[jamin] Perley. *The Federal and State Constitutions, Colonial Charters, and Organic Laws of the United States. Second edition.* Washington: Government Printing Office, 1878. Folio. Two volumes. xii, 1019; 1021-2102pp. Reprint available August 2001 by The Lawbook Exchange, Ltd. ISBN 1-58477-128-3. Cloth. $395.

Pothier, R.J. *Treatise on the Contract of Sale.* Translated from the French by L.S. Cushing. Boston: Charles C. Little and James Brown, 1839. xvi, 406 pp. Reprinted 2000 by The Lawbook Exchange, Ltd. LCCN 99-10260. ISBN 1-886363-82-X. Cloth. $70.

Pothier, Robert Joseph. *A Treatise on the Law of Obligations, or Contracts. Translated from the French, with an Introduction, Appendix, and Notes, Illustrative of the English Law on the Subject. By William David Evans.* London: A. Strahan, 1802. Two volumes. [1], 578, [1]; iv, 715, [1]pp. Reprinted 2000 by The Lawbook Exchange, Ltd. LCCN 99-26397. ISBN 1-886363-98-6. Cloth. $195.

Pothier, Robert Joseph. *A Treatise on Obligations, Considered in a Moral and Legal View. Translated from the French of Pothier. Translated by Francois-Xavier Martin.* Newburn, N.C.: Martin & Ogden, 1802. 2 vols. in 1 book. Reprinted 2000 by The Lawbook Exchange, Ltd. With a new introduction by Warren M. Billings. LCCN 98-38360. ISBN 1-886363-62-5. Cloth. $75.

Pound, Roscoe. *Jurisprudence.* St. Paul, Minn.: West Publishing Co., 1959. Five volumes. Reprinted 2000 by The Lawbook Exchange, Ltd. ISBN 1-58477-119-4. Cloth. $495.

Powell, Chilton Latham. *English Domestic Relations 1487-1653. A Study of Matrimony and Family Life in Theory and Practice as Revealed by the Literature,*

Law, and History of the Period. New York: Columbia University Press, 1917. xii, 274 pp. Reprinted 2001 by The Lawbook Exchange, Ltd. ISBN 1-58477-096-1. Cloth. $75.

Radin, Max. *Law as Logic and Experience.* New Haven: Yale University Press, 1940. ix, [1], 171 pp. Reprinted 2000 by The Lawbook Exchange, Ltd. LCCN 99-30670. ISBN 1-58477-008-2. Cloth. $55.

Rapalje, Stewart and Lawrence, Robert L. *A Dictionary of American and English Law with Definitions of the Technical Terms of the Canon and Civil Laws. Also, Containing a Full Collection of Latin Maxims, and Citations of Upwards of Forty Thousand Reported Cases, in which Words and Phrases Have Been Judicially Defined or Construed.* Jersey City: Frederick C. Linn & Co., 1888. Two volumes. xxxviii, 1380 pp. Reprinted 1997 by The Lawbook Exchange, Ltd. LCCN 97-38484. ISBN 1-886363-33-1. Cloth. $195.

Reeve, Tapping. *The Law of Baron and Femme, of Parent and Child, Guardian and Ward, Master and Servant, and of the Powers of the Courts of Chancery; with an Essay on the Terms Heir, Heirs, Heirs of the Body. Third Edition, With Notes and References to English and American Cases by Amasa J. Parker and Charles E. Baldwin, Counselors-At-Law.* Albany: William Gould, 1862. xlvi, 677pp. Reprinted 1998 by The Lawbook Exchange, Ltd. LCCN 98-36057. ISBN 1-886363-58-7. Cloth. $75.

Richards, John T. *Abraham Lincoln The Lawyer-Statesman.* Boston: Houghton Mifflin, 1916. Frontis. Illustrated. xii, 260 pp. Reprinted 1999 by The Lawbook Exchange, Ltd. LCCN 99-20587. ISBN 1-886363-94-3. Cloth. $60.

Roby, Henry John. *An Introduction to the Study of Justinian's Digest Containing an Account of its Composition and of the Jurists Used or Referred to Therein.* Cambridge: At the University Press, 1886. cclxxix pp. Reprinted 2000 by The Lawbook Exchange, Ltd. ISBN 1-58477-073-2. Cloth. $65.

Roby, Henry John. *Roman Private Law in the Times of Cicero and of the Antonines.* Cambridge: At the University Press, 1902. Two volumes. xxxii, 543; xiii, [1], 560 pp. Reprinted 2000 by The Lawbook Exchange, Ltd. ISBN 1-58477-074-0. Cloth. $180.

Sandys, Sir John Edwin. *Aristotle's Constitution of Athens. A Revised Text with an Introduction Critical and Explanatory Notes Testimonia and Indices. Second edition, Revised and Enlarged.* London: Macmillan & Co., Limited, 1902. xcii,

331 pp. Frontis. Illus. Reprinted 2000 by The Lawbook Exchange, Ltd. LCCN 99-23952. ISBN 1-58477-004-X. Cloth. $75.

Schechter, Frank I. *The Historical Foundations of the Law Relating to Trade-Marks.* New York: Columbia University Press, 1925. xxviii, 211 pp. Reprinted 2000 by The Lawbook Exchange, Ltd. LCCN 99-41673. ISBN 1-58477-035-X. Cloth. $60.

Schroeder, Theodore. *Constitutional Free Speech Defined and Defended in an Unfinished Argument in a Case of Blasphemy.* New York: Free Speech League, 1919. 456 pp. Reprinted 2001 by The Lawbook Exchange, Ltd. LCCN 99-049361. ISBN 1-58477-053-8. Cloth. $90.

Schroeder, Theodore. *Free Speech Bibliography Including Every Discovered Attitude Toward the Problem Covering Every Method of Transmitting Ideas and Abridging Their Promulgation upon Every Subject-Matter.* New York: The H.W. Wilson Company, 1922. 456 pp. Reprinted 2001 by The Lawbook Exchange, Ltd. LCCN 99-049361. ISBN 1-58477-053-8. Cloth. $85.

Schroeder, Theodore. *"Obscene" Literature and Constitutional Law. A Forensic Defense of Freedom of the Press.* New York: Privately Printed for Forensic Uses, 1911. 439 pp. Reprint available December 2001 by The Lawbook Exchange, Ltd. LCCN 00-58815. ISBN 1-58477-154-2. Cloth. $85.

Schulte, Joh. Friedrich von. *Die Geschichte der Quellen und Literatur der canonischen Rechts.* Stuttgart: Verlag von Ferdinand Enke, 1875. Two volumes. Reprinted 2000 by The Lawbook Exchange, Ltd. LCCN 99-087494. ISBN 1-58477-089-9. Cloth. $225.

Schwartz, Bernard, editor. *The Code Napoleon and the Common-Law World. The Sesquicentennial Lectures Delivered at The Law Center of New York University December 13-15, 1954.* New York: New York University Press, 1956. x, 438pp. Reprinted 1998 by The Lawbook Exchange, Ltd. LCCN 98-34100. ISBN 1-886363-59-5. Cloth. $65.

Schwarz, Philip J. *Twice Condemned: Slaves and the Criminal Laws of Virginia, 1705-1865.* [Baton Rouge: Louisiana State University Press]. [1988]. xvi, 354pp. Reprinted 1998 by The Lawbook Exchange, Ltd. LCCN 98-4424 ISBN 1-886363-54-4. Cloth. $75.

Scott, Henry W. *The Courts of the State of New York: Their History, Development and Jurisdiction: Embracing a complete history of all the Courts and Tribunals of Justice, both Colonial and State, established from the first settlement of Manhattan Island and including the status and jurisdiction of all the Courts of the State as now constituted.* New York: Wilson Publishing Co., 1909. Reprinted 2001 by The Lawbook Exchange, Ltd. LCCN 99-10259. ISBN 1-886363-84-6. Cloth. $95.

Scott, James Brown. *James Madison's Notes of Debates in the Federal Convention Convention of 1787 and their Relation to a More Perfect Society of Nations.* New York: Oxford University Press, 1918. xviii, 149pp. Reprint available September 2001 by The Lawbook Exchange, Ltd. ISBN 1-58477-164-X. Cloth. $65.

Scott, James Brown. *The Spanish Origin of International Law. Francisco De Vitoria and His Law of Nations.* London: Humphrey Milford, 1934. 19a, 288, clviii pp. Frontispiece and portrait. Reprinted 2000 by The Lawbook Exchange, Ltd. LCCN 00-036835. ISBN 1-58477-110-0. Cloth. $90.

Scott, S.P. *The Civil Law Including the Twelve Tables, The Institutes of Gaius, The Rules of Ulpian, the Opinions of Paulus, The Enactments of Justinian, and the Constitutions of Leo: Translated from the original Latin, edited, and compared with all accessible systems of jurisprudence ancient and modern. In Seventeen Volumes. In seven books.* Cincinnati: The Central Trust Company, 1932. Reprinted 2001 by The Lawbook Exchange, Ltd. ISBN 1-58477-130-5. Cloth. $750.

Sears, John H. *Trust Estates as Business Companies. [Second Edition].* Kansas City, Mo.: Vernon Law Book Company, 1921. xx, 782 pp. [1921]. Reprinted 1998 by The Lawbook Exchange, Ltd. LCCN 97-32423 ISBN 1-886363-41-2. Cloth. $95.

Shumaker, Walter A. *The Cyclopedic Law Dictionary Comprising the Terms and Phrases of American Jurisprudence, Including Ancient and Modern Common Law, International Law, and Numerous Select Titles from the Civil Law, the French and the Spanish Law, etc., etc. with an Exhaustive Collection of Legal Maxims. Second Edition by James C. Cahill.* Chicago: Callaghan and Company, 1922. xii, 545 pp. Reprinted 2001 by The Lawbook Exchange, Ltd. LCCN 99-11404. ISBN 1-886363 85-4. Cloth. $150.

Spooner, Lysander. *An Essay on the Trial by Jury.* Boston: Bela Marsh, 1852. 224 pp. Reprint available November 2001 by The Lawbook Exchange, Ltd. LCCN 00-058811. ISBN 1-58477-156-9. Cloth. $70.

[St. Germain, Christopher]. *The Doctor and Student or Dialogues Between a Doctor of Divinity and a Student in the Laws of England Containing the Grounds of Those Laws Together with Questions and Cases Concerning the Equity Thereof Revised and Corrected by William Muchall, Gent. to which are added two pieces concerning Suits in Chancery by Subpoena.* Cincinnati:Robert Clarke & Co., 1874. xiv, 401pp. Reprinted 1998 by The Lawbook Exchange, Ltd. LCCN 98-11338. ISBN 1-886363-49-8. Cloth. $65.

Stammler, Rudolph. *The Theory of Justice.* Translated by Isaak Husik. New York: The Macmillan Company, 1925. xli, 591 pp. Reprinted 2000 by The Lawbook Exchange, Ltd. LCCN 99-054019. ISBN 1-58477-066-X. Cloth. $95.

Stevens, Robert. *Law School: Legal Education in America from the 1850s to the 1980s.* Chapel Hill: The University of North Carolina Press, [1983]. xvi, 334 pp. Reprint available September 2001 by The Lawbook Exchange, Ltd. ISBN 1-58477-199-2. Cloth. $85.

Stimson, Frederic Jesup. *Glossary of Technical Terms, Phrases, and Maxims of the Common Law.* Boston: Little, Brown, and Company, 1881. iv, 305pp. Reprinted 1999 by The Lawbook Exchange, Ltd. LCCN 98-50813. ISBN 1-886363-70-6. Cloth. $60.

Stimson, Frederic Jesup. *Popular Law-Making. A Study of the Origin, History, and Present Tendencies of Law-Making by Statute.* New York: Charles Scribner's Sons, 1910. xii, 545 pp. Reprint available November 2001 by The Lawbook Exchange, Ltd. LCCN 00-022513. ISBN 1-58477-094-5. Cloth. $85.

Stokes, I.N. Phelps. *The Iconography of Manhattan Island 1498-1909.* New York: Robert H. Dodd, 1915. Six volumes. Reprinted 1998 by The Lawbook Exchange, Ltd. LCCN 97-30604. ISBN 1-886363-30-7. Cloth. $750.

Stone, Harlan F. *Law and its Administration.* New York: Columbia University Press, 1915. vii, 232 pp. Reprint available November 2001 by The Lawbook Exchange, Ltd. LCCN 00-021508. ISBN 1-58477-093-7. Cloth. $70.

Story, Joseph. *A Familiar Exposition of the Constitution of the United States:* Containing a Brief Commentary on Every Clause, Explaining the True Nature, reasons, and Objects Thereof; Designed for the Use of School,

Libraries and General Readers. With an Appendix, Containing Important Public Documents, Illustrative of the Constitution. New York: Harper & Brothers: 1865. 372 pp. Reprinted 1999 by The Lawbook Exchange, Ltd. LCCN 98-50811. ISBN 1-886363-71-4. Cloth. $60.

[Story, Joseph]. **Story, William.** *Life and Letters of Joseph Story, Associate Justice of the Supreme Court of the United States and Dane Professor of Law at Harvard University, edited by his son, William W. Story.* Boston: Charles C. Little and James Brown, 1851. Two volumes. xii, 574; viii, 676 pp. Frontispiece. Reprinted 2001 by The Lawbook Exchange, Ltd. LCCN 99-058777. ISBN 1-58477-071-6. Cloth. $195.

Story, Joseph. *Commentaries on the Conflict of Laws, Foreign and Domestic, in Regard to Contracts, Rights, and Remedies, and Especially in Regard to Marriages, Divorces, Wills, Successions, and Judgments. Second Edition. Revised, Corrected and Greatly Enlarged.* London: A. Maxwell, 1841. xxxiv, 927 pp. (misnumbered in original, PP. 753-756 omitted.) Reprinted 2001 by The Lawbook Exchange, Ltd. ISBN 1-58477-145-3. Cloth. $125.

Story, Joseph. *Commentaries on the Constitution of the United States.* Boston: Little, Brown and Company, 1858. Two volumes. xxxiii, 735, 702pp. Reprint available September 2001 by The Lawbook Exchange, Ltd. ISBN 1-58477-193-3. Cloth. $250.

[Story, Joseph]. **Story, William W., ed.** *The Miscellaneous Writings of Joseph Story, Associate Justice of the Supreme Court of the United States and Dane Professor of Law at Harvard University, edited by his son, William W. Story.* Boston: C.C. Little and J. Brown , 1852. x, 828 pp. Reprinted 2001 by The Lawbook Exchange, Ltd. LCCN 99-058559. ISBN 1-58477-072-4. Cloth. $125.

Tayler, Thomas. *The Law Glossary: Being a Selection of the Greek, Latin, Saxon, French, Norman and Italian Sentences, Phrases, and Maxims, Found in the Leading English and American Reports, and Elementary Works.* New York: Lewis & Blood, 1856. 580 pp. Reprinted 1995 by The Lawbook Exchange, Ltd. ISBN 1-886363-12-9. Cloth. $65.

Taylor, John. *Construction Construed and Constitutions Vindicated.* Richmond: printed by Shepherd & Pollard, 1820. iv, 344pp. Reprinted 1998 by The Lawbook Exchange, Ltd. LCCN 97-49411. ISBN 1-886363-43-9. Cloth. $65.

[Taylor, John]. *A Defence of the Measures of the Administration of Thomas Jefferson. By Curtius.* Washington: Samuel H. Smith, 1804. 136 pp. Reprinted 1999 by The Lawbook Exchange, Ltd. LCCN 99-24139. ISBN 1-886363-97-8. Cloth. $60.

Taylor, John. *An Inquiry into the Principles and Policy of the Government of the United States.* Fredericksburg:Green and Cady, 1814. With an introduction by Roy Franklin Nichols, Yale University Press, 1950. 562pp. Reprinted 1998 by The Lawbook Exchange, Ltd. LCCN 98-11147. ISBN 1-886363-46-3. Cloth. $75.

Taylor, John, of Caroline. *New Views of the Constitution of the United States.* Washington City: Printed for the Author, 1823. [4], 316pp. Reprint available November 2001 by The Lawbook Exchange, Ltd. ISBN 1-58477-079-1. Cloth. $70.

Thomson, Richard. *An Historical Essay on the Magna Charta of King John: to which are added, the Great Charter in Latin and English, the charters of liberties and confirmations, granted by Henry III and Edward I, the original Charter of the forests, and various authentic instruments connected with them: Explanatory Notes on their Several Privileges; A Descriptive Account of the Principal Originals and Editions Extant, Both in Print and Manuscript; and Other Illustrations, Derived from the Most Interesting and Authentic Sources.* London: John Major and Robert Jennings, 1829. xxxii, 612 pp. Reprinted 2000 by The Lawbook Exchange, Ltd. LCCN 99-40987. ISBN 1-58477-030-9. Cloth. $95.

Tiedeman, Christopher G. *A Treatise on the Limitations of Police Power in the United States Considered from both a Civil and Criminal Standpoint.* St. Louis: The F.H. Thomas Law Book Co., 1886. lxv, 662 pp. Reprinted 2001 by The Lawbook Exchange, Ltd. ISBN 1-58477-122-4. Cloth. $110.

Townley, James. *The Reasons of the Laws of Moses from the "More Nevochim" of Maimonides. With Notes, Dissertations, and a Life of the Author.* London: Longman, Rees, Orme, Brown, and Green, 1827. xi, 451 pp. Reprint available September 2001 by The Lawbook Exchange, Ltd. ISBN 1-58477-168-2. Cloth. $95.

Townsend, William H. *Lincoln the Litigant.* Boston: Houghton Mifflin Company, 1925. [ix], [117] pp. Frontis. Illus. Reprinted 2000 by The Lawbook Exchange, Ltd. LCCN 99-16499. ISBN 1-58477-021-X. Cloth. $60.

Trayner, John. *Latin Phrases and Maxims: Collected from the Institutional and other Writers on Scotch Law; with Translations and Illustrations.* Edinburgh: William Paterson, 1861. iv, [2], 356 pp. Reprinted 2001 by The Lawbook Exchange, Ltd. LCCN 00-067012. ISBN 1-58477-174-7. Cloth. $75.

[Trials]. [Witchcraft Trials]. *Curious Cases and Amusing Actions at Law Including Some Trials of Witches in the Seventeenth Century.* Toronto: The Carswell Co., Limited, 1916. vii, 234 pp. Reprinted 2000 by The Lawbook Exchange, Ltd. LCCN 99-032361. ISBN 1-58477-012-0. Cloth. $65.

Tucker, Henry St. George. *Commentaries on the Laws of Virginia. Comprising the Substance of a Course of Lectures Delivered to the Winchester Law School. With an Introduction by David Cobin and Paul Finkelman.* Richmond: Shepherd and Colin, 1846. Two volumes. 34, 468; 24, 512 pp. Reprinted 1998 by The Lawbook Exchange, Ltd. LCCN 97-10313. ISBN 1-886363-26-9. Cloth. $175.

Tucker, Henry St. George. *Limitations on the Treaty-Making Power Under the Constitution of the United States.* Boston: Little, Brown, and Company, 1915. xxi, 444 pp. Reprinted 2000 by The Lawbook Exchange, Ltd. LCCN 99-31589. ISBN 1-58477-015-5. Cloth. $75.

Tucker, St. George. *Blackstone's Commentaries. With Notes of Reference to the Constitution and Laws, of the Federal Government of the United States, and of the Commonwealth of Virginia. In Five Volumes, with an Appendix to Each volume, Containing Short Tracts upon Such Subjects As Appeared Necessary to Form a Connected View of the Laws of Virginia As a Member of the Federal Union.* Philadelphia: William Young Birch and Abraham Small, 1803. Five volumes. Reprinted 1996 by The Lawbook Exchange, Ltd. LCCN 96-12566. ISBN 1-886363-15-3. Cloth. $450.

Twiss, Benjamin R. *Lawyers and the Constitution: How Laissez Faire Came to the Supreme Court.* With a foreword by Edward S. Corwin. xii, 271 pp. Princeton University Press, [1942]. Reprint available September 2001 by The Lawbook Exchange, Ltd. LCCN 00-067114. ISBN 1-58477-138-0. Cloth. $75.

[Twiss, Sir Travers]. *The Black Book of the Admiralty, with an Appendix.* Monumenta Juridica. Edited by Sir Travers Twiss. Four volumes. 4, xciii, 491, [2]; 4, lxxxvii, 500, 31; 4, lxxxvi, 673, [1], 31; 4, clii, 559, 32 pp. LCCN 97-38809 ISBN 1-886363-39-0. 1871. Reprinted 1998 by The Lawbook Exchange, Ltd. Cloth. $495.

[Upshur, Abel Parker]. *A Brief Enquiry Into the True Nature and Character of Our Federal Government, being a review of Judge Story's Commentaries on the Constitution of the United States. By a Virginian.* Petersburg: Printed by Edmund and Julian C. Ruffin, 1840. 132pp. Reprinted 1998 by The Lawbook Exchange, Ltd. LCCN 97-11151. ISBN 1-886363-44-7. Cloth. $45.

Valmaer. [pseud]. [Ream, Michael]. *Lawyer's Code of Ethics. A Satire.* St. Louis: The F.H. Thomas Law Book Co., 1887. 143 pp. Reprinted 2001 by The Lawbook Exchange, Ltd. LCCN 00-021508. ISBN 1-58477-047-3. Cloth. $65.

Vinogradoff, Paul. *Custom and Right.* Oslo: H. Aschehoug, 1925. 110 pp. Reprinted 2000 by The Lawbook Exchange, Ltd. LCCN 99-0474851. ISBN 1-58477-048-1. Cloth. $45.

Vinogradoff, Paul. *Roman Law in Mediaeval Europe.* London: Harper & Brothers, 1909. 136 pp. Reprinted 2001 by The Lawbook Exchange, Ltd. LCCN 00-039068. ISBN 1-58477-109-7. Cloth. $65.

Vinogradoff, Sir Paul. *Outlines of Historical Jurisprudence.* London: Oxford University Press, 1920. Two volumes. 428; x, 315 pp. Reprinted 1999 by The Lawbook Exchange, Ltd. LCCN 98-42298. ISBN 1-886363-64-1. Cloth. $150.

Walker, James. *The Theory of the Common Law.* Boston: Little, Brown and Co., 1852. xxiv, 130pp. Reprinted 1998 by The Lawbook Exchange, Ltd. LCCN 98-9522. ISBN 1-886363-45-5. Cloth. $65.

Warren, Charles. *History of the Harvard Law School and of Early Legal Conditions in America.* New York: Lewis Publishing Company, 1908. Three volumes. xiv, 543; iv, 560; 397 pp. Illustrated. Reprinted 1999 by The Lawbook Exchange, Ltd. LCCN 99-29193. ISBN 1-58477-006-6. Cloth. $275.

Wheaton, Henry. *Elements of International Law: with a Sketch of the History of the Science.* Philadelphia: Carey, Lea & Blanchard, 1836. xiv, 375 pp. Reprint available December 2001 by The Lawbook Exchange, Ltd. LCCN 00-066335. ISBN 1-58477-170-4 . Cloth. $80.

White, Edw. J. *The Law in Scriptures. With Explanations of the Law Terms and Legal References in Both the Old and the New Testaments.* St. Louis: Thomas Law Book Company, 1935. xxiv, 422 pp. Reprinted 2000 by The Lawbook Exchange, Ltd. LCCN 99-059102. ISBN 1-58477-076-7. Cloth. $80.

Whiting, William. *War Powers under the Constitution of the United States. Military Arrests, Reconstruction & Military Government. Also, Now First Published, War Claims of Aliens with Notes on the Acts of the Executives & Legislative Departments During Our Civil War & a Collection of Cases Decided in the National Courts. 1864. Tenth edition.* Boston: Little, Brown, and Company, 1864. xvii, 342 pp. Reprint available December 2001 by The Lawbook Exchange, Ltd. LCCN 99-049360. ISBN 1-58477-055-4. Cloth. $80.

Whitney, Henry C. *Life on the Circuit with Lincoln. With Sketches of Generals Grant, Sherman and McClellan, Judge Davis, Leonard Swett, and Other Contemporaries.* Illustrated. Boston: Estes & Lauriat, 1892. viii, 601 pp. Reprinted 2001 by The Lawbook Exchange, Ltd. ISBN 1-58477-115-1. Cloth. $110.

Wiener, Frederick Bernays. *Briefing and Arguing Federal Appeals: With an Appendix of Late Authorities Including References to the Supreme Court's 1967 Rules.* xvi, 506 pp. Washington, D.C.: BNA Incorporated, 1961. Reprinted with a new introduction by Bryan A. Garner. Reprint available September 2001 by The Lawbook Exchange, Ltd. LCCN 2001031682. ISBN 1-58477-183-6. Cloth. $85.

Wiener, Leo. *Commentary to the Germanic Laws and Mediaeval Documents.* Cambridge: Harvard University Press, 1915. lxi, 224 pp. Reprinted 2000 by The Lawbook Exchange, Ltd. LCCN 99-23969. ISBN 1-58477-005-8. Cloth. $60.

Willoughby, Westel W. *The Supreme Court of the United States. Its History and Influence in our Constitutional System.* Baltimore: The Johns Hopkins Press, 1890. 124 pp. Reprint available September 2001 by The Lawbook Exchange, Ltd. LCCN 00-068896. ISBN 1-58477-147-X. Cloth. $60.

Woodbine, George E. *Four Thirteenth Century Law Tracts. A Thesis Presented to the Faculty of the Graduate School of Yale University in Candidacy for the Degree of Doctor of Philosophy.* New Haven: Yale University Press, 1910. vi, 183 pp. Reprinted 1999 by The Lawbook Exchange, Ltd. LCCN 99-29294. ISBN 1-58477-007-4. Cloth. $50.

Woolsey, Theodore D. *Divorce and Divorce Legislation, Especially in the United States. Second Edition Revised.* New York: Charles Scribner's Sons, 1882. x, [9]-328 pp. Reprinted 2001 by The Lawbook Exchange, Ltd. ISBN 1-58477-118-6. Cloth. $75.

[Worrall, John and Edward Brooke]. *Bibliotheca Legum Angliae. Or, a Catalogue of the Common and Statute Law Books of This Realm, and Some Others Relating Thereto: Giving an Account of Their Several Editions, Ancient Printers, Dates, and Prices, and Wherein They Differ. [With a Supplement to 1800]. Part I Compiled by John Worrall, Part II and Supplement Compiled by Edward Brooke. Parts I, II and Supplement bound in one volume.* London: Printed for Edward Brooke, 1788-1800. [15], 272, [26]; viii, 40, 49-255, [1]; [3], 45, [2] pp. 1788-1800. Reprinted 1997 by The Lawbook Exchange, Ltd. LCCN 97-12962. ISBN 1-886363-29-3. Cloth. $110.

Wright, John S. *Citizenship Sovereignty.* Chicago: Published for American Citizens, the True Maintainers of State Sovereignty, 1864. Reprinted 1998 by The Lawbook Exchange, Ltd. LCCN 98-15940 ISBN 1-886363-55-2. Cloth. $65.